EVEN ON SUNDAY

Robin Blaser, Vancouver, British Columbia, c. 1997–98
(Photo by Daniel Collins)

EVEN ON SUNDAY

Essays, Readings, and Archival Materials on
the Poetry and Poetics of Robin Blaser

with New Work by Robin Blaser

Edited, and with an introduction by Miriam Nichols

THE NATIONAL POETRY FOUNDATION
ORONO, MAINE 2002

06 05 04 03 02   1 2 3 4 5

Published by the National Poetry Foundation, University of Maine, Orono, Maine 04469-5752. Printed in USA. Distributed by University Press of New England, Hanover and London. The paper used in this publication meets the minimum requirements of the American National Standard for Information Sciences—Permanence of Paper for Printed Library Materials, ansi z39.48-1984.

Design by Betsy Graves Rose. *Front cover photo*: Robin Blaser, early 1990s. Photo by Kenneth Taranta. *Back cover photo*: Morning cappuccino in the Campo dei SS Apostoli, Venice. Photo by David Farwell, May 1997.

This publication was made possible in part by a grant from the Stephen and Tabitha King Foundation.

Library of Congress Cataloging-in-Publication Data

Even on Sunday: essays, readings, and archival materials on the poetry and poetics of Robin Blaser: with new work by Robin Blaser / edited, with an introduction by Miriam Nichols
    p. cm.
    Includes bibliographical references.
    ISBN 0-943373-65-4 (pbk.: alk. paper)
    1. Blaser, Robin—Criticism and interpretation. 2. Poetics. I. Blaser, Robin. II. Nichols, Miriam.

PR9199.3.B63 Z64 2001
811'.54—dc21

                                                                    2001044226

CONTENTS

ACKNOWLEDGEMENTS

Maureen Donatelli, my research assistant at the University College of the Fraser Valley, has worked on the tapes I selected for publication from *Astonishments* over the 1998-99 academic year, correcting the original transcript against the tapes and tracking the sources for Blaser's readings. Her work on this difficult material has been very helpful. Irene Niechoda has also read the corrected manuscript and offered her excellent editorial advice as well as professional copy-editing skills. Steve Evans, my editor at the National Poetry Foundation, has been indefatigable in his careful attention to the manuscript of this collection in its entirety, including my endless footnotes; without him it simply could not have been published. I am also deeply indebted to Robin Blaser for his generous help with sourcing the cited material in *Astonishments*, for his cooperation in providing the archival photographs, and for consenting to an extended interview.

EVEN ON SUNDAY

Robin Blaser with grandparents, Sophia Nichols and "Grandpa Auer" (Sophia's second husband), and dog, Blackie, Idaho, 1926

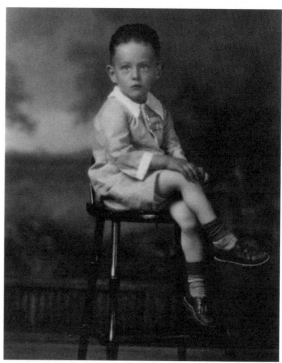

Robin Blaser, about four years old

GREAT COMPANION: DANTE ALIGHIERE I

Robin Blaser

> *The speech born-in-one's-house is that*
> *which we acquire without rule*
> —*De Vulgari Eloquentia* I.1

> *The language for which we have no words, which*
> *doesn't pretend, like grammatical language, to be*
> *there before being, but is 'alone and first in mind,'*
> *is our language, that is, the language of poetry.*
> —Giorgio Agamben: *Idea of Prose*

> *Face to face, but without seeing each other from*
> *now on, the gods and men are abandoned to writ-*
> *ing. This abandonment is the sign given to us for*
> *our history yet to come. It has only just begun. My*
> *god! We are only beginning to write.*
> —Jean-Luc Nancy: *The Inoperative Community*

entering the territory—*map is not territory*—the   Korzybski
boy looked up from the book he held in his lap,
startled that it seemed the size of half of himself
it was so large compared to Emerson, Poe, Hawthorne,
Melville, Dickinson, Longfellow around the house—
Gustave Doré's *Inferno* of the dark forest, where the
boy's mind multiplied the leopard, lion, and wolf in
his heart—heart and mind were then entwined—entered
the writhing trees, drew back from Geryon, as if to
hide, touched the page of flames that were not rain-

drops, swept his hand over the streaming anguish in
the air, felt the chill black of the ice around
winged Lucifer, who chewed on something with two
legs that he didn't want to imagine—in bed
at night after saying "please, if I die before I wake,
I pray the Lord my soul to take"—which was very hard
to think about—he returned before he slept to Dore's
imagery—under the covers with a flashlight—and nearly
always forgot the two small figures high on a rocky pro-
montory, who looked up at the stars—territory is not
map—there, *going from inside out and outside in*, he   Ruth Padel
could not yet think how ancient he was, where *the phe-*
nomena of consciousness are the phenomena of religion—
this is the boy of the house in Idaho, a railcar, painted Union Pacific yellow, by the railway tracks, golden-
rod garden of wand-stems—grandmother Sophia Nichols
whose telegraphic mind knew the distances—in the sagebrush desert during the Great Depression—entangled with 1930
Dante before and after he learned to read—the innocence
of walking there is forgotten—

  "That means," said I, somewhat amused, "that we   Kleist
would have to eat of the tree of knowledge a second time
to fall back into the state of innocence."
  "Of course," he answered, "and that is the final
chapter in the history of the world."

I address Dante, who is our contemporary, like us,
speaking out of human violence—who is implicit in our
use of our mother tongues—who is initial and continuously implicated in the courage of poetry—whose art
records *an attachment to the letter that lay at the*   Saussure
mysterious origin of poetry—the dazzlement—who is
concealed in the depth of our culture like a blind spot— Sollers
whose journey in poetry reverses the metaphysics of a
transparent language—whose daring in the realms of the
sacred proposes *il poema sacro*—propositions of the mind
in that scattered territory—of whom the story is told

that *at the moment he began the Comedy all the rhymes of*   cited/
the world presented themselves and asked to be includ-   Sollers
ed—of whom Mandelstam, studying Italian in order to
read him, writes:

    When I began to study Italian and had barely fami-   trans.
liarized myself with its phonetics and prosody, I sud-   Harris &
denly understood that the center of gravity of my speech   Link
efforts had been moved closer to my lips, to the outer
parts of my mouth. The tip of the tongue suddenly turn-
ed out to have the seat of honour. The sound rushed to-
ward the locking of teeth. And something else that
struck me was the infantile aspect of Italian phonetics,
its beautiful child-like quality, its closeness to in-
fant babbling, to some kind of eternal dadism. . . . Would
you like to become acquainted with the dictionary of
Italian rhymes? Take the entire Italian dictionary and
leaf through it as you will. . . . Here every word rhymes.
Every word begs to enter into concordanza. The abundance
of marriageable endings is fantastic—the astonishment
that is Dante, of whom Yeats wrote in his 1914 poem *EGO*
DOMINUS TUUS:

              The chief imagination of Christendom,
              Dante Alighiere, so utterly found himself
              That he has made that hollow face of his
              More plain to the mind's eye than any face
              But that of Christ—

but it is not the self that made this face so plain to
our mind's eye after him, and certainly not his arguments for Church and Empire, but more likely the colours
he gave to language—first, in his room *una nebula di*   *La Vita*
colore di fuoco—then, within this colour of fire, a   *Nuova*
figure spoke in the high language of divinity—*Ego domi-*
nus tuus—eros and nakedness that overwhelm—he thought
he saw *una cosa, la quale ardesse tutta*—the voice said,
Vide cor tuum—he had not recognized his heart in flames
where it was eaten—this discovery of Beatrice in the

shaping of a world—the colours of this event in language fly in the flag of Italy—

the face moves among the beautiful letters, never still
in the alpha/omega, the A through Z of our vernacular
tongues—born in the house of the heart's mind that is
the mind's heart—*purposed to make it known to many*—   *La Vita Nuova*
that they might flame in their alphabets—*saluting all*
the fedeli d'Amore that they might answer—Dante, drawing upon the Provençal experience of the reason of poems,
brings us to Amors—Giorgio Agamben tells us *Amors is*
the name the Troubadours gave to the experience of the
advent of the poetic word. . . . It is difficult to under-
stand the sense in which poets understood love, as long
as we obstinately construe it according to a secular
misunderstanding, in a purely biographical context. For
the Troubadours, it is not a question of psychological
or biographical events that are successively expressed
in words, but rather, of the attempt to live the topos
itself, the event of language as a fundamental amorous
and poetic experience—the *loved experience* is found in
the poetics of unmapped territory—thus, the *New Life*
is the possibility larger than and other than the mere
expression of the sentiments of subjective reality or
of the self, which is as much a lifetime creation as
is the poesis of the traditional soul—this event of our
vernacular speech—not to be confused with *language as*   Michel de
an object of knowledge constructed by philosophers and   Certeau/
linguists, but a part of language, a mode of language   Godzich
use, that is a discourse—with the heart of—*actual*
social interaction and practice—witness Sordello—   *Purgatorio* VI
disdegnosa—mourning Sir Blancatz—
            And so mortal is the harm (to the virtues   trans.
            That I have no suspicion that it will ever   Ezra Pound
            be undone, except in this wise, that
            they take his heart out, and have it
            eaten by the Barons who live un-hearted,

then they would have hearts worth something—
love's reason reasoning, which Dante tells us it would
be shame not to explain, enters into the discourses of
the territory called world—the poetic is the language
of the mapless—

Dante's gift is continuously contemporary in the shape
he gave his poem's discoursing—out of the advent of
language one's life in language, as if life were the
home of it—where the intimacy of sound discloses the
Amors of othernesses—in *La Vita Nuova*, the interplay
of love and reason, poem and prose, Dante and Beatrice,
friends and beloved ladies opens into a territory—even
Beyond the widest of the circling spheres—where *The
Comedy* entangles the amorous with the discoursing of
myth, cosmology, philosophy, theology, history, economics, and current issues—even as Beatrice's colours—
white, crimson, and green—circle my early morning cof-
fee cup, while I write—this is the polyphony of *The
Comedy*—the ever changing polyphony of amorous thought—

the gift of *the amorous and poetic experience* so entangled—the face haunting the curious laughter of the
syllables—that we might speak an ethics out of this
mapless century of ourselves—"at home," so to speak,
in the unredeemable and irreparable—transmigrators—
of humanism, of religions, of absolutes, of ignorant
hierarchies—when the sublime collapses upon us—as it
did upon Dante—we are inside the condition of it—
marking our footsteps among its uncanny pieces—holding
on to the love of our ordinary lives—hearted or un-
hearted—Dante, "the Tuscan Homer," as Vico called him,
is exemplar of the necessary *poiesis* in a vast terri-
tory—*not exactly human*—even as we take up the task of   Hannah Arendt
our ongoing departure from the *totality he confronted*—   *Men in Dark Times*
                                                                  Sollers

in the difficult matter of God in the streets—*facilis*   *Aeneid* VI.126
descensus Averno—it is easy today to descend to Aver-
nus, as the Sibyl tells us in the voices of Posillipo—
there the door of Dis is open twenty-four hours a day—
like the doors of the current return to religion—whose
concern is with the definition of abomination and exclusion—

in *La Vita Nuova*, Dante proposes that love, which is   Sollers
meaning, which impels speech

the *Inferno* does not come to rest in those brutalities
of God's judgment—it is there that *speech is fixed*   Sollers
once and for all—words stop dead in the depths of a
bloody and frozen silence—the entire human body is devoured—in agonizing contrast to the love that eats the
flaming heart—Philippe Sollers, in his brilliant contemporary reading of Dante, notices that self-interest—
the closed self—is a fundamental characteristic of the
damned, which has consequences: *Language turns upon and*
possesses he who believed he possessed it but in fact
was only one of its signs—

the reader who stops there in the drama of closed meaning will lose Dante—including the Dante who haunts our
discordant departure from Christendom—the *Inferno* fascinates with its imagination of the condition of irre-
deemable loss—the lost *good of the intellect*—we rebel
at the theological imprisonment and abandonment—and suspect that Dante now and again does so too—in this ice-
house of language words, we think, must thaw—we are,
perhaps, closer to rebellious Rabelais than we know—
when Pantagruel *hears thawed out words*:
    he threw on the deck in front of us handsful of   trans.
frozen words, which might have been sugared almonds,   Burton Raffel
like so many pearls of different colours. We saw bright
red words, green words, blue words, black words, golden

words. And after they had been warmed for a bit between
our hands, they melted like snow and we actually heard
them, but without understanding a word, for they were in
a barbarous language. . . .
. . . Panurge asked Pantagruel to give him more. Pantagruel observed that giving words was like making love.
"Then sell me some," said Panurge.
"Selling words," said Pantagruel, "is more like
what lawyers do. I'd prefer to sell you silence and
make you pay more for it. . . ."
But still he threw three or four handsful on to
the deck. And we could see sharp words, bloody words
(which, according to the pilot, sometimes went back to
the place where they'd been spoken, only to find the
throat that uttered them had been slit open), horrible
words, and many others unpleasant to see. And when
they'd melted, we heard: hin, hin, hin, hin, tick,
tock, whizz, gibber, jabber, frr, frrr, frrr, boo, boo,
boo, boo, boo, boo, boo, boo, crack, track, trr, trr,
trr, trrr, trrrr, on, on, on, on, wooawooawoooon, gog,
magog, and God only knows. . . .

Cosi gridai con la faccia levata—this I cried with   *Inf.* XVI.76
lifted face, from among the sodomites—

Inferno—facing Dante's theology—even out of a Roman Catholic
childhood—of the immutable and unchanging—
recognizing that it is the vocabulary of his cosmology—
of creation and continuation—in the body of thought—
this entanglement of language and death—mortality's
speechlessness—repetitious or masquerading in our own
vocabulary of such territory—I walk into a crisis of
where Hell is—out of this cosmology—gone in the
teeth—among twentieth-century Constitutions and religious pretensions—Yes! to be "clean of these hell-
obsessions" in another world, as Pound said, discovering
Hell on the surface of the earth—where, as in Dante,

the present might be found—this sense of exit and departure—"from the first canto to the last, the poet's
path was the path of the living man"—at stake in the
poesis—finding the life of form—in so vast a territory—*practices of the self and of freedom within these
games of truth*, turning round and round in, say, your
marvelous kitchen—to impart relish—I read this great,
vulnerable poem—materiality of language—materiality of
form—materiality of men's and women's bodies envisioning—as if they were my own—thus, to unravel the *Western paradigm of one sole truth*—that cannot find the
place of its totality—founded on sacrifice—there or
here—our immortalities cannot help with this—Churches,
States, even Atheisms are given to personifications of
totality—exchanging bed linens—you can vote for a
water glass of democracy on the side-table—they never
apologize for time misspent, not even in the theories
of themselves—now and again, they rehabilitate some
lives—

Ernst Kantorow

Frederick II

Michel Foucau

Michel de Cert

The Mystic Fab

I was talking to Galileo the other day about his re-
habilitation—he was disdainful—we wondered who or
what is speaking in such ethics of thought—certainly
not time regained, let alone eternalized—we were standing there in Rome—in the Campo dei fiore—at the foot
of Giordano Bruno's monument. He jumped right off his
pedestal and said, "Listen, kid, it's better to burn."
"Hell," I said, astonished, "I'm 72." —we three then
walked along talking about Bruno's dialogues and son-
nets, dedicated to Sir Philip Sidney, *De gli eroici
furori*, and of Plato's curious blending of the words
Eros and heros—"the name heros is only a light al-
teration of Eros from whom the heroes sprang"—of what
it was like to write of heroic frenzies—

Cratylus

in canto X of the *Inferno*, we come upon the open tombs
of those who questioned immortality—Epicurus, who

argued that happiness is the chief good, "and all his
followers"—the last great Emperor of the Holy Roman
Empire (the title lasted until 1806), Frederick II
(d.1250)—of whom it is said that he had a man impri-
soned in a sealed wine vat and left him to perish under
watch to prove that the soul died with the body, if it
could not escape—and among them Guido Cavalcanti's
father and father-in-law, so condemned while Guido was
still alive, neither of whom had so experimented with
human destiny—only Florentines in the midst of religious and political strife, who questioned immortality—the crown of such totality—where in modern
terms a fortuneteller paradises—

I think of the friendship and estrangement of Dante
and Guido, whom Dante names "the first among my
friends" in *The New Life*, of whom, in *Hell*, he sends
the message to his father that he is still living, who
is recalled in the Purgatorio for the glow of his poems—

Guido, vorrei che tu e Lapo ed io　　　　　*Purg.* XI.97
Fossimo presi per incantamento . . .

in Shelley's beautiful sonnet, which translates it:

Guido, I would that Lapo, thou, and I,　　　Sonnet VI
Led by some strong enchantment, might ascend
A magic boat . . .

in Robert Duncan's version from among the sodomites:

Robin, it would be a great thing if you, me and Jack Spicer
Were taken up in a sorcery with our mortal heads so turned
That life dimmed in the light of that fairy ship . . .

there's an ancient prejudice to the effect that one　　　Robert Musil
is born and dies a human being

A completed foundation of humanity should, how-
ever, signify the definitive elimination of the sacri-
ficial mythogema and of its ideas of nature and cul-
ture, of the unspeakable and the speakable, which are
grounded in it. In fact, even the sacralization of
life derives from sacrifice: from this point of view
it simply abandons the naked natural life to its own
violence and its own unspeakableness, in order to
ground in them every cultural rule and all language.
The ethos, humanity's own, is not something unspeak-
able or sacer *that must remain unsaid in all praxis*
and human speech. Neither is it nothingness, whose
nullity serves as the basis for the arbitrariness and
violence of social action. Rather, it is social
praxis itself, human speech itself, which have become
transparent to themselves—

Giorgio Agamben
Language and
Death

"So!" Jack Spicer said, early in our friendship,
"you're one of those who eat their god."

1945

in unmapped America, the Puritans had a ferocious
time with omniscience, which proposed predestination
of human nature, one by one—now, when you get down
to brass facts, who in this community should be
allowed to receive the body and blood of Christ?—
the answer: the successful—speaking in the voice
of—the coherence of—capitalism—

———

in *ESTHÉTIQUE DU MAL,* Wallace Stevens writes: *The death*
of Satan was a tragedy / For the imagination—and asks,
What underground?—it was a dismissal from usefulness—with the shift of Hell to the surface of our
own task, Purgatory and Paradise also shift to the
imagination of the *irreparable*—

like you, I walk *in contemporary culture—the move-*
ment of perpetual departure—I walk *the forest of*
innumerable sounds—I talk with a *haunted tongue*—
how does *the body get form?*—and clothe itself—

the entire Comedy, Philippe Sollers writes, *is an*
apprenticeship in thought, vision, and writing—from
the *frozen silence* to a new poetry—*The Purgatory, in*
fact, is a continuous image of the poetic condition—
Dante walks and questions—perhaps the poetic condition is a matter of interrogation—certainly, it is
for us, as it was for him—he walks as if he were in
the place of language—in Sollers words, *to the dis-*
continuity that rediscovers the silence and otherness
of a new language—the spontaneous, intimate language
that is opposed to Hell—and *approaches, through suc-*
cessive ruptures the "umana radice" (human root)—in
other words the root of a language exempt from
guilt—there in the place where love dictates—I
enter with you *la divina foresta spessa e viva*—the
divine forest green and dense—in apprenticeship—
so, Robert Duncan would celebrate Dante's seven hun-
dredth birthday in 1965, writing of "the sweetness and
greatness" of the Divine Comedy—

we have been walking and climbing all the days of our
lives in a forest fire of language—one calls for the
good of the intellect—it is existentially given—
another calls for the grace note time can be in order
to know oneself—when suddenly a voice calls,
"O voi"—O, you there in your little barc—as one
might from the upper deck of a liner call, "You there
in your dinghy, watch your shores before you lose
your bearings"—we enter the Odyssean language of the
Paradiso—*L'acqua ch'io prendo già mai non si corse—*
in waters that have never been sailed before—we are
warned that we may become lost in the *waves of the*

phrases from
Michel de Certeau

Purg. XXIV.54-56

marvelous—among the light substances, if we do not
have the *intelletto d'amore, as through smooth and
transparent glass*, this discourse with cosmos—*the
glorious wheel*, the radiance speaking, horizon brigh-
tening, a swift fire in a cloud, the sun struck
rubies of conjugated souls—the ladder of splen-
dours—(*La mente, che qui luce, in terra fumma*—the
mind that shines here, smokes on earth)—the mind
that is the sky *ensapphired*—crystalline, where the
sewer of blood and filth is not forgotten but absent—
suddenly, Dante looks down to see the earth—*il varco*   *Inf.* XXVI
folle d'Ulisse—my mind looks back, as Dante's did,
to Ulysses in the *Inferno*, clothed in that which
burned him—who tells us, "I could not conquer within
me the passion I had to gain experience of the world
and of the vices and worth of men"—he talked his companions into making wings of their oars for their mad
flight—until, as he says, "the sea closed over us"—
in the *Purgatorio*, the siren in Dante's dream sings   *Purg.* XXIX.22
of *Ulisse* mid-sea—here, in the *Paradiso*, Dante
looks back through the dangers of language traveling,
Odyssean, eager, and infinite—*come all'ultimo suo*   *Par.* XXX.33
ciascuno artista—as with every artist at his or her
limit—living sparks, rubies, the river of topazes—
the laughter of flowers—to find this rose in the   *Par.* XXX.117
farthest petals, which Charles Olson calls *the
longest lasting rose*—

Dante's Hell, Purgatory, and Paradise are signposts—
of tradition, which implicates us—of shifts in their
landscapes, which implicate us—in imagination of
language—Hell, where we are lost in the unredeemable
time of our own century—Purgatory, renames the
poetic condition—the experiment of writing—the feel
of writing—Paradise, where words wander in the *wild-
wood*—Dante's *Paradiso* remains in the arms of Bea-

trice—for hers is the first name of the love that
moves his language among the stars—this is, of
course, heresy, as the Dominicans recognized when
they condemned him in 1335—

The gods prevent the supreme undecidedness of man; Jean-Luc Nancy:
they close off his[/her] humanity, and prevent him *The Inoperative*
[/her] from becoming unhinged, from measuring up to *Community*
the incommensurable. . . . The gods forbid that man
should be risked further than man. And most serious
of all, they take away his death.

    What there is to say here can be said very sim-
ply: religious experience is exhausted. It is an
immense exhaustion. This fact is in no way altered
by the upsurge in the political, sociological, or
cultural success of religions (. . . Jewish, Islamic,
or Christian fundamentalism; sects, theosophies,
gnosis). There is no return of the religious: there
are the contortions and turgescence of its exhaustion.
Whether that exhaustion is making way for another
concern for the gods, for their wandering or their
infinite disappearance, or else for no god, that is
another matter: it is another question altogether,
and it is not something that can be grasped between
the pincers of the religious, nor indeed between
those of atheism.

coming upon *the inability of man, who is lost in* Agamben:
time, to take possession of his own historical nature *Infancy and History*

poets who took the initial steps into our uncovered
Hell ran wildly into a dark forest—*una selva oscura,*
say,

Shelley, living at Lerici on the Gulf of Spezzia in
1822, starting to write *The Triumph of Life*—beauti-

ful *terza rima* in honour of Dante—bring him into a
vision—he thinks he sits beside a public way where
he sees "a great stream / Of people there . . . hurrying to
and fro, Numerous as gnats upon the evening gleam"—
"one might torrent"—a chariot comes "on the silent
storm of its own rushing spendour"—and in it sits
"a Shape, as one whom years deform"—and the chario-
teer, "A Janus-visaged Shadow," drives the "wonder-
wingèd team"—whose shapes are lost "in thick
lightenings"—"a triumphal pageant of a captive
multitude" that becomes a "sad Pageant"—half to
himself, he asks, "And what is this? Whose shape is
that within the car? And why—"—when suddenly a
voice answers, "Life!"—so,

That what I thought was an old root which grew
To strange distortion out of the hillside,
Was indeed one of those deluded crew,

And that the grass, which methought hung so wide
And white, was but his thin discoloured hair,
And that the holes he vainly sought to hide,

Were or had been eyes—

this is Jean-Jacques Rousseau—displacing the fierce
dignity of Virgil in Dante's *Comedy*—Rousseau, whom
Shelley had revered as emblematic of "political and
metaphysical transition"—of originary language—
of revolutionary possibility—of human liberty
through opppositional writing—of the stake in desire
of any one of us—

in Shelley's vision, we see the Chariot herd, tether,
and roll over the wise, the famous, age and youth—
now, Rousseau insists upon this endless passing on
of life—but Shelley interrupts:

'*Mine eyes are sick of this perpetual flow*
Of people, and my heart is sick of one sad thought—
speak!'
Rousseau replies with the story of his own love—
when "the bright omnipresence / Of morning . . . / And the
sun's image radiantly intense"
'*Burned on the waters of the well that glowed*
Like gold, and threaded all the forest's maze
With the winding paths of emerald fire . . .

'*A shape of light*'

Rousseau tells us that he asked that she "Pass not
away upon the passing stream"—she offers him a cup
to "quench his thirst":
'*I rose; and, bending at the sweet command,*
Touched with faint lips the cup she raised,
And suddenly my brain became as sand

'*Where the first wave had more than half erased*
The track of deer on desert Labrador;
Whilst the wolf, from which they fled amazed,

Leaves his stamp visibly upon the shore,
Until the second bursts;—so on my sight
Burst a new vision, never seen before.'

shadows, phantoms, ghosts—"like small gnats and
flies"—"like discoloured flakes of snow"—which the
"youthful glow melts" and the snow extinguishes—even
Dante, whom the poem honours with its rhyme, is seen
on the "opposing steep" and will be swept away as the
chariot climbs—Rousseau continues:
'*Desire, like a lioness bereft*

Of her last cub, glared as it died; each one
Of that great crowd sent forth incessantly
Those shadows, numerous as the dead leaves blown

'*In autumn evening from a poplar tree.*
Each like himself and like each other were
At first; but some distorted seemed to be

'*Obscure clouds, moulded by the casual air;*
And of this stuff the car's creative ray
Wrought all the busy phantoms that were there,

'*As the sun shapes the clouds; thus on the way*
Mask after mask fell from the countenance
And form of all; and long before the day

'*Was old, the joy which waked like heaven's glance*
The sleepers in the oblivious valley, died;
And some grew weary of the ghastly dance,

'*And fell, as I have fallen, by the wayside. . . .*'
again Shelley cuts into this continuous flow of despair, leaves us and the poem with only his own question in six words —
     '*Then, what is life? I cried?*' —
before he drowned —

Shelley and Rousseau — like many of us — were enamoured
of an absolute — the universal from which human freedom might escape into a community of meaning —

the shift of Hell to our own surface changes the beginning and the end of time — the sacred powerline of
our totalities — alpha and omega reverse — unredeemed —
into our own responsibility — the task of a community
of meaning —

I think of Wittgenstein: "to imagine a language means   *Phil. Inv. 19*
to imagine a form of life" —

and of his remarks to 'the heretics' club: "and how
I shall describe the experience of wonderment before
the existence of the world, with these words: the
world thus is experienced as a miracle. I am now
tempted to say that the correct expression for the
miracle of the world, albeit as expressing nothing
within language, is the existence of language itself."
and I ponder Giorgio Agamben's reply: ". . . if the most   *Infancy and History*
appropriate expression of the wonderment at the exis-
tence of the world is the existence of language, what
then is the correct expression of the existence of
language?

"The only possible answer to this question is
human life, as ethos, as ethical way. The search for
a *polis* and an *oikía* befitting this void and unpre-
supposable community is the *infantile* task for future
generations."

---

in this task of hell—indebted to Dante—I hear Ezra
Pound's magnificent, poetic interrogation of the
great crystal—stained by anti-Semitism and twentieth-century political shame—among us now, as if
they owned a percentage of the human mind of—this
viscid Western paradigm—transmuted into silence—

"To what is the poet faithful?" Agamben asks, un-
covering a vocation—faithful to the immemorial, for
which we have used the word gods—faithful to the emptiness of language—faithful to what is *first in
mind*, word by word and daily yet unformed—
in 1963, an Italian reporter named Luigi Pasquini met
Pound in the Tempio Malatestiano in Rimini:
    "When I reach him he is standing in the sacristy
of the church, a tiny room that formerly housed its
relics. Above the door is Piero della Francesca's

fresco depicting Sigismondo Malatesta as he kneels
before his patron saint. Pound is standing beneath
it, surrounded by people.

I approach him slowly, nervously, until I am directly before him, face to face. I look him in the
eye, and inquire: 'Ezra Pound?'

He does not respond. He stares at me, silent, and
his mouth hints at a smile.

I insist, and repeat his name. He gazes at me,
arching his eyebrows for a moment, but says nothing.

I fear I must be mistaken and address my glance
to the woman beside him. She peers up at him, then
nods, reassuring me that it is him.

I offer him my hand, and he takes it in his own.
I do not tell him my name, but I make clear that I
know his books. . . . He understands, it seems. He
gives a sign of assent, but continues to remain
silent.

Our hands are still clasping each other. 'This is
the hand of the great American poet,' I offer. ('la
mano del grande poeta americano!')

And at last his voice emerges, his first words,
uttered in a tranquil Italian accent without a trace
of an Anglo-American inflection: "I am not great."
('Non grande.')

Swiftly I reply: '—you are among the greatest.'
('Grandissimo.')

But the conversation falters, and I grow uncertain. Through friends I had heard that he was living
in Rapallo, but a stray remark from Miss Rudge indicates they have just come from Venice. I try to
take up the topic: 'Where are you living now: in
Rapallo? Or in Merano with your daughter, or in
Venice?'

He will not reply. He looks at me again, with a
mocking gaze.

I persist: 'Rapallo, Merano? Venice, Rome?'

Nothing. He is still silent, his gaze fixed on me,
like someone playing a guessing game.
I press on: 'So where are you living now?' I
continue, 'Where?'
At last he lowers his head, slowly, and puts his
mouth to my ear so that no one can hear us. His
voice is a whisper, rasping: 'I live in hell.'
This leaves me bewildered. Here we are in a
church, in a sacristy in fact (even if it is the
sacristy of a paganizing temple)—in a place, in
short, as far as possible from Erebus or the underworld of Lucifer. And yet he says we're in hell. I
fail to understand and want to pursue it: 'Which hell
do you mean? The hellish tourism? The inferno of the
war, here in Rimini? The hell of Rome? Of Italy?
Of the world?'
He is silent again. At last he moves his hands:
he places them before his stomach, and slowly lift-
ing them to the level of his heart, as the traces of
light in his pupils become like glowing coals, he
whispers a suffocated scream: 'Here is hell. Here.'"   cited in
L. S. Rainey:
*Ezra Pound: The
Monument of
Culture*

–Robin Blaser
25 August 1997

Author's note: "Great Companion: Dante I" was commissioned by Annalisa
Goldoni, as the keynote address for a Dante conference in June 1997 at the
Universitá G. D'Annunzio, Pescara.

Blaser at the Campus Textbook Exchange, Berkeley, c. 1951

CRITICAL ESSAYS AND READINGS

Blaser sitting outside the library, Berkeley, c. 1952

INTRODUCTION: READING ROBIN BLASER

Miriam Nichols

I

For most of his writing life, Robin Blaser has had a readership consisting of a modest handful of writers in Canada and the U.S. with ties
to mid-century New American poetry. A participant in the Berkeley
scene of the late 1940s and 50s with Robert Duncan and Jack Spicer,
Blaser was included in Donald Allen's influential anthology of 1960,
The New American Poetry, and he has since been given cameo spots
in accounts of the period, such as Ekbert Faas's *Young Robert Duncan*
(1983), Michael Davidson's *San Francisco Renaissance* (1989), and
Peter Gizzi's edition of Spicer's lectures, *The House That Jack Built*
(1998). In the Spicer biography, *Poet Be Like God* (1997), by Lew
Ellingham and Kevin Killian, he plays a larger role, albeit a supporting one. The 1999 release of proceedings from a Vancouver conference of 1995, held to mark the publication of the collected serial
poems in *The Holy Forest* (1993), is the only book-length collection of
commentaries centered on Blaser, and despite some cogent and
attentive readings, quite a number of these pieces have more to do
with Blaser's "public world" or literary friends and interests than with
the work itself.[1] *The Recovery of the Public World*, edited by Charles
Watts and Edward Byrne, does point however toward a larger readership that remains to be developed. Blaser's life as a poet, by his own
reckoning,[2] dates from 1955, a stretch of forty-five years at the century's end, and those he does count as companions in the art are among
some of the best known avant-garde writers of the mid- to late century in the U.S. and Canada: Robert Creeley, Charles Olson, Robert
Duncan, Jack Spicer, Frank O'Hara, John Ashbery, and Charles
Bernstein in the U.S.; George Bowering, Daphne Marlatt, Michael
Ondaatje, bpNichol, Steve McCaffery, and Phyllis Webb in Canada.

In part, the subdued reception of Blaser's work is simply attributable to circumstance. Until the Coach House Press release of his collected serial poems in 1993, Blaser's publications consisted of anthologized poems, essays, and small press chapbooks. When Blaser left San Francisco in 1966 to take up permanent residence in Vancouver, he had recently published the early books of what is now *The Holy Forest*, but at that stage the shape of the poem was not apparent and the chapbooks and anthologized serials—*Cups*, *The Park*, *The Faerie Queene*, *The Moth Poem*, and *Les Chiméres*—were too new, too disjunctive, and too slender in volume to attract the attention of American academics. Once in Canada, he was out of sight.

In Vancouver, Blaser's arrival was preceded by pockets of local interest in the New American poetry. The late Warren Tallman, then teaching in the Department of English at the University of British Columbia, and his partner Ellen were American immigrants and Ellen knew the Berkeley poets from her student days at the University of California. In a series of privately organized readings and lectures at the Tallmans' home, and in public events like the 1961 University of British Columbia Festival of the Contemporary Arts and the 1963 Vancouver Poetry Conference, the Tallmans brought Robert Duncan, Charles Olson, Allen Ginsberg, Denise Levertov, Jack Spicer, Margaret Avison, and Robin Blaser to Vancouver. Response to these visits included *Tish 1-19* (1961-1963), a poetry newsletter edited by Tallman's students and inspired by Duncan's 1961 lectures, that since has become a signpost for the beginnings of an important strand of postmodernism in Canadian writing.[3]

But this glowing response to the "wonder merchants,"[4] as Tallman called them, was an isolated phenomenon. Peter Orlovsky's cutting remark to Ginsberg in 1963, recorded in *The Indian Journals*, that Ginsberg was washed up as a poet and might as well go teach in Vancouver,[5] serves as an unflattering reminder that in the 1960s, the city was at land's end of the map in terms of international cultural happenings. Among Canadian academics beyond Tallman's circle, however, it was the nation and national identity that mattered, rather than the international. A strong push for the creation of a Canadian canon and for legitimization of Canadian studies in university programs was afoot, and this academic initiative had precedent in public policy with the creation of the Canada Council for the Arts in 1957 and legislation favoring Canadian media. Blaser's arrival coincided with a growing irritation with American cultural dominance and a call for a stronger Canadian identity. Moreover, highly influential critics and writers like Northrop Frye, D. G. Jones, and Margaret Atwood were interested in thematic criticism that could bring forward "Canadian content," rather than the formal experimentation and philosophical questions that interested Blaser. As late as 1994, George Woodcock, one of Canada's most prolific nationalist critics, breezily dismisses Blaser's work for its American lineage and formal strategies. Reviewing *The Holy Forest*, he says

> It is true he has been here for almost a quarter of a century, teaching at Simon Fraser, but his links with the Canadian tradition are much more tenuous than his links with the Pacific Northwest and the San Francisco Bay area poetic complex of the late 1950s and 1960s, when he first emerged as a member of a San Francisco circle that had links with the Black Mountain school of poets in the eastern U.S. and traced its ancestry largely to Ezra Pound.
>
> In this sense Blaser remains rather on the American side of the Pacific Northwest complex and his poetry does not relate very closely to what has been written by Canadians in the last 30 years. He writes with a curious textual density that reminds one of the Pound of the *Cantos*, with closely integrated virtuoso patterns of associate images rather than an easily acceptable current of thought. His work has a feeling of monumentality, but what the monument celebrates is hard to determine, so esoteric is his work. (35)

As these comments might suggest, Woodcock is as impatient with "textual density" as he is with the "American side" of things.

But there are reasons beyond the circumstantial for the long silence on Blaser's work. Apart from the Berkeley tag and a postmodern reflexivity which he shares with any number of American and Canadian writers, Blaser is elusive. The vocabulary of his poems and essays frequently *evokes* the poetic and theoretical trends that have come along during the course of his writing life, but it also suggests an errancy in relation to those trends. He has been called a philosophical

poet, and the frequent citations from his readings in philosophy that
find their way into the work seem to bear out the comment.[6] Certainly
The Holy Forest is thinking poetry. But the reader looking for evidence
of this or that philosophical system will find instead a rhetoric that
bends philosophy toward poetic performance and Blaser's own reading of modernity. The title of the 1974 essay, "The Stadium of the
Mirror," for instance, comes from Jacques Lacan's phrase, "*le stade du
miroir*," "translated for the metaphor" (59), Blaser says. The deliberate
mistranslation suggests that Lacan is here made to serve a poetics; the
poetics does not instantiate Lacan—a state of affairs that may put off
the reader unprepared to investigate, or hostile to non-academic usage
of this kind. To this sort of errancy, Blaser adds the juxtaposition,
sometimes in the same essay or poem, of poets and philosophers who
propose conflicting discourses: Alfred North Whitehead, Charles
Olson, Jack Spicer, Robert Duncan, Maurice Merleau-Ponty, Jacques
Lacan, Michel Foucault, Martin Heidegger, Octavio Paz, Samuel
Taylor Coleridge, William Blake, Percy Bysshe Shelley, Michel
Serres, Michel de Certeau, Hannah Arendt, Jacques Derrida, Gilles
Deleuze, Cornelius Castoriadis, and Stéphane Mallarmé jostle each
other in the poems and essays. The list could be lengthened, but the
point is that citation cannot be read as filiation. In "The Violets"
(1983), an essay on Olson and Whitehead, Blaser calls Olson's use of
Whitehead "companionable" rather than "systematic" (72), suggesting
that Olson found stimulation for and confirmation of his poetics in
Whitehead. The same could be said of Blaser's own companionable
approach to other writers; they are fellow travelers in thought who
turn up in the same places and may share perspectives there with the
poet on particular issues.

   Blaser's awareness of his maverick status sometimes registers in his
work as humor—nowhere more dryly than in the transcript of a talk
delivered at the 1986 conference on Jack Spicer in San Francisco and
subsequently published with proceedings of the event in *Acts 6: A
Book of Correspondences for Jack Spicer* (1987). In the mid-1980s, language writing was the most radical and talked about of new American
poetries, at least in the poetry world of older New American poetry
fans. At the same time, poststructuralist theory reigned supreme in
North American English departments. Conference participants
included a significant contingent of language writers and supporters,

generational successors to Spicer who were most interested in his linguist's sense of "the sentence and prose forms" in Ron Silliman's
phrasing (67), or in the possibilities for poststructuralist readings of his
work.[7] Ironically, both Silliman and Blaser titled their papers after
Spicer's last words, "My Vocabulary Did This To Me," and the two sat
on the same panel. On this occasion, Blaser chose to discuss Spicer's
"discourse of cosmos" and to position the poetics of dictation in a
genealogy of the mystical tradition that included St. John of the Cross,
St. Theresa of Avila, St. Ignatius of Loyola, and John Donne (104-05).
His subject matter could not have been more contrary to the temper
of the moment, and as if to underscore the point, he challenged poststructuralist reading practices as ahistorical in the course of the talk—
all this with a wry awareness of swimming against the current: "I am
not talking *abracadabra*. I am not arguing that our critical minds and
our readers' minds rush back to supernaturalism, to religion and so
forth. I've *read* Edward Said, I'm not *dumb*" (102). The last claim is the
hook. Indeed, Blaser *has* read Edward Said and a great many others,
but it is *how* he reads them that is not so apparent.

The focus of this introductory essay is on reading Blaser, as the larger intention of this collection of essays and archival materials is to
demonstrate and enable closer readings of his work. I am not, of
course, proposing a one-person revival of New Criticism, nor am I or
any of the contributors here anti-theory. But writers may be "disappeared" in any number of critical generalizations about national,
generational, or theoretical identities, and this kind of erasure is particularly evident in the history of Blaser's reception. I began to work
on this collection because I wanted a text that would encourage discussion on what is specific to the work of this poet. Particular to
Blaser, however, is the constructing of singularity through acts of creative reception; reading Blaser means, first, an attention to how
Blaser reads.

II

On *Astonishments*, a series of autobiographical audio tapes recorded
with Warren Tallman and others in 1974, Blaser locates the beginnings of his project in his arrival at Berkeley and initiation into Anglo-
American modernism.[8] As a student at the University of California

from 1944 to 1954, Blaser studied renaissance, medieval, and romantic
literature, but off campus he participated in a lively community of students, writers, and artists engaged in making new forms of art. Robert
Duncan, then resident at the communal Throckmorton Manor, con-
ducted a reading group for friends and acquaintances interested in the
moderns, in part to express disapproval of the way that they were then
taught at the University. In this group, which Blaser refers to as
Duncan's counter-university ("Vocabulary" 98), there were readings of
Yeats, Pound, Eliot, Joyce, Mallarmé, and Lorca. What Blaser heard
there—and later he would add Nerval and de Sade to the list—was a
wreckage of the epistemological foundations of western philosophy
and religion, and the consequent disappearance of a public world
view. Still very much a Catholic boy at nineteen, Blaser says of his
arrival at Berkeley that "the Idaho kid didn't know that the manhood
had died into itself as closed form and thought, closed into his need,
into his grief, into himself as measure, his will then imposing upon all
things and turning them into a human image losing the actual interaction between self and world" (Side 19).[9] The young Blaser, says the
older one, "tried to join the world and found it absent, the world itself,
and all the images in the world, so the visibility, the manhood as
humanitas or whatever you want to call it, the human element is no
longer a visibility in the world at all but . . . a closure of relationships,
interrelationships, a lyric voice that speaks only of itself and closes into
itself, no longer narrates the world and the actual astonishment of the
world" (Side 19).

Blaser's apprenticeship in poetry began, then, with a recognition of
the collapse of metaphysical certainty announced by the moderns,
but on the tapes Blaser also speaks of "the unrecognized disaster of a
world devoured into the human [form], rather than a world disclosed
in which we are images of an action, visibilities of an action, an
action which otherwise is invisible, larger, older, and other than ourselves" (Side 19). The "*unrecognized* disaster" (emphasis added) is
that the old humanism has merely given place to a skepticism that is
as ahistorical as what it is meant to replace. This reading of modernity—and Blaser hears the postmodern as a corrective to modernism
rather than the advent of a "great divide"[10]—suggests an *anxiety* that
runs contrary to that everywhere expressed in critical writing of the

last four decades. However disparate the camps, the dominant manner of theorizing modernity is as a struggle to demystify the exaggerated claims of various authoritative traditions, and to construct new, more equitable ones. The perceived danger derives from ideologically veiled structures of domination, whether of omniscient authorship (to go back to Barthesian arguments); compulsory gender and sexual roles (feminist and sexual difference theorists); theologies of consciousness (targeted by poststructuralists and psychoanalytical critics); or economic and cultural imperialism (the province of Marxist and postcolonial critics). Blaser is not insensible to the dangers posed by the state or other social institutions and systems, but he takes exception to the immunity from historical contingency that theoretical languages sometimes appear to grant themselves. Citing René Girard in "The Violets," he writes:

> The cultural heritage of humanity is regarded with suspicion. Its only interest lies in its "demystification."
> Humanity, we are told, has fallen victim to a vast mystification unrecognized until now. This is cultural nihilism, and it is often associated with a fetishistic cult of science. Because we have discovered the "original sin" of human thought, we think ourselves free of it. (63)

The contemporary tendency to dismiss the past Blaser hears as "'scientific angelism.'" It constitutes "an apocalypse of the objective or of a generalized humanity which can be seen as an objectivity," he says. "It is also a disguised superstition" (63). In the same essay, Blaser remarks that "[i]t is one of the curiosities and discomforts of conversation and of lecturing, when one is involved in the presentation of, say, Dante or Giotto or Michelangelo that one meets embarrassment, even hostility, before the contents among so many people. . . . Many have fallen into time, so to speak, and seem unable to go forwards or backwards" (82). "No foundation" means a shift in the *status* of knowledge, such that all cultural orders become historical, and hence traversible; if one can "go forward and backwards" as Blaser says, it is because no order grounds the others. In a different context, Merleau-Ponty makes a similar point: if a truth appears to be ultimate, he argues, "that is itself the mark of a certain cultural epoch"

(20). Thus where a discursive tradition, like that of the sacred, has simply been struck off the agenda for many contemporary writers, Blaser argues that such a discourse is a mode of thought, and a part of cultural history; it does not simply vanish when its status changes. From this point of view, the contemporary task is the rethinking of relationships, such as those of the sacred, that have fallen out of belief and into history. The "polar logic" that marks much of Blaser's poetry and prose instantiates one such investigation into the sacred.

Blaser finds a first and stellar example of the changed status of knowledge and of polar thinking in the thirteenth century, rather than the twentieth. In "The Hunger of Sound" from *The Boston Poems* (1956-1958), he records a childhood introduction to *The Divine Comedy*

> Read Dante without words.
> (By Doré.)
>   I try now to remember
> what I thought of hell.
>   A small head
> bent over the big pages.
>   And now
> borrowed the terrible trees
>   and
> the whole image of Dante. (*Holy* 390-91)

On *Astonishments*, Blaser again returns to "the little boy opening the big Dante book" (Side 19), and then moves to Ernst Kantorowicz's reading of a Dante "that wasn't the baby-book Dante." At Berkeley, Blaser studied medieval political philosophy with Kantorowicz, who, he says, "*put you into time*" (Side 19; emphasis added). The chapter of *The King's Two Bodies* (1957) most relevant to his reading of Dante, he says, is "Man-Centered Kingship," where Kantorowicz discusses the significance of Dante's distinction between earthly and spiritual life.[11] Unlike more orthodox writers of the time who made God and his ecclesiastical representatives the supreme authorities on earth, Dante distinguished historical life from the divine; the moral and ethical from the spiritual; the emperor from the pope; the terrestrial from the heavenly paradise. This allowed him to present the earthly paradise as the work of a human collective ("*humanitas*"), to be made with the help of the pagan virtues (Prudence, Fortitude, Temperance, and Justice). These could be achieved without divine assistance, while the Christian virtues (Faith, Hope, and Charity) could only be given by grace. Dante, says Kantorowicz, "transferred the age-old struggle about the superiority of either pope or emperor to a plane differing from the customary argumentations when he referred both powers to their absolute standards, those of *deitas* and *humanitas*" (460).

The significance of this reading of Dante to Blaser lies in Kantorowicz's emphasis on Dante's conferring of agency and responsibility on all people for the composition of the earthly good, while withholding ultimate reality from that composition at the same time. In Blaser's view, Dante faced conditions parallel to those he and other New Americans had to confront at mid-century, namely the breakdown of belief, the loss of metanarratives, and the task of reimagining a world. On the tapes, Blaser says:

> one had no sense of how crucial this thing of the thirteenth-century was, that the world image is disappearing then and Dante takes it on to battle and quarrel for the nature of the world image, whether it would be god-given or man-given. . . .
>
> . . . .
>
> what you were getting out of Kantorowicz is that it is [the] thirteenth century that for the first time discloses history as a process, the first time, so that when we get to our period and have to quarrel through Marxist views of history and all of that, we are literally, for my mind, doing something that I discover through Dante first with comfort and with astonishment. . . . (Side 20)

Here Blaser draws from Dante the notion that history is processive, and without an objective teller; while it is unavoidably undergone, it cannot be constructed as an object of knowledge. Dante registers the historicity of human knowing by reserving the transcendent point of view for God. On the same tape, Blaser says,

> I think one of the most fearsome notions in the world, and it's only in the modern period when they have refused to think in oppositions, [is] if you think of time without an opposite you simply—you have resolved into the worst kind of—well, an inadequate thought. It's like taking the body and forgetting there's a mind or something the way some people like to do too. (Side 20)

Yet Blaser does not read Dante as simply dualistic; rather he sees the possibilities of a triadic imagination that is neither conventionally idealist nor materialist:

> Body, intellect, and soul are three different things and you must work with a triad. . . . And it is so important that you keep the triad rather than what we live in where material and immaterial forms—and all you do is reverse back and forth. You're either a theosophist—spiritualist—or you're a materialist and both of you seem stupid to me. (Side 20)

This last remark comes as a kind of throwaway on the tapes, but the rejection of both materialism and idealism is a key point of poetics, and one that Blaser is prepared to reiterate decades later. In "Of the Land of Culture," from *Streams II* (1986-1991), he writes:

> the shills said, confidentially, cultural haven is under one of these three walnut shells, named O.T., N.T., and materialism— try your luck! (*Holy* 335)

The missing third position, I propose, is that of the realist, a position which Blaser elaborates in his discussion of Spicer in "The Practice of Outside" (1980).[12] In this essay, he describes the "real" as "a polarity and experienced dialectic with something other than ourselves . . . . The doubleness of a man and a world are recovered to operate in the language" (275).

A pivotal term in Blaser's poetics, the "real" is opaque with conflicting histories of usage and hence a term most likely to tempt the reader to import meanings that will resonate oddly in a Blaserian context. It is also a complex term which leads into the various dimensions of Blaser's poetics; to inquire into the significance of the real is to find oneself investigating an epistemology, an aesthetics, and an ethics. Before "The Practice of Outside," Blaser had explored the "doubleness of a man and a world" in "The Stadium of the Mirror," and it is in this earlier essay that he first takes up the duplicity of the real. In "Stadium," he also brings in citations and pieces of vocabulary from theorists who might appear to make odd bedfellows, such as Merleau-Ponty and Lacan.[13] Blaser's vocabulary and choice of companions thus invite questions about the epistemology of the poetry. Andrew

Ross's reading of Olson in *The Failure of Modernism* suggests what a hostile reader might do with a term like the real.[14] I will therefore turn to the sense of the word as it comes into Blaser's writing and the philosophies he brings to the work; in the remainder of the essay I will follow the real as it is played out in serial form, and the ethico-politics of the poems.

III

Blaser opens "The Stadium of the Mirror" with a distinction between Language and the syntax of the individual speaker; the former is "a permanence . . . that surrounds the impermanence of our words" (53). Moreover, language is composed of both sound and silence: "If we take the order of language to be the arrangement of words without noting the silence between words and at the beginning and end of sentences, we have lost the protagonist language is,—to make of it a totality of wisdom that does not compose the real, but imposes upon it" (53). In the course of this essay, Blaser also pairs speech and language, language and silence, language and experience, and the body and language in chiasmatic relationships; at a higher level of generality, the chiasm links form and its Other. In a passage that is key to the polar thinking of the poems and later essays, Blaser says that "[t]he Other is not an object, but acts chiasmatically (Merleau-Ponty's word). Not a stillness. Not a rest. Always the opposite and companion of any man's sudden form. This is the unrest given to thought. And to our invisibility" (55).

In "The Primacy of Perception," a 1946 address to the Société française de philosophie, Merleau-Ponty proposes to treat perception as "[i]mmanence, because the perceived object cannot be foreign to him who perceives; transcendence, because it always contains something more than what is actually given" (16). While Merleau-Ponty's chiasmatic linking of perceiver and perceived has encouraged some readers to discover in his thinking a "phenomenological dream of a meaning" hidden in things, the passage also makes perception irreducibly perspectival and this is an important point for Blaser.[15] Cornelius Castoriadis has noted that Merleau-Ponty's insistence on the *primacy* of perception earned him the "compliment of relative silence" (122) during the 1970s and 80s, because his project seemed so contrary to those of poststructuralists, Foucauldians, and Lacanians who stressed the derivative and determined status of consciousness. Yet by making perception both primary *and* perspectival—by making knowledge non-totalizable—Merleau-Ponty moved toward a version of the epistemological shift into modernity: "The perceived happening can never be reabsorbed in the complex of transparent relations which the intellect constructs because of the happening," he writes (20). And then, "if this is the case, philosophy is not only consciousness of these relations; it is also consciousness of the obscure element and of the 'non-relational foundation' on which these relations are based" (20)—a "foundation" that cannot become fully an object of knowledge. From here, he proposes that knowledge be situated historically:

> When I think the Pythagorean theorem and recognize it as true, it is clear that this truth is not for this moment only. Nevertheless later progress in knowledge will show that it is not yet a final, unconditioned evidence and that, if the Pythagorean theorem and the Euclidean system once appeared as final, unconditioned evidences, that is itself the mark of a certain cultural epoch. Later developments would not annul the Pythagorean theorem but would put it back in its place as a partial, and also an abstract, truth. Thus here also we do not have a timeless truth but rather the recovery of one time by another time, just as, on the level of perception, our certainty about perceiving a given thing does not guarantee that our experience will not be contradicted, or dispense us from a fuller experience of that thing. (20)

There is an important point embedded in this passage that goes far in explaining Blaser's interest. Perspectivism does not just mean the impossibility of ever fixing upon a transcendent point of view, but also the impossibility of not having a position; *one cannot not be somewhere*, even though "somewhere" is historically contingent and never *fully* sayable. If the Pythagorean theorem may be rethought at a future date, then so may Merleau-Ponty himself or anyone else. The question of whether or not the chiasm suggests some immanent, extralinguistic meaning and therefore remains in the realm of idealist philosophy requires a separate argument, but such an interpretation must surely be troubled by the fact that Merleau-Ponty positions idealism as one mode of historical knowledge among others. This is where the chiasm does its work in a way "companionable" to that in Blaser's "Stadium of the Mirror": any somewhere has an elsewhere, or to go back to Blaser's phrasing, "[t]he Other is the opposite and companion of any man's sudden form."

It is on this point of the Other as non-totalizable, as harbouring absence, that Lacan enters Blaser's meditation on the real alongside of Merleau-Ponty. In the "Stadium" essay, Blaser cites the Lacanian notion of "foreclusion": it is a *"sort of 'original hole,' never capable of finding its own substance again since it has never been anything other than 'hole-substance'"* (57). "Hole substance" here serves as another figure of the missing point of view, the Mallarméan flower absent from every bouquet. In a passage that coincidentally draws out the polar thinking which Blaser finds in both Merleau-Ponty and Lacan, Slavoj Žižek describes the real as the place of the impossible: "it is impossible to *occupy* its position," he says, and "it is even more difficult simply to *avoid* it" (*Sublime* 156; emphasis original). Žižek's *Sublime Object of Ideology* postdates "The Stadium of the Mirror" by fifteen years, and he is not a source for Blaser, but his description of the real brings forward the *affective* dimension of Lacanian thinking: as the site of the impossible, the real is that which cannot be undergone. It is the *exterior surface* of specular consciousness (inseparable in Möebius fashion from the "interior"), and as such it would include materiality, futurity, and death—the nothing that withdraws from every appearance of something. In his polemic against deconstruction, Žižek also aligns philosophical metalanguages with the real because, in his view, such languages assume the place of the impossible by refusing to accept limit.[16] While the deconstructive point is that no position is exempt from the operation of *différance*, Žižek's contention is that a position must be taken, even if one knows it to be unstable. The notion that the impossible can neither be avoided nor experienced, suggests that the real can only be *felt* as polar, even if it is constructed as not prior to or separable from specular consciousness.

This thinking of polarities opens what is really a nexus of readings and companionships which extend Blaser's findings in Dante and situate them among contemporary writers. Olson and Whitehead, for instance, precede Merleau-Ponty and Lacan. In *The Special View of*

History, Olson draws attention to Whitehead's reformulating of the content of the word "God": in Whitehead's language, God's consequent nature is the sum of actualities in the world; his primordial nature is the infinite potential of the world to become (Sherburne 227). As Olson translates, the "Primordial—the absolute—is prospective. . . events are absolute only because they have a future, not from any past" (16). What Olson identifies in Whitehead is a displacement of the Other from its traditional locus in religion as a supernatural origin, to the future, where it functions as the possibility of creativity. By definition, the future is a place that can neither be occupied nor avoided, and it is thus real in Žižek's sense of the term; to make it primordial is to profoundly change the nature of form. If the origin is ahead, rather than behind, then form emerges retrospectively, from a process that does not predetermine its specificity and that is without a *telos*—a wandering that does not know where it is going, but only where it has been. This idea is key to the serial poem, and I will return to it.

In a much more recent engagement that postdates "Stadium," and *The Holy Forest*, Blaser finds another instance of polar thinking in Giorgio Agamben's *Infancy and History*.[17] Beginning with Walter Benjamin's remarks on the end of experience in "The Storyteller," Agamben pushes back the date of the "death of experience" to the introduction of prosthetics in the sciences and the emanationist narratives of the neo-Platonics. Scientific prosthetics expropriated the world from the senses; emanationist versions of creation blurred the distinction between human and divine knowing. In different ways, both prepared for Cartesian rationalism which began with the demand for certainty. The *alternative* to certainty Agamben locates in classical tragedy, where the human way to know is limited to the undergoing or suffering-through of events. Divine knowing, in contrast, is complete and simultaneous. If we follow Agamben through to Montaigne in this narrative, then the eventual "enlightenment" which awaits the human subject is death, and experience is ("undergoing") the means by which the subject approaches this limit.

The point of intersection between these disparate companions of Blaser's is the perspectivism: whether they write it as death, lack, the real, the impossible, the future, or simply the Other, all withhold something from human knowing—as, of course, did Dante. The story of modernity that Blaser constructs from these readings thus clearly belongs among those that have challenged the universality of rationalism and argued for situated knowledges. To turn again to "Stadium," Blaser says, "The first *Image-Nations* began a movement that became a consciousness. A reversal of the consciousness I did not believe, but had been taught—the ownership of the poet, the transparency of the language, the imposition of form upon the real, the cogito" (54). In his subsequent movement into the internally contentious turf of contemporary theory, Blaser constructs a position that troubles the boundaries of both phenomenology and poststructuralism. If "form is alive" ("Stadium" 54), perspectival, and "otherous" (Blaser's word), it cannot be thought as presence; if it has to do with consciousness, it is not well described as "disseminative drift."[18] In an article on "White Mythology," Bernard Harrison remarks on the "French seventeenth-century feel" (533) of Derrida, meaning that deconstruction is linked to the Cartesianism it dismantles, whereas other philosophies are not (Wittgenstein is Harrison's example). Since Blaser drops the demand for certitude through his reading of Dante, his project is better described as alongside, rather than coincident with deconstruction. The difference is clear in a piece like *Aporias*, where Derrida deconstructs the concept of death.[19] While the undoing of this concept affects our ability to *know* it, the deconstruction does not erase death as the advent of the impossible or the limit of that which it possible to *undergo* ("*the aporia can never simply be endured as such*" [78]). Another way to say this is that death is a corollary of consciousness, not of material becoming. It is never some death-in-general to which I draw near, but always "my death."

And here is another knot in the nexus. The familiarity—the intimacy—of death is a recognition of Jean Cocteau's *Orphée*, a film vital to Spicer's *Heads of the Town Up to the Aether*, and thoroughly familiar to Blaser. When Cocteau's Orpheus is run down by Death's leather-clad, motorcycle-riding minions and wakes to find himself in hell, he is confronted by the "Princess," who asks, "Who am I?" Orpheus correctly answers "*ma morte*," and falls in love with her. This scene ties death to consciousness as the (beloved) Other, which is to say it reveals death as the *affective* limit of consciousness. The film also ties poetry to a journey towards the borders of consciousness, and hence to

the pursuit of the singular—there at the edge of its end, where the
form begins to show. This is a fascination that Blaser repeatedly claims
for poetry. In "The Fire," he argues "the personalness of language and
form" (18); in "Stadium," he says that "poetry always has to do with
consciousness" (56); in "The Recovery of the Public World," he
assigns to the social sciences the study of group behaviours or trends
(18-19), and to the arts, the history of consciousness (36).

This narrative of the modern suggests two possible claims. The
more modest of them says that poetry is that discourse which deals
particularly with affective relations, and thus remains concerned with
the phenomenal *effects* of language. The bolder thesis, however, and
this is the one that Blaser seems to favor most often, is that all
thought, including skepticism, is affective at base—that certitude, the
quest for it, and the critique of it constitute the history of a scandalous
deification of human knowledge—*"the god tumbling down into a
fake-humanity / in the man catapulted to a false-divinity"* (Holy 204).[20]
This seems to be Blaser's position in "'My Vocabulary Did This To
Me'": "These new methods of reading that sometimes lead us into
marvels of a changed intelligence—linguistic, structural, decon-
structionist—rich and challenging as they are, become dangerous
when they become hegemonic, and to my reading, thereby *ahistorical*" (103). Polar thinking holds open "the sacred vacant lot" (*Holy*
278), on the premise that the historical narrative requires its constitutive Other. The larger project of the poems and essays then becomes
the working through of a poetic form capable of reenacting the historicity and dynamism of the real, where "real" in this context means
reality understood as the ongoing composition of and contestation for
a collectively made world that is rendered historical through its dis-
junction from ultimates—the latter variously figured as Lacan's real,
Mallarmé's missing flower, or Dante's *paradiso*. In Olson's phrasing,
what is needed is an art "equal, that is, to the real itself." For Blaser,
this would mean the serial poem.

IV

In "The Fire," Blaser describes his version of the serial and Spicer's
as an Ovidian *carmen perpetuum*, "a continuous song in which the
fragmented subject matter is only apparently disconnected" (17). This
description of the form calls attention to the dis/continuity of seriality.

On one hand, the sequences that compose *The Holy Forest* seem to succeed each other chronologically as so many discrete fields of attention. *Cups* and *The Park* are situated in the landscapes of Blaser's Idaho childhood; *The Moth Poem* turns on the movements of its central figure in domestic space; in *Syntax*, language is the locus, as the title of the sequence suggests, and so on. On the other hand, serials like the *Image-Nations* or *The Truth Is Laughter* are interspersed with the others, demonstrating in a typographical way that the units of the poem do not close. Ovidian form supposes the continuity of the contiguous; Daphne becomes a laurel tree not because tree and woman are more alike in some essential way than they are to other things, but because woman and tree are contiguous at a moment of transformative intensity.

This dis/continuity of the contiguous has a philosophical genealogy in Leibnitz's expressivist aesthetic, and in the Möebius-like relationship between the inner and outer of things with which Leibnitz proposed to displace the ontology of the discrete. As Deleuze shows in *The Fold*, this line of thinking includes Whitehead's "philosophy of organism" as well as Leibnitz's monodology; his own adaptation of the monad to open-ended nomad represents a contemporary version of form as fold.²¹ In the *Forest*, the workings of the fold are apparent in the way that the poems read and explicate each other. *Cups*, for instance, could stand as Blaser's *Vita Nuova*. It is chronologically first of *The Holy Forest* serials, and in it Amor draws the poet into a commitment to the Other, as Dante was bound to Beatrice. In *Cups*, this scene translates as marriage to the world-tree (poe-try or holy forest) rather than a woman:

> Upon that tree there was a ring.
>
> HI HO HUM
>
> The ring surrounded the darkest part.
>
> HA HA HA
>
> The ring imagined a marriage bout.
>
> FIRE FIRE FIRE (*Holy* 12)

The Moth Poem replays this scene between the *Cups* poet and Amor in quite a different key. The moth beating against piano wire, window, or mirror suggests an image of the mind's desire for the world, like that of Dante for Beatrice, or the legendary desire of the moth for the stars. Yet the two sets of images alter as well as inform each other. In *The Moth Poem*, Dante and Beatrice have modulated into Psyche and Cupid, where Psyche is no longer a butterfly, but a moth and *blindly* attracted to light.[22] For the moth, the *paradiso* manifests as the dangerous lure of a lamp or flame that will destroy on contact (the real as the place of the impossible; the real as death). The moth image thus defers the reach for reconciliation between mind and world (*union* with the Other) as imagined in Dante's *Paradiso*. Instead, the image directs us to the deferral of consummation through the discipline of "unknowing" which Spicer and Blaser both associate with the serial poem: in Spicer's words, "'You have to go into a serial poem not knowing what the hell you're doing'" ("Practice" 277). The allusions to Dante and Amor in *Cups*, however, contribute to the significance of the moth-Psyche-Cupid images in *The Moth Poem*, even as the latter modify the way we read the former and interpret the "marriage."

The brush fire of *Cups* is another, related image that accrues significance through retrospective reading. Dante's dark wood—desert sage brush for Blaser—into which the poet has been led by Amor catches fire with the energy of his passage (Blase-r), and "Shapes / of poems / fly out of the dark" (6); similarly, in *The Moth Poem*, a moth emerges, phoenix-like, from a full ashtray (58). As images of fire multiply throughout the *Forest* we begin to see that the Dantean journey toward the paradisal rose has morphed into the undergoing of the purgatorial fires of experience where the "point is transformation of the theme" rather than completion (171).

In Blaser's version of the *carmen perpetuum*, each serial rereads the others, and as the possibilities for connections multiply, the domain of the poem expands. This rhizomatic branching yields a form that is retroflexive in the sense that Olson gathered from Whitehead: the beginning is always ahead, rather than behind. Always the definitive trope that will ground all the others is to be found in the next poem, the one that hasn't been written, even though every trope contends for that (impossible) position. This means that the *Forest* can be read backward as well as forward: backward because later serials "explain" the earlier ones; forward not only because the earlier poems inform the later, but because every image, in its potential for new recontextualizations, exceeds explanation. In a later poem, Blaser wryly puts himself "in the tree tops" (*Exody*), from which vantage point he sees that "the *unfolded fold* is important and onliest" (352). But this high-up point of view is still earthbound; the fold is what the poet can see from his particular tree. If "form is alive"—if metaphor is open to contiguity—then the fold, too, will eventually morph into something else.[23]

Despite the absence of a grounding trope, Blaser's seriality entices the reader into a hermeneutic approach, not only because the poems are fraught with lacunae that tempt her to fill them in—"what the clothes man called the 'world-tissue' / does have a hole in it, 'must be,' / he said, 'darned-up again'" (*Holy* 182)—but also because the citations and references suggest a large, latent content, and the interlocking of the images seems to demand exegetical tracking. However, this is precisely how readers, including the poet, are set wandering. To show more particularly how the *Forest* both calls for and deflects exegesis, I will follow Blaser's serializing of just one prominent image.

In "The Hunger of Sound," Blaser writes, "My emblem became a tree," a choice that seems to be borne out by the sheer number of trees that come into the poem, as well as the title of the collected serials. The tree image seems a good candidate for a seminal metaphor and an invitation to read hermeneutically. Here it is as a language tree in "Sound":

> The child says, 'Draw me,'
> and my hand trembles like a tree
> first planted in chaos.
> Hear the words sound a child's joy.
>   What is uprooted.
> Hear the wind howl at a world of exact proportions.
>   A shape that was like him.
> Hear the sound inhabit the mind,
> bells in an orchard.
> The words knock against chaos. (*Holy* 388)

In this verse paragraph, words emerge from the indefiniteness of sound and bring the child into a world of measure ("exact proportions"). But the planting of the language tree is also an uprooting. The phrase "What is uprooted," written as a statement rather than a question, makes "what" the subject of the sentence. "What" or "whatness" becomes thinkable with language, which is to imply that language ushers in the discrete, and therefore uproots an undefined something from preverbal indefiniteness.

What follows in the next verse is number; the child counts leaves, birds, and blossoms on "10 fingers," and the tree becomes an orchard. In this counting, language is displayed as measure and relationship, but also as the flowering of speech in a perpetual spring(ing) forth of form and meaning. This image itself then blossoms out into a continuing meditation on language that runs through the *Forest*. In the first *Image-Nation*, for instance, the "trees" "wander and roll" (61), while in the last *Image-Nation* of the collection, "Proto-Indo-European trees" emerge through the human working of the environment: "*hewing down a tree with a stone axe, / the physical difference between an elm and a linden, or even an / English and a live oak would be obvious*—calluses—*gone to / thought*" (368). Or in *Pell Mell*, "The Ruler" recalls "The Hunger of Sound" in another account of the childhood acquisition of language, where the wooden ruler, a "measure of the old foot" (242), becomes a liminal object between culture and nature. A piece of a tree, the ruler is also a human product; an artificial device for measuring, it nonetheless derives from the body—a (man's) foot. Ruler of the world that it shapes, language also "carries" physicalities that it cannot fully bring to presence. These few examples of the linguistic trees in the *Forest* could be substantially expanded and the interpretation pushed in different directions. What I am tracking here, however, is not one particular exegetical line, but a demonstration of what happens when the reader accepts the poet's invitation and tries for exegesis. The same set of tree images in "The Hunger of Sound" could be followed into quite other territory.

The "orchard" in the passage I have quoted above cannot but resonate with the Orchard of Blaser's youth, one of the small railway depots in the Idaho desert where Blaser grew up; in fact, a few lines later, Orchard appears with a capital "O." The language tree, then, is also a family tree and the immediate question this reading raises is that of the role of autobiography in the writing of the *Forest*. Indeed, autobiography plays no small part in the poem and in creating the obscurity of which Blaser has been accused for many years. There is no one of the serials which does not include references to personal experience, and these are often cryptic. In "The Fire," Blaser writes, "I want here to create the image of a field which is true history, and autobiography, as well as land, place and presence" (18). Blaser then turns to the psychology of Edith Cobb, in this early essay, to describe the autobiographical dimension of his poetics. Citing Cobb, he says: "'I became acutely aware that what a child wanted to do most of all was to make a world in which to find a place to discover a self. This ordering reverses the general position that self-exploration produces a knowledge of the world'" (17-18). He goes on to say:

> Edith Cobb in her interest in biological psychology moves to describe what she names a "cosmic sense," which in a separate essay, Margaret Mead describes as "a human instinctual need for a perceptual relation to the universe." This is the scientific basis for the proprioceptive process which Charles Olson speaks of. In this context, I am arguing not for my pretentions as a poet, but for what the poetry reflects, if it is entered. That the poet does the job of entering this world and continues through his life to record that entrance is a fact, not pretence—that it is personal, original, and singular is also fact. (18)

If "land, place and presence" are folded together as they are in the Olson-Whitehead view of things, and of course in the baroque that Blaser comes to later, then autobiography is unavoidable; the folding of inner into outer in proprioception makes of the self a singular expression of "land, place and presence" rather than a separable subject inserted into the world. What is autobiographical is the manner in which any one of us receives the world as it is given to us: "imagination," Blaser says, "is more a power to take in and hold than it is a power of making-up" ("Fire" 18). We might call it a point of view.

Autobiography, as Blaser begins to work with it in "The Fire," thus quickly becomes more complex than so many personal references to be tracked down because it is at once a performance of the poem's epistemology and a lyric treatment of the singular. What might happen if we could recover all the autobiographical allusions in the *Forest*? On this route, I find Philippe Lacoue-Labarthe helpful, although his *Poetry as Experience* (1986) is not a source for Blaser and has been released in English translation only in 1999. Writing about Celan in this slim little book, Lacoue-Labarthe comes to connect "the banished singularity of the subject" with "what amounts to the same thing, the question of idiom, of 'pure idiom,' if that can exist" (14). The obvious connection between this inscribing of idiom and Blaser's thinking is of course, Jack Spicer. "We make up a different language for poetry / And for the heart—ungrammatical," Spicer writes (*Collected* 233), and his "Martian" plays off the idea of a pure idiom that would deliver the subject in its absolute authenticity.[24] An impossible project. But Lacoue-Labarthe has more. He describes Blanchot's and Levinas's readings of Celan as "gnomic," meaning that "they found their arguments on phrases lifted from Celan's poems (his verse contains many such isolatable bits, as does all 'thinking poetry')" (14). The latter could be said of Blaser, and the temptation to lift "isolatable bits" is strong. In contrast to this reading strategy, however, is Peter Szondi's exhaustive tracking of Celan: Lacoue-Labarthe writes that Szondi's is "the only one [analysis] to completely decipher a poem, down to its most resistant opacities, because it is the only one to know what 'material' gave rise to the work: the circumstances remembered, the places traveled to, the words exchanged, the sights glimpsed or contemplated, and so on. Szondi scouts out the least allusion, the slightest evocation" (14). Lacoue-Labarthe concludes that the resulting translation leaves almost nothing out—"*almost*," he emphasizes, "because we must still explain, beyond Szondi's delight at having been present in the right place at the right time, a poetry based on the exploitation of such 'singularity,' and thus. . . forever inaccessible to those who did not initially witness what the poetry transformed into a very laconic 'story' or a very allusive 'evocation'" (14-15).

This account of the reading of Celan's poetry seems to me applicable to Blaser's work, and it raises more questions about the possibility of writing the singular. If, in every utterance, the particular withdraws from the abstraction that every language is, if all experience is about absence (missed particularities to the perceiver as well as to potential readers or witnesses), and if, as in Blaser's serial poem, every tree turns into a orchard and every image into a nation of them, can the singular be written? This was Celan's question, Lacoue-Labarthe says, and it was also Spicer's. For Spicer, singularity was the "absolutely temporary": an immediacy that, like Lacan's real, is only ever apprehendable as absent. For Blaser, more accepting of mediation and partial knowledge than Spicer, the singular inheres in how one receives and inflects a given world, as well as in a summoning into the work of the unsayable. But for neither poet can singularity be paraphrased. The once-only of an event, a love, or a life, is always less and more than a meaning: less because it includes materialities like silence, rhythm, the semiotics of the non-human world, as well as unrepeatable patterns and contiguities that exist below the level of the concept; more, because any such event may generate endless interpretation. As Blaser writes in *The Moth Poem*, "there is no meaning here, / there is all meaning here" (56). But now the family tree, it seems, has become a linguistic one again.

In "The Hunger of Sound," language is both excess and lack; it makes possible the blossoming of speech as well as the violent uprooting of the speaker from the semiotic flow of nature; it awakens the desire for unique expression even as it despoils its own immaculate conceptions. In this poem, Orchard (both the grove and the train depot), is matched by the "terrible trees" and "the whole image of Dante." Here is the "dark wood" of cultural and spiritual uncertainty that was the occasion for Dante's venture and that has now become a beginning for Blaser. Later, in the preface to *Syntax*, Blaser writes of a *"cultural orphanhood* that has hunted me since childhood" (159). But the "terrible trees" in "The Hunger of Sound" are specifically those of the suicides of the thirteenth canto: Blaser's "Bent to return the torn leaves / and cracked bark / to their wounds" refers to the Florentine suicide who, in the shape of a bush, is torn by hounds in canto XIII of the *Inferno* (173-74). The suicides are punished for a despair that comes of their failure to love and imagine the world as larger than their own misery. For rejecting the human body, they are trapped for eternity in plant forms. The "terrible trees" thus modify the "orchard"; they suggest that the linguistic wood and the individuation which it enables (autobiography) bring alienation as well as possibility. The trees simultaneously liberate the child and entrap him in a medium that brings him consciousness of limit and death. This is the language tree in its affective dimension, as existential agony and cross. The Dantean answer (the Christian answer) to individuation is love—hence the entrance of Amor in *Cups*, the serial that immediately follows "The Hunger of Sound" chronologically. What Blaser comes to call public love in the later poems and essays is "a crossing, an 'intertwining'" ("Practice" 294) of self and world such that neither is separable from nor reducible to the other—and we are back, via the curved space of the poem, at a dis/continuity of form that serves as both an aesthetic and an epistemology in the *Forest*. And of course we are no closer than when we began to a definitive reading.

I began this segment of my discussion by suggesting that the poem lures the reader into an exegesis that simply turns into a labyrinth. The image of the wandering Jew on the leather back of a rocking chair from Blaser's childhood home speaks to this reading experience at the end of the *Forest*: poet and reader are constantly moving without ever getting out of the woods. However, this is exactly what the poem asks us to do: *not* to abandon the work of exegesis because it is without end, but to let ourselves be pulled into it—tricked as Spicer would say—and therefore also tricked into the work of constructing a world. Our reading of Blaser would then parallel his reading of others; as we read and combine the images or try to explicate them in the more exchangeable currencies of other discourses—philosophy, aesthetics, or politics—we not only begin to create our own world, but also to expand our field of attention. I have argued that Blaser locates creativity in the imaginative reception of the given; with him, then, we are invited to participate in this kind of creativity, with the difference that the poem—the record of his attentions—now becomes the object of ours.[25] The farther we follow the poet into *his* forest, the bigger it gets, the bigger we get, and the more *our* forest it becomes. This, I suggest, is the ethical dimension of the poem. The more expansive the point of view, the more "we" includes, the better able we are to extend ourselves beyond the narrowness of self-interest and respond to the perspectives of others. In Blaser's writing, this fold of the ethical brings into contiguity poetic and political thinking.

V

On political philosophy, Blaser has acknowledged a debt to Hannah Arendt throughout his writing life, and in key ways her thinking touches the perspectivism that Blaser adapts from Whitehead and others such as Olson and Merleau-Ponty. First, Arendt constructs the *polis* as a "space of appearance" where agents come to be subjects processively, through action and speech. Her account of the public actor thus bears a formal resemblance to Whitehead's description of the "actual entity" as that which comes to itself through numerous acts of response or infoldings of its surrounds.[26] Secondly, Arendt's interest in narratives, rather than historical trends or forces, and specifically in narratives that achieve coherence only in retrospect, is an important point of intersection with Whitehead on Blaser's map of modernity and with Blaser's own serial poetry.[27] This narrated quality of Arendt's *polis* also constitutes an ethical hinge between the aesthetic and political through the implied refusal to flatten particularities into abstractions; the "what-ness" of socially assigned identity, for instance, is of less interest to Arendt than the "who-ness" of the agent, and this implies a radical conception of who may participate in public life—a point to which I will return. Thirdly, Arendt conceives of the *polis* as creative and outside the logic of means and ends; in *The Human Condition*, she describes public life in Aristotelian terms as the "work of man' *qua* man" (185). Arendt glosses this phrase as "actuality." "The human sense of reality," she says, "demands that men actualize the sheer passive givenness of their being, not in order to change it but in order to make articulate and call into full existence what otherwise they would have to suffer passively anyhow" (187). Through action and speech, and the stories that preserve them, we concretize the world. As well, the more perspectives we witness through the narratives of others, the better we are able to think with them, even those with whom we may not empathize, and the better able we are to construct a shareable world in which human plurality might be recognized and honored. Hence the expansiveness characteristic of Blaser's notion of creativity becomes in Arendt a political virtue, adapted from Kant's "enlarged mentality" as a criterion for the reflective judgment that an inductive deliberative process requires.[28] Margaret Canovan importantly suggests that the Arendtian *polis* exists "not to satisfy needs but to bestow significance on human life" (188). In Arendt's words, the "revelatory character of action as well as the ability to produce stories and become historical. . .together form the very source from which meaningfulness springs into and illuminates human existence" (*Human* 296-97).

These characteristics of Arendt's political thought, and particularly her attachment to the expanded point of view, places her alongside not only Whitehead on Blaser's map of modernity, but also Dante and Olson. Dante consigns to the *inferno* those who have whittled the world down to the size of their own desires or expressions of will.[29] Whitehead makes complexity the subjective aim of God, and what he calls the "lure for feeling" a cosmic urge toward its maximization.[30] Moreover, agency, for these poet-philosophers as well as for Arendt, resides in the possibility of responding creatively, and with attention, to what comes as given. In "The Kingfishers," Olson tersely summarizes the significance of this kind of creativity: "not accumulation but change, the feed-back proves, the feed-back is / the law" (*Collected* 89). "Feed-back" is the key term. For Dante, it means the double translation of complex, earthly events into moral narrative and back again; for Whitehead, feedback is a process through which an "actual entity" forms itself by selecting or rejecting elements of its surrounds; to Arendt, it suggests a deliberative process where public decisions are made inductively by examining narrativized data; for Blaser, it is a serialized reading and writing process that explicates what has come-to-pass by refolding it into new configurations.

Arendt's account of the *polis* and political agency, however, depends on a highly controversial alignment of binary distinctions between the political and the social, freedom and necessity, public and private—distinctions that Blaser reproduces. In "The Recovery of the Public World" he writes that the "social has to do with the problems of large numbers of people: food, shelter, clothing, sanitation— in a word, necessity" (18). Freedom, on the other hand, is the "not-determined aspect of human nature" and Blaser locates it first in renaissance humanism before crediting Arendt: for Pico della Mirandola in *The Oration on the Dignity of Man*, "freedom is always beyond necessity, poverty, and terror" (23).[31] In order to bring out the issues at stake in the Arendtian strand of Blaser's poetics, I want to digress here to consider some of the arguments that Arendt's readers have raised on this point.

In the question period following a conference in her honor at York University in 1972, Arendt's interlocutors fasten on this point of distinction between the social and political. Mary McCarthy wonders what someone is supposed to do on the public stage if the social is excluded (Hill 315). Albrecht Wellmer asks for an example of a social issue that is not also political (318). C. B. Macpherson takes exception to Arendt's defining of "a lot of key words in ways unique to herself: you know, social *versus* political . . ." (322). Examples of similar objections on other occasions include Hanna Pitkin's wonderings in print about what can be left to discuss once the social is excised from political space; Pitkin imagines, with reference to Arendt's Grecophilia, groups of "posturing little boys clamoring for attention" (272).[32] Sheldon Wolin argues that Arendt never understood that an economy is not merely production and consumption but also a "structure of power" (295). Feminists of Arendt's generation like Adrienne Rich and Mary O'Brien have read the public-private split as displaying "an exclusively male perspective" (O'Brien 110), and they take Arendt's curt treatment of the domestic sphere as a devaluation of life-affirming, woman-identified perspectives.

Although recent rereadings of Arendt, including feminist readings, offer a richer range of interpretations than I can indicate here, even supporters argue the necessity of renegotiating her distinctions. In one such revision, and in defense of Arendt, Seyla Benhabib suggests that it isn't the content of the social that needs to be separated from the political, but rather the manner in which content is handled. Actors in the public sphere may behave as clients and promote their own interests, or they may put into practice the Kantian "enlarged mentality" and act politically by taking into account the perspectives of others in composing the good of a common world.[33] Alternatively, David Luban has noted that Arendt's distinctions amount to a difference between the logic of "in order to" and "for the sake of" (84). If the *polis* has to do with the latter, what comes up in it cannot be measured by predetermined criteria of the good or bad, the useful or worthless, because it is in this space that these abstractions are to be given historical substance. But this is just the sticking point for

Arendt's critics: in side-stepping the logic of means and ends ("in order to"), Arendt withholds moral prescription, and thus does not offer up social justice. As Luban suggests, she is out of step with most political theorists because she tries for meaning, rather than predictability or control, in human affairs (86).

The more common alternative to Arendt's model of agency and the "not-determined" *polis* is embedded in arguments that begin by assuming that the body politic and its agents are over- rather than underdetermined: this is a starting point for Marxist, Foucauldian, psychoanalytic, and deconstructive positions and their feminist inflections. In addition to this line of thought, there is a second that is skeptical about the possibility of "doing" politics at all under current economic conditions, and Arendt herself takes this argument up in relation to her own description of public space. In the first category are arguments such as James Bohman's in "The Moral Costs of Political Pluralism." I cite Bohman as an example simply because of the take-it-for-granted currency of his complaint that formal equality in the political realm is meaningless without social justice; in other words, he assumes, and rightly in my view, that social position significantly determines what one may do and who may participate in public affairs. Bohman's focus in this piece is on the Little Rock incident. In her notorious essay on the desegregation of schools in 1960s Little Rock, Arkansas, Arendt withheld her support on the grounds that the state should not intervene in the right-to-associate. Bohman points to Arendt's understanding of totalitarianism as dependent on the elimination of diverse *civic* spaces and organizations in discussing the high moral price she seems willing to pay to keep social space unregulated. Accepting Arendtian pluralism as desirable, however, Bohman suggests that it may be better served by measures that seem formally contrary to it. Special rights for minorities (political inequality), or interventions promoting distributive justice (social regulation) may result in more, not less diversity of voice in the public realm.[34] This move may be more attractive morally than Arendt's position, and as Bohman says, it may be the most effective means of promoting access to the public sphere and thus maintaining some semblance of diversity, but it does not account for the creative component of the Arendtian *polis*. To make plurality the desired *outcome* of a *prescrip-*

tive political process has the effect of displacing deliberative freedom with an agenda that is simply to be enacted. The prescriptive measures Bohman proposes are similar to those which Arendt seemed to think belonged to the social sphere and could be managed bureaucratically.[35] The unpalatable idea that Bohman draws out of Arendt's Little Rock argument is that deliberative freedom does not necessarily produce social justice. Mary Dietz, in her overview of feminist readings of Arendt is blunter on this point: "If strategic action does indeed reside in the question of justice, then justice is something that Arendtian politics—whose focus on freedom resolutely downplays the 'what-ness of doing' in favor of the 'who-ness of speaking'—is unable to accommodate" (40).

I do not propose to argue Bohman's issue away; his objection really says that social justice must precede the kind of public creativity Arendt calls political. But then Arendt raises some questions for Bohman too. Who sets the agenda for whom, and how is it to be enacted, or is "enforced" the better term? At what point in the process might there be room again for deliberative freedom? From Arendt's point of view, real, rather than sham enfranchisement is the only adequate response to a demand for social justice—not the suspension of deliberative freedom. But this is where the second counter-argument to Arendt's vision of the *polis* comes in, the argument which says that under current social and economic conditions, such a *polis* is impossible. Arendt is the first to make it. In *The Origins of Totalitarianism*, she situates the eclipse of political by economic considerations in nineteenth-century imperialism. To summarize a complex analysis, nationalism and imperialism converged, she says, when the unequal distribution of wealth had brought about the accumulation of available capital in excess of what could be absorbed domestically by the European nation states. In addition, the "human debris" remaining from every crisis of industrial growth—the permanently unemployed—represented excess labor (150). Imperialism "solved" the problem of what to do with both excess wealth and excess labor, collapsing political into economic interests. What the bourgeoisie wanted, Arendt says, was to create stable investment zones through the extension of bureaucratic control abroad, but without offering political representation. With the identification of eco-

nomic interest as the basis of the body politic—the triumph of
Hobbesian man, in Arendt's view—imperialist thinking could extend
to domestic as well as foreign affairs.[36]

In "The Public Spheroid," an essay on Blaser and Arendt, Jerry
Zaslove calls this analysis of Arendt's a "theory of 'trash'": it sketches
out "the degradation and humiliation of peoples in the name of the
economic" (443). The current globalization of capital extends and
intensifies this triumph of the economic over the political, or what
Arendt would call the private over the public sphere. It easy to agree
with Bohman, then, that equality in name only is inadequate, and an
obvious task, in the face of need, is to focus on social problems. But
if the end of improved access to public life is taken to be better distributive justice *alone*, or the achievement of predetermined goals,
then Arendt's point has been missed. The component of her thought
that is quite foreign to contemporary thinking is that which says that
degradation in the name of the economic extends to the owning
classes as well as the poor—that public life is not solely about the production and distribution of wealth. Here is how Blaser articulates the
matter:

> Marxism is an instrument, and an excellent one, for social anal-
> ysis and the understanding of the problems of necessity for large
> social bodies, and, perhaps, when the wreckage of its twentieth
> century practice has been cleared away, it may become an instru-
> ment for the founding of social justice. In the meantime, the
> problem of reality—what do we mean by the real? ("Violets" 62)

What is missing when the *polis* dissolves into a sum of private interests and needs is reality itself. In *The Human Condition*, Arendt writes
that:

> To live an entirely private life means above all to be deprived of
> things essential to a truly human life: *to be deprived of the reali-*
> *ty that comes from being seen and heard by others*, to be deprived
> ·of an 'objective' relationship with them that comes from being
> related to and separated from them through the intermediary of
> a common world of things, to be deprived of the possibility of
> achieving something more permanent than life itself.
>
>   (53-54; emphasis added)

This shareable world and mutual witnessing of lives is where the arts intersect with the public sphere, and it is what Blaser reaches for in his performance of a poetry that imagines the "real." The heterogeneity of contemporary societies does not change this task, but sets the conditions of it. Arendt's concept of public space as a "space of appearance" is telling here, because it leaves room (empty space) for an understanding of the "common" as that which might be constructed were enfranchisement to be genuinely extended to anyone who wanted it, rather than a "common" that conceals hegemony as a set of "norms."[37] This distinction informs Blaser's treatment of practical political issues in "Even on Sunday," a poem about contemporary and historical discrimination against homosexuals written for Gay Games III in Vancouver, 1990. In this piece, Blaser offers a poetics of the singular as a response to the social assignment of identity. The latter he attributes to the Enlightenment ideal of equality, quickly turned to compulsory "normality":

> ... an Enlightenment which first and foremost posited
> an *equality of men and women, including homosexuals*—religion and sexuality go hand in hand in the apple-light
>
> it was not to be merely law, like free speech, but a *mental practice*
>   what developed, in the guise of a Darwinian terror advancing in evolutionary form, was the lion body with a man's head, walking in the garden, so that *the underlying principles of liberty and equality, not even taking fraternity into account, inordinately encouraged combatting all*
> *forms of outsiderdom in favour of what Ihab Hassan calls 'quantities of normed*
> *phenomena'*—normed existence excludes the *existential given*, not being
> alive in the full sense of body and soul—and *extends, not merely perverts*
> that which calls itself normality into political form but Mayer[38] asks, *what*
> *is it then if the precipitating step outside, into the margins, is a condition of*
> *birth, a result of one's sex, parentage, physical or spiritual makeup?*
> *Then*
> *one's existence itself becomes a breaking of boundaries*

> we can thereby return to ourselves a *measure of freedom,* and take
> form—
> the work of a lifetime—in this breaking of boundaries—
>   against,
> as Mayer says, *a global disposition of thought toward annihiliation,*
>   *which*
> *thinks to admit only majorities in the future and is determined to*
>   *equate*
> *minorities with 'worthless life'* Worthless are the Jews, there the
>   blacks [and
> aboriginals], somewhere else (and everywhere) the homosexuals, women
> of the type of Judith and Delilah, not least the intellectuals keen on
>   individuation. . . . (Holy 348-49)

I have quoted at length because this passage so clearly lays out an
Arendtian case for the "who-ness of speaking" as against the coercive
assignment of "what-ness," and it suggests where an Arendtian vision
might find practical application—in initiatives, for instance, that
extend the franchise and challenge the equation of socially defined
groups with "worthless life."[39] Yet neither Blaser nor Arendt propose
to do this through what has come to be understood by identity
politics, insofar as such a politics means the staging of a particular set
of group interests. As Norma Cole notices in her notes for this collection on "The Fire" and *The Moth Poem,* the kind of collectivity
suggested in Blaser's work is without an identity. Cole juxtaposes to
Blaser this passage from Giorgio Agamben's *The Coming Community*:
"'What the State cannot tolerate in any way, however, is that the singularities form a community without affirming an identity . . . that
human beings co-belong without any representable condition of
belonging.'"

This line of thinking offers one way of addressing the problem of
access for those who have been "othered," but it does not address the
question of the *efficacy* of the political process, raised by the sweeping disenfranchisement of nearly everyone from meaningful political
participation under transnational capitalism. This latter problem is
not so clearly engaged by the contesting of boundaries or demands
for access to public policy-making in its present forms. The critical
dissent around Arendt's public-private distinction has obscured an
element of the argument that is even more apparent now than when

Arendt wrote it. To state what is obvious and everywhere announced, the privatization of the public sphere, which Arendt anticipated as world alienation in *The Human Condition* and *The Origins of Totalitarianism*, means an uncoupling of public debate from economic decision-making, so that deliberation, even if it were to occur, would lack executive power. In "As If By Chance," Blaser comments on this reversal of the political and economic:

> **the political**, which, by manipulation, is over the stunned
> *polis*, in order to manage production, distribution, and
> consumption of wealth, becomes political economy—thus,
> what is under becomes what is over, and *vice versa*, to define
> realities without earth and sky which are cultural habitudes
> (*Holy* 324)

For Blaser, and Arendt too, there is no *polis* under such conditions. In "Even on Sunday," Blaser writes that "the *polis* is at the 'bottom of the sea'" (346), and certainly there is nothing in the poems or essays that holds out the hope of imminently *recovering* a public world. As Zaslove has noticed, the postwar task of imagining a new public world, post-the-modern—a Paterson (Williams), a Gloucester (Olson), a "grand collage" (Duncan)—has been truncated, both by the processes of globalization and, in the smaller literary-academic world, by the shift of attention from constructivism (ethics and aesthetics) to deconstruction (epistemological collapse) in 1970s and 80s critical theory. As Zaslove remarks, after Cornelius Castoriadis, "no poet can everytime heal the world he has lost with that one more poem" (450). Perhaps, though, a poet may wound, when he calls us to remember that the present conditions of social and political life are neither natural nor inevitable. Here is Blaser again, in "Even on Sunday":

> I think
> of that recent hustle in the United States, offering the end of history
> like a dinky-toy, democracy, pinking, blueing, and off-whiting in
> plastic
> —'My goodness!' everyone said, 'They've discovered Hegel!' and
> *Time*
> *Magazine* thought he was little known—and I said, 'My goodness!
> Francis Fukuyama, so we finally got here, there, anywhere'

> so to be reminded once again of Puddin'head Wilson: *It was*
>   *wonderful*
> *to find America, but it would have been more wonderful to miss it*
>
> *this unified mankind*—for that's who's there, quantity or lump, at the
> end of a materialist's or an idealist's history—*conceived*, Mayer writes,
> *as a homogenized humanity. Woe to outsiders* (350)

Blaser's poetic response to determination—*"homogenized humanity"*
or economic "inevitabilities"—whether enforced through hard-
edged, state-sanctioned repression, compulsory social norms, or the
soft tyranny of the market, is the on-going performance of the unpara-
phraseable, the singular, and the contingent.

In *The Community of Those Who Have Nothing in Common*,
Alphonso Lingis writes that, confronted with otherness, "[m]y sociological, political, anthropological, and biological understanding
reestablishes my imperative alone on my thought; my explanations
justify my own understanding and my own intentions" (28). Lingis is
exploring here an "imperative" of the other that is not simply identifiable through "laws and codes" (29), and what he brings out in this
passage is the effort of attention required to witness singularity—as
opposed, say, to observing a set of attributes. This is the kind of attention that connects the aesthetic, ethical, and political dimensions of
Blaser's thinking. If creativity is a form of reception, it requires attention to the world, whether the desired result is the composition of a
self, a poem, or a public sphere. In "The Fire," Blaser writes, "I am
sometimes lost when a reader finds me uninteresting or too obscure,
his interest too soon exhausted to come to any meeting" (15). Now,
more than three decades after "The Fire" was written, and at a historical moment that offers the distractions of "thick" technology, this
attention deficit is not just characteristic of the hasty reader, but also
of a culture unable—or unwilling—to hold onto complexities more
intricate than those of the exchange relation. The chances for a poetry that honors the singular are slim in such a context. In 1964, Jack
Spicer could say, "No / One listens to poetry" (*Collected* 217). For the
ones who do, however, a dissenting poetry such as Blaser's offers the
strenuous pleasure of a real meeting.

VI

The critical essays, parallel texts, and archival materials of this collection circle around and around this imagination of meetings and
the love of the particular it entails. For some readers this means attention to the reader-writer, or I-You interchange; for others it means
thinking through Blaser's construction of the subject, the Other, or
the collective. George Bowering's reading of "lake of souls," a major
poem from *Syntax* (1983) is deceptively casual and homely—a sec-
tion-by-section walk-through of the poem during which Bowering
plays the uninitiated näif in lines like, "the poem begins so beautifully, as a person without theoretical training might say." This strategy is designed to show how the poem enacts its parataxis (and without help from theory): "Parataxis is Blaser's poetic and his politics,"
Bowering says, and his phenomenological reading, for all its dramat-
ic naivety, moves to the quick of *Syntax*. Beginning with Olson's
observation that Blaser has "no syntax," Bowering demonstrates that
"no syntax" means "conjugation rather than subjugation," with implications that stretch from the arrangement of words on the page to the
ordering of lives in the world. The model of collectivity Bowering
sees in this poem is companionable, and compares, in his view, to
that of the Okanagan people:

> there is a principle called *en'owkin*, which spirit visits people
> who come together to formulate civic, political and educational
> plans. In council, anyone from any social position can express
> feelings and ideas. They do not debate. When everyone who
> wants to speak has spoken and everyone has heard all questions
> and suggestions, the best possible solutions are agreed upon and
> the others are not forgotten.

David Sullivan arrives at the relational in Blaser's writing from a
different angle—a study of the second person pronouns. His
"'Companions are horizons': 'I,' 'You,' Robin Blaser and Emily
Dickinson" takes Jonathan Culler's "Apostrophe" as a point of departure for a discussion of Blaser's scare-marked "'you.'" Sullivan argues
that Blaser subverts the "conventions of aesthetic distance" in order
to implicate the reader in the ethics of the I-you interchange and in
this he sees an affinity between Blaser and Emily Dickinson, who

appears in Blaser's "Image-Nation 12 (Actus." Both poets, he says, "force readers to confront their own perspective and take responsibility for how they treat others."

Norma Cole's "A Minimum of Matter: Notes on Robin Blaser, 'The Fire' and *The Moth Poem*" is not an expository essay as are most of those in this section. Rather her notes, a collage of dense, incisive quotations and comments—a Cole's Notes for poets—pull out a wide range of issues from Blaser's early writing. Opening with a citation from Merleau-Ponty's *The Visible and Invisible*, Cole remarks on the "invisibility of the crucial" in "The Fire," and Blaser's preference for images over concepts in the representation of invisibilities such as "'the heat of one's sense of the war [Vietnam], or a place, or a body, or of the extensions of these, the earth, the existence of gods, and so forth.'" With equal economy, Cole points to the singularity Blaser is after as vital to his sense of both the poetic and political.

Andrew Mossin and Scott Pound each take up Blaser's linking of the singular and the collective through readings of the *Image-Nations*. In "Recovering the Public World: Robin Blaser and the Discourses of Subjectivity and Otherness in *Image-Nations 1-12*," Mossin discusses the ethics of the writer-text-reader connections in Blaser's *Image-Nations*. The "enjoinment and separation" which Arendt sees as essential to the *polis* (a common world that relates and separates at the same time), Mossin discovers in Blaser's treatment of the image and the serial form. In the *image* nation is the particularity that is key to public space: "Blaser would have us recognize that we only begin to recognize the terms of our humanness when we achieve perception of the particular in discourse with an other or others." The image-nation becomes a site where poet and reader co-create a meeting. For Scott Pound it is the "unworking of totality," or what he calls the atopian quality of the *Image-Nations*, that "defines the poem's relations to community." Pound argues that "ideology happens when content is permitted to devour form"; Blaser's *Image-Nations* are readable as a form of ideology critique in that they resist the thought of totals through the inscription of "'indeterminate, various, resistant finitude.'"

Pound values those elements of Blaser's writing that are congenial to language writing, namely the rejection of naturalized speech and the disappearance of the subject as organizing principle ("language as a field of possible relations supplants the 'I'"). Peter Middleton takes on the question of Blaser's relationship to both New American poetry and language writing in his "An Elegy for Theory: Robin Blaser's Essay, 'The Practice of Outside.'" Middleton notes that the objection to the New American poetry—Olson's version of it in particular—was the anachronistic view of the subject that this poetry was understood to hold. Andrew Ross's notion that Olson sought a subjective power *over* language (rather than recognizing the subject as a language effect) exemplifies this kind of complaint. Middleton, however, builds an argument for Blaser's poetic as "a route not yet followed by poststructuralist theory in literary and cultural studies." In "performing the real," Middleton says, Blaser makes "world and language [into] activities, and not conditions, entities or systems." Middleton's argument is also a response to a general turn away from New American poetry which has included Blaser, but without specific attention to the work, and he proposes to reposition Blaser through a theoretics of performance.

Fred Wah's *Music at the Heart of Thinking* poems, written for this collection, are Blaser riffs within a much larger serial. Wah's pieces relate to Blaser's as a jazz performance relates to a melody. In *MHT* #111, for instance, Wah picks up the central thought of *Syntax*—that word and world order are various—in a poem that imagines the materiality of form. He begins with "The Truth Is Laughter 13," a found poem for Blaser, "originally written in Eskimo syllabics" by Joe Panipakuttuk:

> . . .*we got near the musk oxen*
> *and I found out they were carrying*
> *something on their backs   I thought*
> *to myself they must be carrying*
> *their little ones, but I soon learned*
> *that this was part of the animal*
> *when you see musk oxen for the first time*
> *they have a huge back on them* (Holy 178)

Like Blaser, Wah lets word and world cross chiasmatically in a poem that brings out the materiality of both, and of course subverts any "purety" [sic] of meaning.

The purety of spelling rests in the bole of a
cottonwood tree out of the way of those musk-ox-
like syllables in the distance with their potent loads
on their backs each letter a nameless squirrel all
eyes and spasm chittering deep under the
encephalo roof.

Not only does Wah perform the sense of Blaser's piece but he also
enacts the difference-in-repetition that for Blaser characterizes creative reception. Blaser quotes Panipakuttuk, but of course the English
translation is really a transfiguration of the first poem, as Wah's poem
transfigures Blaser's in pushing toward the semiotic non-sense hidden
in the semantic—letters chittering like squirrels. The next Wah poem
begins appropriately with a comment on quotation: "Citation that
close is a way to deflect being full of / yourself. . . ."

   Like Wah, Paul Kelley focuses on the non-semantic component of
Blaser's poetry—what does not communicate—in order to pull out a
meditation on the poetic construction of the singular. Kelley begins
his reading of Blaser's "The Iceberg" (from *Pell Mell*) by thinking
about silence as something the poem composes as particular, contextual and "multiguous" rather than mere background: silence "sets
free the no-longer heard, the unheard, in each word." Kelley reads
Blaser's poem—and poetry itself—as iceberg, and his engagement is
with that portion which is submerged. Poetry does not argue or recommend, Kelley says; rather it conjures singularities that history, philosophy, or politics elide. What is concealed in the concept, written
over on historical records, or leveled into quantitative measurement
in the theater of *realpolitik* (who has the most power), spills out in
poetry's solicitation of "subjectivity . . . composed of scars and cracks
of its history as well as the longings which, unsatisfied, make of history a history of such dissatisfactions. . . ." Kelley turns to love, the traditional subject of the lyric poem, and the "emotion of particularity"
(Blaser's phrase), to link poetry and politics through the third term
of the ethical. Without ethics, love is mere "*sexus*," and politics self-
perpetuation (an inversion of means and ends). Poetry's resistance to
the instrumental—its seeming irrelevance to social issues, its courting
of particularity, its ateleological wandering, or its embarrassing
passion—is precisely its relevance to any kind of life worth living, and

by no means in just a soft, feel-good sense. The play of memory and desire which poetry sets in motion creates a distance, Kelley says, which brings the present givens of self and world into critical question.

The Archival section of this collection consists of a selection of materials I have drawn from the early, middle, and recent stages of Blaser's writing life. Kevin Killian has assembled a revealing discussion from 1956 between Spicer, Blaser, and Duncan on eastern versus west coast poetry from cards housed at the Bancroft Library at Berkeley. Killian's fine, contextualizing commentary on these materials requires little addition. Likewise, my interview with Blaser of July 1999 speaks for itself; Blaser talks about many of the issues raised in the essays here, and as well introduces his latest work, a libretto for an opera on the last supper of Christ, with music by Sir Harrison Bertwhistle.

The *Astonishments*, however, require some explanation. There are twenty-two tapes in all, some transcribed and some not, all unpublished except for the sections that appear here, and one in *The Capilano Review* 6 (1974) under the title "The Metaphysics of Light." As I have noted (endnote 8), the tapes were made in 1974, at the home of Warren Tallman, with Dwight Gardiner, Angela Bowering, Martina Kuharic, and Daphne Marlatt in attendance. When I began to work on Blaser's poetry as a graduate student at Simon Fraser, Tallman gave them to me, and I then took them to Special Collections in the Bennett Library at Simon Fraser where they are now housed. By today's standards, the technology used to make these recordings was not good and the tapes were stored in a shoebox in Tallman's basement for some years. While they have been cleaned by SFU's technical support staff, there are still moments that are difficult to hear. The transcript I am presenting here has been checked for errors against the tapes by my research assistant, Maureen Donatelli, and I have checked the final copy again myself. Robin Blaser has also been very generous in helping to track references and in supplying the texts from which he read on the tapes in 1974. Where the tapes have not yielded to our combined attentions, or where the conversation stutters into dead-ends, I have resorted to ellipses.

The stories I have selected from the very many of *Astonishments* are not chronologically consecutive, but they are complementary. The first begins as a talk on the "geography of the imagination" (to borrow that phrase of Guy Davenport's), but Blaser quickly comes to Dante and his importance to the forming of a poetics at Berkeley. The "Great Companion" poem on Dante, written in 1997 and published in North America for the first time in this collection, is anticipated by this section of *Astonishments*. My second selection has a significant section on James Joyce, who Blaser sees as the twentieth-century response to Dante. I have found these stories and the others on *Astonishments* crucial to my reading of Blaser. Typically the talks offer riches in indirection. Rather than deliver a thesis, lecture-style, they are always coming to a point. What else would one expect from Blaser? *Pli selon pli.*

–*Miriam Nichols*
Vancouver, August 1999
Revised, July 2000

NOTES

1. *The Recovery of the Public World*, advertised as "a conference and poetry festival in honor of Robin Blaser, his poetry and poetics," was held from June 1-4, 1995 at the Emily Carr Institute of Art and Design in Vancouver. Sponsors for the event included Simon Fraser University, the Emily Carr Institute, the Fine Arts Gallery at the University of British Columbia, the Western Front, and the Kootenay School of Writing (the latter two are artist-run centers).

Conference proceedings now have been published under the title *The Recovery of the Public World*, and this title repeats that of Blaser's essay in *Reflections on Cultural Policy: Past, Present, and Future*, edited by Blaser, Evan Alderson, and Harold Coward. Confusingly, the title comes from Melvyn A. Hill's collection of essays on Hannah Arendt: *Hannah Arendt: The Recovery of the Public World*. There are thus four different referents for the same name: Hill's collection, Blaser's essay, the 1995 Blaser conference, and the conference publication. Parenthetical references to "The Recovery of the Public World" ("Recovery") in this volume will refer to Blaser's essay.

2. In "The Fire," Blaser writes, "I am thirty years old before I begin even tentatively to accept the title of poet" (20). "Thirty years old" would be 1955, the year that Blaser was awarded an M.A. and an M.L.S. from Berkeley and left for a position at the Widener Library at Harvard. *The Boston Poems* (1956-1958), written while working at the Widener, are the earliest pieces he preserves. On *Astonishments*, however, he recalls writing volumes of Whitmanic verse as a teenager and in "Lake of Souls," from *Syntax* (1979-81), he reproduces "Song in Four Parts for Christ the Son," first

published in *Occident*, a Berkeley campus magazine, in 1947.
3. Introducing *TISH 1-19*, a collection in book form of the student poetry newsletter, *Tish*, Frank Davey writes:

> The impulse to create **TISH** had been sparked by Robert
> Duncan during three nights of lectures, July 23, 24, and 25, 1961,
> at the Vancouver home of Warren Tallman. Tallman, a professor
> of English at the University of British Columbia who had already
> influenced George Bowering, Fred Wah, and myself as students
> in his general poetry class, had begun in 1959 to make contact
> with the San Francisco poetry scene—partly at the suggestion of
> his wife [Ellen Tallman] who had known several of its poets dur-
> ing her college days. . . .
>   While Duncan was only the first of many avant-garde writers
> (including Creeley, Ginsberg, Levertov, Spicer, Olson, Blaser
> and Avison) that Tallman's energies would bring to Vancouver,
> his visit, which included more than nine hours of lectures,
> unquestionably had the greatest impact. (8)

Davey cites Duncan's accounts of little magazines like *Origin, Black Mountain Review*, and *The Floating Bear* as inspirational. *Tish* was edited by George Bowering, Frank Davey, David Dawson, James Reid, and Fred Wah.
4. "Wonder Merchants: Modernist Poetry in Vancouver during the 1960s" is the title of an essay by Warren Tallman.
5. Ginsberg writes:

> All month since I came back from Bodh Gaya Peter unwelcom-
> ing & silent & determined on his separate music & untouchable
> energies—slow drift to we silent & curt answers, neither raising
> voice in my sadness or he in his irritation and no long talk except
> one night on Morphine he telling me I'm washed up & sold out
> to go teach in Vancouver broken poetry vow he judged. . . . (208)

6. Reviewing *Syntax* for *Canadian Literature* in 1984, Judith Owens writes:

> Robin Blaser's latest book, *Syntax*, confirms his reputation as a
> philosophical poet whose difficult but brilliant work has earned
> an admiring, if still small, audience. (95)

7. Jed Rasula, for example, brought a "fragmentary and necessarily partial sketch" of "a reflection on the impetus behind my essay 'Spicer's Orpheus and the Emancipation of the Pronouns,'" published in *Boundary 2* (1977). The Deleuzean sketch which follows in *Acts* 6 is called "The Body Without Organs in the Underworld" (95-96).

8. See my introduction to *Astonishments* in the last section of this essay. The tapes were recorded in the spring of 1974 at Warren Tallman's home, with Angela Bowering, Daphne Marlatt, Dwight Gardiner, and Martina Kuharic. Frank Davey and George Bowering were briefly present but did not attend the series. *Astonishments* is currently housed in Special Collections at the W. A. C. Bennett Library, Simon Fraser University.

9. The late Charles Watts of Special Collections, SFU, numbered *Astonishments* for easier reference. Watts assigned a number to each side of every tape. These are the numbers I will use for parenthetical reference.

10. In "'My Vocabulary Did This To Me,'" Blaser writes:

> . . . the intelligence of context is vocabulary, and syntax— whether hypotactic, the author imperiously in charge of the sentence; or paratactic, the author *perhaps* democratically among things. The intelligence of context is vocabulary and syntax, as everyone knows who has truly dealt with Modernism and whatever it is that has followed from Modernism to correct the practice of it—that is the practice of Modernism. (98)

11. *The King's Two Bodies* was published after Blaser left Berkeley, but Kantorowicz workshopped the book much earlier in his classes. See Blaser's comment on this point in the July 1999 interview in this volume.

12. In "The Practice of Outside," Blaser cites Spicer's idea that he (Spicer), Duncan, and Blaser were the "three immortals" (324), and much could be done with the triangular relationship between them. With some finessing of terms, Spicer might be cast as the materialist, Duncan the idealist, and Blaser the realist, for instance. Or there is the Freudian triangle through which Kevin Killian reads Blaser in *Poet Be Like God*:

> Blaser has spoken of the "triangular imagination" shared by himself and his two Berkeley peers. We all know the Freudian side effects of triangulation—the forced, shifting identification into father, mother, child. Blaser's own great personal beauty created a vortex, a hole out of which a certain madness, a *folie*, was given its head. His epic-length *The Holy Forest* continually recasts the relation of language and person into that of a deeply wounded relation to words themselves. (370)

13. A precedent for Blaser's frequent citations and piecemeal use of other writers is to be found in Walter Benjamin and Hannah Arendt's description of Benjamin as the "pearl diver." The well-known passage I have in mind is from Arendt's introduction to *Illuminations*:

> Insofar as the past has been transmitted as tradition, it possesses authority; insofar as authority presents itself historically, it

becomes tradition. Walter Benjamin knew that the break in tradition and the loss of authority which occurred in his lifetime were irreparable, and he concluded that he had to discover new ways of dealing with the past. In this he became a master when he discovered that the transmissibility of the past had been replaced by its citability and that in place of its authority there had arisen a strange power to settle down, piecemeal, in the present and to deprive it of "peace of mind," the mindless peace of complacency. (38)

14. In *The Failure of Modernism*, Andrew Ross attributes to Olson a number of grotesque positions. Olson rejects "the traditional order of symbolic relations which bind us together within a commonly intelligible network of codes" (97), Ross says, and this is tantamount to psychosis. Discussing Olson's spiral forms, he finds that "when it comes to looking for moral guidance, Maximus consults his own genitals . . . he [Maximus] notes the resemblance of his twisting public hairs to the Lybian ostrich feather, which . . . may once have adorned the crown of Egypt, as the symbolic 'spiral of entry' which marked off the coronation ceremony as a divine *rite de passage*" (124). Or commenting on Olson's correspondence with Edward Dahlberg, Cid Corman, and Robert Creeley, Ross remarks on "Olson's practice of setting up relations of debt that often resemble forms of *blackmail*" (134). These charges of madness, moral perversity, and criminality, however, seem to pale beside Ross's discovery of Olson's principle failing: epistemological naivety.

> For Olson, this lived sense of the "real" is bound up within his ambitious attempt to modify the classical realist position of reflecting or reproducing the world "as it really is." (98)

According to Ross, Olson's search for a renewed sense of form was based on the assumption of "an *a priori* and empirical field of reality to which language must find a relation of adequacy" (101). For a response to Ross, see Peter Middleton's essay in this collection.

15. In "A Dialectics of the Real" from *The Recovery of the Public World*, David Marriott writes on the contiguity of Merleau-Ponty and Lacan in Blaser's "Stadium of the Mirror." Marriott takes the view that Merleau-Ponty's *chiasmus* represents an ideal unification of mind and world. The phrase I have cited comes from this passage:

> The world upon which perception opens is not a domain of pure presences but "an ambiguous field of horizons and distances," an overlapping and intertwining of the visible and the invisible. The figure that typifies this overlapping and intertwining is, for Merleau-Ponty, that of chiasmus. "We place ourselves . . . in us *and* in things," writes Merleau-Ponty, "at the point where, by a

sort of chiasmus, we become the others and we become the world." In this chiastic encounter with and appropriation of otherness may be found Merleau-Ponty's phenomenological dream of a meaning-laden imbrication of the viewer and the viewed, body and the word, subject and object in the flesh of the world. (351-52)

Marriott argues that Merleau-Ponty takes language as secondarily representing "an ontology of meaning . . . concealed or captive in the thing" (352). As well, he attributes this view to Olson and "the phenomenological poetics of many American poets writing in the 1960s" (352), and then goes on to suggest that Blaser moves beyond the "illusion of immanence" to introduce a Lacanian aporia into the *chiasmus*. This reading of Merleau-Ponty is, I think, contestable. Consider, for instance, Castoriadis's reading of the *chiasmus* as indicating the collapse, rather than the shoring up, of foundational thinking in "The Sayable and the Unsayable."
16. Here is Žižek's quarrel with deconstruction:

> The post-structuralist position constantly repeats that no text could be totally non-metaphysical. On the one hand, it is not possible to get rid of the metaphysical tradition by a simple gesture of taking distance, of placing oneself outside it, because the language we are obliged to use is penetrated by metaphysics. On the other hand, however, every text, however metaphysical, always produces gaps which announce breaches in the metaphysical circle: the points at which the textual process subverts what its 'author' intended to say. Is such a position not just a little too convenient? To put it more bluntly, the position from which the deconstructivist can always make sure of the fact that 'there is no metalanguage'; that no utterance can say precisely what it intended to say; that the process of enunciation [sic] always subverts the utterance; is *the position of metalanguage* in its purest, most radical form. (154-55)

Whether or not deconstruction does constitute a metalanguage is another issue for debate, but what Žižek brings out so well here is that a claim to exteriority is at once impossible to make good and to avoid. Every articulation has its constitutive aporia: it carries the real along as an absence that has never been a presence.
17. Blaser introduced Agamben to me in conversation in 1995. See also his remarks on Agamben in the July 1999 interview in this volume.
18. The phrase "disseminative drift" is Bernard Harrison's. See his "On 'White Mythology'" 521.
19. It is death as such that Derrida deconstructs, and in this his *focus* is different than is that of Blaser. In *Aporias*:

I hope that I have convinced you my purpose was not to justify a
passage beyond knowledge, anthropothanatology, biology, or the
metaphysics of death toward a more radical, originary, or fundamental thought, as if the limit were a known edge between, on
the one hand, anthropology (be it even a fundamental anthropology) and, on the other hand, ontology, an existential analysis,
and more generally a more questioning thought of death in general. On the contrary . . . my discourse was aimed at suggesting
that this fundamentalist dimension is untenable and that it cannot even claim to have any coherence or rigorous specificity.
(79)

Where Derrida targets the concept of death-in-general, Blaser simply makes death
particular in his tying of it to consciousness. Polar thinking is not about the producing of consciousness, but about the undergoing of it.
20. The italicized phrase in Blaser's poem "further," comes from Hermann Broch's
Death of Virgil:

oh nothing was so near to evil as the god tumbling down into a
false-humanity, or the man catapulted toward a false-divinity,
both lured toward evil . . . (131)

21. In his conclusion to *The Fold*, Deleuze suggests that the contemporary monad
has become nomadic—that it straddles diverging worlds and unresolved dissonances,
unlike the Leibnitzean monad which expressed a single, harmoniously-centered
world (137). For a fuller presentation of the nomad, see Deleuze and Guattari's *A
Thousand Plateaus*, especially the introductory chapter on the rhizome (3-25), and
the chapter titled "Treatise on Nomadology: The War Machine" (351-423).
22. Compare Blaser's moth with Robert Duncan's monarch butterfly, in the titular
poem from *Roots and Branches*, "awakening transports of an inner view of things"
(3).
23. For another discussion of Blaser's fold and its philosophical genealogy, see Steve
McCaffery's essay in *The Recovery of the Public World*, titled "Blaser's Deleuzean
Folds." McCaffery takes careful note of the affective component in *The Holy Forest*
which I have stressed in my discussion of polarity:

The Holy Forest as both a monadography and a nomadography?
What does this claim require? It demands initially an affective
(as opposed to a systematic) reading of the seriality. . . . Affective
reading entails both monadic and nomadic vectors. A relishing
of the particulate alongside an open acceptance of the non-totalizable. (381)

My claim, however, is that Blaser makes any figure which might be given to the "non-totalizable" treatable as bounded; the fold becomes one in a series of tropes rather than the one which explains the others. The uprooted tree, rather than the rhizome, is a trope perhaps closer to the specificity of Blaser's poems, because the former is both mobile and "particulate"—and yet of course, it too, may give place to another.

24. See Spicer's Vancouver lectures:

> a few years ago at North Beach John Ryan and I decided to start talking in Martian, just to bug the tourists. And after a while we could actually converse in Martian to each other, with no recognizable linguistic things or anything else. But right now I could speak in tongues and it wouldn't be anything but some kind of switch that you pull. It's perfectly possible for me to fake an unknown language. So I don't know. On the other hand, the experience of Tzara and others may mean that there's some way there. (*House* 12)

25. The kind of relationship Blaser sets up with the reader differs from that supposed to be reader-directed and sometimes attributed to language writing. *The Holy Forest* requires careful attention to the writer's line of movement, meaning that allusions have to be looked up, references tracked, and so on. The writer thus seems to be manipulating the reader's attention, but in the process of following this lead (and yet the poet of the serial does not know where s/he is going), the reader *cannot not* begin to compose. In the *Forest*, the absence of a dominant metaphor, a transcendent point of view, or a *telos* forces readerly choice at every step: where to put one foot down in front of the other? Yet as Susan Howe has so clearly demonstrated in her many poems that read other writers, even texts that do present omniscient voices are heavily marked with materialities that undo the definitive exegesis. And as Howe also shows, true attention to a text is a creative act. Blaser makes this readerly creativity explicit, by letting the poem stand as a record of meetings that demands of the reader what it demanded of him. In "The Truth is Laughter 12":

> *a radiant finger points*
> (*Holy* 177)

26. Deleuze offers a more radical version of this process of becoming-through-infolding, but Whitehead seems the more appropriate reference here because his philosophy of organism retains the possibility of wholeness, even if the whole is potential rather than actual (God in his primordial aspect is the potential fullness of the cosmos). Similarly, the historical narratives that engage Arendt give us history as that which is always coming to a point, like the serial poem. The last word must be deferred, because only someone "outside" the story could write it, but the process has in it an urge toward completion (Whitehead's "lure for feeling"). Deleuze's becom-

ings, on the other hand, simply *spread*, without that quality of movement from point to point characteristic of narrativized processes.

27. On the retrospective narrative, Arendt writes that "whatever the character and . . . content of the story may be . . . its full meaning can reveal itself only when it has ended" (*Human* 171), and then of course only to observers rather the actors themselves. As I've noted above, Whitehead's primordial God is similarly "outside," and in the serial poem, where the poet himself is inscribed as a point of view, the final trope cannot be written.

28. I am selecting from Arendt's thoughts on judgment those that seem most illuminating in relation to Blaser, but in the context of Arendt's *oeuvre*, selection is simplification. I offer the following passage from Ronald Beiner's "Interpretive Essay," published with Arendt's Kant lectures, as an indication of conundrums that I cannot engage in an essay where Blaser, not Arendt, is the focus. Here is Beiner:

> In the earlier formulations we find discussions of the relation of judgment to "representative thinking" and opinion, leading one to suppose that judgment is a faculty exercised by actors in political deliberation and action. . . . But this approach is implicitly denied in her later account. We have already mentioned that in "What is Freedom?" Arendt aligns judgment with intellect or cognition, in stark contrast to her eventual denial that judgment is an intellectual faculty or is indeed cognitive at all. In unpublished lectures delivered in 1965 and 1966, Arendt went to the opposite extreme, defining judgment as a function of the will. . . . And in one context she even went so far as to say that "whether this faculty of judgment, one of the most mysterious faculties of the human mind, should be said to be the will or reason, *or perhaps a third mental capacity*, is at least an open question." (138-39)

29. In a note to canto VII of the *Inferno*, John Sinclair points out that Dante divides sins of incontinence between those of the flesh and spirit. The worst of the latter, he says, is "the sluggish, persistent bitterness of the souls which are so mastered by their resentments that they refuse the light of the sun, the goodness of God" (108). These sins of weakness are matched by sins of will, the latter punished in the lower circles of hell. Again, as Sinclair says, the crimes involve a turning away from fellow men, God, or nature (God's art) (152-53).

30. Donald Sherburne, to whose helpful *Key to Whitehead's Process and Reality* I have repeatedly turned, explains God's workings in the world this way:

> As superject [datum for others], God offers for each actual entity, as its subjective aim, a vision of what that entity might become. This subjective aim constitutes the ideal for growth on the part of the actual entity that would result in maximum

ordered complexity in the world were it realized in fact—this is God's mode of operation in the world, designed to produce the kind of world that, physically prehended by his consequent nature, would result in maximum intensity of satisfaction for him. (244)

31. Importantly, Arendt distinguishes freedom from sovereignty:

> If it were true that freedom and sovereignty are the same, then indeed no man could be free, because sovereignty, the ideal of uncompromising self-sufficiency and mastership, is contradictory to the very condition of plurality. No man can be sovereign because not one man, but men, inhabit the earth—and not, as the tradition since Plato holds, because of man's limited strength, which makes him depend upon the help of others. All the recommendations the tradition has to offer to overcome the condition of non-sovereignty and win an untouchable integrity of the human person amount to a compensation for the intrinsic "weakness" of plurality. Yet, if these recommendations were followed and this attempt to overcome the consequences of plurality were successful, the result would be not so much sovereign domination of one's self as arbitrary domination of all others, or, as in Stoicism, the exchange of the real world for an imaginary one where these others would simply not exist. (*Human* 210-11)

32. Despite the provocative caricature of Arendt's *polis*, Hanna Pitkin argues for revision rather than rejection of Arendt's political theory. In the article from which I've taken this phrase, titled "Justice: On Relating Private and Public," she searches for a link between the social and political realms: "The danger to public life comes not from letting the social question in, but from failing to transform it in political activity, letting it enter in the wrong 'spirit'" (281). Pitkin therefore joins those readers of Arendt who seek to renegotiate her terms by assigning them to modes of public presentation rather than content.

33. Benhabib agrees with Pitkin on this point of the political and social as modes of public presentation:

> Whichever class or social group enters the public realm, and no matter how class or group specific its demands may be in their genesis, the process of public-political struggle transforms the *attitude of narrow self-interest into a more broadly shared public or common interest*. This, I think, is the fundamental distinction between the "social-cum-economic" and the "political" realms for Hannah Arendt. Engaging in politics does not mean abandoning economic or social issues; it means fighting for them in

the name of principles, interests, values that have a generalizable basis, and that concern us as members of a collectivity. The political for Arendt involves the transformation of the partial and limited perspectives of each class, group, or individual into a broader vision of the "enlarged mentality." (145)

34. Bohman writes that "moral compromise" should be required to meet two criteria:

> They are fair if they . . . correct for persistent inequalities and . . . they make possible continued participation in a common framework of pluralist citizenship. (73)

35. On this point, I have in mind the exchange between Albrecht Wellmer and Arendt at the 1972 conference on Arendt at York University, recorded in *The Recovery of the Public World*:

> ALBRECHT WELLMER: I would ask you to give one example in our time of a social problem which is not at the same time a political problem. Take anything: like education, or health, or urban problems, even the simple problem of living standards. It seems to me that even the social problems in our society are unavoidably political problems. But if this is true, then, of course, it would also be true that a distinction between the social and the political in our society is impossible to draw.
> ARENDT: Let's take the housing problem. The social problem is certainly adequate housing. But the question of whether this adequate housing means integration or not is *certainly* a political question. With every one of these questions there is a double face. And one of these faces should not be subject to debate. There shouldn't be any debate about the question that everybody should have decent housing. (318)

This latter comment supports Luban's argument that Arendt's social-political distinction is a distinction between utility and meaning, or problems to be solved and relations to be established. What Arendt consigns to the social, of course, would be understood more commonly as political. It is worth emphasizing that Blaser follows Arendt here, as in the passage I cite above from "The Violets" (62), where he gives to Marxism the social questions, and then turns to the construction of the "real." 36. Arendt argues that Hobbesian humanity (humanity devoted to murderous self-interest and "power after power") is "not at all the realistic pessimism for which it has been praised" (140), but rather a refashioning of "Man" in the specular image of bourgeois society as it emerged in the seventeenth century. For Arendt, the idea that economic interest is the sole basis of politics is specific to the bourgeoisie; it is not an

inevitable or transhistorical condition of collectives. On the significance of this view
of things to the spread of imperialist thinking, she writes:

> Since the owning and dominant classes had convinced every-
> body that economic interest and the passion for ownership are a
> sound basis for the body politic, even non-imperialist statesmen
> were easily persuaded to yield when a common economic inter-
> est appeared on the horizon. (*Origins* 153)

37. Arendt's concept of what should constitute access to the political world in a
democracy is characteristically distinctive. While in practice politics is not for everyone, Arendt says, anyone who wants the public life should have it: the elite should
be self-selecting. Here she is in *On Revolution*:

> From the viewpoint of revolution and the survival of the revolu-
> tionary spirit, the trouble does not lie in the factual rise of a new
> élite: it is not the revolutionary spirit but the democratic mental-
> ity of an egalitarian society that tends to deny the obvious inabil-
> ity and conspicuous lack of interest of large parts of the popula-
> tion in political matters as such. The trouble lies in the lack of
> public spaces to which the people at large would have entrance
> and from which an élite could be selected, or rather, where it
> could select itself. The trouble, in other words, is that politics has
> become a profession and a career, and that the 'élite' therefore is
> being chosen according to standards and criteria which are them-
> selves profoundly unpolitical. It is in the nature of all party sys-
> tems that the authentically political talents can assert themselves
> only in rare cases, and it is even rarer that the specifically politi-
> cal qualifications survive the petty manoeuvres of party politics
> with its demands for plain salesmanship. (277-78)

Craig Calhoun, in his discussion of Arendt in "Plurality, Promises, and Public
Spaces" notes that "Civil society is first and foremost a realm of freedom *from* politics. But public freedom is freedom *in* politics. . . . Real freedom, then, consists of
freedom to enter into public life" (253-54).
38. Blaser's note says that the Mayer of "Even on Sunday" is Hans Mayer, and the
citation is from *Outsiders* (*Holy* 351).
39. Calhoun, in the essay I have cited above (note 38) raises the possibility of multiple publics:

> It is normal, however, not aberrant, for people to speak in a num-
> ber of different public arenas and for these arenas to address mul-
> tiple centers of power (whether institutionally differentiated
> within a single state, combining multiple states or political agen-

cies, or recognizing that putatively nonpolitical agencies such as business corporations are loci of power and are addressed by public discourse. How many and how separate these public spheres are must be empirical variables. (250-51)

WORKS CITED

Agamben, Giorgio. *The Coming Community.* Trans. Michael Hardt. Minneapolis: U of Minnesota P, 1993.
_____. *Infancy and History: Essays on the Destruction of Experience.* Trans. Liz Heron. London: Verso, 1993.
Allen, Donald M., ed. *The New American Poetry.* New York: Grove, 1960.
Arendt, Hannah. *The Human Condition.* New York: Doubleday/Anchor, 1959.
_____. Introduction. *Illuminations.* By Walter Benjamin. Ed. Hannah Arendt. New York: Schocken, 1969. 1-55.
_____. *On Revolution.* 1963. New York: Pelican, 1977.
_____. *The Origins of Totalitarianism.* San Diego: Harcourt/Harvest, 1973.
Beiner, Ronald. "Hannah Arendt on Judging." *Lectures on Kant's Political Philosophy.* By Hannah Arendt. Ed. Ronald Beiner. 1982. Chicago: U of Chicago P, 1989. 89-156.
Benhabib, Seyla. *The Reluctant Modernism of Hannah Arendt.* Thousand Oaks: SAGE, 1996.
Blaser, Robin. *Astonishments.* Audiotapes. Vancouver, 1974.
_____. "The Fire." *Caterpillar* 12 (1970): 15-32.
_____. *The Holy Forest.* Vancouver: Talonbooks, 1993.
_____. "The Metaphysics of Light." *Capilano Review* 6 (1974): 35-39.
_____. "'My Vocabulary Did This To Me.'" *Acts* 6 (1987): 98-105.
_____. "The Practice of Outside." *The Collected Books of Jack Spicer.* By Jack Spicer. Ed. Robin Blaser. Santa Barbara: Black Sparrow, 1975. 271-329.
_____. "The Recovery of the Public World." *Reflections on Cultural Policy: Past, Present and Future.* Ed. Evan Alderson, Robin Blaser, Harold Coward. Waterloo: Wilfrid Laurier UP for The Calgary Institute for the Humanities, 1993.
_____. "The Stadium of the Mirror." *Image Nations 1-12 and The Stadium of the Mirror.* London: Ferry, 1974. 53-67.
_____. "The Violets." *Line* 2 (1983): 61-103.
Bohman, James. "The Moral Costs of Political Pluralism: The Dilemmas of Difference and Equality in Arendt's 'Reflections on Little Rock.'" *Hannah Arendt: Twenty Years Later.* Ed. Larry May and Jerome Kohn. Cambridge: MIT, 1997. 53-80.
Broch, Hermann. *The Death of Virgil.* Trans. Jean Starr Untermeyer. 1945. San Francisco: North Point, 1983.

Calhoun, Craig. "Plurality, Promises, and Public Spaces." *Hannah Arendt and the Meaning of Politics.* Ed. Craig Calhoun and John McGowan. Minneapolis: U of Minnesota P, 1997. 232-59.

Canovan, Margaret. "Politics as Culture." Hinchman and Hinchman 179-205.

Castoriadus, Cornelius. "The Sayable and the Unsayable." *Crossroads in the Labyrinth.* Trans. Kate Soper and Martin H. Ryle. Cambridge: MIT, 1984. 119-44.

Dante, Alighieri. *The Divine Comedy.* Trans. John D. Sinclair. 1939; rpt. New York: Oxford UP, 1981-82.

Davey, Frank. Introduction. *TISH 1-19.* Ed. Frank Davey. Vancouver: Talonbooks, 1975. 7-11.

Davidson, Michael. *The San Francisco Renaissance: Poetics and Community at Mid-Century.* Cambridge: Cambridge UP, 1989.

Deleuze, Gilles. *The Fold.* Trans. Tom Conley. Minneapolis: U of Minnesota P, 1993.

Deleuze, Gilles, and Felix Guattari. *A Thousand Plateaus.* Trans. Brian Massumi. Minneapolis: U of Minnesota P, 1987.

Derrida, Jacques. *Aporias.* Trans. Thomas Dutoit. Stanford: Stanford UP, 1993.

Dietz, Mary G. "Feminist Receptions of Hannah Arendt." *Feminist Interpretations of Hannah Arendt.* Ed. Bonnie Honig. University Park: Pennsylvania State UP, 1995. 17-50.

Duncan, Robert. *Roots and Branches.* New York: New Directions, 1969.

Ellingham, Lewis, and Kevin Killian. *Poet Be Like God.* Hanover: Wesleyan UP, 1997.

Faas, Ekbert. *Young Robert Duncan: Portrait of the Poet as Homosexual in Society.* Santa Barbara: Black Sparrow, 1983.

Ginsberg, Allen. *The Indian Journals.* San Francisco: Haselwood/City Lights, 1970.

Gizzi, Peter, ed. *The House That Jack Built: The Collected Lectures of Jack Spicer.* Hanover: Wesleyan UP, 1998.

Harrison, Bernard. "On 'White Mythology.'" *Critical Inquiry* 25.3 (Spring 1999): 505-534.

Hill, Melvyn A., ed. "On Hannah Arendt." [conference discussion]. *Hannah Arendt: The Recovery of the Public World.* New York: St. Martin's Press, 1979. 301-39.

Hinchman, Lewis P., and Sandra K. Hinchman, eds. *Hannah Arendt: Critical Essays.* Albany: State U of New York P, 1994.

Kantorowicz, Ernst. *The King's Two Bodies.* Princeton: Princeton UP, 1957.

Lacoue-Labarthe, Philippe. *Poetry as Experience.* Trans. Andrea Tarnowski. Stanford: Stanford UP, 1999.

Lingis, Alphonso. *The Community of Those Who Have Nothing In Common.* Bloomington: Indiana UP, 1994.

Luban, David. "Explaining Dark Times: Hannah Arendt's Theory of Theory." Hinchman and Hinchman 79-109.

Marriott, David. "A Dialectic of the Real." Watts and Byrne 351-55.

Mayer, Hans. *Outsiders.* Cambridge: MIT P, 1982.

McCaffery, Steve. "Blaser's Deleuzean Folds." Byrne and Watts 373-92.

Merleau-Ponty, Maurice. *The Primacy of Perception*. Ed. James M. Edie. Northwestern UP, 1964.

O'Brien, Mary. *The Politics of Reproduction*. Boston: Routledge, 1981.

Olson, Charles. *The Collected Poems of Charles Olson*. Ed. George F. Butterick. Berkeley: U of California P, 1987.

——————. *The Special View of History*. Ed. Ann Charters. Berkeley: Oyez, 1970.

Owens, Judith. "Fertile Forms." *Canadian Literature* 103 (1984): 93-97.

Pitkin, Hanna Fenichel. "Justice: On Relating Private and Public." Hinchman and Hinchman 261-88.

Rasula, Jed. "The Body Without Organs in the Underworld." *Acts* 6 (1987): 95-96.

Ross, Andrew. *The Failure of Modernism: Symptoms of American Poetry*. New York: Columbia UP, 1986.

Sherburne, Donald, ed. *A Key to Whitehead's* Process and Reality. 1966. Chicago: U of Chicago P, 1981.

Silliman, Ron. "'My Vocabulary Did This To Me.'" *Acts* 6 (1987): 67-71.

Sinclair, John P. Commentary. *The Divine Comedy: Inferno*. By Dante Alighieri. Trans. John P. Sinclair. New York: Oxford UP, 1961.

Spicer, Jack. *The Collected Books of Jack Spicer*. Ed. Robin Blaser. Santa Barbara: Black Sparrow, 1980.

——————. *The House That Jack Built: The Collected Lecture of Jack Spicer*. Ed. Peter Gizzi. Hanover: Wesleyan UP, 1998.

Tallman, Warren. "Wonder Merchants: Modernist Poetry in Vancouver during the 1960s." *Godawful Streets of Man*. *Open Letter* 3/6 (1976-77): 175-207.

Watts, Charles and Edward Byrne, eds. *The Recovery of the Public World*. Burnaby: Talonbooks, 1999.

Wolin, Sheldon. "Democracy and the Political." Hinchman and Hinchman 289-306.

Woodcock, George. "From the Impenetrable to the Lewd." *B.C. Bookworld* (1994): 35.

Zaslove, Jery. "The Public Spheroid—Following the Paths in the Millennial Wilderness, or, 'Lost Without a Utopic Map' in the Spheres of Hannah Arendt and Robin Blaser." Watts and Byrne 432-53.

Žižek, Slavoj. *That Sublime Object of Ideology*. London: Verso, 1989.

ROBIN BLASER AT LAKE PARADOX

George Bowering

2.

The dying Charles Olson told Robin Blaser, I would trust you on the image, but you have no syntax, or something like that. Here is a famous Blaser image:

Supper Guest

> leaning over the white
> linen which casts
>
> a pale light
> over his face (*HF* 44)

—which seems to present no problems in reading its syntax. But the rest of this single-sentence poem without a period at the end carries us as a moth might fly, on a path better glimpsed than followed, to rest in a corner. The image is part of *The Moth Poem*, written "for H.D." It often favors the carefully advancing well-lit stanzas that H.D. liked in her later days, but it does not adhere to classic sentences the way that H.D.'s *Trilogy*, for instance, does.

Do we know what Olson meant by "syntax," and do we know why Blaser called his 1983 book *Syntax*? Was Blaser taking up Olson's challenge, or was he proving that he had another meaning for "syntax" in mind? There is a clue, one knows, in the "Preface" to the book:

> I read, walk, listen, dream, and write among companions.
> These poems do not belong to me.

Note that he begins the way a grammar teacher's examples do: I
(verb) *etc.*

Syntax means the way things are gathered, tactics for getting language together. Words, specifically, listen among fellows. A grammar
of something is a set of principles showing the way it works. The
rules, a strict grandma might say, a program for letters. But syntax: I
guess that as synthesis is to thesis, so syntax is to tactics.

Now the thing about tactics is that they are thought out in advance,
not as far in advance as is strategy, but practiced and planned toward
expectations and an end. They are the practical science of deployment. We can hardly be talking about a typical Blaser poem here, not
that zigging moth.

Once I got a letter from a faithful reader of Blaser: ". . . really,
there's only one question about Blaser that needs to be answered:
what's the effect on his thought of having no cognitive syntax?
(i.e. the question behind that is about parataxis, and how effective it
really is. Blaser, for instance, is a much better poet than an essayist.
When he gets into trouble (i.e. becomes inscrutable) in the poetry,
it's because he starts looping ideas and images together, making a
marvel."

Parataxis is Blaser's poetic and his politics. In his book *Syntax* it
serves his purpose well as conveyor and indicator of any message we
might want to coax from a poetry. For one thing, parataxis usually
shows up more in speech (formal or street-level) than it does in writing, and "companions" use the occasion of bread-breaking to retire
from their lone studies to share words with one another. For another
thing, parataxis makes conjugation rather than subjugation. So in his
"Great Companions" series, Blaser will not use the old meditative
play that would treat the great dead poets as masters; and in *Syntax*
he will not treat the radio, overheard transit talk, graffiti or tombstone
inscriptions as vulgarity to be "lifted" into poetic order by a bard's
quotation. If Blaser is looping idea and image, he is not converting
one into material for the other.

The difficulties presented by Blaser's essays I will leave unre-
marked. But it seems to me that for a lot of readers (i.e. people used
to buying poetry books as unselfconsciously as they buy snowtires) the
difficulty in reading Blaser's poetry is not the zigging of the sentences,

but the learned referentiality. I am also persuaded that this is the reason for the ignoring of Blaser by the regular Canadian literature critics who like the untroubled sentences and straight-ahead similes they can purchase in the lyrics of autobiographical Canadian poets. They want to find out about an individual's exemplary pain at the loss of a father to cancer, or the ways in which killer whales and the rest of nature can be compared to human beings, to the shame of the latter. They do not want difficulty, either of allusion or lexical presentation—how often have you heard, for instance, from reviewers and others that they used to like Erin Mouré's poetry before she got all caught up in deconstruction and reflexivity?

※ ※ ※

After a few volumes of *Image-Nations*, hard to find, expensive to buy, and filled with erudition, readers were greeted in 1983 with *Syntax*, published by Talonbooks, and full of jokes. Lots of short poems and found poems. Lots of quotations from philosophers and poets, too, but plainly attributed: "(phrases from Valéry and Geoffrey Hartman, March 24, 1981)".

Through it all one hears Blaser's mind (or brain, is it?) *reading* (or listening) and all at once writing, a word-compiler among a compilation of words.

How hard can it be, then, to come to the table and understand a poem like "lake of souls (reading notes"? When Blaser wrote "these poems do not belong to me," could he have meant that they belong to the reader? Or could he have been saying that they are not in the business of belonging?

In *Syntax* there is no table of contents, but nearly all the poems' titles are indicated by upper-case letters—for instance the often used "THE TRUTH IS LAUGHTER." There are two titles that are in lower-case italics. One, *"alerte d'or,"* is made out of "phrases from Valéry and Geoffrey Hartman." The other is the poem under consideration. There are also two poems whose titles are presented in lower-case Roman type, a one-liner called "graffito," and the last page, which could be thought title-less. In the table of contents of the collected books, *The Holy Forest* (1993), this last one is called "'further'," indicating that it has no title but is marked off by its first word as something more than an ending to the stuff on the previous page.

In *The Holy Forest* the titles do not have upper-case letters, and the title "lake of woods (reading notes" has no italics, though like "*alerte d'or*" and "graffito," it is differentiated by its having a lower-case first letter.

Well, so what? Robin Blaser's system is a lot like Robert Duncan's, and Jack Spicer's (and bp Nichol's): the various parts of "lake of souls (reading notes" are marked differently, but they come together, even the enclosed 1947 Blaser*kind* poem "Song in Four Parts for Christ the Son," to form this eleven-page poem called notes. And "lake of souls (reading notes" joins a lot of pieces called "The Truth is Laughter" and others to form a book called *Syntax*. But then "lake of souls (reading notes" enters as part of *Syntax* into a much larger book called *The Holy Forest*. It is not difficult to imagine that *The Holy Forest* is part of a large book being written by Blaser and his companions. You are not out of the woods just because you happen upon the opening of a field. The poems, said Blaser in his 1967 essay "The Fire," are "a continuous song in which the fragmented subject matter is only apparently disconnected" (238).

Does that mean that the reader is "free" or "bound" to connect? Or to find possible connections? Or to read like a person who knows little about this and less about that? I, for instance, have liked Blaser's poems since I first saw them in the early sixties, but have always been intimidated by them, believing as I always did in graduate school that everyone else knew more about the subject than I did. So I usually take a tack that is supposed to disarm other sailors. I approach a poem as if one can believe everything one reads, and then register my surprise when that proves not to be so. Sorry for the personal note—I won't let it happen again.

*   *   *

So, "lake of souls" one reads in lower-case, and already one is lost, hopeful of being found, because that sounds so nearly familiar—is this lake to be found somewhere in Dante, or an Egyptian story about

Osiris, or somewhere in Blaser's favored Gnostics or Sufis? There is a lake of souls somewhere in Chinese stories, but Blaser is not calling these "reading tones," and we will not get any Chinese reading here. Of course we do not know, the syntax been adumbrated, whether that word "reading," so lately a verb, is some other part of speech. Are these notes made while reading, or notes being read, or notes doing some reading? Surely not what a lake of souls is doing? Adumbration of syntax can make one feel so rich. So *rich*, and lamenting a want of confidence.

Then the poem begins so beautifully, as a person without theoretical training might say. It opens with traditional timing, a summer dawn full of birdsong—and the poem will seem to end eleven pages later, returning not to dawn's light or the eve's onset, but mixing dark with light and (in this longest piece followed only by an "envoi" and a "further") getting us back to the aurora borealis that started *Syntax*.

The poem begins with beautiful sound, even while talking in the vulgate ("things move about quickly"), a simple response to the familiar calls of birdsong. Yet we know that this will be a longish poem about the poet's place in the relationship between belief and lone practice, because we can't help hearing it as a reply to Robert Duncan's poem on the way poiesis gets going. "The light foot hears you and the brightness begins," Duncan said, puzzling us somewhat. Now "the period dissolves and becomes a curve of notes." Duncan's poet seems to be writing the whole night long, stopping when dawn is rumored. Blaser's noting of sources will begin when day wakes, probably telling Duncan and us that he is not so much spooky as Eosic in his invitation of muse and mind.

The only two published poems in Blaser's "Great Companions" series are the ones for Duncan and Pindar, the poet that Duncan credits with the first line of his poem.

Here the birds rather than the bards seem to start this poem about reading. But does one "read" birdsong? There is a bird song at the end of every sentence this morning, but we don't know who is forming the sentences; and bird songs go up and / or down their scale. The period dissolves from a little dot to become, presumably, an undetected part of a solution, and if there is no end to syntax, there is no syntax. Otherwise reading, the only "period" we yet know of is "dawn," when things that move about quickly are likely birds, those light-foots that in poetry bring messages from heaven to earth.

If the subject is grammar, this is demonstrative, and indefinite is a pronoun. Or the spiritual condition signaled by the birds is a doubly negated (in-, de-) finite. Yes, says the bird's line-ending, it is. As if syntax has a secret the poet is challenged by. But it is morning: the condition is not a dream, not the message enjoyed by a Romantic poet or a Duncan. Wide awake at dawn, this poet is making a thematic statement, as few are wont these days to do. Flirting or arguing with Jung, he declares that we all share this condition not in a collective reverie, but in the day's light. Poetry, furthermore, is not passed from master to younger savant, but available to all, produced by earthly graffitists. Hence parataxis rather than authors. If there is such a thing as the sullen art, it is a solitude we join among us to reach. In becoming civilized we learn—

Oh no. Solitude comes from sole. Solution comes from lose. The reader is always in danger of getting things backward when he gets cute.

* * *

Having fallen upon the word "civilization," Blaser thinks of the civilized seeking refuge from the barbarians. Their lesson, learned by them or not, will be that there is no such thing as privilege if the unprivileged are not in sight, that the barbarians are already inside us, where they belong. The bird's song curves—it does not merely rise or fall like a civilization.

Cavafy's poem is marked by plenty of punctuation and subordination, italicized, quoted syntax. It is the outside of Blaser's poem's inside. *Those people* (the purported, demonstrated others) *were some sort of solution*, in which a whole period might be dissolved. But they did not arrive as they were supposed to, on the dot. There never was a fall of Constantinople. It was everybody's language.

* * *

Birds are not the most intelligent of earth's creatures. If their chattering gets written down, it is done by human writers, the same people that copy words out of the library at Alexandria or off the windows of a city bus. When that happens that song becomes "everybody's language," and poets rightly address skylarks and cuckoos.

Here I will have to admit that I can get my little feet better on Blaser's image than on his syntax:

> the spiritual condition which is everybody's language
> of the world is not finally as small as my own solitaire

Of course "finally" echoes "indefinite." Of course "solitaire" echoes "solitude." But is "solitaire" a game or a jewel? I would like to say that Blaser is typing up the argument of his whole (page and) book—the declaration that the experienced poet now values the ensemble world of language above any gem-like singularity—silver knobs (hmm), single jewels, shining verses. Casement windows.

On the first page of this eleven-page poem there are many v's and l's, the work of love. But there are also five words with "sol" in them. Is this working on a reader earlier than syntax, signifying a kind of sun's dawn? How many ways can Blaser make his point at once?

✳ ✳ ✳

The second page is autobiographical prose, the prose writer the poet Blaser. He tells of his learning early the Nicene Creed, issued in Constantinople, home of Cavafy's family. Blaser says that he learned it in Latin, French and English, but we know that it was first written in Greek. It is a wonderful foil for the poet's demotic argument, because (1) it declares a belief in pure patriarchal order: *Credo in unum Deum Patrem Omnipotentem, factorem coeli et terrae, visibilium omnium et invisibilium*, and (2) it reaches for the "universal," being the only creed that was to be accepted by Christian churches East and West, Catholic and Protestant.

Yet Blaser introduces it with an image of "pouring over the crazy-quilt." I like to think that he is remembering a literal family comforter. The crazy-quilt is made for family memories, and made with an originary design, caught-as-caught-could. Neither does it declare anything like the universal of the cosmic Maker. It is all image, no syntax. Things go side by side, composition. It is homely.

Blaser inscribes his own public Idaho when he twists some sagebrush into this patch of the poem. Yet sage is ancient and mediterranean (from earth's center before frontier America); it was supposed to promote memory and wisdom, Blaser's two topics here.

But before he can bring his thought to a completion, the old grammar teacher's definition of the sentence, he is led at the end of his line not to birdsong this time, but to bee's sound, murmuring, beyond the Greeks to Sanskrit. Then to nowhere, and then to Berkeley in 1945. The Nicene Creed was not really a profession of belief but a submission to discipline. Blaser will seem to be a kind of musical apostate.

* * *

In the next patch or square, which like all the notes abjures uppercase letters to begin sentences because there is no more beginning than ending, Jack Spicer is both "beloved friend" and new acquaintance. Quilt-makers make new covers out of old clothes; lyric autobiography happens at dawn. Crazy Spicer is in 1945 even more ecumenical than the Council of Constantinople, being both "Presbyterian and a Buddhist." He made a campy remark about young Idaho's Catholicism. On Easter Sunday next year Robert Duncan, an even stranger mixture of religions, does likewise. Remembering the effect of this shock, the poet nearly lets this thread ravel, as the words loosen their connections to one another, gaps in the lines.

Finally, in the year after the poet became a legal adult, he published a poem about a kind of Apocrypha Jesus, in the campus magazine. It was praised, we are told, by one Keith Jones. Blaser holds his needle and tells us that now, or rather at the time of the poem's composition, Jones is a "labour leader / among the grapes." A nice touch, this praise from a man who would be surrounded by both lowly work and the fruit of sacrament. Prose and poetry. Hesiod and Dionysus.

Blaser's reading notes now reprint the four stanzas (with Yeatsean Roman numerals) of that student's poem. It is titled "Song in Four

Parts for Christ the Son." Each line begins with a capital letter, and so do these words: Your, He, God, Him, Love and Our Lady. There is lots of end-rime, and periods at the tail ends of its short sentences. It is redolent of roses and dancing. It alternates iambs with anapests, like a child walking and skipping. It is a love song that affirms a Christian relation while challenging, or at least modifying it. It is sort of like a Yeats poem stripped by H.D. Finally, it affirms a Christ lover dancing instead of sticking to a tree. It is so well finished that it ends with a couplet, both of whose lines end with periods. There is not a bird within earshot, except the unheard peacocks.

Blaser must be copying all those satisfied periods to join his two young friends in making fun of the young poet. Certainly that is the function of Anna Russell, the great singer who makes fun of opera's egos. If singers have a resonance where their brains ought to be, they have echoing empty heads. They may be ecstatic but unquestioning, satisfied with their echoing achievement, convinced that they know the score.

We are going to learn that Blaser is hearing Anna Russell on the radio, another composer of these notes, of this book of poems.

Then, "I think of," says the poem for a second time, this time of Oscar Wilde, who is the necessary satirical contemporary of Yeats, the fifth homosexual writer mentioned so far, and the peacock model for Anna Russell's wit. Mr. Wilde made a deathbed conversion to Catholicism, and upon hearing about it, James Joyce said that he hoped that it was insincere. When Oscar Wilde gets into a poem, the temptation is to say that all bets are off. In any case, Blaser avers that he thinks about Wilde's poem "nonsensically." But that's a problem, too: maybe nonsensically is a synonym for asyntactically. That would make sense, then, and our troubles have only begun. If I were gathering this poem, I would stop listening for echoes, and find something to read.

* * *

René Girard has been here almost from the beginning, or he has almost been here from the beginning. The "indefinite spiritual

condition" we share, like syntax, said the dawn poet, "is a violence /
or a love." The twenty-one-year-old poet said "Love" while addressing
the Sacred. Girard's book is called *Le violence et le sacré*.
    (Here's a simple fact. This poem is made of various prose and verse.
It is aimed at coming to a form, as words come to be, there. In this
way it is not unlike a credo.)
    It has to be getting later in the morning or the day. The piece is
getting to be more like reading notes, or affirmative quotations drawn
not from autobiographical memories become writing, but remembered reading, others' writing, brought to the light of this day.
Thoughtful bricolage. This Girard says to us that theorists in our
spiritual condition relegate sacrifice not to the earthly body but to the
imagination. We eat not our god but our co-composers' imagination.
The feat allows us not into high heaven but into speech.
    So now Blaser does not write "I think" but rather "speaking." And
even though he gets to William Blake not by subordination but by
association, he breaks into plain speech to pretend that we have
syntax, the orderly coming: "let's get our principles straight—" Oh,
sure! Don't we have a suspicion that Blake may have got here because
a few pages and some decades back the young poets were in "Blake's
Restaurant on Telegraph Avenue"? Thus was the poem wired from the
beginning. Let *us* get *our* principles via twisted threads.
    The Blake passages tell us of further ecumenicity, which means the
occupied world. Human beings are themselves occupied by Blake's
famous Poetic Genius, angel or spirit or demon, those agents whose
job it is to interrupt the natural order of mortal provinces. Blaser's
paradox is Blake's orthodox—the interruption of human ways is the
work of all humans treading them. Thank god the radio is still on, the
radio that Jack Spicer compared poets to. Anna Russell "interrupts"
again, messing with a traditional song, turning its ancient soothing
measures into a rackelly-backelly refuse heap, comic disorder,
proving that the truth is laughter. She's got a bad attitude. Hey, we
discover over and over, she can really *sing*!
    Girard's interesting argument about the place of the sacred in a
world bereft of the transcendent has inescapable implications for
poetry, as long as we do not lose the notion that poetry has agency in
the world, as long as poetry is not simply descriptive of the world or

little autobiographical bits of it. All those mundane lyrics you see in all those magazines, all those little things that are pumped out in a belief that their job is to deliver pictures of the world to you, are manufactured in a desultory faith in a simple kind of transcendence. The world transcends the poem, they say—here's a little path into the world. No, don't thank me. I'm only doing my job. It goes on my c.v.

* * *

Some people probably say who was Charles Olson to make judgment on Blaser's syntax anyway? Look at Olson's poems and prose, this for instance:

> the Mountain of no difference which I
> have climbed as other men and other men will
> have no other choice than: there is no other
> choice, you do have to listen to that Angel and
> 'write' down what he says (you don't your
> other Angel does and you obey him
> to the degree that it is impossible to
> keep doing, that's for sure!

But you might see that Olson's poem works its info exactly by way of its subtly turning phrases with their instant new decisions. If there are to be images, they will be by-products of the syntax. Olson is interested in the way everything goes together. In 1963 he told me that he was hoping to find out that Chinese is an Indo-European language!

* * *

But violence is his, as the Lord sayeth, and then there is no Lord, so much for the Ten Commandments and all other writing handed down from a mountain or a congress. The sacred is that which we are scared of. Before a one-god was made, each peril had its own holy overseer. Before *that* system was set up the source of the terror had no name at all. All religions are one, indeed.

In the young Blaser's nimble poem the day belonged to the dancers. But Girard, writing a quarter-century later, said "Violence is the heart and soul of the sacred." It has become as othered, as superhuman as natural disasters. I think that Blaser is lamenting the loss of responsibility in human behavior, and that it all started to go when angels and demons no longer awed men. I also think that I am on the edge of losing the poem here, losing its argument. Or maybe the poem is in danger of losing its way. It happens. But anyone who grew up reading T. S. Eliot can see how this poet has been making this poem called reading notes, not with a clausal syntax but with an assemblage of voices. I think I remember that Eliot, or an Eliotist, mentioned a "syntax of images." Critics of Eliot were fond of saying that he and his like did violence to poetic order to achieve effects consonant (or dissonant) with the twentieth century. Call it politics.

So the crude graffito that Blaser brings from the toilet. In what has no likelihood of veracity, the anonymous writer (perhaps a puny freshman) claims to have been born on one of the geographical symbols loved by Romantic poets such as Shelley, and raised in another. But then he claims to be some sort of unlovely and isolate satyr, a brainless lout with a predilection for simple bangs.

The word barbarian was invented echoically to indicate foreign people who do not speak "our" language, who have no more idea than songbirds do of our grammar. It is becoming necessary to figure out Blaser's attitude here, how much irony we are getting, because if some people make only babbling noises, even if the barbarians ride within the gates of each reader's soul, how does that square with poetry that belongs to no one sophisticate who makes notes on erudite reading early in the morning when some poor sods are getting ready to go to work or the welfare office? Are we really looking at the dark side of the asyntactical? Are some of those birds saying "caw"?

Bernard-Henri Lévy tells us in Blaser's note that in our time totalitarianism was invented (though he must be leaving out the great religions), and that it leads to the barbarian state, and that this state of affairs is a result of atheism. The violence of politics had to become an independent entity in order to replace external gods. Lévy will not give it the status of the divine, saying rather that it takes residence in the space unoccupied by divinity, by authority. A syntax starts with an authoritative beginning: see *Genesis* I and *John* I, the beginnings of long poems in which the authors both claim order and assign it to a higher authority.

Geoffrey Hartman takes up the argument of Girard and Lévy and specifically relates the ejection of the old gods to the sprawling victory of free verse. He regrets the artifice of traditional verse that offered insight and beauty that were great because the poet's language transcended the noise of the barbarians. He presumably allows a community of poets, but will not welcome into that community the composers of gravestone wit and unambitious graffiti. Geoffrey Hartman is not a purveyor of laughter, and he would certainly not ascribe truth to it. He sees poetic diction as a gatherer—in other words as a selector of the most desirable in language.

What is Blaser's purpose here? Does he support a priestly cult, as he has in earlier times been accused of doing? Is he giving the elitists their voice in a kind of dialectic? Is he making a potential critic write in interrogative sentences? Is he changing his position as the poem grows longer, or moving from side to side in the space he has found to be his own? We remember that a poet writing "reading notes" has no obligation or reason to go back and revise a first page, where he might have written that the depths of our indefinite spiritual condition, like syntax, "are not a / privilege but everybody's." Potentially everybody's, maybe.

Among the Okanagan people, there is a principle called *en'owkin*, which spirit visits people who come together to formulate civic, political and educational plans. In council, anyone from any social position can express feelings and ideas. They do not debate. When everyone who wants to speak has spoken, and everyone has heard all questions and suggestions, the best possible solutions are agreed upon and the others are not forgotten.

One supposes that a poem can work that way. An answer does not have to be traceable to an origin. Graffiti ≠ gravity.

* * *

Percy Shelley may not have loved living in the middle of paradox, but it would be hard to find a poet more paradoxical. He was an atheist whose poems, including *The Triumph of Life*, are hung on religious imagery. He was both a Platonist and a believer in historical perfectibility. In fact *The Triumph of Life* may have been unfinishable because in it he made his last effort to reconcile his amazing idealism with his equally committed empiricism. He was the most intellectual of English poets, but we remember his emotional outbursts, his ecstasies and mournings. He was loved and condemned for his advanced ideas, but he systematically set out to write poems in every form known to classical traditions, and to make them otherwise even more complex.

The Triumph of Life is written in Dante's *terza rima*, as if in contemporary answer to the trinitarian. "The deep truth is imageless," said Shelley, and the mortal's only way toward it is via images that must be expunged because of their delightfully flawed nature. If Charles Olson were somehow tuned to the source of Shelley's imagination (well, it was in *Queen Mab* that we first found the term "human universe") he may have been speaking of limitation when he told Blaser that he trusted him on image but not on syntax. If the truth is laughter, the surviving Blaser might say, it could be laughter that is to be heard in the depths beneath images. But whose laughter? What skeptic's? Well, Shelley, in *The Triumph of Life*, called reality "the realm without a name." It is the place in which men's linked thought is without error. Even the greatest of mortal thinkers, Shelley's championed "sacred few," can only touch the word with "living flame" before disappearing.

The depths of our "spiritual condition," said Blaser this morning, are not privileged but shared by all, and are likely the well of syntax. Shelley was the master of syntax, and custodian of its origin and diverse complexity. That is one of the reasons for Blaser's quoting of Shelley's lines about dawn here. Of the two sentences he quotes, the second takes up thirty-one five-beat lines. Even portions of that sentence work wonders: consider the meaning tempered by the turns that start "But I, whom thoughts which must remain untold," and end "Was at my feet, and Heaven above my head,—."

The deep truth is imageless. The truth is laughter. If there is a mini-essay hidden in the sprawl of these reading notations, that's it.

"A violence / or a love," said Blaser at dawn. When William Hazlitt reviewed Shelley's poem in 1824, he remarked a "violence of contrast," complaining that the poet never succeeded in getting out of his paradox. Shelley did not signal his surrender to Life by abandoning the poem; he knew that he was acknowledging it by writing as much as he did. All poets who attempt great things get the joke eventually. In *The Triumph of Life* Shelley uses light as his main image, the energy that usually makes images visible. He is not simple, but here is a simple diagram of the light: the distant stars, especially the most faint, stand in for the potential Imagination. But the sun, standing in for Nature, obliterates the light of the stars. Then Life, figured as a fiery chariot, replaces the sun's light. What is Life, the poem asks at its end, where traditional readers have seen its stopping as premature. Might as well ask metaphysical questions of a tiger. Shelley went out and gave up his spark to those other elements, wind and water.

Here we should pay attention to the most obvious gesture: Shelley's morning is cast as noted reading by Blaser in his morning's verses, another bright bird heard from, morning's sweetest minion. Shelley knows where he is going, you say. He is using *terza rima*. He implies a paradiso. But he is no nineteenth-century Catholic—he ends with a question, and it is not the *meaning* of life that he is after. Thus Blaser's "notes" effect the shape of his poetic.

Shelley's lines are beautiful—we can thank both poets for bringing us that, even while we remember admonishments regarding beauty from Baudelaire, Pound, and Spicer. But in Shelley's conscious beauty trap the volcanoes are "smokeless altars"—the revolution (see Shelley's late iconography) is dormant or at best potential. The birds are obedient and end in a period, something that the poet is reluctant to do, either for the next ten stanzas or at the end of the poem. All nature follows the patriarchal Sun. Only the poet offers a "But," and because of it acquires a trance and then a vision, which in these notes we are not vouchsafed. What Shelley shows us is an admixture of Nature and something else. It will not bring about worship. Worship is obeisance to a source of syntax not readily available to the worshiper, who normally goes to the end of his own. The Metaphysicals made a trope out of that: their syntax failed and that failure led them to visionary and paradoxical images they could report while insisting that truth lies beyond even them.

* * *

Herakleitos, Modernism's favorite Greek because he proposed paradox and parataxis, did not like Hesiod, the systematical and confident chronicler of order. Hesiod was mundane, Herakleitos incendiary. Hesiod built bridges, Herakleitos burned them behind him. He was never going to cross that river again anyway.

Ecumenical Blaser is reading a Herakleitos translated by a Catholic poet who died in water. His God is neither taxonomic nor edible; He is a mixture of opposites. Like Shelley's imagination, he is fire, and takes on the qualities of that which he creates. Blaser might have included H.D.'s "Pygmalion" in his notes:

> Now am I the power
> that has made this fire
> as of old I made the gods
> start from the rocks?
> am I the god?
> or does this fire carve me
> for its use?

Burning bright, indeed.

Remind yourself that Blaser is gathering voices to make a sequence inside a sequence inside a sequence made by those gatherers gathered. He is assembling a self, a plural self to argue a poetic different from the positivist "I" who plays a role in many reactive poems in many anthologies. If Blaser's notes and the noted are replete with the terms of spiritual language, it is not because this is a poetry designed to praise the transcendent; this is a sacred poetry itself. If paradise is around us in fragments, as Ezra Pound wrote in his Pisan prison, one can assemble those fragments in a poem as they are disbursed in a life. Look at them, perhaps, in Sufism's half-light, defined by Luther as the "being of man," Blaser's "indefinite spiritual condition." What do fragments tell us of syntax?

> Le Paradis n'est pas artificiel
> but spezzato apparently
> it exists only in fragments unexpected excellent sausage

the smell of mint, for example,
Ladro the night cat

I am always reminded of "Canto LXXIV" when I read "lake of souls (reading notes."

* * *

J. S. Bach gets onto the last page of the poem because in 1981 Robin Blaser was supposed to be writing *Bach's Belief* for the Curriculum of the Soul series, and he was making reading notes for that. When the booklet finally arrived in 1995, one could see that it is composed the way in which Blaser's poems and lectures are composed, with a reading mind among a gyre of quoted texts. (When Blaser gave courses at Simon Fraser University he appeared in the classroom with a pile of thick books, bookmarks hanging out of them like tongues.) If Bach knew Luther's definition for the being of man, Blaser will define being as soul. More properly:

> *soul*—that mysterious word, contracted by loss of syllables into a single sound and with which Christianity grabs at belief with a muscle-bound hand—originally meant *life itself, animate existence*—such quickness—subsequently made obsolete by crossdressing in immortality—its original sounds **saiwalas* "corresponding formally" to Greek αιολοσ, <u>fleeting</u>, <u>flitting</u> movement —of, say, earth, air, water, and fire—each of them <u>*lief.*</u>

We know that Blaser is by now that normative 1980s postmodern who sort of believes as Pound did that meanings *inhere* in the language and can be followed and saved by good linguistic order, but that it is at the same time somehow unknowable by the creature participating himself in flux.

And here we are, both in and out of our paradox at last.

We in the North are not creatures of new dawn or twilight, but rather denizens of science's spooky *aurora borealis*, back at the beginning of Blaser's *Syntax*. Ha ha.

The northern lights give their green light to our daytime, but it comes to us out of the blackness at the pole's night. Staying away from upper-case letters, Blaser offers us even this mysterious last stanza with its troubled predicate agreement, with shepherd and mother, images that Catholics also appropriated. That black milk, I think, is commodious enough to form a lake of souls, so much so, if you are following Pygmalion-like, that the lake might be *constituted* of souls, our shared life.

If I were to feint and dribble my way out of this essay the way that Blaser departs a poem, turning to give another little wave, I might suggest that you contrast this lake of souls to the sea of faces and limbs and torsi that the racing craft drive through in William Carlos Williams's poem "Yachts."

An apology anyway. This essay of notes has been long and centrifugal because Robin Blaser with his skirl of books *leads* you astray or away to get you here.

WORKS CITED

Blaser, Robin. *Bach's Belief.* Canton, N.Y.: The Institute of Further Studies, Glover, 1995.
_____. "The Fire." *The Poetics of the New American Poetry.* Ed. Donald Allen and Warren Tallman. New York: Grove, 1973. 235-46.
_____. *The Holy Forest.* Toronto: Coach House, 1993.
_____. *Syntax.* Vancouver: Talonbooks, 1983.
D[oolittle], H[ilda]. *Collected Poems 1912-1944.* New York: New Directions, 1983.
Duncan, Robert. *The Opening of the Field.* New York: Grove, 1960.
Olson, Charles. *The Maximus Poems.* Berkeley: University of California, 1983.
Pound, Ezra. *The Cantos of Ezra Pound.* London: Faber & Faber, 1954.
Webber, Jean, and the En'owkin Center, eds. *Okanagan Sources.* Penticton: Theytus, 1990.

"COMPANIONS ARE HORIZONS": "I," YOU," ROBIN BLASER, AND EMILY DICKINSON

David Sullivan

Friendship . . . does not allow us to speak of our friends,
but only to speak to them: it does not allow us to make
them the theme of conversations . . . but is the movement
of the understanding in which, speaking to us, they keep,
even in moments of the greatest familiarity, their infinite
distance.
                              —Maurice Blanchot, *L'Amitie* (326)

the Belovèd   is the   murmur
inside   the work
at the edge
          of the words

the silence   is the other
at the edge   of my words
a

          move
               ment
the words drink us up

who is speaking

dear beings, I can feel your hand
                              —Robin Blaser,
          "Image-Nation 5 (erasure" (*Holy* 117-18)

97

In Robin Blaser's work there are two impulses in relation to the reader which push and pull against each other. The first is a desire to pull the reader into the orbit of the poet's world, to have him or her take on the position of the scare-marked "you" Blaser addresses.[1] When the reader catches the thread of Blaser's thought, makes connections between disparate poems and pulls out the references to other authors, he or she may feel a kinship to this person whose signature ties together the diverse voices of the tapestry-like assemblage of poems that make up *The Holy Forest*; the reader may feel a friendship forming.

But it is impossible not to recognize the second, concurrent desire, which is to push the reader away, to remind him or her constantly that the reader is not—and cannot be—entirely at ease with the friendship Blaser invites, for the text demands further, ever-more-nuanced responses. To this end Blaser uses the scare-marked "you" to bracket off even the closest of friends as necessarily distant. Their status as coherent *cogitos* is constantly in question, as is his own. It is the recent impulse to totalize through demanding each subject be a unitary body with a single voice which Blaser is questioning—"the disaster of anthropomorphism, which in modern terms becomes the substitute for all other totals," as he says in "The Stadium of the Mirror" (62). What Blaser is courting is an open-endedness which does not rely on the stability of identities, but instead presses against the unstable and dynamic edge where the I/you relationship forms itself.

It is in this push-pull dynamic that the *Image-Nation* poems are born. As Blaser has written, "The danger of [the early *Image-Nation* poems] was that the I, the poet, and the manhood of the poems in the distance of the work would become only a spectator. Like the naiveté of trying to gain outwardness, or rather its semblance, by erasing all the I's of a poem and substituting other pronouns" ("Stadium" 55). In "The Stadium of the Mirror," printed with *Image-Nations 1-12* in 1974, Blaser recognized that putting the "I" into question could not be accomplished through erasure, but only through a more confrontational addressing of that construction—as performed in the *Image-Nations* to come. It would not be through a syntax-less nullifying of the addresser instance that this confrontation would take place, but through a super-abundance of addresser instances—some coming from other writers, some from the imagined author (himself a changing construct through time), and some partaking of both realms.[2] In this way the position of the "I" would be the unstable state of language's coming to find a form, and "anthropomorphism" would be only "a superstition" ("Stadium" 66).

In this same essay Blaser also addresses the relation of the *Image-Nations* to the reader, or to the writer's desire for a response, to that Other, He says that "The Other is not an object, but acts chiasmatically. . . . Not a stillness. Not a rest. Always the opposite and companion of any man's sudden form. This is the unrest given to thought" (55). The Other is called for as a man finds form(s), defines himself (his selves), comes to be (multiply). That restlessness inheres in the knowledge that one is always misheard and misperceived. Further, a definition is always necessary, and will always lead to other misconceptions, *ad infinitum*. The Other is not an object, nor even a subject, rather, it subjects the writer to a restlessness that surrounds his work with all that remains unsaid.[3] Blaser's *Image-Nations* simultaneously opens to the reader, encouraging participation, and shuts down that very possibility as only a semblance of contact. The power of these serialized poems comes precisely from what they promise but never quite deliver; what they court from the reader, and yet refuse to grant; what they seduce the reader into feeling, and what they suggest can only be found elsewhere. The poems make me restless in turn; they make me return to myself altered, changed, broadened; they make me seek out other selves within and without me.

This push-pull dynamic begins with the earliest *Image-Nations* and continues to the ever-deepening and ever-more-diverse later poems. If there are two items that are put into question in these poems consistently, they are the "I" of the writer and the "you" of the reader. In Jean-François Lyotard's vocabulary, Blaser questions the addressee and addressor poles, as well as the meaning and referent that the words themselves make manifest.[4] Rather than being statements about the world, the *Image-Nations* attempt to perform worlds. Elsewhere in "The Stadium of the Mirror," Blaser writes that "the spiritual . . . [is] active in the composition of the real" (55). He is staging the questioning of the I/you relation in his writing through jockeying between addressor and addressee instances so self-consciously that neither can be assumed to be stable, but always in motion, shifting. And by insisting that the referent is not something external to the poems, he argues that "meaning is a kind of movement" within the poems themselves (61); the pun "move / ment" occurs repeatedly throughout the series to underscore this point.

Blaser's first two *Image-Nations* poems introduce the central problem of the too-easily passed over I/you relationship established by any writing. It is tacitly assumed that most writing issues from an individual who has consciously composed the words we read. Likewise, it is usually assumed that the individual imagined, even if writing in a locked diary, the possibility of others reading his or her words. By putting into question the identity of the poem's speaker—by having the scrim of others' words overlay his own—Blaser frustrates any easy definition of who the speaker "is."[5] Likewise, by frequently bracketing with scare-marks the "you" of his poems he reminds us of our own ambiguous status: are we friends, who imagine we have some privileged information that will allow access to the worlds of the poems? or astute readers? or curious bookseller browsers who happened to alight on a page of *The Holy Forest*? or Blaser himself, rereading his words? How do we read? And how does the reading alter us? Who do you imagine is being addressed *now* at the present moment, under the rubric of this "we"? What are you doing with these words "I" am writing? (these words "I" wrote?) How does their function alter as I become their reader with 'you'?

In "Image-Nation 1 (the fold," the speaker baldly declares that "the participation is broken" (*Holy* 61). The romantic fiction of an easy correspondence between a person (the writer, author, or speaker) and another person (the reader, audience, or hearer) will be refused. Instead, the "we" will "meet in paradise"—not a transcendent place outside of the poem—but within its movement in which "the I consumes itself" (61). The stated goal, therefore, is to eradicate the divisions between separate unitary individuals; to confront not only the barriers between the writer and reader, but within the selves that make up each entity so labeled. The poems that make up the serial will attempt to be events "in which the world and the sacred are alive," and each is made manifest in its multiplicity ("Stadium" 53).[6]

On the next page "Image-Nation 2 (roaming" introduces the scare-marked "you" which figures so prominently in the series. At first the address to "you" seems to exclude general readers, for it refers to a specific, precisely described event:

> but there, it was
> there   'you' saw
> the head of a horse burn,
> its red eye flame   'you' stepped
> to the fireplace where the meta
> morphosed log lay without a body
> and put 'your' hand over the seeing (*Holy* 62)

We can picture the scene. The fire has burned down in the fireplace when one of the two people notices that the log resembles a horse's head, with a red flame for an eye. The addressee then steps forward and covers that "eye." Written out this way the pun on "eye" becomes prominent, and the action of the "you" who covers the "eye" clearer. The corresponding pun on the "blazing" log—winking in and out of view—which stands in for the poet is also folded into this scene. In this way the private act has been made public, and in the retelling, the two individuals have begun to change, to metamorphose.

The stanza which follows confirms that a change has taken place:

> turned by that privacy
> from such public perils as words
> are, we travel in company with the messenger (62)

Not only is the log "turned," but the persons have been "turned" out, faced—awkwardly—towards the reader who is not—or not only—"you." The presence of readers, how they position themselves in relation to the private act the poem makes public, is therefore put into question. Words become the public peril that the writer risks, hoping that something of the event's sacredness is also carried along in the transformation.

It is the ability for a second person address to be simultaneously specific and general that allows it to compound readerly temporalities; to keep functioning as an event that happens to each reader. The degree to which the addressee is specified limits the degree to which a reader will feel addressed by the writing, though Blaser's successful second person addresses—as in "Image-Nation 2 (roaming"— implicate each reader and put into question his or her status as a third party witness. His most effective addresses do not employ the mindlessly general "you" of popular songs, nor do they circumscribe the addressee so narrowly—through proper names and the use of topographical or temporal co-ordinates—that only one "you" could be meant;[7] instead they examine the impulse to send and receive messages. Every reader is, by definition, a receiver, though rarely implicated in the circuit of communication so directly. Not only does Blaser put himself on trial, but also each reader who is willing to accede to his displacements of readerly complacency.

Second person addresses are performative when they successfully implicate the reader as a potential addressee; when "we" become a participant in the event. This "we" is a strange community, since each is addressed individually by the seemingly singular "you," yet each imagines other similarly addressed individuals. Therefore, these addresses can never be entirely limited by their initial context; they engage each new reader. For example, when Blaser's poem "Giant" ends with the lines: "you're somewhere less than perfect, / but reading the story" (*Holy* 278), it is impossible *not* to think that the speaker of the poem is addressing you, the reader, who has just read about a child's perceptions of the world of toys that make him feel giant-like. The reader has, in some sense, been placed in the position of looking down at this child's world, only to have the seemingly omniscient speaker of the poem look down on him or her in turn.

This inability to limit addresses in the second person makes for syntactically convoluted sentences and embarrassing ambiguities when a critic attempts to write about them because the province of each "you" must be specified anew. In Jonathan Culler's insightful chapter "Apostrophe," which provokes many of the questions I pursue here, Culler argues that they "may complicate or disrupt the circuit of communication, raising questions about who is the addressee, but above all they are embarrassing: embarrassing to me and to you" (135). Culler's use of address in this sentence is meant to embarrass the reader who is positioned by it, and part of that embarrassment is that the writer claims to know that the reader's reaction will be. The word "embarrass" is derived from the Portuguese word for noose, "baraca," so that the term originally meant that one's head was metaphorically caught in a noose.[8] If I am *not* embarrassed then I have side-stepped the address which sought me out, escaped the noose, and I can tell myself he is referring to other readers. But this would be a strategy to mitigate my embarrassment by transforming the address into a *technique* rather than an *event*; I would describe the address rather than receive it. This strategy, Culler writes, is a way to repress or transform the reader's embarrassment by turning apostrophes into descriptions.

Blaser's apostrophes not only disrupt conventions of communication by the embarrassing shifts around the addresser and addressee poles, but by overstepping temporal and spatial frames as well. Culler claims that "Apostrophe resists narrative because its *now* is not a moment in a temporal sequence but a *now* of discourse, of writing . . . . Apostrophe is not a representation of an event; it if works, it produces a fictive, discursive event" (152-53). I agree with Culler's characterization of a successful apostrophe as being an event, but rather than resisting narration, I would argue that an apostrophe compounds narrative times, so that the time in which one examines the trope also becomes part of the trope's functioning. In "Image-Nation 5 (erasure," the lines,

> I tell you of my sexual prowess
> in love   to gain your attention
> at the edge of this
>   movement (115)

radically disrupt the time frame of the poem. The reader must ask him or herself who is speaking, and to whom? Though the words may echo the adolescent speaker of *The Mu'allaqah*, whom the poet quotes directly elsewhere, these words could also be the speaker's own bravado as he cheekily gains the attention of the reader through his bragging. Therefore, I would argue that rather than inscribing a narrative *within* writing, successful apostrophes inscribe narratives *around* each new reading.

Yet Culler avoids the most embarrassing addresses by focusing almost entirely on apostrophes to inanimate objects, while avoiding the more complex addresses to a person for whom a reader in some way substitutes.[9] His examples display only the embarrassment of having someone address a tree (as in Yeats's "O chestnut tree, great-rooted blossomer"), until the final poem, Keats's interrupted sonnet "This living hand." But here Culler fails to explore the layered puns involved in Keats's handwriting an address to "you" *about his hand's writing*, at the margin of an unfinished fairy tale of transformation and abduction. Instead, Culler merely states that "We know too little about apostrophes to assert what actually happens when an apostrophe succeeds, but this poem. . . is a daring and successful example of the attempt to produce in fiction an event by replacing a temporal presence and absence with an apostrophic presence and absence" (154). Culler characterizes this poem as a "fiction," in which temporality is replaced by an apostrophe, but his argument has been about the ambiguous status of apostrophe *as* a fiction; if the apostrophe works, the event of the reader being addressed *happens*. Therefore, the apostrophe does not replace temporality, it compounds it. Culler's work exposes an embarrassing feature of many lyric poems, but then elides it in favor of the simpler apostrophic "O" directed at inanimate objects.

Blaser's apostrophic writings court the moments of embarrassment which Culler avoids, and question conventional circuits of communication by divulging seemingly intimate revelations in ambiguous second person addresses. He simultaneously manifests and questions the need for a reader to ascribe personal import to poems by his ambiguous syntax, punning language, and scare-marked "you." These ambiguities do not playfully dissolve all judgments, but shifting the contexts within which second person addresses are heard and read frustrates conventionalized meanings, and puts the writer and reader into discomforting play. I write "heard," because part of Blaser's linguistic power is the ability to suggest present tense conversations, or spoken interpolations, and "read," because it is through their material manifestations, which can shift temporally and spatially, that these words generate productive ambiguities. Blaser faces us through his poems in multiple guises; he puts his best faces on.

I use face as a verb which connotes a direct response to another person, whether that action is one of *dissembling*—in which one

presents a knowingly false front, or *assembling*—in which one presents a seemingly composed self. To face someone can mean to adopt
a dramaturgical mask which helps one survive a difficult situation—
what Erving Goffman would call a performance front[10]—or it can
mean to face up to a painful or difficult confrontation without shrink-
ing from the inadequacy of any response—what Emmanuel Levinas
calls answering the "infinite which commands in the face of the
other" (*Otherwise* 97).[11] Writing can be a way of articulating an identity, of composing oneself in composition, yet it is also, necessarily, a
splitting of oneself through the act of articulation.[12]

   Jacques Derrida, in an interview with Jean-Luc Nancy, expresses a
similar idea in phrases which recall Levinas's writings:

> The singularity of the 'who' is not the individuality of a thing that
> would be identical to itself, it is not an atom. It is a singularity
> that dislocates or divides itself in gathering itself together to
> answer to the other, whose call somehow precedes its own iden-
> tification with itself, for to this call I can only answer, have
> already answered, even if I think I am answering 'no.' ("Eating
> Well" 100-01)

It is from this position of having to answer, even if it is to explain why
one cannot answer the call of the other, which Blaser examines. His
poems issue from a person whose identity is part of what creates, and
is created by, his poetry. And I read this act of creation of a self, or the
authoring of one's selves, through and in writing, as part of the answer
he gives. If he questions the supposed transparency of the author in
the early *Image-Nations*—"The naiveté of trying to gain outwardness,
or rather its semblance, by erasing all the I's of a poem" ("Stadium"
55)—the later entries in the serial question the opacity of the author
that suggests permanence and stability.

   I do not want to reduce the poetic utterances to mere biographical
data, nor do I want to treat them as devoid of any relation to the
person who wrote them, but to negotiate my way between these two
extremes. I want to reveal the way the poems both function *in* the
poet's life, as potential communications which can alter the relationship between a sender and a receiver, and the way they may function
out of the poet's life, as potential communications which can alter

multiple receivers and their attitudes towards others. I call this process poetic biography. Rather than focusing on what the *person* did, a biographical poetics focuses on what the *writings* did (and do). My belief is that the phrases we make, make us as well, and that our identities are shaped and re-shaped by the way we phrase them to ourselves and others in the constantly evolving process of living and writing.[13] Blaser's poetic evolution suggests this shift of identities as he becomes a reader of his own writings—particularly in the *Image-Nations* poems. It is this double movement that poetic biography seeks to recover. It seeks the shifting foci of a person's identities as these manifest themselves in different writings, rather than an identity which is coherent over time. Paradoxically, the examination of these foci produces correspondences which suggest a persona, if we understand by that term the coherence of the faces we present to ourselves and others under a proper name.[14]

A poem by Blaser which is addressed in the second person situates an addressor and an addressee because it establishes a point of contact between them: the poem. The poem itself establishes one referent which the addressor and the addressee share, if only because they are both situated within its language. The "I/you" structure the poem necessarily implies—though it may use neither term—places the addressor and the addressee in a linguistic relationship regardless of their prior communications. In some poems the addressee instance may be definitely marked, often through specific biographical material or a proper name, at other times the addressee instance may apply to any "you" willing to situate her or himself as the reader of the poem. The first I call a "proper address," the latter I call a "proprietary address." Both "proper" and "proprietary" are rooted in the word *proprius*, meaning own or particular, but whereas the first phrase suggests some*one* who is an identifiable individual, the second suggests some*thing* that is transferable and can be appropriated by others.

As the poem which immediately precedes the section "Companions" apostrophically suggests: "I desire / you as companion of poems language too, physical / among things, desires" (306). It is not simply Blaser, the signatory of these poems, who desires our interest, but the poems themselves seem to be invested with desire; they want to be figured out, heard, responded to. Of course this is an illusion—the poems don't have sentience—but they seem to once their author has created them, and found himself created through what he discovered in their unexpected interplays.

If a proper address is necessarily implicated in ethical considerations since the "I/you" structure seems to substitute for persons who lived, a proprietary address is implicated only in aesthetic considerations since the "I/you" structure seems to situate characters for whom particular persons may or may not substitute themselves. For Blaser, however, the address situation never seems entirely fictive; that is, at no time does the "you" seem to be without a relationship to a person or persons. This is the relationship between the second person addressed in the poems and the persons for whom those addresses and proprietary addresses insist that the addressor and addressee instances substitute for persons, while simultaneously insisting that we, as readers, are not distanced third parties, but similarly answerable to living persons in our own lives. Such poems cannot be contained in their historical moment and necessarily implicate readers in their second person addresses; they implicitly call into question the way we answer the needs of living persons whose phrases have gotten through to us.

The relationship between these addressed writings and the living persons for whom their addressor and addressee instances substitute make these aesthetic productions uncomfortably extra-literary. As Stephen Owen has written:

> To treat a fictional character as a living person is an unwarranted but comprehensible sentimentality; to treat someone who lives or has lived as a merely fictional construct betrays an uglier impulse. (112)[15]

The ugly temptation "to treat someone who lives or has lived as a merely fictional construct," as Owen writes, is what these poems of address directly confront by denying conventions of aesthetic distance. In addition, by virtue of their frequent second person addresses they implicate us, as readers, and implicitly question the more or less adequate way in which we face those in our own lives. I stress interactions with living or yet-to-be-born persons because it is only those who are incarnate that our actions can affect—the dead do not profit from our deeds. Jacques Derrida, in a piece on Friedrich Nietzsche, makes a distinction between the person who lived (or lives), and the putting of "one's name on the line" by staging "signatures." If writing is a type of staged performance which one authors, then the name signed to that writing can have a changing value in the lives of other persons and institutions whether or not the person who signed that name is living. Derrida writes:

> At the very least, to be dead means that no profit or deficit, no good or evil, whether calculated or not, can *ever return again* to the bearer of the name. Only the name can inherit, and this is why the name, to be distinguished from the bearer, is always and *a priori* a dead man's name. . . . What returns to the name never returns to the living. (*Ear* 7)

Poetic biography is the name I give to this process of distinguishing between what a person recorded in her writings, and what her name inherits.

Through his poetry Blaser faces effacing. The use of gerunds in the phrase—"facing effacing"—suggests two related activities which combine the personal and the poetic: the first focuses on the poet's own actions—"facing" can mean to turn towards another human being while "effacing" can mean to turn from them and deny their existence; the second focuses on what these actions produce— "facing" can also mean the surface of something written, such as a poem, and "effacing" can mean the obscuration of that writing.[16] Therefore, this phrase can refer to the poet's actions in relation to others, as well as to what those actions produce in and of themselves. Poems of address paradoxically manifest the poet's desire for contact with other persons (to have the poems of address be phrases which will be answered) and an opposing desire to forego such contact (to have the poems of address, in themselves, be all the answer that is necessary). The first requires living persons whom the poet cannot wholly manipulate, the second only requires characters whom the poet can create.

Though the making of characters is something we all engage in— inasmuch as we tell ourselves stories whenever we think, write, speak, or dream—Blaser negotiates with others whose needs cannot be displaced by simply substituting characters for them. Even as he attempts to efface other persons, to claim that he does not need to answer them, he articulates a desire to answer their needs. By "answering needs" I mean taking actions that will alleviate the physical or psychological discomfort of another human being, or to respond to someone's stated or unstated desires. Poems of address *may* serve such a function, but they may also serve as a means to avoid more direct action. Blaser, in his frequent use of second person addresses, manifests a desire to answer the needs of others and to be answered in turn.

Through the use of second person apostrophes Blaser simultaneously turns towards an other by directly addressing him or her, and turns away from the incarnate person by addressing him or her in writing. The word apostrophe means "to turn away" (from "*apo-*" away from, and "*strephein*" to twist or turn), and derives from the motion of the classical Greek chorus when it turned from one side of the stage to the other. This root suggests that the elevated diction of an apostrophe which comments on what occurs removes it from the situation of an answerable address. Poetry is a genre which is commonly rarefied, at one remove from written communication in prose, and thus resistant to be answered by an addressee. Since poetry is conventionally treated as a debt-free aesthetic object which we enjoy without incurring any responsibility for our responses, Blaser's poems discomfort. This implication of the reader distinguishes Blaser's second person addresses from others and allows them to confound conventional limitations. Apostrophes are difficult to write about because writing itself asserts that the poem is finished, and yet these poems compound narrative times by always, to some extent, addressing the reader. Though we conventionally read poems at a distance, without feeling directly implicated in the actions of the words on the page, Blaser draws us nearer through his puns, word games, ambiguous typographic techniques, and scare-marked "you."

The figure of the sea in Blaser's *Image-Nations*—particularly in "Image-Nation 12 (Actus," and "Image-Nation 24 ('oh, pshaw'"—is an image for the distance and nearness of friends. They are distant, since they are always absent from the scene of writing, and yet near, since writing serves as a way to make distant "you"s present again. This image, and the corresponding pun on seeing and being seen which often accompanies it, is a way for Blaser to investigate the meaning of correspondences between persons. Blaser's poems are acts of exposure, of being seen, and of subterfuge, of being seen only as one wants to be seen. Like Odysseus, the figure he adopts in "Image-Nation 24 ('oh, pshaw,'" Blaser's journeys are simultaneously revealing and reveiling.

This sea imagery in the *Image-Nations* is clarified through the figure of Emily Dickinson. At first these may seem widely divergent individuals, since Dickinson wrote tight, speaker-driven, formally rigorous poems in 1800s New England, while Blaser writes sinuous, literature-driven, expansively polyglotal poems in late-1900s San Francisco and Vancouver. Yet both question the social constraints and religious tenets of their times, and both attempt to construct an alternative spiritual life to that which they see taking place around them. In the process, each artist involves the reader in a radically discomforting way that—when recognized—forces readers to confront their own perspective and take responsibility for how they treat others. The image for this confrontation is often that of being seen, and in their turning towards the reader they look out from their words and address us; thus compromising the aesthetic distance which we assume separates our own lives from those of the artist. It is this commonality with Dickinson that Blaser draws out and incorporates into his own poems. *The Holy Forest*'s project is to establish another way of presenting the world, one involved in bringing out correspondences between persons, whether living friends or literary acquaintances, which place the reader's own position in question.

Blaser's use of Dickinson towards the end of "Image-Nation 12 (Actus," echoes her own poem about "I." I want to examine this poem at length to establish the connection I am drawing out between these two writers. The opening gambit of poem 789 is undermined by the poem's own formal and linguistic divisions. It reads:

> On a Columnar Self—
> How ample to rely
> In Tumult—or Extremity—
> How good the Certainty
> That Lever cannot pry—

And Wedge cannot divide
Conviction—That Granitic Base—
Though None be on our Side—

Suffice Us—for a Crowd—
Ourself—and Rectitude—
And that +Assembly—not far off
From furthest +Spirit—God—

+Companion—not far off
from furthest Good Man—God—

+Faithful
(789)

The solitary "I" suggested by the "Columnar Self" is not, after all, very ample, nor very stable. Though there are numerous poems in which Dickinson portrays an "I" in relation to others who have either failed to arrive, left, died, been unkind, or participated in some transient moment of face-to-face interview, rarely is the "I" of the poems "ample" or "Certain." In addition, the possibility that each "How" is an interrogative pronoun undermines the reading of each as an exclamatory adjective; instead of declaring a conviction each may be asking a question (How ample *is* it to rely "On a Columnar Self"?).[17] Finally, the line that stresses that there is no division is itself divided: "divide / Conviction," so that the "Lever" and "Wedge" which the poem claims to refute are in fact embedded in the poem's very form. The poem's breezy declarations which project the speaker's certainty can also be read as wavering postulations which reveal the speaker's doubt.

If the initial supposition of "ample" solitude is unstable, the second supposition of a crowded solitude is even more problematic. The confusing syntax at the end of the poem reflects the effort required to make one many, and it seems necessary to read line seven again to make sense of it. If what "Suffice Us" is "That Granitic Base," then line eight is a parenthetical comment which serves to emphasize the solitary nature of the one who is convicted. The speaker uses plurals self-reflexively: "Our Side," "Suffice Us," which suggests the crowd before the crowd has been delineated. This confusion forces the reader to maintain multiple readings while parsing out the poem, so that the reader, rather than being assured of an "ample" and secure base, is instead standing on shifting sand.

The final list of whom this "Crowd" contains does little to settle the issue, for it complicates the numbering even by its first term. "Ourself," is neither "myself," nor "ourselves," but hovers ambiguously between the two so that when the poem was first printed in the 1929 *Further Poems of Emily Dickinson* the editors felt it necessary to change the word to "Ourselves."[18] The second term, "Rectitude," suggests that the rightness of the speaker becomes itself a form of company to which she can turn, and the truth of the statement can be willed by repetition in a hall-of-mirrors delusion of multiplying selves.

The final term again involves multiple readings, for the "Assembly" that is part of her solitude is not far from the furthest spirit, who is "God." This suggests that what is near the speaker in her crowded solitude is connected to that which is furthest away from the speaker, "God." But an alternate reading is that the "Assembly" (which is "not far off / From furthest Spirit") is "God," which would make "God" plural. The writer was uncertain about which reading she wanted to convey because the first variant would replace "Spirit" with "Faithful," and thereby stress that the "Assembly" is "Faithful," while the second variant emphasizes the other interpretation by having "God" be a "Good Man's" "Companion," though neither reading satisfactorily resolves the tension between singular and plural nouns. The singularity which began the poem has, by the end of the poem, been fractured not only within it, but within any reading of the poem. The poem's own contention that "a Columnar Self" suffices is undermined by the poem's syntactical ambiguities.

In addition, the insistent voice of the poem suggests a person who has a stake in establishing solitude as a privileged state. The poem positions the reader on the outside (since "None be on our Side"), and claims not to need her. But the fact that the poem was written down, and later recopied into a sheaf of papers and bound, presupposed a potential reader who is not the speaker. Despite all the protestations to the contrary, the writer of the poem must rely on readers if the speaker's solitary singing is to be heard, and I hear that voice desperately arguing for an unmaintainable solipsism. The I fractures even as it asserts its indomitable unitary nature.

It may be this same type of simultaneous self-proclaimed self-sufficiency, *and* unending need for a response from others, that Blaser was calling up when he quoted Dickinson in "Image-Nation 12 (Actus": "*I am glad you cherish the sea*, Emily Dickinson wrote, *we / correspond though I never met him.*" Dickinson makes selves where there aren't any (she sees the sea as a "him" which she hymns). Yet her address to "you" establishes that they have a common correspondent, a natural link which they both "see," the sea. The use of the term "correspond" suggests two possibilities: that of letter writers who never met (and Dickinson, particularly at this stage in her life, had many of those), and that of analogic correspondences (and Dickinson often used the image of the sea as a metaphor for the unbridgeable distances that separated her from her friends).[19] Dickinson may have retracted increasingly from physical contact with her friends, but her daily letters and hundreds of addressed poems continued to present their absences.

The letter Blaser chose to quote (and he had taught seminars on Dickinson, so he was well aware of her works) is a late letter to Mabel Loomis Todd, the lover of her married brother, who had previously urged Dickinson to publish some of her poems.[20] At the time of the letter Todd, who had become a good friend of the poet, though she had never seen the recluse, was in Europe traveling—hence Dickinson's playful signing the letter as being from "America," which underscores her own interrogation of identities. Towards the end she asks Todd to "Touch Shakespeare for me," presumably through the statue of the playwright in England.

Blaser takes up on this suggestion by paraphrasing Shakespeare immediately after quoting this letter. The quote wasn't chosen at random, however, for it comes from *Anthony and Cleopatra*, which was one of Dickinson's favorites, and which she used as a reference point for much of her correspondence with the other woman in Dickinson's brother's life: his wife, Susan Gilbert. This passage, which shows the faithful love of a servant for his master who is in love with a woman who is killing him, mirrors Dickinson's own triangular relationship with Susan Gilbert. It is this close friend of Dickinson whom the poet was in love with—though what the nature of that love was is still being contested.[21] So the single line that Blaser quotes embodies overlapping and complex relationships that Dickinson negotiated between through writing poems and letters. The importance of this Shakespeare play to the poet is stated in a letter she wrote to Joseph Lyman after she had recovered from an eye treatment enough to be permitted to read: "How my blood bounded! Shakespeare was the first; Anthony and Cleopatra where Enobarbus laments the amorous lapse of his master. . . . Give me ever to drink this wine . . . I thought I should tear the leaves out as I turned them" (76).[22] Blaser quotes from the scene of Anthony and his servant Eros, which echoes Enobarbus's first act testimony to his love for his master. The homoerotic undertones of the servant's self-immolation at Anthony's unknowing behest is emphasized by Blaser through his isolation of the name Eros. These final lines emphasize the homoerotic undertone which inform all the writers clustered together by Blaser in this "Image-Nation": Montaigne's friendship with Boetié, Ch'u Yuan's with his master, and Dickinson's with her sister-in-law.

There are two more correspondences with *Image-Nations* poems that the line from Dickinson's letter suggests and that I want to draw out more fully. The first is to "Image-Nation 10 (marriage clothes," which is an extended meditation on soul mates examined through the lenses of various writers. Already this recalls Dickinson's own writings on and to her beloved friends, and her attempts to somehow come to terms with her love of perishable humans and the jealous Christian God she grew up being taught to fear. But even more intriguing is the etymology of soul which Blaser records in this earlier *Image-Nations* poem:

> *Saiwala is the oldest recorded*
> form of the word
>   soul   blending with *awa*,
> *closely related to the word 'sea'* (133)

Since these lines occur just a few poems before the quotation from Dickinson, their import is readily accessible. They suggest that Dickinson's playful anthropomorphic treatment of the sea corresponds to her deep yearning to find a connection to God through a human representative. Whether this was a lover, a preacher, or a force of nature, makes little difference, it indicates how strongly she felt a need for a soul mate. Indeed, Dickinson herself makes the connection between the word "sea" and "soul" in poem 76: "Exultation is the going / Of an inland soul to sea," which suggests that the soul's expansion in daring to extend itself is like an individual launching out onto the sea.

But this etymology also suggests another connection between Blaser and Dickinson, for just as she never saw the sea, so the twentieth-century poet had never seen the sea while growing up in Idaho. His only contact with a semblance of sea-ness occurred when his front yard's geography was transformed by a storm. On the following page of "Image-Nation 10 (marriage clothes," he writes that "sacred / geography   turns in the wind / uprooted / the sea runs over the railbed" (134). And in "Image-Nation 12 (Actus," directly before he quotes Dickinson, Blaser writes about "the work folding / a dragon at the edge   of the sea   my enlargement / of the pond / where   the story went / wild   fiery   under the leaves" (140). To understand this event in Blaser's young life, in which a small pond became a "sacred" literary "sea," we have to skip ahead to "Image-Nation 24 ('oh, pshaw,'" where the story of the heavy rains are told in detail.

In this heavily autobiographical poem we get a wonderful description of Sophia Nichols, Blaser's grandmother, overlaying the rain-swollen geography of Idaho with sea-faring imagery from Odysseus's "Homeward journeys of the soul." This imagery was already introduced in "Sophia Nichols," a poem in *Charms*, which included the lines: "Sophia Nichols . . . of //the Odyssey and the homing stories of the soul,   the sea / imaginary" (100). In the revisiting of the earlier image there is preponderance of dashes—Dickinson's most conspicuous grammatical mark, whether writing poems or letters—and seeing and the sea are punned with through Blaser's description.

once the rains were so heavy the water rose up the opposite em-
bankment, nearly reaching the railbed, and stayed for days—
'a sea,' Sophia Nichols said, never having seen one, and it
was wide and stretched along the tracks as far as I could see—
we needed supplies from the commissary across there—Carnation

condensed milk, I remember—and we plotted a way to cross that
sea—the tin tub and a shingle, just the right size boat and paddle
for me, we thought—round and round it went, being round, and
drifted from shore meandering—she tossed me a broom, which
luckily floated near enough to reach it—'see if you can touch
bottom,' she said—I could—'so push,' she said—and I made it
there circuitously, pulled my tub up on the beach, got the supplies, and returned—'circuitously Odyssean,' she said, having
spent hours those rainy days telling me stories of Odysseus,
which were, she said, homeward journeys of the soul—whatever
you find *that* is, she seemed to say. . . (358)

The storyteller's device of repeating "she said" brackets this off as an
oft repeated oral tale in the family and makes us aware of our position
as an audience to the telling. The story has now become part of the
poet's lore.

When this long narrative ends it does with a surprising turn toward
the reader, where the chances of finding that companionable Other,
and of giving individuals something worth reading, is described as a
crap shoot. The speaker in the poem hopes for "a nick . . . or a natural," which could be seen as two modes of touching the addressee.

> I tell 'you,' my love, these tales—*fold according to fold*—
> my chances—it may be
>
> a crap game—hoping for a nick—7—or a natural—11—
>
> on a startled day—the ashen boy—becomes—exodic (363)

They are tales because they have become part of the verbal self-
narrative that was told about the speaker and that the speaker now
takes on and tells himself. This is not to question their veracity, but
simply to remind the reader that such tales are highly selective and
often rearranged manifestations of the past. By repeating them in his
poems Blaser is presenting himself—not simply as he is, exposed—
but as he would have himself seen. On that day when chance startled
him out of the conventional Idaho flatland he turned from being an
ashen boy to being exotic, and beginning his exodus. The smaller
voyage across the "sea" becomes symbolic of Blaser's larger voyage in
life. He is no longer spent ash, dry and lifeless, but ablaze with light.

The *Image-Nations* serial is more than an act of imagination; it is the creation of an amalgamated nation of friends who correspond with, to, and for each other. What Blaser imagines is that another nation can be built up if one tracks down the correspondences between various literary and literal friends. This trend can be discerned in the earliest *Image-Nations* poems, in which the words "fold," "other," "correspondence," "friends," "movement," and "suddenness," occur repeatedly, as well as in the later, more prosaic ones.

The expanding series, each one nesting within the open parenthe-sis of the previous poem's title, builds on every previous poem. If you consider the series as an ever-deepening exploration of the first poem's themes, and each subsequent parenthetical title an addition, then the title of the whole piece would read: "Image-Nation (the fold (roaming (old gold (erasure (epithalamium (l'air (morphe (half and half (marriage clothes (the poiesis (Actus (the telephone (the face (the lacquer house (anaclitic variations (opercula (an apple (the wand (the eve (territory (in memoriam (imago-mundi ('oh, pshaw,' (exody." Notice how correspondences or groupings of parenthetical titles serve to knit this weave tighter: the rhyme of "fold" and "gold," "erasure" and "l'air," "morphe" and "half"; the two strung together "the" lists; and the final opening out of exody which continues the folding in of the first title through its suggestion of Biblical nomadic wandering and the excretion or exertion of an uncontainable body.

As the distance traveled through this series increases, the replication of folds and patterns also increases, so that one of the last quotations in "Image-Nation 25 (exody" is from Deleuze's *The Fold,* the subtitle of the first: "A *'cryptographer'* is needed, someone who can at once account for nature and decipher the soul, who can peer into the crannies of matter and read the soul." Notice the double direction of this quote, which Blaser stresses in his introductory remark about "*the pleats of matter, and the folds of the soul,*" for it requires that someone be able to see what is outside, in the natural environment—that holy forest of variegated plant life, and what is inside, in the nature of being human—that holy forest of cranial mental life. What is needed is someone who sees correspondences between these things, who does not settle for the distinctions and divisions others labor under, but courts the places where the pleats overlap. Some*one* perhaps, is too strong a term, since Blaser stresses that no one alone can accomplish this task; by definition it must happen between persons — however they are embodied. And in the last lines of this last poem of the present version of *The Holy Forest*, Blaser suggests that it may be closer to a something that contains the words of many persons that will be able to answer this need. When he writes about the most personal of items, the eyes of the "wandering Jew or nomad" which stared out from the leather of the faded rocker of his childhood home no matter where one moved in the tight yellow trailer, he says that those "eyes follow me or 'you'" (370). In this instance, as in many others, the scare-marked "you" includes the reader only if he accedes to this work, if she responds to it, and to the "I"s which produced and are embodied within it. The response is not so much to the person Robin Blaser, but to what the constellation of words he's assembled ask of you.

If his work has been successful it has brought you into its folds, made you a participant in the looking outward, into the natural world, and inward, into the sea of your so-called "soul," and given you a means to correspond with others.[23] If you accept this final gesture towards an "evolutionary love," then you are engrossed in the tale of the "thousand and one celebrations" (371) that unfold from parenthetical poem to parenthetical poem in the ever-widening and ever-deepening movement of the *Image-Nations* series — itself a parenthetical insertion into the tapestry of *The Holy Forest*. The last words echo the thousand and one nights, with its suggestion of erotic attachment and unending pleasures, as well as the sensual central panel of Bosch's "The Garden of Earthly Delights," which dominates the last *Image-Nation* in the current version of *The Holy Forest*.[24] If Blaser's craft is well stocked, then a reader will be able to find someone to couple with, some other that responds to or awakens her desires. It is such couplings that *The Holy Forest* courts and creates; a paradoxical annihilation of separation through facing that inevitable separation; a gesture that in its very impossibility becomes a statement of faith in the imagination's possibilities: *"dear beings, I can feel your hands"* (117).

Or, as Dickinson says in an invitation to the reader that simultaneously reminds you of her corporeal existence, and of all those whom you haven't yet responded to:

More hands—to hold—These are but Two—
One more new-mailed Nerve
Just granted, for the Peril's sake—
Some striding—Giant—Love—
                                                           (263)

Love of another—whether found in a physical embrace, a "new-mailed" letter that seems to embody the person, or a "coat of mail" encasing someone's pain—always puts us in peril. We risk ourselves in the uncontrollable friendship with a beloved, but in that risk is the possibility of being made giants who can participate in our "thousand and one celebrations" (371).

NOTES

1. The reference to the 'you' of the poems as being "scare-marked" occurs in a talk Robin Blaser gave at the Kootenay School of Writing in Vancouver, 1994, which I was able to listen to when my friend Miriam Nichols loaned me a cassette of the event.
2. Miriam Nichols makes a similar point when she writes that *"The Holy Forest* is always also a story about a man who loses his way in a dark wood. This important narrative strand in the poem is based on a Whiteheadian redefinition of subjectivity: the subject is not a Cartesian cogito, but a 'point of view' and continuing event" (10). And Jean-François Lyotard writes: "It is not the thinking I that withstands the test of universal doubt, it is time and the phrase" (59).
3. A similar idea is expressed by Paul Kelley in "Things Left Out," an essay first delivered as a paper at the Recovery of the Public World Conference in June, 1995, and published in *The Recovery of the Public World*, edited by Edward Byrne and Charles Watt. He writes that in "a language prior to, or beyond systematicity of significations—there is no small element of 'shock' which, in its reverberations, gives the *point* to experience, a point which is brought by the other, not only as the one who has been forgotten but as the one who is not—and never has been—known" (321).
4. For a detailed discussion of these issues see Jean-François Lyotard's *The Differend.*
5. Again, from "Stadium of the Mirror": "I knew from Mallarmé that the language went on speaking—older and other than ourselves. There was also the sudden discovery that silence is not the contrary of speech (Merleau-Ponty), but its violent opposite" (61). Similarly, Paul Kelley writes: "silence is not the end of speech and communication but their origin as well as their trembling passage" (320).
6. Miriam Nichols stresses the importance of this project in her writings: "Blaser re-opens a discussion about the sacred at a time when many intellectuals have abandoned the idea; in the process, he lays bare the theologisms which continue to inhabit our secularity" (33).

7. The relationship between a proper name, which is an independent marker without signification *per se*, and spatial or temporal co-ordinates is adopted from Jean-François Lyotard. In *The Differend: Phrases in Dispute*, he writes that "reality has to be established, and it will be all the better established if one has independent testimonies of it. These testimonies are phrases having the same referent, but not immediately linked to each other. How can it be known that the referent is the same? *The same* signifies in these systems, the referent loses the marks of a current 'given': there, *at that very moment*. The place and the moment where it was given can become the object of as many validations as one would like" (38-39). The type of addressed writings I discuss forces the reader to consider the situation *"here, at this moment"* and put into question conventional displacements.

8. All etymologies are derived from *Webster's Third New International Dictionary of the English Language*.

9. In the introduction to his book, Culler writes about the "striking but puzzling feature of the ode and lyrics generally, the invocation of or address to absent beings and various non-human entities: souls, skylarks, sofas" (x). The embarrassment is clearly reserved for the joking list while the absent beings are passed over in silence. The untitled introduction to Derrida's *Postcard* comes closer to specifying the embarrassment I am addressing. He states that the reader will have "a disagreeable feeling" which "places you in relation, without discretion, or tragedy. It forbids that you regulate distances, keeping them or losing them" (5). Though I have profited from reading this text, I find Derrida's playful addresses lacking in the urgency that is a vital element of Blaser's poetry.

10. See Erving Goffman's *The Presentation of Self in Everyday Life*.

11. Elsewhere Levinas writes: "To utter 'I,' to affirm the irreducible singularity in which the apology is pursued, means to possess a privileged place with regard to responsibilities for which no one can replace me and from which no one can release me. To be unable to shirk: this is the I" (*Totality* 245).

12. Robin Blaser puns on his name throughout *The Holy Forest* (the title of which itself invokes birds and the potential for fire) in the ubiquitous images of birds, bird songs, fire, and blazing. Similarly, Dickinson plays on names, identities, and uniqueness in a late letter to Mary Bowles, when she writes: "Please address to my full name, as the little note was detained and opened, the name being so frequent in town, though not an Emily but myself" (*Letters* 624). Though the name is common because it can be found in many places, attached to many persons, there is "not an Emily but myself." The address eventually found her because only she could answer its call.

13. I quote another introduction, from a book which has highly influenced my thinking about the identities of and in writing, Jean-Luc Nancy's *The Birth of Presence*. "This is . . . a thinking about 'presence.' Not the firmly- standing presence, immobile and impassive, of a platonic Idea. But presence as a to-be-here, or to-be-there, as a come-to-here, or there, of somebody. Some *body*: an existence, a being in the world, being given to the world. No more, no less, than *everybody*, everyday, everywhere. No more, no less than the finitude of this existence, which means: the matter of fact that

it does not have its sense in any Idea (in any achievement of 'sense'), but does have it in being exposed to this presence that comes, and only comes" (ix).

14. In *The Differend* Lyotard writes that "the proper name is a designator of reality, like a deictic. . .the independence of the mark in relation to the current phrase comes from the fact that it remains invariable from one phrase to the next even though what it marks is found sometimes in the position of addresser, sometimes in the position of addressee, sometimes in the position of referent" (39).

15. Though Stephen Owen is discussing readers, I believe that the observation is valid for writers as well.

16. I cite information derived from Webster's *Third New International Dictionary* to draw out these etymologies more thoroughly.

> To efface: to eliminate clear evidence of something written, painted, or otherwise marked upon a surface by abrasive or lev-elling action; to remove from cognizance, consideration, or memory; to withdraw oneself entirely from attention; to make oneself inconspicuous and modestly or shyly unnoticeable.

> Face, probably derived from the Vulgar Latin word *facia*, which is from the Latin *facies*: form, shape, face; and connected with the Latin word for to make or do, *facere*.

The first root word is a noun which designates the thing that is made or shaped, while the second is a verb denoting the act of making. The word "face," therefore, has an etymological relation to something that is formed or made, as well as the act that produced it.

17. James McMichael pointed out this possibility to me.

18. See Thomas Johnson's three- volume edition of *The Poems of Emily Dickinson*, (596).

19. For example, in poem 640, "I cannot live with You—" the speaker ends by pro-claiming:

> So We must meet apart—
> You there—I—here—
> With just that Door ajar
> That Oceans are—

20. See Richard Sewall's two-volume biography of the poet for a further amplifica-tion of these relationships. Though this substantial work is a good starting place, Sewall leans towards a more conventional reading of Dickinson's love interests and all but disregards her 40-year tumultuous friendship with Susan Gilbert.

21. Cristanne Miller writes, "Questioning the extent of Dickinson's sexual experi-ence is of less importance and interest than acknowledging the force of her passion-ate nature. This reclusive poet is remarkably frank in letters and poems about her

own passion" (200). Similarly, Suzanne Juhasz, in "Reading Emily Dickinson's Letters," writes: "However much some feminist critics want to dwell upon Dickinson's homoerotic impulses toward Sue, I would maintain that she did not conceive of enacting them in anything like a literal or physical way, which is what gave her the security to express those feelings" (178).

22. The lines of the servant that Dickinson refers to are the same that she often paraphrased in her letters to Susan Gilbert. "For his ordinary pays his heart / For what his eyes eat only. . . .Other women cloy / The appetites they feed, but she makes hungry / Where most she satisfies" (II,ii, 274-75, 287-89). It is interesting that Enobarbus's love for Anthony is paralleled by Eros's at the end of the play, so that the section Blaser chooses to equate echoes his earlier scene.

23. In a personal letter to me, Edward Byrne made a similar observation. "Companionship, which is central to *The Holy Forest*, is a democratic concept. . . egocentric, having to do with a kind of angelism, a surrounding of oneself with beings of an angelic sort. . .masters, students, readers, lovers. But it is a self-conscious egocentrism, which allows a constant decentering, a self-effacement or the infinite proliferation of centres that it implies (democracy)."

24. The critical work which Blaser draws on most heavily is Michel de Certeau's *The Mystic Fable*. "The Garden," de Certeau writes (and here we might substitute the name of *The Holy Forest*), "cannot be reduced to univocity. It offers a multiplicity of possible itineraries, the traces of which, as in a labyrinth, would constitute so many stories. . . . The painting seems both to provoke and frustrate each one of these interpretative pathways. . . . Bosch has been called a raving lunatic: quite to the contrary, he makes others rave. He turns on our meaning producing mechanisms" (51-52). It is a similar project that I believe Blaser is engaged in.

WORKS CITED

Blanchot, Maurice. *L'Amitie*. Paris: Gallimard, 1971.
Blaser, Robin. Lecture. The Kootenay School of Writing: Vancouver, 1994.
_____. *The Holy Forest*. Toronto: Coach House, 1993.
_____. "The Stadium of the Mirror." *Image-Nations 1-12*. London: Ferry Press, 1974.
Byrne, Edward. Personal letter to the author. July 27, 1996.
Culler, Jonathon. *The Pursuit of Signs: Semiotics, Literature, Deconstruction*. Ithaca: Cornell UP, 1981.
De Certeau, Michel. *The Mystic Fable: Volume I. The Sixteenth and Seventeenth Centuries*. Trans. Michael B. Smith. Chicago: U of Chicago P, 1992.
Derrida, Jacques. *The Ear of the Other: Otobiography, Transference, Translation*. Trans. Peggy Kamuf. New York: Schocken Books, 1985.
Derrida, Jacques and Jean-Luc Nancy. "'Eating Well,' or the Calculation of the Subject: An Interview with Jacques Derrida." *Who Comes After the Subject?* Ed. Eduardo Cadava, Peter Connor and Jean-Luc Nancy. New York: Routledge, 1991. 96-119.

_____. *The Post Card: From Socrates to Freud and Beyond.* Trans. Alan Bass. Chicago: U of Chicago P, 1987.

Dickinson, Emily. *The Letters of Emily Dickinson.* 3 vols. Ed. Thomas H. Johnson and Theodora Ward. Cambridge: The Belknap Press of Harvard UP, 1958.

_____. *The Lyman Letters.* Ed. Richard B. Sewall. Amherst: U of Massachusetts P, 1965.

_____. *The Poems of Emily Dickinson.* 3 vols. Ed. Thomas H. Johnson. Cambridge: Belknap Press of Harvard UP, 1955.

Goffman, Erving. *The Presentation of Self in Everyday Life.* New York: Bantam, 1959.

Juhasz, Suzanne. "Reading Emily Dickinson's Letters." *ESO: A Journal of the American Renaissance.* 30.116 (1984): 170-92.

Kelley, Paul. "Things Left Out." *The Recovery of the Public World.* Eds. Edward Byrne and Charles Watts. Vancouver: Talon, 1999. 319-25.

Levinas, Emmanuel. *Otherwise than Being or Beyond Essence.* Trans. Alphonso Lingis. The Hague: Martinus Nijhoff, 1981.

_____. *Totality and Infinity.* Trans. Alphonso Lingis. Pittsburgh: Duquesne UP, 1969.

Lyotard, Jean-François. *The Differend: Phrases in Dispute.* Trans. Georges Van Den Abbeele. Minnesota: U of Minnesota P, 1988.

Miller, Cristanne. *Emily Dickinson: A Poet's Grammar.* Cambridge: Harvard UP, 1987.

Nancy, Jean-Luc. *The Birth to Presence.* Trans. Brian Holmes and others. Stanford: Stanford UP, 1993.

Nichols, Miriam. "Robin Blaser." *Dictionary of Literary Biography. Vol. 165: American Poets Since World War II.* Fourth Series. Ed. Joseph Conte. Detroit, Washington D.C., London: Bruccoli Clark Layman/Gale Research Inc. 57-68.

Owen, Stephen. *Traditional Chinese Poetry and Poetics: Omen of the World.* Madison: U of Wisconsin P, 1985.

Sewall, Richard B. *The Life of Emily Dickinson.* 2 Vol. New York: Farrar, 1974.

(Above) John Wieners, Robert Duncan, Robin Blaser, Allen Ginsberg, and Robert Creeley at SUNY, Buffalo poetry reading, 1968

(Right) Poster for a conference on poetry and politics organized by Stan Persky, University of British Columbia, 1968

A MINIMUM OF MATTER: NOTES ON ROBIN BLASER, "THE FIRE," AND "THE MOTH POEM"

Norma Cole

> *For after all, sure as it is that I see my table, that my vision terminates in it, that it holds and stops my gaze with its insurmountable density, as sure even as it is that when, seated before my table, I think of the Pont de la Concorde, I am not then in my thoughts but am at the Pont de la Concorde, and finally sure as it is that at the horizon of all these visions or quasi-visions it is the world itself I inhabit, the natural world and the historical world, with all the human traces of which it is made—still as soon as I attend to it this conviction is just as strongly contested, by the very fact that this vision is mine.*
>
> > –Maurice Merleau-Ponty,
> > *The Visible and the Invisible*

* * *

> *I desired sunrise to revise itself*
> *as apparition. . . .*
> > –Barbara Guest, *Fair Realism*

* * *

As things seen and heard are not *there*, these same things shimmer, flicker in the heat of the "what is at stake" here. How does *auto-da-fé* shift between declaration of faith and the sentence to be burned alive at the stake?

Robin Blaser's "The Fire," is dedicated "especially to Ebbe Borregard," and was written for an occasion, "for a few in San Francisco, where I read it last March 8th." *We* may read it in *The Poetics of the New American Poetry*, eds. Donald Allen and Warren Tallman, Grove Press, 1973; or in *Caterpillar* 12, July 1970, ed. Clayton Eshleman, a special issue devoted to Robin Blaser and Jack Spicer, indicating a prior "last March 8th"; or possibly in *Pacific Nation* #2, 1968, referring to an even earlier March 8th.

"The Fire" begins with the introduction of the invisibility of the crucial. It goes on to privilege image as representation of this invisible crucial, to value image above concept or idea, and to propose the possibility or desirability of "holding" or "catching" this invisibility in a line "by sound and heat," ultimate ultrasound, shaping . . . what is at stake here, flowers of salt all around. The eidetic diegesis: "I'm haunted by a sense of the invisibility of everything that comes into me (aware that nothing is more invisible than emotion—by emotion, I mean the heat of one's sense of the war, or a place, or a body, or of the extensions of these, the earth, the existence of gods, and so forth— the I-have-seen-what-I-have-seen, recorded by Pound in Canto 2)." (Blaser, "The Fire") *Seen. Recorded. Desired.* In what order?

1968 also saw publication of Robert Duncan's *Bending the Bow*, from New Directions, the "Introduction" a crisis that coheres, beginning with "The War." The culmination of this critical turbulence is "Articulations," itself beginning with Dante and exploding "our composure" with its announcement of "the Satanic person of a President," sparking the subsequent charges of "Passages 13   The Fire":

> *Hell breaks out   an opposing music.*

this other fire ignited by

> *. . . those who would be Great Nations   Great Evils.*

The heat or affinity of these conflagrations evokes, by the negation of the negation, the shape—elusive—of something that in 1990 will come to be invoked as *La communità che viene, The Coming Community* (Agamben): "What the State cannot tolerate in any way, however, is that the singularities form a community without affirming an identity [Cities were imaginary—like oceans. The name of a man would be a town. (Blaser, "The Fire")], that human beings co-belong without any representable condition of belonging. . . ."

In "The Medium," the relationship between its musicality and the tempering of others' scales, as well as the narrative of the timing, are perceptible here in or as "a darkness," a rhythm reflecting its "reluctance." In another matrix or in other verbal conjunctions this would not or does not occur, would not be obvious. And yet once posited it is not cagey or even subtle but direct and immediate, the "something" of experience. There seems to be another speech back of this speech. "The Medium" scores emotion inchoate in "invisible pencil," on Blaser's table

as "Atlantis/draws back from the shine on the water," from Atlantis to water a precision, a meticulousness of microtonal attention, anticipating the flow of a/the *next* line where "the crumbling pieces flow unattached." And then, you have to trust that someone on the other side of the "*pure transparency*" will not flip the switch, locking you in, or was it under? A rocking motion is a kind of compass.

The spotlight generated by rhythm or ideology posits speculation about the relationship between rhythm and ideology, "heard, seen and spun," a question for the millennial turn at hand. Odysseus is space man, Penelope the figure of time itself. Now we are in imagined memory, Atlantis, moth-time.

Where, so to speak, a public language has closed itself in order to hold a meaning, it becomes less than the composition of meaning. It stops and relegates both the language and its hold on the "real" to the past. The place of language in the social, as performance of the "real," is displaced to a transparency and becomes an imposition rather than a disclosure.
        –Robin Blaser, "Statement"

The safety of a closed language is gone and its tendency to reduce
thought to a reasonableness and definiteness is disturbed.
— Robin Blaser, "The Practice of Outside"

Distance is non-metrical, that is, not exactly measurable, spinning
in the multiple readings of (e)motion from "cloud" to "crowd"
("Paradise Quotations"). Every paradise hovers in this little distance.
"From the Marysville Buttes a cut/northeast, up lava flows / towards
Paradise—not that city / but the Single One / of all our meeting. . . ."
(Kenneth Irby, "Fragments"). In this same issue of *Caterpillar* can be
found eight poems from *The Holy Forest*. Except for "The Translator:
A Tale," from *The Moth Poem* (1962-1964), all are from *Charms* (1964-
1968).

The image develops *in static*. The static is motion generated by the
image or arising spontaneously between the image and its reader. "it,
it, it, it," the "unexpected myth," the paste imitation which is also the
real jewel, locked up in a vault, out of sight. Neither perception nor
possession is the poetry. The undefended eye, that is, the open eye
catches, is caught by words, that is, by air. Its rhythm is a mirror
simultaneously reflecting and deflecting. Like a song, or like words
displaced in a dream, it appears to be heard, it disappears. Prosody
speaks with some authority, as the shape of *"the white rose of Eddy-
foam"* persists through time.

"The Supper Guest" arrives in a "minimum of matter" (Merleau-
Ponty) and an "infinitely small vocabulary" (Spicer). "I love waits
with cold wings furled . . . ," said H.D. As though the Nerval translations already inhabited these rooms, the music is familiar yet
unrecognizable, words anticipate themselves, "a gift, a promise of a
debt" ("Salut"; *Holy* 55). According to its own concordant logic, the
instrument has a blind spot, this "language a darkness." In deference
to this darkness itself, we separate in silence.

"I have found in the serial poem a way to work from my displaced,
uncentered 'I' in order to be found among things — relational, at least
to what I can. Recent theory tells us writers that the author is gone from

his/her authority. That seemed real enough before theory ever hit home. And, without authority, a conversation went on. . . .so, I guess "The Moth Poem," though back there, is still working at my initial sense of the multiplicity of times, persons, gods, things, thoughts, places, and stuff—folding—"
     –Blaser, "Statement"

Poetry the true fiction
     –Barbara Guest, *Fair Realism*

PG: *Obviously part of the joy is that it's bigger than you are.*
MP: *Certainly.*
PG: *And it works because one keeps reading back into it, one keeps finding oneself in that figure.*
MP: *And maybe that becomes a figure of itself, for that idea of imaginary community in which poets tend to dwell with others. Not to say that it's outside the real, but it's constructed through the imagination and sometimes in opposition to the principles of reality that are laid on us, all of which say "you should not be doing this."*
     –"Interview with Michael Palmer," Peter Gizzi

"Deeper—there is the defense of longing for love against the practice of love. . . . But the work is solitary, and seen thus: one has strength in the solitude that takes the place of loneliness for solitude is within the practice of love. The mute entrance towards fulfillment."
     –Robert Duncan, letter to Robin Blaser, 28 February, 1959

Citation is invocation, cross-referenced. The "imaginary community," or "community to come," never at hand, pregnant with contradiction, has its points of agreement; unavoidable tautology, since it is defined by its points of agreement. Time and space are conventions that exist in relation to such points of agreement. Loss, the uncompromised "solitary," provides the bottom line, reading uncalibrated memory. There is no "general view" of experience; perhaps the promise of "the non-invasive association of memory" (Michael Emre, conversation)

at which point we agree enough to speak about how something is made, as though blood flows through rope, blew through a rope.

Context can promote citation as authority, legitimacy; desire can mark it as the celebration of companionship, proofing faith, proving the being among. Its agency is felt reality, its work fiery apprehension.

"The world, like every in-between, relates and separates. . ." (Hannah Arendt, *The Human Condition*) also reads as "The work, like every in-between, relates and separates. . . ." "An emphasis falls on reality" (Barbara Guest, *Fair Realism*). Which challenges a prevailing tide not merely consisting of forgetfulness but of the violent refusal of complexity in the name of stylish variety, the refusal of form (whether it involve history, context, a figure and ground relationship) in the name of the "random violence" playing over or behind or around us.

But "the near object and the far object are not comparable." (Merleau-Ponty)

a song}　　　　　　　　　　—think about
I made}　　　　　　　　　　space *drawn* by syntax i.e.
a coat}　　　　　　　　　　delivered in the tensions and questions
　　　　　　　　　　　　　　of syntax

What is *agreement* (north) held up against (measured? against?) *convention* (North?) We are north of you, or the eight-ply of the heavens are all folded into one darkness North of you. . . . "Need" does not arise from "things." Remembering (*mnesia*, from *mneson*, mindfulness) and the need to speak arise from the absence of . . . as departure is a prerequisite for any arrival.

our articulations,　 our
　　　　measures.
It is the joy that exceeds pleasure.
　　　　–Robert Duncan, "The Dance"

. . . *—what I love about poetry is the astonishment of language—its surprising abilities—that poetry guards the materiality of language— its workability—its careful steps. . . .*
　　　　–Robin Blaser, "Hello"

Shocking greeting, "you, priest, must know why you strike" ("Salut") easily misreads as, rhymes with, "you, priest, must know why you write," a reading-into-assertion foregrounding the reversal ever present in statement. Unexpectedly flipping the reader's "statement" into (the reader's?) "question," image re-establishes its right to represent faith bursting into flames.

The actual fire has raged around the crystal. The crystalline poetry to be projected, must of necessity, have that fire in it. You will find fire in The Walls Do Not Fall, Tribute to the Angels, *and* The Flowering of the Rod. [Dec. 15, 1949]
But The Walls Do Not Fall *is, in a sense, like certain passages of* The Gift, *runic, divinatory. This is not the "crystalline" poetry that my early critics would insist on. It is no pillar of salt nor yet of hewn rock-crystal. It is the pillar of fire by night, the pillar of cloud by day. It is divinatory, I say, for it seems to indicate, even to predict that Cloud of Witnesses, the starry cloud or star-nebula, as I later call the group of young RAF pilots: John, Lad, Larry, Ralph and Charles tap out their message, with (as one of them spelt clearly on the table) o-t-h-e-r-s- m-a-n-y.* [Dec. 30, 1949]
This was an actual experience:
    he stands by my desk
    in the dark.
[Jan. 5, 1950]
"H.D. by *Delia Alton* (Notes on Recent Writing)"

And full of contradictions. Book of images, present like any permanent, elusive event. *Elusive*: On the way (via the OED) to "elusive" we run across "dogstones," and note that this is the name for various species of *British Orchis*, "from the shape of the tubers."

Elusive: from the Latin ppl. stem *elus-* of *eludere*, to elude, *e-* (out) + *ludere* (to play). Out of play, from play, a product of play: one obsolete sense is "baffle" or "fool," "to disappoint."

The music of this "obsolete" ex-ludic disappointment, baffling, inheres:

"My Dear—

we end with you
circling your garden. . .
the circling continuing in downturning spiral, the vocalic {long i—
long e—short a} trajectory from the first words, "My Dear" to the
final "somebody else's idea" recapitulated in the final word, "idea"

Elusive: Another obsolete sense, to while away (tedium). 1660, R.
Coke, *Justice Vind*. "Men seek . . . company to divert themselves, so
to elude the length of time." To escape by dexterity or stratagem (a
blow, attack, danger, or difficulty); to evade the force (of an argument;
to evade compliance with or fulfillment of (a law, order, demand,
request, obligation, etc.); to slip away from, escape adroitly from (a
person's grasp or pursuit, *lit*. and *fig*.) [How to distinguish *lit*. from
fig.?] Milton, *Paradise Lost*, ix, 158, "Of these [the flaming Ministers]
the vigilance / I dread, and to elude, thus wrapt in mist / Of midnight
vapour glide obscure. . . ." Of things, to elude inquiry, notice, observation, etc. To remain undiscovered or unexplained. 1878, Tait &
Stewart, *Unseen Universe* vi, §177, "So infinitesimally small as to
elude our observation."

With assiduous application to "O-t-h-e-r-s-/-m-a-n-y" reading through
things, to build through-composed or clear-composed work, without
device as safety net; but, rather, to be startled by form's dynamic
insistence.
"I looked at my paper and suddenly I saw that the, all the music, was
already there."
        —John Cage, Notes for "Daughters of the Lonesome Isle"

The accidental vision becomes the incident. "How to follow the gaze
that stares into its future-past?" is just a question, like "Where is the
country with the all-night bookstores?" Realism is a character that
believes in . . . us? Is it fair in the sense of just? Or just beautiful in
and for itself, because we say so? Poetry believes in reality and references the investigatory philosophy of the crisis of "the destruction of
experience" (Giorgio Agamben), always having anticipated it. Not

only is reality's visibility in question, so is its name, "emotion." We call it "emotion," or sometimes "experience." Is it, then, outside experience? Or only in the possession of the specificity of "having one"?

I have worked since 1955 to find a line which will hold what I see and hear, and which will tie a reader to the poems, not to me.
   –Robin Blaser, "The Fire"

The idea of the moth's or the poem's resistance to "having seen," or caught: The generative nature of this resistance: The resistance of the image to *being seen* generates the poem. Fair realism eludes its image as the elusive image is being sung. "It is essentially reluctance the language / a darkness, a friendship, tying to the real / but it is unreal" (Blaser, "The Medium," *Holy* 45).

WORKS CITED

Agamben, Giorgio. *The Coming Community*. Trans. Michael Hardt. Minneapolis: U of Minnesota P, 1993.
Arendt, Hannah. *The Human Condition*. Chicago: U of Chicago P, 1958.
Blaser, Robin. "The Fire." *Pacific Nation* 12 (1968). Rpt. in *Caterpillar* 12 (1970). Rpt. in *The Poetics of the New American Poetry*. Ed. Donald Allen and Warren Tallman. New York: Grove, 1973.
_____. "Hello." *Sulfur* 37 (1995).
_____. "Statement." *The New Long Poem Anthology*. Ed. Sharon Thesen. Toronto: Coach House, 1991.
_____. "The Practice of Outside." *Collected Books of Jack Spicer*. Ed. Robin Blaser. Santa Barbara: Black Sparrow, 1975.
_____. *The Holy Forest*. Toronto: Coach House, 1993.
D[oolitle], H[ilda]. "H.D. by Delia Alton (Notes on Recent Writing)." *Iowa Review* 16 (1986).
Duncan, Robert. *Bending the Bow*. New York: New Directions, 1968.
_____. "The Dance." *The Opening of the Field*. New York: New Directions, 1960.
_____. Letter to Robin Blaser. 28 February 1959.
Guest, Barbara. *Fair Realism*. Los Angeles: Sun & Moon, 1989.
Irby, Kenneth. "Fragments." *Caterpillar* 10 (1970).
Merleau-Ponty, Maurice. *The Visible and the Invisible*. Trans. Alphonso Lingis. Evanston: Northwestern UP, 1968.
Palmer, Michael. Interview with Peter Gizzi. *Exact Change Yearbook* 1 (1995).

Blaser in London, 1959

RECOVERING THE PUBLIC WORLD: ROBIN BLASER AND THE DISCOURSES OF SUBJECTIVITY AND OTHERNESS IN *IMAGE-NATIONS 1-12*

Andrew Mossin

There may be truths beyond speech, and they may be of great relevance to man in the singular, that is, to man in so far as he is not a political being, whatever else he may be. Men in the plural, that is, men in so far as they live and move and act in this world, can experience meaningfulness only because they can talk with and make sense to each other and to themselves.

–Hannah Arendt, *The Human Condition* (4)

For he saw the mouths of men gaping at each other full of terror, no sound wrenched itself from the dry clefts and no one understood the other. It was the last step of silence on earth, it was the ultimate silencing of men; and beholding this his mouth also yearned to open in a last mute cry of horror. Still while seeing it, almost before he had really seen it, he no longer saw anything. For the visible had vanished into most abrupt darkness, the light of dream quenched, the landscape disappeared, the flames quelled, the people evaporated, the mouths abolished, this was night, timeless, spaceless, wordless, toneless, the most empty blackness, an empty night without form and without content. . . .

–Hermann Broch, *The Death of Virgil* (219)

In a profound sense, poetry always remains at the beginning, where the body is involved in thought — the passion that a man reaches for the world before he has any sense whatever of an uncreated thing like happiness. This involves the "process of image" and the "rhythm of it." The reading of a poem is the re-enactment of the images of contact with the world.

–Robin Blaser, "Particles" (39)

I

When Robin Blaser and Robert Duncan had their falling out in late 1965 over ostensibly poetic matters related to their translations of Gérard de Nerval's sonnet sequence, *Les Chimères*, what became most immediately apparent perhaps were the fundamentally different ways in which they understood the poet's role in the writing process and the nature of poetic language. The pairing of Blaser and Duncan (one that inevitably abuts the third figure of this grouping, Jack Spicer) still makes sense on a number of levels, notably their shared roots in the San Francisco Renaissance and lifelong friendships with one another. But reading both the poetry and essays Blaser produced in the wake of this disagreement confirms the degree to which, Duncan and Blaser's similarities in a cosmologically and mythologically oriented poetics notwithstanding, we are in the presence of two very different sensibilities.[1] I want to begin my discussion here of Blaser's resolutely "public" poetics, his assertion of the intersubjective nature of poetic discourse, by underscoring a separation in attitude and stance that in certain respects goes to the heart of Blaser's project. For while Duncan's mythopoetic and vatic approach has remained a predominant force behind Blaser's cosmology of "great companions," Blaser's own increasingly individuated stance and profoundly ethical struggle for the terms of his poetic practice find their fullest expression in his meditation on self and other, individual and *polis*, and on the language in which individuals in a society communicate a vision of public life.

Taken together, these issues suggest the dense topographical terrain of *The Holy Forest*, the collection that includes the bulk of Blaser's work in poetry from 1956 to 1993. The comprehensiveness of this effort is made clear in the essays that, together with this volume, form a singular contribution to post-war U.S. and Canadian poetries and to continuing efforts to produce and sustain a genuinely public art. The "forest" of Blaser's title serves as a metaphor for that uncharted realm—that wilderness—in which "I" and "other," self and world, co-exist in indeterminate yet palpable relation. "Forests are where one is lost, and sometimes found," Blaser tells us in "The Stadium of the Mirror" (1974), the essay that accompanies the poems in the first book publication of *Image-Nations 1-12*. This volume decisively sets

the stage for Blaser's later inquiries into the nature of social and public life, the instability and ineffability of language, and the trans-
parencies and fractures of poetic subjectivity.

In poetry and prose that argue against the sufficiencies of the
Cartesian self, Blaser offers a profound critique of philosophical and
poetic models that insist upon notions of unified subjectivity. In an
argument that has vivid implications for Blaser's work in *The Holy
Forest*, Wlad Godzich suggests that the work of contemporary
philosophers such as Michel de Certeau and Emmanuel Levinas
poses a direct challenge to post-Enlightenment positionings of the
self as arbiter of the "real":

> Against a notion of the truth as the instrument of a mastery being
> exercised by the knower over areas of the unknown as he or she
> brings them within the fold of the same, Levinas argues that
> there is a form of truth that is totally alien to me, that I do not
> discover within myself, but that calls on me from beyond me,
> and it requires me to leave the realms of the known and of the
> same in order to settle in a land under its rule. Here the knower
> sets out on an adventure of uncertain outcome, and the instru-
> ments that he or she brings may well be inappropriate to the
> tasks that will arise. Reason will play a role, but it will be a sec-
> ondary one; it can only come into play once the primary fact of
> the irruption of the other has been experienced. (xvi)

It is in this propositional space deeply inflected by the presence of the
other and otherness that Blaser's poetry makes manifest a middle-
ground of activity and intellection. Here, self as such is neither
aggrandized nor dismissed. Rather, its role is shifted away from the
private and intimate concerns of the individual toward the world
shared in common, which constitutes for Blaser a site of meeting in
discourse, of the public and political. As Blaser suggests in "The
Stadium of the Mirror," he would seek to inscribe in the public space
of poetic thought an "effort to recover the primary language in which
the world and the sacred are alive" (53).

Blaser's model of public and social reality, developed over the last
forty or so years, stems directly from his early exposure to the work of
Hannah Arendt, who taught a graduate course at Berkeley in 1955 on
European political theory. While Blaser wasn't able to attend this

course, Arendt's presence on campus and the subsequent buzz surrounding her discussions of contemporary Western political and
social philosophy had a great impact on Blaser and Spicer and the
circles in which they traveled. As Blaser has described this early period, "[t]he excitement on campus gathered in crowds—Thus the
community there could carry by conversation and constant talking
what was going on in political philosophy—or, rather, the philosophy
of politics—Spicer and I were particularly interested, since our philosophical adventures had led hardly at all to polis/politics."[2] Starting
with *The Origins of Totalitarianism* (1951), the importance of whose
first preface Blaser has acknowledged numerous times over the years,
Blaser began to track Arendt's work, to find corollaries to his own
developing sense of a historically and philosophically grounded poetics. As an orientation point to Blaser's own thinking through of matters, the last paragraph of Arendt's 1950 preface remains pivotal:

> We can no longer afford to take that which was good in the past
> and simply call it our heritage, to discard the bad and simply
> think of it as a dead load which by itself time will bury in obliv-
> ion. The subterranean stream of Western history has finally
> come to the surface and usurped the dignity of our tradition.
> This is the reality in which we live. And this is why all efforts to
> escape from the grimness of the present into nostalgia for a still
> intact past, or into the anticipated oblivion of a better future, are
> in vain. (ix)

Along with *The Human Condition* (1958), *The Origins of
Totalitarianism* provides a critical vocabulary for Blaser's subsequent
inquiry into the nature of political experience and cultural knowledge in the twentieth century. It is in *The Human Condition*, though,
that Arendt delineates in particularly cogent ways the public and
social realms of human endeavor, providing a foundation for Blaser's
thinking that is important at least to sketch in here, as her sense of the
terms "public" and "social" differs from common contemporary
usage in which they have become all but interchangeable.[3]
    According to Arendt, modern formations of the social have their
roots in the ancient Roman and Greek distinctions between the "private," understood as that pertaining to one's household and personal
affairs (including the harvesting of crops, seeking of shelter, and other

necessities of existence), and "the public" (or *res publica* as the Romans termed it), that arena of interaction in which, as Margaret Canovan has observed, "human beings gather to form a space among themselves, and in that space can see their common world from different points of view and therefore talk about their common affairs" (111). As Arendt outlines it, only with the collapsing of the private into the social (realms that had seemed antithetical to the ancients) in the mid- to late- eighteenth century, do we begin to see the emergence of the social as the dominant governing force within Western European cultures. With the formation of mass society and increased industrialization in the early nineteenth century, the private and public realms were both subsumed into the conformist totality of the social. Arendt's assessment of the social as "a kind of pseudo-public realm, a distortion of authentic public life" (Canovan 117) is unequivocal and perhaps not surprising, given her own experiences as a survivor of the global fascism of the 1930s and 40s:

> The rise of mass society . . . only indicates that the various social groups have suffered the same absorption into one society that the family units had suffered earlier; with the emergence of mass society, the realm of the social has finally, after several centuries of development, reached the point where it embraces and controls all members of a given community equally and with equal strength. But society equalizes under all circumstances, and the victory of equality in the modern world is only the political and legal recognition of the fact that society has conquered the public realm, and that distinction and difference have become private matters of the individual. (41)

As Arendt goes on to suggest, the modern period's organization of life processes around labor and work, those factors necessary for sustaining life and aspects of experience once relegated to the private realm of individual households, has resulted in a situation where "society is the form in which the fact of mutual dependence for the sake of life and nothing else assumes public significance and where the activities connected with sheer survival are permitted to appear in public" (46).

If Arendt reserves a good deal of hostility for the conformist and survivalist aspects of the social, she does so in light of what she views as the erasure of the public realm's ancient role as that space in which

excellence (*arete* as the Greeks called it, *virtus* in the Roman distinction) could be made evident before all members of the *polis*:

> While we have become excellent in the laboring we perform in
> public, our capacity of action and speech has lost much of its for-
> mer quality since the rise of the social realm banished these into
> the sphere of the intimate and the private. . . . No activity can
> become excellent if the world does not provide a space for its
> exercise. Neither education nor ingenuity nor talent can replace
> the constituent elements of the public realm, which is the prop-
> er place for human excellence. (49)

The loss, in Arendt's view, has been all but total and has resulted in
a "banishment" of that world-in-common wherein the individual
could understand both his own difference and singularity as constitutive modes of being, of relation, rather than, as in the sense perva-
sive to modern society, homogenization, indistinctiveness, isolation.

The public, in Arendt's account, is the made place of the world,
fabricated in common by human activities engaged to a commonly
understood end. "To live together in the world means essentially that
a world of things is between those who have it in common, as a table
is located between those who sit around it; the world, like every in-
between, relates and separates men at the same time" (*Human* 52). As
contemporary theory has argued, there are a number of problems in
such a formulation of social reality, in particular the notion of a
"world in common"—especially as that world is currently more likely to be fractured and unevenly shared, with certain groups and sectors of the political and social realms possessing more power and economic capital than others, while many factions and individuals are
marginalized or left out of the picture entirely. Yet, it is important at
the same time to recognize that Arendt's conception of the public
world is very much part of a historical *ethos* in which, as she writes in
her preface to the first edition of *The Origins of Totalitarianism*: "It is
as though mankind had divided itself between those who believe in
human omnipotence (who think that everything is possible if one
knows how to organize the masses for it) and those for whom power-
lessness has become the major experience of their lives" (vii). For
Arendt, and to a certain degree for Blaser as well, the public realm
holds out the only sustaining hope for the survival of civil discourse

and preservation of cultural knowledge. Despite what nearly fifty years of further erosion of Western political and intellectual life have taught us, Arendt's vision of the public realm is no idealized or nostalgic construction; rather, it remains the gathering point that "prevents our falling over each other" (52), while preserving a space for discourse, for public and reciprocal identities to engage one another.

For Blaser, these distinctions are vital and pervade the commentary of his essays. As is clear, Arendt's propositions go directly to the heart of his formulation of a poetics of public feeling and political concern. At stake is a version of public life that is intimately related to the tangible realities of poetry and the potential for a common (i.e. public) language of political investment. As Blaser suggests in his 1969 essay, "Particles":

> Poetry has moved since early in the century to the inclusion of political content, not because the relevance of poetry can be defined by its political or ideological content, but because the public world is sick and has in many places disappeared for lack of particularity. Nothing is shared and no vision of a shared world is possible. (36)

Blaser's linking of politics and political projections of social reality with the language arts extends upon Arendt's conception of the public as that site in which discourse among individuals may occur. And it is here, Blaser argues, that twentieth-century poetry has most meaningfully engaged the public arena of its concern, by providing a space for the reader to renew contact with his or her worldly self:

> What has to be understood is that form and content combine in an activity which reveals meaning, grasps the mind of the reader, so that he is forever changed, because, if he has understood, there has been a meeting. And that meeting has permanence since it is held in public words. (37)

It is this meeting that marks the poem as a public—as opposed to a solely private—occasion. "We return again and again to the importance of language in its activity of holding on to the world and life in that world" (40).

Blaser's comments resonate with the principled valuations of willed
testimony and public projection, based upon a measured understanding of the ways in which discourses of poetry and poetics must
go hand in hand in a cultural environment often hostile to the undertaking. Thus, his is a world view tempered by recognitions of the
technocratic and ideologically impervious aspects of commerce and
global consumerism that stand in opposition to (or, more accurately,
surround and attempt to nullify) the possibility of a genuinely public
art. These recognitions find renewed articulation in one of Blaser's
more recent essays, "Recovery of the Public World" (1993), in which
he attaches Arendt's forceful commentary to a project meant to
engage once again

> [t]he durability of the world. We can hardly understand it, even
> though it has only changed technologically. Where the durabil-
> ity of the world is our primary concern, we uncover, alongside
> the discourses of the social and the political, the related—or
> should-be related—discourse of the arts and the sacred. But
> durability has become unattractive with built-in obsolescence,
> and our culture sets the latter discourses aside, unless they can
> become an exchange value. What was the durable in-between of
> the world is now an abstraction, or a series of them, drawn from
> the characteristics of large numbers of people. (30)

Rather than setting the discourses of the arts and the sacred apart
from the manifold processes of society-at-large and maneuvering
these discourses toward a space of privilege and sacrosanct regard,
Blaser links them to what he calls "our worldly project in language"
("Recovery" 31) and suggests that only once we begin to revivify the
lost connectives of our cultural past can we claim to have presented
ourselves to the world—or to each other. "We need to know how old
we are," Blaser writes, a comment which simultaneously suggests that
the effort must be multi-disciplinary and educational—a working
back to understand how and from whence we have come (37).

    Blaser's long-standing commitment to a poetics of public statement
and cultural intervention has been emphasized by a number of poets
and critics. Among the more recent is Miriam Nichols, who lays the
groundwork in her article, "Three for Public: Steve McCaffery,
Nicole Brossard, and Robin Blaser," for a reappraisal of Blaser's

recognition of the ways in which the public, political, and poetic are inflected by the numinous, cosmological, and non-visible that form a corollary world of (other) meaning. In the work, such recognition manifests itself in Blaser's avowedly utopian impulse to go beyond language and its deictic functions, to move in a poetic discourse and landscape in which the visible objects of the world are imaged by what is absent, rather than what is named. As Nichols suggests:

> The element in the poem which communicates nothing and takes place nowhere reinvests the visibles of the moment with the potential to be otherwise—in opposition to a cultural econo-my which forecloses the possibility of being otherwise than rep-resented. Poetic *utopoi* thus imply that knowledge is an activity rather than the condition of knowing something—and hence that difference, when it appears, is irreducible to more of the same (not for sale). Poetry is not only about the expression of dif-ferent forms of subjectivity or different public behaviours, differ-ent linguistic formations or different historical thought worlds, *but also and always a continuing reclamation and renewal of the means of producing thought.* (99; emphasis added)

Viewed from this standpoint, Blaser's is a recognizably utopian poet-ic project. As co-participants in this production of meaning and thought, we enter Blaser's poems painfully aware that whatever pat-tern we may discern in the movements of the language, it is a change-able and multiply fashioned one—subject to sudden alterations and variable degrees of silence.

Rather than fetishizing the poem's difficulty and valorizing the knowledge base from which the poem emerges, a knowledge base often inflected with images of mastery and authorial control, Blaser refutes the exclusionary impulse, insisting instead upon the genuine, urgently felt difficulty of the undertaking. As he suggests about the writing of the early *Image-Nation* poems, it is a difficulty underwrit-ten by the investigative nature of the poems' activity:

> It is my purpose to make it difficult for the first *Image-Nations* . . . . I wish in this way to suggest what it is that haunted their composition. I could have wound up there inside the lyric logic of the disappearance—of myself, a syntax, the whole damn cul-tural grid. While then the image would have remained the

> possibility of an entrance, magically, still the danger was that the
> I, the poet and the manhood of the poems in the distance of the
> work would become only a spectator. ("Stadium" 55)

Situating the first twelve of the *Image-Nations* at a point at which they
are most defenseless to charges of obscurity and inward referentiality,
Blaser begins to articulate and define the project that has occupied
his attentions and energies to the present day: to reclaim for poetry a
position of public assertion and accountability. If the loss of the lyric,
ego-based "I" is part of the cost of this endeavor, Blaser would seem
to suggest that continuing efforts to preserve this "I" result in a flawed
epistemology that has even graver consequences for the continuing
cultural life of poetry—and the public knowledge it proffers.

"No serious poetry can be described as self-expression," Blaser
warns in "Particles" (38). In so doing, Blaser clearly doesn't intend a
dispensing with the personal; rather, he wants to suggest that no valid
contemporary poetic discourse can emanate from a space configured
only in terms of its relation to the poet's life experience. The "I" is significant only in so far as it exists as one part of the poetic encounter—
a meeting that is always involved in "activities of content—of passion
and thought—the relation of a man to the world as the world calls to
him" (38). If the "I" retains expressive force at all, it is as a gathering
point, a dictated site of words and worlds that inform the poet's development:

>   . . . . I know nothing of form
>   that is my own doing   all out
>   of one's self   our words were
>   the form we entered, turning intelligible
>   and strange   at the point of
>   a pencil
>   (*Holy* 124)

Language in this undertaking is neither limit nor ultimate presence;
rather, it suggests the folded, perceptible form of a public and intimately known actuality. The imaged "I" of this work exists neither in
isolation from what it expresses nor in mimetic relation to the experience rendered in the poem's language. Instead, the subjective self
remains "both visible and invisibly continuous. At an edge. At the

edge of his thought and feeling" ("Stadium" 55).

Blaser's major contribution to poetic thought and practice in the latter half of this century may rest on his rigorous rethinking of the entire set of relations that includes writer, text, reader, and the discourses that link them to each other. In suggesting the terms of a meeting, a correspondence, bound to an activity of thought, Blaser establishes a poetic that is intermedial and, in the best sense of the term, oppositional. The radical potential of this endeavor lies in its recognition of the public value and immediacy of a contemporary poetic that refuses to collapse under the weight of cultural and social conditions that call for nostalgic and otherwise false epistemologies of experience. Like Pound and Olson, two of the "masters" most often cited by Blaser in his naming of the tradition, Blaser's is a critical art of reappraisal and cultural repositioning; more clearly from our present vantage point, his work proposes an ethics at the center of a poetics—the essentializing, totalizing one that would investigate the terms by which any of us writes poetry in the technology driven *ethos* of global capital and cultural forgetting:

> this thought of the end is the modern
> sweetness and terror, but it simplifies to terror
> alone—the societal dream of itself as absolute
> reality, then practiced as uniformity and barbarism,
> is the oily turntable of the roundhouse where we
> repair the engine again and again—it is the
> absolute humanism that is repulsive (*Holy* 188)[4]

The purpose, for Blaser, as for any one interested in the revivification of public (which is to say, poetic) discourse, "is toward a reopening of words—towards the violence and dynamism of Language" ("Stadium" 58). What emerges from the poems, then, is a version of subjectivity that relies less on narratives of personal statement (solipsistic veracities of the self-expressive) than on the force of communally achieved knowledge. The poems, in their processive exploration of the overlapping realms of self and other, body and spirit, world and text, are the recognizably principled accounts of this endeavor.[5]

It is in *Image-Nations 1-12*, the composition of which spans a period from the late 1950s through the early 70s, that Blaser begins to explore formally and contextually the ways in which poetry may reflect a world and selves within that world. As the first "Image-Nations," titled "(the fold," makes clear, the series will be as much "about" its own procedures as about the nature of language and the subjective "I" limned within the poem's landscape:

> the participation is broken
> fished from a sky of fire
> the fiery lake pouring itself
> to reach here
>
> that matter of language caught
> in the fact   so that we
> meet in paradise   in such
> times, the I consumes itself
>   (*Holy* 61)

The propositions of an "I" that consumes itself in the grandeur of its own radiant expectancy clash with the poem's effort to define a space of speaking, a midway locale of initial encounter. As the poems make evident, it is a locale of intensely imaged particulars, in which the "I" is both observer and observed:

> white trees, rings around them,
> wander and roll, the fog breaks,
> the sky, blue in the window
>
> sits up there, out of reach,
> hands full of *beautifuls-uglies*
> *justs-unjusts,   halves-doubles,*
> pulls the strings . . .
>   (*Holy* 61)

Causality and the perceptible realm are made part of a discourse on the nature of observable experience and the role of the subject in mediating the flickering images of exteriority. As in Maurice Merleau-Ponty's description of the chiastic meeting of the incorporeal and invisible/corporeal and visible: "the seer and the visible reciprocate one another and we no longer know which sees and which is seen" (139).

Later, in "Image-Nation 5 (erasure," Blaser works further at this model of composition that, as he notes in "Stadium of the Mirror," was already "negligent, uneasy, inarticulate" (55). In so doing, he sets out in fractured lines of nearly obliterated connectives the rough outlines of an argument:

> the words do not end   but come back
> from the adventure
>   the body at the edge
> of their commotion
>   the nonsense
> the marvelous clarity
>   in the pool of the
> heart
>   (*Holy* 113)

The poem, in its left/right configuration, poses a dialogue between language and the physically bounded universe ("the body at the edge") of thought and feeling. In these "traces," the position of a self is at stake, as are the incarnational properties of language:

> we quarrel over the immortal Word,
> many times one falls out of the mortal
> there suddenly   the missing   outward
> journey
>   (*Holy* 113)

The lines fold one into the next in a blurring of the binary of subject/object, as the spiritual reality of the "Word as Flesh" forms a kind of seam, interleaving the mortal and immortal in language, compressed almost to the point of inarticulateness:

> the co-herence   falls, like rain,
> into the syllables
>   this in-herence
> of a golden poem
>   translating
> blood, dancers,
>   and whirling

drunken lives
                    into a tense
    music
    of a hollyhock
    (*Holy* 115)

Here the related discourses of Gérard de Nerval, Stéphane Mallarmé, and Jalal ud-Din Rumi, each of which has been an intricately interwoven aspect of the poem's meditation on the visible/invisible, real/unreal, are brought forward in a language of heightened lyricality. The encounter is made in language, yet, as Blaser's poem records, its experience is one that cannot be limited to language alone.

Blaser's question—"what exactly do we experience in poeisis" (*Holy* 317)—is given added force in the context of a refusal to sentimentalize or aestheticize the first person singular, which, as Blaser reminds us, is "neither first, nor a person, nor singular" (*Holy* 317-18). His comment is meant as a playful yet deeply serious rebuke of theoretical and poetic models that would attempt to resolve the matter through the simplifying *dicta* of egocentrism. As he has suggested in his 1989 essay, "Poetry and Positivisms: High Muck-A-Muck or 'Spiritual Ketchup'":

> We have . . . in the twentieth-century poetry that is unable and unwilling to depend upon the direct and simplifying clarity of the ego at the center, a concern with the arrangement of words which both renews and disturbs our relation to words and to the rhythm of form—so to compose the representable alongside the nonrepresentable. (25)

What is stressed here and elsewhere in Blaser's critique of the ego-based lyric (a critique that finds echoes in Yeats and Pound and particular resonance in the work of Olson) is the intermediate position, through which a useful interrogation of concept, meaning, and perspective may occur. No one position can be claimed as complete as the poet confronts the realities of poem and language, realities formed of the discourses of sexuality, spirituality, philosophy, and religion. It is a flowing-out and through, a disappearance, rather than an emplacement or a presence, that we as readers encounter:

a Nervalian movement   of
astonishment   an arm around
a hollyhock   or foxglove,
as if we dressed in them,

a flowered man   the bees
disturb   the stillness   seeking
sweetness in the pockets
an art as natural as *lunch poems*
or an extravagant   speaking   out of
the *gnostic horse's mouth*

a translation of oneself into the Other
(*Holy* 114)

This "translation" is one that, as Blaser repeatedly suggests, can never
be completed; rather, the fluctuating nature of the poem's movement
records the drifting back and forth across the divides of self and other.
The poet's job becomes that of repeatedly renegotiating this transla-
tional "edge" out of which the form of the poem and its language
arise:

the task of a man   and his words
is at the edge
                    where we are
translated   restless   men
the quarrel over the immortal language,
one may believe in a god-language
behind us,   but god moves to the end
of our sentences
                    where words   foment
a largeness
          of visible
and invisible worlds
they are a commotion
of one form
(*Holy* 116)

In this "one form" (a unifying construct that echoes Duncan's notion
of the poem as "living force"), language is the contact point, but not,
as Blaser is quick to point out, the source. Here it is useful to keep in
mind a discussion from his 1967 essay, "The Fire":

> I am trying to describe the foreignness, the outsideness, as a kind
> of metaphor for the sense I have of the process that leads to a
> poem, which again is outside, when made, and it is akin to trans-
> lation, a word which in its parts holds the meaning of the word
> metaphor, the bringing over. . . . The heat I'm after is not simply
> the personal heat of the meeting, the recognition, but a heat and
> a passion which are of the nature of existence itself. The person-
> al, yes, but then the translation of the personal to correspond
> with larger and larger elements, images of earth, is a process of
> inclusion—a growth of sensibility, in Valéry's phrase, but also a
> making which is not self-expressive. (243-44)

In Blaser's conception of it, the discourses of self are inextricably
bound to discourses of worldliness—political, social, religious, mystical—that provide a context, an outside, which the poem's language
continually negotiates. As Blaser has aphoristically framed the matter:
"The seat of the language in the Other is the necessary exploration"
("Stadium" 62). By which I take him to mean that only through a
genuinely dialogic poetic practice, one not seeking the self-affirming
closures of a transcendent or idealized subjectivity, can poetry begin
to suggest the repleteness and incommensurability of worldly experience.

"Difficult voices speak to us," Blaser writes in "The Stadium of the
Mirror" (60). Blaser's remains one of the most difficult of our era,
largely due to this concerted attempt to work out the problematic
nature of public discourse (written, spoken, lived) and its historically
pinioned, culturally determined character. Shaking free of the disso-
lutions and ideological fictions of the contemporary social condition
is, as Blaser's writing career attests, no easy trick. One risks, among
other things, not being read or being read incorrectly (a situation
addressed with particular bitterness in the correspondence between
Duncan and Blaser during the course of their Nerval dispute);
seeming out of step with the cultural, social and artistic *zeitgeist*;
or simply being dismissed out-of-hand for "obscurity, crazyness [sic],
and personalism" ("Stadium" 58). Yet, as Blaser notes, there
are consequences of failing to follow through on what is essentially a
retracing (however partial and incomplete it must remain) of the
maps of our shared cultural reality:

The forgetfulness of our cultural condition destroys our ability to think. Since the meaning of the term [*humanitas*] has become questionable in one discourse after another—indeed, murdered by way of some of them—I think our sense of our humanity is central to whatever we may believe. We began, I'm told, in conversation with God; we've come to converse, if we converse at all, only with ourselves. ("Recovery" 24)

Caught in the discourse of forgetfulness that is our contemporary situation, Blaser's poetry seeks to re-establish the links, to create a poetry of public accountability and inter-personal delight in "the depths beneath the surfaces in which each 'simple, separate person' swims" ("Hello" 87).

I I

"Unless the *Image-Nations* are read by image, there is no saving grace," Blaser asserts in the opening sentence of "Stadium of the Mirror" (53). This insistence upon image is clear enough from the title of the series itself. For "*Image-Nation*" proposes the public discourses of both *image* and *nation*: the nation as image, the image as nation, and both as correspondent realities of *imagination*. From these "small lighted words," Blaser points to the public properties of a work devoted to the particularity of images as *these occur in the writing itself*. The importance for Blaser of the individual image as it relates to his concern for the communal and public is perhaps best summed up in this passage from "Particles":

> Greek and Roman political experience argues that to act intelligently in the public realm requires a vision of things. The words themselves, vision and things, are telling. Vision, full of that sense of seeing and image, which are basic to knowing—and things—even bits and pieces. *There is no vision of things without the emotions of particularity.* (36; emphasis added)

As Blaser suggests, there can be no meaningful politics without an accompanying vision of the world and of the objects that compose a world. In this, Blaser again aligns himself with Arendt, whose notion of the seen as that which is made public is carried over into Blaser's formulation of a poetics of "image-nation." As Arendt writes in *The Human Condition*, "[e]verything that appears in public can be seen and heard by everybody and has the widest possible publicity. For us, appearance—something that is being seen and heard by others as well as by ourselves—constitutes reality" (50). One must see to become part of the larger, publicly recognizable orders of existence, and seeing requires a receptivity to the images of the world. "How particular the image is," Blaser writes. "This too is part of the activity of discourse" ("Particles" 37).

Both the site of a meeting and the instant of an interchange, the image occurs in the poem's contextual and public space. The image is rendered particular in language that eschews the familiarity of instrumental discourse, in favor of the communal, the open-ended and propositional. Blaser's serially constructed poem-works align themselves with a political envisioning of experience in which poet, poem, and reader are co-creators of a meeting. This, in turn, suggests the deeply political nature of Blaser's lifework. For if the *polis* is dependent on a vision of things, the poem is equally reliant upon the image as that particular site of reciprocity and public speech. This notion of the poetic image finds a powerful analogue in Arendt's depiction of the place held by public discourse in ancient Greek culture:

> For the Greeks the essence of friendship consisted in discourse. They held that only the constant interchange of talk united citizens in a *polis*. In discourse the political importance of friendship, and the humanness peculiar to it, were made manifest. . . . For the world is not humane just because it is made by human beings, and it does not become humane just because the human voice sounds in it, but only when it has become the object of discourse. (24)

Grounded in such talk, Blaser's *Image-Nations* reappropriate the communal sphere as the metaphorical site of the poems' interchange. Rendering the singular a key component of the public and pluralist interchange of the poem's effort, Blaser would have us recognize that we only begin to recognize the terms of our humanness when we achieve perception of the particular in discourse with an other or others.

The image, then, exists for Blaser not merely as a literary conceit of modernist writing, but as the foundational impression, the site of both adjoinment and separation, wherein the public world is articulated and envisioned. Because it cannot be completed as such—it is complete already—the image resists hegemonic narratives of totality and closed meaning. Part of a world of publicly actualized poetic discourse, the image reveals itself as part of a discretionary movement among shifting points of contact:

> the powers are brought
> to birth   and again the vocabulary
> loses them   image—imageless
> Plotinus says our effort is to make
> the visible invisible   but here the
> invisible would not be borrowed   may
> you have *a radiant world compelling*
> *adoration*   the tree waits to be visible
> (*Holy* 119)

Like the tree awaiting visibility and concretion as a part of experience, the poem and its language suggest a pool of visible and invisible relations; the mind cannot entirely grasp their meaning, yet the context of an activity that can neither be denied nor entirely articulated has been suggested by the poem's movement in time. It is in this shifting movement between the visible and the invisible, the image and the imageless, that Blaser meaningfully draws out the terms of the poem's public enactment.

Blaser's emphasis on the particular, the discrete detail, likewise suggests an awareness of those distilled aspects of perception that together inform the composition and unfolding realities of poetic content. Meaning occurs in the synaesthesic moment when image recommences in perception. Blaser's imaging of thought ("the words are meaningless / until they emerge in the action they are / images of" [*Holy* 126-27]) is a direct consequence of his rigorous effort to bind the poems to real activity and a process-oriented understanding of poetic endeavor. The poems are, in this way, *effort-ful*, procedurally self-conscious of their instigations and developmental movement. Unravelling, unfurling, keeping pace with the objects that come into view ("a bone, a ball, a top / an apple, a mirror, a skein of wool" [*Holy* 127]), they entice and incite with the prospect of newly-found observation and knowledge of the world.

Divestment and initiation accordingly become signature motifs of the work. As Blaser writes in his 1975 essay, "The Practice of Outside," on fellow-poet and Berkeley companion, Jack Spicer, "[t]he condition of that beginning again in language and meaning is between our manhood, the anthropology of our thought, and everything outside its orders. It is, at times, almost a *divestment* of the memory of words. Undressed words" (285). The *Image-Nation* poems similarly adhere to a poetics of divestment, in which the poems resist completion and the ordering narratives of normative syntax to engage an "image of an action" wherein reader and writer are invested in the con-joint project of poetic thought:

> but there, it was
> there 'you' saw
> the head of a horse burn,
> its red eye flame 'you' stepped
> to the fireplace where the meta
> morphosed log lay without a body
> and 'your' hand over the seeing
>
> turned by that privacy
> from such public perils as words
> are, we travel in company with the messenger
> (*Holy* 62)

This arc from the "I" to the "you" is a critical marker of Blaser's public positioning of his text. For, as he suggests, in the correspondent acts of seeing, of in-sight, the "you" and the "I" are transformed into the plurality of a "we" brought into existence through the imaged perceptions of a publicly held language. Thereby the standard questions posed of the lyric—*Who is speaking? Who is listening?*—achieve via Blaser's poetic stance distinctive variation: *What are the circumstances in which 'I' speak and 'you' listen? What is the basis of the relationship formed there?* Piece by piece, image by image, the work seeks, in its negotiation of the multiplicity of realities and forms governing any single act of perception, not so much a coherence of utterance as an engagement in the processes by which any of us can be said to "speak" or "act" alone or together.

III

Olson said, 'I'd trust you
anywhere with image, but
you've got no syntax' (1958)
–Blaser, "Diary, April 11, 1981" (*Holy* 183)

The context of Olson's comment to Blaser and Blaser's response, scribbled on the back of a postcard—"Who's the image boy round here?"—are now part of the public record.[6] What is remarkable in the context of Blaser's development over the next several years was the use he made of what just as well could have seemed a throwaway comment at the time. Blaser's reception of the implicit challenge and rebuke of Olson's remark, and his willingness to engage this comment as an ongoing intellectual project (leading him to title his 1983 collection *Syntax*), tell us much about the highly responsive—and patient—nature of Blaser's poetic process. As his essay, "Stadium of the Mirror," makes clear, the absence of syntax was a decidedly conscious move—borne out of a need to free the poem from its manifest cultural markings and resituate the work at the edge of language: "The first tentative effort was to remove that syntax which had been a misapprehension—in order to let the image speak out of the absence the Other had become" (54). This "absence," marked by the disruptions and dislocations of syntactical order, relates in key ways to Blaser's attention to the cosmological realities of poetic discourse, realities that when thwarted slide into the false propositions of a transcendent subjectivity. "The absence of syntax," Blaser writes, "becomes polar to another language—of presences alongside absences, of speech alongside a silence of words, of a visibility tensed alongside a love which traces its invisible open-work" ("Stadium" 56-57).

Blaser's terminology is key, for it reinforces the investigatory positioning of the work, its attempt to "relearn" its own procedures and arrive differently at a place open to contact with a world positioned between appearance and disappearance, absence and presence. In refusing the confines and conjectures of a culturally inherited syntax—and it is a refusal writ large in the work—Blaser turns to the serial as the constitutive formal marker of his poetic practice. While seriality doesn't replace syntax in *Image-Nations*, it clearly fulfils the function normally reserved for syntax, that is, to order and regulate language, in response to the social necessity for comprehensible speech. Blaser's need to understand the composite exigencies of culturally given syntax before grounding his poetic texts in its legitimizing and controlling discourses results in disjunctions in the earlier work. Enfolding discrete observation and detail in the poem's movements, Blaser enlists serial form as a method (i.e. a practice of *both* outside and inside) to inquire into "the violence and dynamism of Language" ("Stadium" 58). It is an approach that, as Blaser recognizes, has its costs in the account it gives of the visible and invisible world: "The serial field is honest, if dangerous ground . . . [that] constantly circumscribes an absence that brings its presences to life. An indefiniteness that is one of the providing aspects of the world" ("Stadium" 61).

If *The Holy Forest* is the book of that "story of persons, events, activities, images, which tell the tale of the spirit," then the poetics that informs the early *Image-Nations* poems reveals the individual panels of a continuously evolving work. Each is positioned to face the other; there is no one image nor one nation at stake in the unfolding narrative. Rather, connections are made, lost, and re-made throughout the series, the full meaning of which cannot be ascertained from the reading—or writing—of any single poem. As Blaser suggests in "The Fire," "the beauty of the idea that you can write a single poem is a lie" (20). Spicer's work in and following his *After Lorca* provides a model here of serial composition that deeply informs Blaser's own project. The poems move notationally in the ordering of the series and the book, a critique of the traditional self-sufficiencies of the lyric. In so doing, seriality remains far more than simply a formal principle of ordering. Rather, it suggests work generated by *attention to what is happening.* In Blaser's account, the serial poem

> has to be a renewed language and information that becomes a kind of map. Ideally, Jack worked in that long form without looking back and without thought of the previous poem, so that the poet could be led by what was composing. The serial poem is often like a series of rooms where the lights go on and off. It is also a sequence of energies which burn out, and it may, by the path it takes, include the constellated. . . . A "necessary world" is composed in the serial poem. ("Practice" 278; emphasis added)

Necessary because it insists upon the public context of poetic making. And upon the reality of the images that compose the poem. Like Spicer's lemon—"The lemon [should] be a lemon that the reader could cut or squeeze or taste" (*Collected Books* 33)—the images that come into the serial poem are entirely real and entirely invented. "Things do not connect; they correspond," Spicer says later in the same "imaginary" letter to Lorca. Similarly, the serial poem continually suggests correspondences and clusters of meaning that accumulate and overlap over time. The work thus engages, as Blaser puts it, "a reopened language [that] lets the unknown, the Other, the outside in again as a voice in the language" ("Practice" 276).

It is in this emphasis on the unknown, the cosmologically and linguistically other (as differentiated from, but related to, contemporary post-colonial discourses of the other and otherness), that the serial poem proposes an endeavor of public making, a process in which the activity of thought is imaged in the fragments of discursive writing. As Rachel Blau DuPlessis has argued in her essay, "The Blazes of Poetry," "The interest in making a serial poem is in establishing what kinds of links can be presented between any two units, and among all units. How each is modified in relation to the existence of others. Thus it is an image of sociality (community)" that emerges from the "sutured" bits of language (8-9). The *Image-Nations* develop from this intense awareness of the circumstances of the serial as a compositional and ethical mode invested in the collective, the gathered-together, and communal. Its work traverses a space of the multi-voiced rather than the "voice," the polyvalent rather than the singular, the random rather than the predetermined.

Moreover, as "Image-Nation 5 (erasure" suggests, the historically contingent and culturally specific work in the series is yet another marker of the particular, the discrete detail, from which meaning is made. These perceptible instants of public recognition become

> like small poems read from
> vast stages   the images of the war
> in Vietnam   burn up   out of the
> words,
>   where they are not
> added to the real
>   but compose it

> where the body
> burns
> in bubbles of fat
> and re   opens
> into something
> without lineaments
> (*Holy* 114)

Read as one part of those "small poems," the image of a burning body is exacting and horrific in its allusion to a signal episode in the history of post-colonial warfare: the United States' napalming of North Vietnamese civilians during the Vietnam War, images of which were seen on the nightly broadcast news and in the print journalism of the period. As a response to an actual historical incident *in extremis*, the poem's language records the terror of the event, while suggesting an attendant dis-ease, as the imaged body gesturally transforms "into something / without lineaments," that is to say, into a form without trace or outline. The dissolution of the physical combined with the stark appearance of burning flesh compose a space that is at once unreal and palpably horrific. As suggested by the language of this poem, Blaser's is an unsettling version of human eventuality, one always at the edge of depiction and cognitive understanding. The path through the forest remains, like the language of the poetic series, discontinuous, manifest, hidden and potentially terrifying.[7]

While it would be overly simplistic to draw direct parallels between the political-historical events of the period and Blaser's writing of this or any of the other poems in *The Holy Forest*, the question arises: to what extent does the serial form, as engaged by Blaser, Duncan, Spicer, and others, anticipate and in certain ways relate to the events of the Vietnam War and the Civil Rights, anti-war, and other mass protest movements of the 1960s and early 1970s? As DuPlessis observes, "One 'answer' seems to be the articulation of the many and the one. Both [George] Oppen's and Blaser's serial works (and Duncan's too) are marked by the Vietnam War and the post-war crisis of recognition of the wounds to democratic culture carried out in the name of the American imperium" (7).

Certainly, in ways that "Image-Nation 5" makes explicit, the poem is one part of a critical response in the public language of poetry to events that exert great pressure on the poem and its formal procedures. Seriality may compose a necessary world, but the world met in the serial work will inevitably suggest the problematic and discontinuous nature of the human historical present in which any poem is written. Governed by this view is Blaser's acute sense of what lies at stake in any contemporary discourse in which poetry plays a singularly pertinent part. From "The Fire":

> That we have reached a point now where such discourse must include the nation, our politics, the scholarship in which we tend to lay down images of poetic thought—is obvious. This is a kind of memory theatre in which the poet with his craft is after not some thing or place remembered, but present. Nothing would be more painful or costly to the mind, and ugly in the sense that great poetry may be very ugly, than a poetry in which the present war was present, held in sight and sound and intellect. (30)

The move is at once toward a credible place of public response and authentic feeling and away from a poetics and poetry that would remove itself from present circumstance, whether political, social, or personal. To do so, as Blaser suggests in "Image-Nation 9 (half and half," is to invite the situation in which

> . . . public life has fallen asleep
> like a secret name   the wrong-reader
> will say he has pity for others
> where the thought is born in *hatred*
> *of pity*, which is *only feeling*   the action
> we are only images of   hates pity
> and its *reduction of horror to sentiment*
> (*Holy* 126)

This perception of public life as having "fallen asleep" exists as a generating concern and intellectual *topos* throughout the early (and late) *Image-Nation* poems. Again, Blaser sets the model of sentimentality (or false feeling) against the politically and culturally thought-out purposefulness of action, imaged in a language of public statement. The implication that each of us is a part of unfolding narratives of social and political life and that the choices we make in these areas form paradigmatic concerns of our moral being is foregrounded by the investigatory traces of the series. In the language of Blaser's poem, ". . . the words are meaningless / until they emerge in the action they are/images of" (*Holy* 126).

IV

Governed by such images, by what can be ascertained in the pictures drawn by language, *Image-Nations 1-12* hold forth the possibility of a genuinely dialogic poetic. The poem becomes, in Blaser's sense of it, "a translation of oneself into the Other" (*Holy* 114). As he suggests, it is in the process of encountering images in language that we inhabit a transpersonal site of knowledge in which the distinctions of "I" and "Other" achieve particularity and clarity. Recovering a location that is "perched among words," writer and reader are positioned to engage in public meaning and making:

                                    where words   foment
              a largeness
                           of visible
              and invisible worlds
              they are a commotion
              of one form

              the voice is *recognizable*
              as fragments
              of a greater language,
              a live and changing
              face
                           (*Holy* 116)

"Speaking speaking / as if woven" (*Holy* 120), Blaser sounds out a dimension of worldly reality imaged in the scatterings of material—the "bits and pieces"—that provide the content of and context for a continuing discourse of the real. Indeed, the notion of "scattering" occurs as yet another apt description of the work accomplished by *Image-Nations*, poems that engage in profound acts of scattering. For Blaser, the related image of Orpheus provides a foundational metaphor for his work in poetry: "It is precisely in the image of the scattered body and mind of Orpheus that I place whatever I know about the poetic process—that scattering is a living reflection of the world" ("Fire" 26). As such a remark suggests, Blaser's work has been deeply informed by a decidedly heterodox and multiphasic approach to the formation of cultural and poetic knowledge. His is a view of the poem and poetic process that insists upon the validity of "an activity which reveals meaning, grasps the mind of the reader, so that he is forever changed, because, if he has understood, there has been a meeting. And that meeting has permanence since it is held in public words" ("Particles" 37).

Blaser's "forest" resonates as a metaphor of precisely these instances of public and ethical concern, which have been brought into relation by the poet's recognition that, as he suggests:

> The Other is present and primary to our speaking. There is no public realm without such polarity of language. The operation of its duplicity is the poetic job. A peril and an ecstasy. The traffic around a heart which is heartless. The characters do not speak only of themselves, since they are images of an action. *Transcendence is not a position somewhere else, but the manner of our being to any other* (Merleau-Ponty). A co-existence. ("Stadium" 59; emphasis added)

This doubling of speech remains the manifest sign of a poetry committed to the splendors and terrors of thought, and recurs as a primary motif for Blaser. As Jed Rasula has remarked, "Blaser's work is positioned *with care* at the interface of visible and invisible, thought and unthought, original and derivative. Its doubling is conjugal" (100).

Alluding as it does to the combined and inter-related discourses of culture, politics, theology, and history, Blaser's work attests not so much to the "tale of the tribe," to recall Pound's phrase, but to the multiple narratives of self and other that are by their very nature public *and* social realities. "*I am not   there where I am the plaything / of my thought,*" Blaser writes, citing Jacques Lacan, in "Image-Nation 10 (marriage clothes," "*I think about what I am / there where / I do not think I am thinking*" (*Holy* 135). This "There-Where" is fundamental to Blaser's conception of poiesis as, to paraphrase Arendt, "thinking what we are doing." It is as well a portion of the idealized and real world-in-common: that space in which each of us is implicated in processes of public making that are dependent on multiple strands of individual and communal meaning and meeting. "The world is never separately—by simplicity's trick—social, political, artistic, or sacred, but, rather, it is made of an entanglement of discourses having to do with men, women, earth and heaven" ("Recovery" 18). The image of this entanglement is one in which "the light and shadow become / the substance of men and women" (*Holy* 129).

In working through Blaser's own involvement in issues of poetic form and politics, as these are manifest in his poetry, statements on poetics, and scholarly prose, I have sought to suggest both the scope of his concerns and the range of materials and discourses brought to bear on a project of manifestly public concern, "the territory, the largeness, in which we try to live and think" ("Poetry" 21). At the same time, the ethical component of this endeavor needs to be underscored. As in the philosophical writings of Levinas, whose concerns with the Other and the ethical imperatives of discourse provide meaningful corollaries to the work discussed here, Blaser's *Image-Nations 1-12* evince the interrogative rigor of a project that seeks to unpack the discourses of Self and Other and reclaim for poetry its public function and usefulness in the world of ideas. In the radical potential of images cast by this work, Blaser strives to recover a location, a space deep within our human and cultural memory, in which the separations that have become endemic to our public, private, and social existences may be diminished, if not eradicated, through the transformative work of a language held in common. The idealism and utopian import of this stance needs to be seen alongside the pervading realism of Blaser's engagement. Between Self and Other and selves and others, Blaser has situated his lifework—and, by extension, those readers who form its community—within a humane and plurivocal space of language. It remains open to each of us to locate ourselves amidst those other "awesome sweet laborers / of something" (*Holy* 240).

NOTES

I am indebted throughout my discussion here to several individuals. In particular, I would like to acknowledge and thank Robin Blaser for his generosity in answering a number of questions related to the work discussed here. I would also like to thank

Miriam Nichols, whose discussion in letters to me of the particular meanings of "social" and "public" as applied to Blaser's work has been a significant influence on the essay in its present form. Finally, I want to acknowledge the contribution of the late Barry Cox, who read and commented on an earlier version of this essay and whose providing of key and hard-to-find essays by Blaser came at a crucial moment in this essay's development.

1. See my "In the Shadow of Nerval: Robert Duncan, Robin Blaser and the Poetics of (Mis)Translation."
2. Personal correspondence with author, August 22, 1996.
3. For a lucid account of Arendt's thinking as it relates to these two key terms, see Canovan, esp. 110-22. Of particular importance for my discussion here is Canovan's observation that the public holds such preeminent status in Arendt's work because "it is only in the public realm that reality discloses itself" (111).
4. I am grateful to Miriam Nichols for bringing this passage to my attention. Blaser's hostility to the essentializing discourses of humanism, those "closures of our thought of reality," is articulated in the sternest terms. For Blaser, emphasis on the multiple and interconnected suggests a resolute rejection of the "version of humanism that collapses into itself, worldless, and leaves the large numbers of people who define it moiling" ("Recovery" 19).
5. As is evident from even a cursory reading of Blaser's poems, they are built through the overlapping motifs of allusion and textual citation, gathering sources into the processive measures of the poem's thought. While this collaging of multiple discourses and sources (of the found, the chance discovered, or the trouvée) remains a signal strategy of modernist writing from Pound onward, Blaser's handling of materials suggests a more relational and less autocratic intent than that of Pound, Eliot, et al. Rather than the imposition of a cultural knowledge base (as in *The Cantos* or even *The Maximus Poems*), Blaser alternatively offers an "opening up" of the terms by which we acquire meaning and knowledge of the world. Opposing systematic argument in favor of elision, obliquity, and suggestiveness, the arrangement of materials in Blaser's poems is very much what they are about. They smudge the traditional equation of form and content as stated by Creeley ("Form is never more than an extension of content") to arrive at form that is content and vice versa.
6. For a full account of this exchange between Blaser and Olson, as well as other matters from their early correspondence, see "Charles Olson to Robin Blaser, Part I: Robin Blaser in Massachusetts—with an introduction to the letters by Robin Blaser."
7. Duncan's best known Vietnam War poem, "Passages 25: Uprising," which appears in his 1968 volume, *Bending the Bow*, provides a provocative counter-example of how socio-political content is brought to bear on poetic discourse. While Duncan's is clearly the more outraged and politically vocal text in terms of its content, it also suggests the limits of a kind of writing that subsumes the current and topical into a poetic language reliant on immediate and emotional responses. Inasmuch as Blaser's poem is "about" the destruction of Vietnamese human life and culture, it remains situated in a Mallarméan *ethos* of absent presence—a poetic stance in which the

potentially overwhelming historical realities of the present are folded into overlapping layers of reality.

WORKS CITED

Arendt, Hannah. *Men In Dark Times.* New York: Harcourt, 1968.
_____. *The Human Condition.* Chicago: U of Chicago P, 1958.
_____. *The Origins of Totalitarianism.* New York: Meridian, 1958.
Blaser, Robin. "Charles Olson to Robin Blaser, Part 1: Robin Blaser in Massachusetts—with an introduction to the letters by Robin Blaser." Ed. Ralph Maud. *Minutes of the Charles Olson Society* 8 (June 1995).
_____. "A Correspondence." *Capilano Review* 2.17-18 (1996): 96-108.
_____. "The Fire." *Caterpillar* 12 (1970): 15-23. Rpt. in *The Poetics of the New American Poetry.* Ed. Donald Allen and Warren Tallman. New York: Grove, 1973.
_____. "Hello!" *Sulfur* 37 (1995): 84-94.
_____. *The Holy Forest.* Toronto: Coach House, 1993.
_____. *Image-Nations 1-12 & The Stadium of the Mirror.* London: Ferry Press, 1974.
_____. "Particles." *Pacific Nation* 2 (1969): 27-42.
_____. "Poetry and Positivisms: High Muck-A-Muck or 'Spiritual Ketchup.'" *Silence, the Word and the Sacred.* Ed. E. D. Blodgett and H. G. Coward. Calgary: Calgary Institution for the Humanities, 1989. 21-50.
_____. "The Practice of Outside." *The Collected Books of Jack Spicer.* Ed. Robin Blaser. Santa Barbara: Black Sparrow, 1980. 271-329.
_____. "The Recovery of the Public World" and "Afterthoughts." *Cultural Policies: Past, Present, Future.* Calgary: Calgary Institute for the Humanities, 1993.
Broch, Hermann. *The Death of Virgil.* Trans. Jean Starr Untermeyer. New York: Pantheon Books, 1945. San Francisco: North Point, n.d.
Canovan, Margaret. *Hannah Arendt: A Reinterpretation of Her Political Thought.* New York: Cambridge UP, 1992.
DuPlessis, Rachel Blau. "The Blazes of Poetry: Remarks on Segmentivity and Seriality with Special Reference to Blaser and Oppen." *The Recovery of the Public World.* Ed. Edward Byrne and Charles Watts. Vancouver: Talonbooks, 1999. 287-99.
Godzich, Wlad. "The Further Possibility of Knowledge." Forward. *Heterologies: Discourse on the Other.* By Michel de Certeau. Trans. Brian Massumi. Minneapolis: U of Minnesota P, 1986. vii-xxi.
Merleau-Ponty, Maurice. *The Visible and the Invisible.* Trans. Alphonso Lingis. Evanston: Northwestern UP, 1968.
Mossin, Andrew. "In the Shadow of Nerval: Robert Duncan, Robin Blaser and the Poetics of (Mis)Translation." *Contemporary Literature* 38. 4 (1997): 673-704.

Nichols, Miriam. "Three for Public: Steve McCaffery, Nicole Brossard, Robin Blaser." *Public 12: Utopias*. Toronto: Public Access, 1995: 97-111.

_____. "Robin Blaser's Poetics of Relation: Thinking Without Banisters." *Sagetrieb* 9. 1-2 (1990): 122-46.

Rasula, Jed. "Taking Out the Tracks: Robin Blaser's Syncopation." *Sulfur* 37 (1995): 95-107.

Spicer, Jack. *The Collected Books*. Ed Robin Blaser. Santa Barbara: Black Sparrow, 1980.

WRITING/REPEATING COMMUNITY: ROBIN BLASER'S *IMAGE-NATION* SERIES

Scott Pound

> *[T]he 'I' that is always beyond itself is a rascal—
> beribboned with the colours of permanence—
> repeatedly forgiving itself for its curious permu-
> tions. Language, which is not simply a structure
> studied by linguists, philosophers, and theologians,
> is a biological gift and a vortex where the 'I' abides.*
> –Robin Blaser
> (unpublished letter to Scott Pound)

Robin Blaser's *Image-Nation* poems[1]—a serial progression of, to date, twenty-five numbered, subtitled poems of variable length and formal distinctiveness—have as their primary characteristic a resistance to absolutism, or that which is without relation.[2] As the flow of meaning appears to approach stasis in a single term, the poem doubles back on itself:

> the starry issue
>   the horizon
>   the beauty
> and terror composed inextricably mingled
> in an unfixed freedom. (134)

This doubling back to the beauty *and* terror "composed . . . / in an unfixed freedom" is repeatedly enacted and variously thematized throughout the series. Here, a beauty that is not somehow traversed by terror is not beauty. Likewise, terror raised to apocalyptic levels is repulsive in its uniformity:

this thought of the end of the end is the modern
sweetness and terror, but it simplifies to terror
alone—this societal dream of itself as absolute
reality, then practiced as uniformity and barbarism,
is the oily turn-table of the round-house where we
repair the engine again and again—it is the
absolute humanism that is repulsive . . . . (188)

This resistance to the absolute in Blaser is an unusual function of repetition: the repeated deployment of resistance, which introduces into Blaser's text a new form of the repetitive exigency—to expose relationality in its active, differentiating moment. Thus everything returns to the edges of words in Blaser. Language must brush up against, fold onto, an Otherness, an Outside, and it must do so repeatedly:

The task of man   and his words
Is at the edge
where we are translated (116)

the Beloved   is the murmur
inside   the work

at the edge of the words
the silence   is the Other
at the edge   of my words (117)

he is to become that
governs   entangles   at the edge

of his words (144)

In reading the *Image-Nations*, not for what they might have to say *about* "community" as an exemplary figure or determining concept, but for the resistance they repeatedly enact to exemplarity itself, I will be attempting to demonstrate how repetition functions within a textual politics by locating community at the level of the text's deployment as a perpetual unworking of what is, in aesthetic and political terms, a too easy transcendence. In the *Image-Nation* series, Blaser demonstrates that community is a matter of repeatedly exposing relations rather than a substance.

The series as a whole is built on several extended parallelisms between its various terms: image and nation, word and body, public and private, visible and invisible, *etc.* These terms are not readable as rigid oppositions but occur as co-present intensities that literally revolve around one another. There are always at least two series simultaneously, but non-symmetrically, entwined: the one texturing as the other etherializes, one sounding as the other colors, one telling as the other shows, and so on. The poems work themselves into a potentially infinite series of crossings and folds:

> the co-herence falls like rain,
> into the syllables
>
>   this in-herence
>
> of a golden poem
>
>   translating
>
> blood, dancers,
>
>   and whirling
>
> drunken lives
>
>   into a tense
>
> music
>   of a hollyhock. (115)

The interplay here between, for example, the textured (rain, blood, dancers, drunken lives) and the etherealized (a golden poem, music) is not a matter of simple opposition but of a dual momentum that exposes, not one series over the other, but the reflection of the one in the other—in other words, relationality itself, or as Blaser says, "*the necessity of exchange between the spheres*" (129).

Relationality is therefore exposed, not as one might expect, through the establishment of a generality that produces "coherence," but rather through the perpetual re-opening of the series to the differences that animate it, producing what Blaser names "co-herence" (with the crucial hyphen) or differentiation itself.

There are two general ways to signify relationality in language: the use of connective words to indicate identity, difference, or levels of subordination (hypotaxis) and simple juxtaposition (parataxis). The irony of parataxis is that, while by definition it is the elimination of connective words and devices of subordination, it is the mode of a relational/differentiated poetics *par excellence*.

wind—words   wind—hair   we . . . (127)

Similarly, nothing can bring words closer together than spacing:

> the blood
>   is light
>
>
>   zero
>
> enacts it. (128)

Of course, it is necessary to view syntax and spacing in non-canonical poetry as significant in themselves and, moreover, as distinct from typical discursive practice, which is necessarily infused with connective tissue and subordination. The effect of Blaser's syntax and spacings (in the early *Image-Nations* particularly) is not a build-up of accumulated significance, but a mere setting in motion: "the meaning plays and composes before our eyes" ("Practice" 278) such that "a 'necessary world' is composed in the serial poem" (279).

"Image-Nation 4 (old gold" is a literal conflagration of images:

> . . . snow did not remain in this
> place, a black garden, the
> surface of the moon, now explained
>
> (Ella Cinders) it is a crust
> of cinders over the red coals, a
> banked fire over which no snow
>
> caught her hair if you walk
> unwary, your feet slip into the
> fire   of strawberries (64)

There is no doubt a referential context to this brief passage, but the necessary world it creates is itself. Even the appearance of a proper name (more a textual event than a person in this poem) extends no further than the next line, its presence purely functional to the poem's movement, refracting as it does aspects of the layered, asymmetrical series of snow/fire, white/black, black/red, fecundity/barrenness, surface/depth, and so on.

If it is true that Blaser begins (and ends) with the repetition of difference, then we must also note the implications of where he does not begin. He, of course, does not begin with the solitary subject. We forget this at a cost, because the absence of subjectivity as an organizing principle in Blaser's poetry is significant. The dislodging of the subject—firstly, as a vehicle for a certain kind of meaning (an interiorized and disengaged meaning); secondly, in contradictory fashion, as both the source of unmediated expression and the means by which the "truth" of such expression is totalized; and thirdly, as a reservoir of momentous but unexamined value—opens up a new space of *poesis* that is without perceptible boundaries.

Blaser defines the poem as "a making that is not self-expression." This comment immediately recalls Olson's critique of the Poundian ego and Spicer's impatience with "the big lie of the personal," but is reducible to neither. Blaser's resistance to the absolute undifferentiated subject resonates formally and politically in ways that are different from that of Olson and Spicer. First, it dislodges the poem from generic limitations. Deprived of its fixity in either the lyric self or the epic world, the serial poem unfolds in a kind of middle distance. The poem thus does not re-present a circumscribed locus whether inside or outside, cosmic or geographical, but repeats the sort of "coherence," or being-with—equally a property of words and bodies—that is the condition of possibility for community. The poem presents

> that matter of language caught
> in the fact   so that we
> meet in paradise   in such
> times, the I consumes itself. (61)

Language "caught in the fact," as opposed to language suspended in benign personalisms or fictive absolutes, provides the precondition for an actual meeting which can and does stand as the literal condition of community. In this passage, the fact of language, as a field of possibilities and inexhaustable relations, supplants the "I" as the site of utopian possibility.

But it is also important in a discussion of Blaser's poetry to distinguish community from cosmology. Atopian is perhaps a better word than utopian since it accounts for the decenteredness of the poem's deployment and avoids the highly idealized implications and textual strategies of utopianism. Community names a relation that stays relation, to modify a Poundianism; cosmology is the end result of a collective of relations, a totality. Since community is for Blaser (as it is for Nancy, Blanchot, and Agamben) first and foremost a possibility, any form of writing that proposes to expose this possibility must resist everything that would hypostasize it in a definitive representation. "Writing/repeating community" then is a form of ideology critique, or as Nancy says in a phrase that Blaser will eventually borrow, "the inscription of our infinite resistance" (81). To paraphrase Blanchot, what matters is to let a possibility manifest itself beyond any utilitarian gain in meaning. The title *Image-Nation* does not denote a totality that the poems represent; it names the activity the poems enact, which is, as Blaser phrases it, "the constant / movement / of a finitide / which re opens" (115).

The poem's insistence on unsublated relation over totality is evident throughout *The Holy Forest*, but probably nowhere as explicitly related to community as in Blaser's treatment of a single word. "Co-herence," which I quoted above, means existing together, side-by-side, rather than "coherence"—the integrity of parts within a whole. More definitive than any sense of building that goes on in Blaser's poetry is the fact of the poem's insistent and repeated unworking of totality. It is, finally, this very unworking that defines the poem as what might be called an event (or example) of *communitas*.[3]

In "Image-Nation 2 (roaming," the traditional model of communication (and thereby of community) as a form of closed circuitry is jarred out of its polar fixity. The "journey" referred to in the opening line does not extend from point A to point B, but occurs "in company with the messenger," which is to say somewhere between origin and end, at the interval (integral) point of relation or "company." The "'you'" of the poem is literally held in abeyance (i.e. enclosed in quotation marks) recalling the "I" of "Image-Nation 1" which "consumes itself" so that, in the line immediately preceding, "we meet in paradise" [emphasis added]. "I" and "you" in Blaser are not discreet entities standing at sites polar to one another, traversed by the message; they are part of a "we" that "journey[s] in company with the messenger" (62). The specificity of this company, irrespective of where it begins or ends, is the focus of the poem.

The work of community is not an essence—that is, not the property of a "message" that might purport to define a collectivity—but an operative function akin to tarrying with the messenger. As Blaser has most recently emphasized it, community is a fact of "the mind's play and the body's extension into relations among things—an indeterminate, various, resistant finitude" ("Hello" 87).

But what is being resisted?

The answer is ideology. Ideology happens when content is permitted to devour form. In the context of the series as a whole, "image" functions as an index to this finitude and as that which keeps ideology—"the oily turn-table of the round-house where we / repair the engine again and again" (188)—at bay. Ideology critique in Blaser's poetry takes place at the level of the "image," which for Blaser is a cipher for the quality of finitude.

"Image-Nation 5 (erasure" begins:

> as the image wears away
> there is a wind in the heart
>
> the translated men
> disappear into what they have
> translated. (113)

For Blaser, the image is the site of primary intensity in the poem, not as figure, but, following Pound, as a nexus of sound, texture, and meaning, an eventfulness rather than a representation. Any poetic mobilization of community would thereby employ a functional as opposed to a representational language: a language of indeterminacy, variance, and resistance. Indeed, it is only "by way of resistance" that community can hope to preserve itself in the face of a totality, which as Blaser tells us, "is very careless of our finitude" ("Hello" 90). The term "writing/repeating community" serves to preserve this sense of functionality and resistance and to distinguish Blaser's poetry from a poetic practice that would otherwise remain suspended in a representation of community. When the eventfulness of the image is elided, sublated, or otherwise erased, as happens in ideological constructions, "there is a wind in the heart" as in "Image-Nation 5 (erasure." The "childish man" of the poem's next line would appear to be the ideologue who disappears into his doctrine, forming a

> . . . still-life
> at the edge of his body
> erasing the body of those opposites
> who are companions. (113)

The translation of specificity (finitude) into uniformity (the absolute) is thus an act of erasure in both linguistic and corporeal terms (language and the body are indissolubly of both orders), but what is erased specifically is not language or the body—these merely assume a smoother texture and a static comportment to the world—but relation or companionability between opposites.

The only way to override relation is to attempt to efface the limits that constitute the finitude of a singular being. The absorption of this specificity into transcendence and thereby the erasure of limits that constitute relation—in short, the becoming absolute of finitude—is the traditional notion of what poetry does. In Blaser, the opposite takes place. Words come back to participate in "their commotion" and "nonsense":

> The words do not end but come back
> From the adventure
>   The body is at the edge
> Of their commotion
>   The nonsense
> The marvelous clarity
>   In the pool of the
> Heart. (113)

The transformation of the heart from a barren landscape into a reservoir sets off a series of transformations at the level of the image. The "childish man" becomes "the flowered man" and we are introduced to a new kind of translation: "a translation of oneself into the other" (114).

This brings us to another moment in the series, in "Image-Nation 6 (epithalamium," when Blaser indexes yet another form of humanist terror: "a terror in the movement / of a man devouring / into his own shape" (121). Indeed, for Blaser interiority is a form of cannibalism: "(to be refreshed from evil // we have eaten ourselves   luxurious / and careless" (127). To write/repeat community means to actively and ceaselessly (repeatedly) disrupt any process of aesthetic or discursive totalization. To write community is to resist ideology through the constant unworking of the coordinates that congeal to form thought-less constructions.

In contrast to the idealizing, cannibalizing process of ideology is the continuous undressing of the wor(l)d in these *Image-Nations*, to show it, not in unmediated nakedness, but as clothed in its own dou-bleness. The insistent doubleness of the poems—"the unfamiliarity of the familiar," "heart-heartless," "visible-invisible," "image-image-less"—exposes, rather than represents, the material condition of rela-tionality. This kind of exposition is a presentation of words at their limit *as words*.

We need to note, however, some qualities about the later *Image-Nations*. An epistemological break of sorts occurs in the series around "Image-Nation 17," skipping "Image-Nation 18," which is more or less formally consistent with the earlier ones. Blaser's touchstones in the earlier poems of the series—arch-modernists like Mallarmé, Pound, Olson, and Whitehead—are updated, and we begin to see references to the progenitors of postmodern discourse—Merleau-Ponty, Lacan, Foucault, Geoffrey Hartman and others. But the effect of this is odd in that it takes the poems in a decidedly different direction; radical parataxis and the friction that it generates between words in the early *Image-Nations* gives way to a highly discursive, meditative style as Blaser seems to embark on a reading of the earlier *Image-Nations* through the veil of baroque art and the mediation of theory. The later poems begin to read less like baroque objects and more like notes toward some supreme fiction, in an elegiac key. Lines like:

> so we've gone from one thing
> to another (213)

and

> I have told many things and want
> to tell more in a short time (255)

situate the poems within a much more discursive and reflective environment than that of the earlier *Image-Nations*.

"Image-Nation 17" is titled "opercula." An operculum is a fish's gill cover and can also denote the lid-like structures in plants or the valve in shells that closes their mouths. It's a wonderful image but also a telling one. The fold of the earlier *Image-Nations* turns into a flap, as if the poems began to be deprived of oxygen. Formally, they lose distinctiveness as Blaser begins to write in increasingly long strings of phrases and appropriates whole blocks of text from other sources rather than a few words. The rhetoric implied in the spacings of the earlier poems is sucked up into the text, and everything starts sticking to the left margin.

The effect of the citations in these later *Image-Nations* is particularly different. The earlier poems include swatches of, mostly, poetry marked by italics. The later ones appropriate whole yards of theory and use them to meditate on earlier works of art. There is a riff on Robert Graves in "Image-Nation 22," a Duchamp meditation in 23, and a long section devoted to Bosch via de Certeau in 25. Whereas in the earlier *Image-Nations* there was a layering of textual events, here we have layers of discursive speculation on substitute cosmologies. Many of the passages Blaser quotes in the later *Image-Nations*, for example from de Certeau, read like descriptions of the event-character of the earlier poems of the serial:

> *coming into meaning and going out—this space is curved inward upon itself, like the circles and ellipses Bosch endlessly generates, there is no entrance, only interpretive delirium, fragments of a language, a lacunary system, a cosmos unsure of its postulates—displaces units of meaning piece by piece.* (368-69)

This change in register is interesting for its own sake as an example of a poem beginning to feed off its own activity. The technique of reflecting on the poem's activity from within the poem itself seems to betray the a-discursive quality of the earlier poems. And yet, the baroque quality of these later meditations does not limit the fluxes that the earlier "Image Nations" commit themselves to.

We are not in Blaser dealing with a major poetic world *à la* Olson or even a cosmology in the full sense of Duncan's use of the term, but rather with an embryonic or virtual world to come: "syllables of a longing for completion" (116) but not the completion itself. Words for Blaser "foment a largeness," but they are not themselves this largeness. Rather they trace and re-trace the limit of their own togetherness; the largeness they foment is the largeness of unassimilable difference that is created when words are permitted to glide off and fold onto one another as things would. The limit they trace then is not one of signification—the limit after which the ineffable takes over—but the limit at which the singular being (not a subject) meets another singular being.

NOTES

1. All references to the poems are from *The Holy Forest*.
2. Miriam Nichols has written a noteworthy essay on "Robin Blaser's Poetics of Relation" in which relationality is viewed as constitutive of cosmology. My own treatment of relationality in Blaser will differ from Nichols's in its attempt to situate relationality with regard to community, the functioning of which I propose is antithetical to that of cosmology.
3. "Unworking" (or "the unworking") is Pierre Joris's translation of Maurice Blanchot's very important phrase (which Jean-Luc Nancy also uses) "*le désoeuvrement*." The term is essential to both Blanchot and Nancy's attempts to think community as a functional though non-productive experience of finitude or "the unworking of social, economic, technical, institutional work" (Nancy 25).

WORKS CITED

Blaser, Robin. "Hello." *Sulfur* 37 (1995): 84-94.
_____. *The Holy Forest*. Toronto: Coach House, 1993.
_____. "The Practice of Outside." *The Collected Books of Jack Spicer*. Santa Barbara: Black Sparrow, 1980. 271-329.
_____. "The Stadium or the Mirror." *Image-Nations 1-12*. London: Ferry Press, 1974. 53-64.
Joris, Pierre. "Translator's Preface." *The Unavowable Community*. By Maurice Blanchot. New York: Station Hill, 1988. xxii-xxv.
Nancy, Jean-Luc. *The Inoperative Community*. Trans. Peter Connor, Lisa Garbus, Michael Holland, Simona Sawhney. Minneapolis: U of Minnesota P, 1991.
Nichols, Miriam. "Robin Blaser's Poetics of Relation: Thinking Without Bannisters." *Sagetrieb* 9.1 -2 (1990): 121-46.

AN ELEGY FOR THEORY: ROBIN BLASER'S ESSAY "THE PRACTICE OF OUTSIDE"

Peter Middleton

BLASER AND THE AMERICAN POETICS ESSAY

Robin Blaser's essay on Jack Spicer, "The Practice of Outside," is one of the small number of key essays on poetics that have helped define the practice of innovative poetry in North America, yet it remains much less well known than those by other New American poets and Language Writers. The genre of the poetics essay itself is small and marginal anyway, and only a tiny number of the essays remain significant much beyond their moment of emergence for any but historians of modern poetry. Almost all these essays have been published by small presses, and they are usually strongly addressed to poets at a specific moment, urging them with retrospective admonitions and prospective possibilities to forge some new and necessary form of poetry. Rhetoric is only part of it. They often display a knowledge of aesthetics, politics, philosophy, and history usually only found in academic papers, but these essays can't rely on the institutional protocols and agendas by which new ideas and interpretations are guided in the academic press. The other side of this is a freedom to let their language fold back on itself in thicknesses of texture and sound, while shouting or whispering visionary pronouncements whose claim to universality may simply extrapolate local, even eccentric, beliefs. It all makes for strain, as excessive formal structures and not quite attained ideas create the friction of too many commas slowing the sentence to stutters, or raise the volume of stridency and passion almost to the point of unintelligibility. These are essays more than usually out on the edge of articulation. They enact the importance of poetry as polemical instruction knowing that poets may resist anything they suspect is a coercion of their practice and critics are likely to reduce it all to documentary evidence of the position and poetry of its author. So the best of these essays are usually unclassifiable prose which remains hard to assimilate into any hermeneutic systematization of an author's poetry, refuses to be a recipe for composition, and resists co-optation as public relations for a literary movement.

"The Practice of Outside," one of the best and most lucid of these essays, is also even more unclassifiable than most. Ostensibly about Jack Spicer, it is also a strong statement of Blaser's own considered poetics as the third and least widely published of the group he formed with Jack Spicer and Robert Duncan in San Francisco in the late 1940s. This is not so much because Blaser is avowedly uninterested in "the poet of a limited biographical occasion" ("Practice" 281), and avoids repeating the usual contemporary practice of reducing discourse to "a sadly limited personality" (280), as because the essay is an elegy. Like the poetic elegy, the essay finds consolation through a substituted figure, and as Peter Sacks argues in his *The English Elegy*, also in the very process of such substitution itself. The absence of Jack Spicer becomes a trope for the absence of the subject in all discourse, which the essay claims Spicer explored in his poetry. Elegiac poets commonly draw upon the discourse of the pastoral. Blaser's shepherds are two recent French intellectuals. The phenomenology of one helped provoke the poststructuralist rejection of the philosophy of the subject; the other helped inaugurate the moment of poststructuralism. From Maurice Merleau-Ponty's posthumous *The Visible and the Invisible* Blaser takes the radical epistemology of indwelling that Merleau-Ponty investigates through the experience of visibility, and its dependence upon the non-visible. Michel Foucault's announcement of the "death of man" in the spirit of Nietzsche's Zarathustran declaration of the death of God, enables Blaser to make an astonishing identification between this trope for a shift in the historical episteme away from the subject-centered knowledge of the past two hundred years, and the death of one particular poet. Foucault's "man" is treated as if he were the modern equivalent of the vegetation god whose death (and expected rebirth) is alluded to in the personification of the seasons in poetic elegy. Sacks asks why a humanized deity should represent nature at all, using the very collective pronoun whose demise Foucault had announced:

Why, after all, should man so bitterly lament the passing of a season that he knows will return unless it is his own unreturning
nature that he mourns? And why should he represent nature by a
human form unless he wants in this instance not only to mourn
his own image but also to identify that image with nature's powers of regeneration? (20)

In Blaser's essay the poet becomes the figure for a historical change
which is then paradoxically implied to be a cyclical process by this
close simulation of the poetic elegy. The author is dead, long live the
author! Instead of a poststructuralism in which poetic intention,
planning, and compositional skill are tied to a humanism of an autobiographical impulse that denies its position in language, Blaser
imagines a poetry of a newly comprehended subjectivity in language
which can make effective representations in public spheres, and not
simply remain closed in a verbal circuit of unbroken self-referential
chains of syntax. How he does this, and how persuasively, is the
theme of this essay.

Blaser's timing was fortuitous. Although Spicer had died in 1965,
the essay only appeared in 1975 as a modest part of the apparatus of
The Collected Books of Jack Spicer, one of the most beautiful books
ever produced by Black Sparrow Press. From about 1972 onward a
rapid shift of paradigms from the New American poetry to Language
Writing altered the discourses of innovative poetics and radically
altered the practice of poetry, and by 1975 the new paradigm was
beginning to cohere. The essay was composed during a brief inter-
regnum when it was possible to formulate a poetics that could draw
upon the *doxa* of the earlier paradigm and the improvisations of the
emergent, in a dialectical argument that was also facilitated by
Blaser's position as an electively Canadian writer. Independence
from any local American poetic *socius* gave Blaser's inwardness with
the American poetry scene a perspective that enabled him to do what
no other poet of the time could have done: reformulate the terms of
the shifting debate with the help of concepts drawn from that French
culture with which Canada has special affinities.

The rapid abandonment of the projects associated with Charles
Olson, and to a lesser extent Robert Duncan, Denise Levertov and
Robert Creeley, by Language Writers, had many causes, but one of

the most commonly cited is the insistence of the self in the New American Poetry. Existential self-display as a guarantee of authenticity was looking stiff and mannered by the early seventies. Charles Olson had died, Robert Duncan had muted himself by deciding not to publish, Robert Creeley was writing little, and Denise Levertov, although still very active, was like many poets, almost completely defining her poetics by anti-war projects. The shift was most evident in the practice, which immediately implied a thorough rejection of the politics and poetics of poetic self-expression, however organic, open, or attentive to speech. Explanations came later, and were usually respectful of the earlier generation, and therefore often cautious in their judgments. A more explicit, if somewhat crude case against the New American ethos was made by the critic Andrew Ross in his book *The Failure of Modernism* (1986), in a psychoanalytic study of Olson. (Ross, an editor of *Social Text*, has been an enthusiastic exponent of Language Writing.) What might seem to be the most enduring feature of Olson's work, his re-theorization of history and the consequent practice in his poetry, is summarily dismissed as failing to be "an organized field of knowledge, despite the efforts of students and critics to round it off as a 'system'" (110). Ross discards the historicism quickly because he does not want to be distracted by epistemological issues from the supposedly more foundational questions about the nature of language. He thinks that Olson mistakenly believed that he could single-handedly reform the language, not realizing that such an attempt to "rewrite the laws of language" reveals such a depth of delusive belief in the possibility of a transcendent subjectivity outside language, when subjectivity is evidently only alight in the cells of discourse, that the poet's state can almost be described as "psychotic" (105). "Olson's attempts, then, to 'make English behave' are a way of idealizing a new fully 'completed man' with linguistic powers over and above the inherited social codes of communication" (104). To Ross this is psychotic disavowal, yet Ross's own description echoes with the elegiac rhetoric of subjectivity in a manner which might suggest other possibilities. Olson, we might say, tries to deny the death of man which Foucault announced, by poetically inventing a maximal man, an ideal whose powers derive from a sovereign power over language, while failing to recognize that this superfigure is merely a demonstration of the tropic power of language itself. Ross, we might say, reads Olson as an anachronistic elegist.

Ross's cursory rejection of Olson's poetry of knowledge means that he loses sight of a dimension of the poetry which even a critic as skeptical of Olson's overall achievement as Robert Von Hallberg still concedes can be defended on cognitive grounds, at least as far as the first volume of *The Maximus Poems* is concerned.

> It is proper for a poetry that desires to communicate knowledge to declare itself bound by the structures of historical accuracy . . . . As long as Olson stayed close to the record he could allow his language to move toward abstraction; he could articulate precepts that were directly related to the specific subject at hand
>
> (212)

The poem achieves this because "the mind guiding the sequence at this point is a generalizing one that transforms facts into instances by articulating propositions" (212). The problem with the later poems is that they don't produce knowledge, just "an order so distinctly Olson's own that it offers readers little else than a show; there are no principles to be abstracted from the subjects of the later poems" (213). Hallberg's balanced assessment presupposes that knowledge exists and can be communicated, that history can be known with an objectivity which makes accuracy a possible value, and finally, and most unpalatably for poststructuralists, that the author's voluntarist will can help shape the formation and presentation of knowledge. A position as extreme as Ross's mix of Foucauldian and Lacanian theory, characteristic of literary theory in the 1980s, has no place for objectivity and mental guides. All knowledge is produced by the ideological workings of power, and the mind is a unified agent only in the mirror of its own imaginary. The effect of Ross's fervent poststructuralism is that Hallberg's judgment that Olson's poetry unfortunately loses its value when it becomes egocentric is turned into the determinist conviction that Olson's beliefs about subjectivity made it impossible for him to achieve a field of knowledge at all. Although Ross says that Olson fails to produce an *"organized field* of knowledge" it is hard to see how Ross's poetics would enable any poetics to do this. Ross's clever reading of Olson's work as a struggle with his own father derives its concepts from that particular synthesis of Foucault, Jacques Lacan, Jacques Derrida and Roland Barthes, which called itself Theory in the 1980s, and the dogmas of this tendentious systematization render him unable to comprehend some of Olson's arguments.

The kind of difficulty which this synthesis might encounter with Olson can be glimpsed in an extraordinary coda to Foucault's *Archaeology of Knowledge* (1969—available in translation in 1972). If the making of poetry can reasonably be described as dependent upon what Foucault calls a "constituent subjectivity" then he seems to be unwittingly banishing the making of poetry not only from the *polis* (a term favored by Olson, partly because of Plato's dismissal of the poets from it), but from the entire world of discourse. At the end of his outline of methodology, Foucault stages a dialogue with a skeptic who is willing to concede the critique of the limitations of structuralism but passionately defends the transcendence of language and reason, whose "constituent subjectivity" is evident in the "profound continuity" of knowledge. At first Foucault concedes nothing. His own earlier work's "essential task was to free the history of thought from its subjections to transcendence" (203). In his final rejoinder to this imagined critic, Foucault offers a concessionary sympathy for the plight of someone whose "transcendental narcissism" makes her still desperately hang on to the belief that language overcomes mortality and time, and as he enters into this articulation of the unbearable sense of loss, he begins to ventriloquise the other's voice:

> How unbearable it is, in view of how much of himself everyone wishes to put, thinks he is putting of "himself" into his own discourse, when he speaks, how unbearable it is to cut up, analyze, combine, rearrange all these texts that have now returned from silence, without ever the transfigured face of the author appearing: "What! All those words, piled up one after another, all those marks made on all that paper and presented to innumerable pairs of eyes, all that concern to make them survive beyond the gesture that articulated them, so much piety expended in preserving them and inscribing them in men's memories—all that and nothing remaining of the poor hand that traced them, of the anxiety that sought appeasement in them, of that completed life

that has nothing but them to survive in? [. . .] Must we admit that
the time of discourse is not the time of consciousness extrapolat-
ed to the dimensions of history, or the time of history present in
the form of consciousness? Must I suppose that in my discourse
I can have no survival? And that in speaking I am not banishing
my death, but actually establishing it; or rather that I am abol-
ishing all interiority in that exterior that is so indifferent to my
life, and so *neutral*, that it makes no distinction between my life
and my death?" (210)

Foucault thinks of the interlocutor as someone who insists on mourning the loss of a power invested in a language previously imagined to
be capable of preserving at least some trace of the very origin of the
interlocutor's being in its cryogenic mausoleum ready for future
technologies of reading to reawaken the remains to life again. Having
cast himself in the role of analyst to the narcissistic ordinary person,
Foucault goes one stage further in his final remarks. Such people
believe, he says, that "they must preserve that tiny fragment of
discourse—whether written or spoken—whose fragile uncertain existence must perpetuate their lives" (211), against the loss of autonomy
to the rules and transformations by which discourse is really maintained. This remarkably determinist, anti-democratic stance, which
belittles the sense of loss he depicts, results from his unwillingness to
consider his theory in terms of a loss to be mourned, yet at the same
time presents his poststructuralist theory as an antidote to mourning.
Yet as Freud showed, the antidote to mourning may be the failure to
deal with it which he diagnosed as melancholy.

Ross's portrait of Olson seems to be borrowed from this interlocutor, as Ross re-enacts this dialogue of poststructuralist superiority to an
attributed mourning for the loss of autonomous agency, in a manner
which was endlessly repeated during the past two decades. Ross at
least has more reason than some poststructuralist critics, for it could
seem as if poetry like Olson's deserves to have its unexamined egoism
checked. In every poem, in every essay, the poet insists on the letter
"I," to the point where his claim to be uninterested in the emotional,
psychological self might seem outrageous. Nor is Olson alone. The
New American poets consistently write the specular consciousness,
and only occasionally recognize that the mirror might be morphing
the self (in John Ashbery's "Self-Portrait in a Convex Mirror"), or

recognize that the words of the poem are, in Philip Whalen's final words in *Self-Portrait from Another Direction*:

> an exorbitance-
> slingstone hurled at a tangent to the circle
> in which it lately whirled
> zipping off in high-speed parabola
> Into the mirror (NOW showing many men) all of them "I"
>   (n.pag.)

The hegemony of the poetic ego led the Language Writers to believe that the earlier generation were engaged in what Charles Bernstein called in an essay published in 1983, the "mapping of consciousness in writing . . . charting the role of the self in mediating human knowledge of the world" (14). This judicious assessment's emphasis on "charting the role of the self" rather than on the "knowledge" is characteristic of the paradigm shift. In the passage that follows, Bernstein offered one of the most intriguing accounts of the generational perspective when he offered his own phenomenological response to the New American poetry, saying:

> The mapping of consciousness in writing does undercut one sense of the sealed-offness from other minds by charting the role of the self in mediating human knowledge of the world. The peculiarities that form the trace of consciousness and make it specific or individual demonstrate the *partialness* of any construction of mind or reality, in sharp contrast to the universality of claim in the tone of many conventional writing modes. This acknowledging and charting of partialness does in fact break the monologic spell of writing seen as a transparent medium to the world beyond it, but it does so only by making a projection of self central to its methodology. In the end, this practice leaves the reader as sealed-off from the self enacted within it as conventional writing does from the world pictured within it; while the trace may frame the reader, it also exteriorizes him/her; while it critiques the suprapersonal transcendental projection, it creates its own metaphysical fiction of the person. The experience is of a self bound off from me in its autonomy, enclosed in its self-sufficiency. The power of this besideness is that it (re)creates the conditions of nature itself, and so is a model of the human experience of it, human relations to it. But I feel not only simultane-

ously outside nature and constituted by nature, but also that I am
constituting it! (14)

Knowledge is still admitted as a legitimate goal of poetry, but now it
has to be local, perspectival knowledge making the observer's stance
visible. The necessarily abstract generality of this historical overview
of recent literary history also has the effect of attributing the importance of this poetry to its metapoetic strategies. Demonstrating the
limited perspective of the knowledge is what the poem is about, not
so much the knowledge itself, which in any case is *only* a construction. Such an interpretation assumes that saying it is a construction is
sufficient to deactivate and fully comprehend it. But perhaps we
ought to be looking at other dimensions of social construction.
Michael Taussig's comment that the mere identification of social
construction as such, which once seemed a productive and conclu-
sive insight, should now be recognized to be only a first step, may be
pertinent here:

> I think construction deserves more respect, it cannot be name-
> called out of (or into) existence, ridiculed and shamed into yield-
> ing up its powers. And if its nature seems to prevent us—for are
> we not also socially constructed?—from peering deeply therein,
> that very same nature also cries out for something other than
> analysis as this is usually practiced in reports to our Academy. For
> in construction's place—what? No more invention, or more
> invention? And if the latter, as is assuredly the case, why don't we
> start inventing? Is it because at this point the critic fumbles the
> pass and the "literary turn" in the social sciences and historical
> studies yields naught else but more meta-commentary in place
> of poesis, little by way of making it new? (xvi)

The poesis of knowledge in the New American poetry may have been
much more than just a demonstration of its constructedness.

Unlike Ross, Bernstein tries to distinguish between the transcendent subjectivity that Foucault elegizes and this new, but still dubi-
ous, metaphysics of self. The self may no longer be a transcendent
and therefore unapproachable guarantee of what is said, but it now
turns into a story of the I, which has no material base. Bernstein then
dramatizes his own feelings about this self, as if to produce his own

counter fiction to it. These New American selves like Olson's are out
of touch, you can't dialogue with them, they hold themselves apart,
as if they were absent in being present. What remains, the trace of
consciousness, is as fixed and autonomous as a statue, a materiality
which assimilates it to the material world (Olson said that "man and
external reality are so involved with one another that, for man's purposes, they had better be taken as one" ["Human" 60]). Then comes
the almost violent affective reaction to this, signaled by an exclamation. This is the claim to be "constituting" the natural world, and
therefore such others as well, based on an appeal to feeling which
allows the essay to admit that this experience may be the very delusion of which Foucault wrote (it is just a feeling after all), and yet at
the same time suggests that such invention may somehow still be possible without restoring an authoritarian humanism. Maybe it is possible for the subject to constitute the world after all. A similar proposal can be traced in other Language Writers. Bruce Andrews's essay
"Constitution / Writing, Politics, Language, the Body" (1982) argues
that in conventional literature "signifying is not ascribed the privilege
of constituting the social world" (155), and this works "to deprive
history and interaction and production of their creativity" (156). What
is needed is a "countersocialization," which will reinstate a degree of
voluntarism, as is implied when Bob Perelman, analyzing Clark
Coolidge's procedures in *American Ones* concludes that in such
poetry, "signification, the primary fact of language, is no longer an
automatic process" (Perelman 34). Bernstein's willingness to allow a
form of "constituent subjectivity" is not an extreme idealism, but a
more materialist belief that certain cultural practices can encourage
a reader to recognize that s/he is at work in the invention of intersubjectivity and knowledge, through a new position as reader, made
aware of the "fact of projection" (16) in the process of writing. The
essay ends by saying of the new poem that "its truth is not assumed but
made" (16), to emphasize the primacy of this writing, and its refusal to
rely on prior authorities for its conclusions.

   What I now want to suggest is that the earlier generation does not
have to be read in quite the way that their successors assume. One of
Ross's evidences for the psychotic tendency of Olson's project is the
well-known claim in Olson's wonderful poetics essay "Human

Universe" that the problem with most existing arts is that they are caught by "the dodges of discourse. . . . For any of us, at any instant, are juxtaposed to any experience, even an overwhelming single one, on several more planes than the arbitrary and discursive which we inherit can declare" (qtd. in Ross 105). To Ross this is further evidence that Olson never allows for doubt, dialogue, or alternatives, and that he thinks that he has direct knowledge of the world that ordinary language subsequently distorts. Ross misses Olson's main point that poetry should aspire to the accuracies of science and other knowledge practices in its representation of its discoveries, and that this requires attention to the effects of language, even if he does also give credence to a version of the recurrent twentieth-century desire for *linguistic* perfectibility. We should note that the idea of being immersed in the world beyond the capacity of any one sense to represent it has many affinities with the work of Merleau-Ponty. An example would be the following attempt to use sight as a trope for the process of making knowledge in *The Visible and the Invisible*.

> Thus since the seer is caught up in what he sees, it is still himself he sees: there is a fundamental narcissism of all vision. And thus, for the same reason, the vision he exercises, he also undergoes from things, such that, as many painters have said, I feel myself looked at by the things, my activity is equally passivity—which is the second and more profound sense of the narcissism: not to see in the outside, as others see it, the outside, to exist within it, to emigrate into it, to be seduced, captivated, alienated by the phantom, so that the seer and the visible reciprocate one another and we no longer know which sees and which is seen. It is this Visibility, this generality of the Sensible in itself, this anonymity innate to Myself that we have previously called flesh, and one knows there is no name in traditional philosophy to designate it. (139)

This is extremely close to Olson's account of the body in "Human Universe," and yet surprisingly it also opens into other directions in recent poetry too, as Blaser shrewdly recognized. Bernstein's desire for intercourse with the self in the poetic text is anticipated here, and perhaps even more surprisingly, so is the dismissal of the fiction of self in favor of an individuated anonymity, an absence of self in the making of truth.

Olson's thought also intersects with some features of Foucault's intellectual history. At Black Mountain College in about 1956, Olson tried to set out an ambitious framework similar in scale although not in execution, to Foucault's later plan.

> Hanging over into the present from the old cosmology are three drags, each of them the offsets of the principle [sic] desire of man for Kosmos during the two millennia and a half preceding us. And the three hang about people's necks like dead birds. They are Void, Chaos, and the trope Man. Or, to put them in the order of their occurrence, Chaos, Man, Void; that is Chaos was the imagined unformed on which the order Kosmos set form. Man was the later child of the same act—a teleology of form as progressive was the hidden assumption of the old cosmology, and Void is what's left when the kosmos breaks down as the interesting evidence of order. Man falls when that purpose falls, and so Void is the only assumption left; that is, Kosmos infers Chaos as precedent to itself and Man as succeeding, and when it goes as a controlling factor, only Void becomes a premise of measure. Man is simply filling an empty space. Which turns quickly by collapse into man is skin and flesh surrounding a void as well. Void in, void out. It is the counsel of despair. Man is matter is now so dated (Spengler, the Adamses) that one can date the removal of it as a measure—1920 (Adams' date for the Doom). It has already been succeeded by a more interesting mentext [sic]: man is, and is in, void.
>   I am suggesting that a period has closed in which any known previous vocabulary applies. (*Special* 14)

This history of thought, although reminiscent of the historicists it cites, also has clear affinities with Foucault's account in *The Order of Things*. Foucault argues that "a new arrangement of knowledge" emerged at the beginning the nineteenth-century, leaving behind the older system of correspondences (the map of Chaos), in which "the historicity of economics (in relation to the forms of production), the finitude of human existence (in relation to scarcity and labor), and the fulfillment of an end to History" were linked together (262). This gave rise to an anthropology, as Foucault calls it, a preoccupation with the question "*Was ist der Mensch?*" as a foundation for what he calls the Kantian questions—"What can I know? What must I do? What am I permitted to Hope?" (*Order* 341). Foucault then argues that nineteenth-century thought tries to "make the man of nature, of exchange, or of discourse, serve as the foundation of his own finitude" and the circular confusion of empirical existence and metaphysical conditions causes anesthesia only curable by following Nietzsche's remedy and eliminating the tropes of God and Man:

> It is no longer possible to think in our day other than in the void left by man's disappearance. For this void does not create a deficiency; it does not constitute a lacuna that must be filled. It is nothing more, and nothing less, than the unfolding of a space in which it is once more possible to think. (342)

The similarity of vocabulary in this dismissal of essentialism, of those who "refer all knowledge back to the truths of man himself," and even those who imagine that there is a being in need of liberation, with Olson's sketchy, uneven program in the student lectures, is not accidental. Although at times Olson does seem close to reinstating some kind of originary humanity the scope of his project does anticipate Foucault's.

The very different poetics of Olson and Bernstein can be mapped in part across the lines of argument traced by the two complex theoretical texts of Merleau-Ponty and Foucault, and one could show that this intertextual opportunity is available to a much wider range of discursive statements of poetics spanning the two movements. The brilliance of Blaser's essay is in part made possible by his tacit recognition of this general possibility of working through the consequences of some current theories of poetry by substituting certain theoretical moments in the two unstable theoretical texts, in order to discuss specific positions taken by contemporary poets without becoming caught too rapidly within literary allegiances. Moreover, the two works of French theory are themselves hard to place in any orthodox history of literary theory represented as a shift from humanist, subject-based studies, to a poststructuralism that locates subjectivity as a linguistic projection. Blaser's choice of theoretical texts was not however made primarily in order to make analogies between continental philosophy and recent poetics. Their choice was largely forced upon him by his wish to compose a prose elegy for Jack Spicer.

SPICER AND THE FALL OF MAN

The Collected Books of Jack Spicer is a characteristically fine production from Black Sparrow Press, printed on a beautifully thick creamy
paper in one of the exceptionally clear typefaces used regularly by the
press, and characteristically idiosyncratic. The cover image of a hand
emerging from a cloud to hold a grail-like cup to a young man in
buckskin sitting under a tree contemplating a row of these strange
double ended cups was printed in a subtle ghostly gray on the gray
paper cover of the hardback edition and unobtrusively embossed into
the cover of the paperback inside a black border. This was not a collected poems. It reproduces all the books that Spicer acknowledged,
all published in small press editions, because in these he created the
"serial poems" which he regarded as his most valid poetic achievement. Out of the poems and their prose poetry accompaniments
emerges a poetics that works with a dialectic of presence and
absence, and the known and the unknown. "Imagine," invites a serial poem "A Fake Novel About the Life of Arthur Rimbaud,"
"Imagine, those of us who are poets, a good poet. . . . If they call him
up into being by their logic, he does not exist" (161). Poets have their
own ontology, and their special rhetorics. "A metaphor is something
unexplained—like a place in a map that says that after this is desert.
A shorthand to admit the unknown" (162). Poetry goes out into the
unknown and makes maps which acknowledge its place beyond the
legitimated knowledge of organized sciences and the academies, and
lets the grail hang in the air, with "No visible means of support . . . /
like June-berries in October or something / I had felt and forgotten"
(194), in the words of the "Book of Percival." *After Lorca* describes
itself as the result not of mere translation of a text from a poet whose
life has not entirely vanished, but as "a kind of casual friendship with
an undramatic ghost who occasionally looked through my eyes and
whispered to me, not really more important to me than my other
friends, but now achieving a different level of reality by being missing" (51), as if in agreement with Merleau-Ponty's description of
vision as the alienation by a phantom. Language is always a preoccupation for Spicer, the trained linguist. When "the syntax changes,"
cultures change, sometimes violently, and nothing is free of syntax,
not even the "I," once "you put a dot or a dash with it" (242). The mere

addition of punctuation to the single letter produces messages like the telegraph's morse code.

Unlike other metapoetic modern work, Spicer's poetry constantly dares the reader to assent to his pronouncements and ponder seriously his exempla of linguistic strangeness in the face of an accompanying gloomy mockery of such effort and the credence that sustains it. The poetics hangs there like the grail just waiting for an opportunity to disappear with a hollow laugh as the unworthy quester reaches for its conclusion. It would be reckless to follow such poems with an un-ironic discussion of their poetics and the condition of poetry, yet this is what Blaser had to do. As if this wasn't enough, the poems also issue posthumous instructions to their editor in a letter published in the poem *Admonitions*, where Spicer dismisses almost all his earlier work, insisting that "there is really no single poem" and that almost all his earlier poems look "foul." He anthropomorphizes them, saying "They cannot live alone any more than we can" (61). The letter takes this heavily ironic analogy further, saying that the earlier discrete poems were "one night stands . . . pointing nowhere, as meaningless as sex in a Turkish bath." This challenges readers to consider the poems within an ethics of homoerotic relationships, and so manages to make the usual abstractions of readerly pleasure, desire, and the work of interpretation more open to re-evalution because the laws and orientations which underpin these terms become evident. There is a strong echo of Spicer's earlier contention in *After Lorca* that poems are like (male) pygmalions brought to amorous life by the poet, who then search for lover-readers, an image which might be a homoerotic counterpart to Bernstein's "sealed off" poem. Some poems are "'easily laid," but Spicer is more concerned about the shy ones, who might make much more loyal partners "properly wed." He suggests this erotic parallel because he is troubled by the question of futures, of what happens to poems after they are written, and wants to avoid an itinerary of objects or an excessively hermeneutic account of reading, and so opts for a then highly trans-gressive homoerotics of intertextuality. He enumerates the options, casual sex, marriage, the classical Greek relationship of older man and young men, and then concludes that it is only in one or possibly two friendships that he finds adequate readers of the poems he writes, "and one of that two really prefers to put them in print so he can see them better" (39). This will turn out to be crucial. Publication and its circulation need to be conceived of as forms of intimate relation for the poetry.

Spicer's extravagant claim at the end of his letter to Blaser that "this is the most important letter that you have ever received" (61) must have lent these arguments considerable force, despite their self-consuming irony, when he began to edit the volume and compose his essay. The volume had to accede to Spicer's own self-evaluation and print just the "books" of the poems which Spicer valued, and the essay had to acknowledge the wider claims on Blaser made in the letter, as well as to measure up to the didactic pantomime of poetics. A mere biographical note would not suffice either. "At first this essay was short and simple—about Jack. But that became a reduction which every twist and turn of the work denied—a biography without the world that the poet earned or a split between the man and the work which drank him up and left him behind" begins the essay (271). Spicer the fatal drinker, Spicer the grail cup, Spicer giving his poetic blood to his successors—these ready-made narratives won't do. Already Blaser's text is beginning to practice its own "outside" as it allows the relative pronoun to convey both hindsight and foresight about the relation of poetry and poet. Was this man who loved to drink himself consumed by the impersonality of his language, or would the attempt to write about the man without the poetics simply end up with an account of a work whose author had been consumed by the supervening discourse? Man and poetry seem to actively disrupt one another's presence.

The essay begins with the confession that its aims have radically changed and ends with a gesture that the writer's friendship with Spicer makes seem utterly appropriate in an obituary essay. Blaser cites Montaigne's moving reference to the friend, Etienne de la Boetie, whose loss had contributed to the melancholy he hoped his essays might relieve: "*Si on me presse de dire pourquoy je sens que cela ne se peut exprimer, qu'en respondent: Par ce que c'estoit luy; par ce que c'estoit moy*" (326). In the first edition Montaigne had simply written: "If you press me to say why I loved him, I feel that it cannot be expressed" (212). It wasn't until the edition published after his death that the words that appeal to an inexpressible ipseity of self could be made public: "except by replying: 'Because it was him: because it was me.'" Montaigne's words are also especially appropriate because Spicer's letter to Lorca about the fate of poems was constructed in terms of Montaigne's analysis of friendship. Montaigne discusses the affinities between friendship and kinship ties, and concludes that such relations, "commanded by the law and the bonds of nature," preclude the freedom of choice evident in friendship. Heterosexual love and marriage fare little better, even though they do evince autonomy, because passion fluctuates, marriage is a complex bargain full of reciprocal duties, and women, believes Montaigne, in a display of male superiority, are incapable of the "mutual confidence" of friendship. This only leaves one kind of love that Montaigne can think of, Greek homosexual love, and having first covered himself by calling it "abhorrent to our manners," he goes on to give a positive, somewhat Platonic account of the way such relationships could foster "valour, wisdom, justice" in the younger passive partner, the "Beloved" (210). He acknowledges the force of those who claim that these relationships help sustain the public sphere, but then implies that the erotic element is redundant by claiming that those relationships that are valuable end in friendship anyway. Yet his own language for the lost friendship that helped prompt him to write, draws upon a discourse that has always been used to describe erotic love. Strong echoes of Plato's *Phaedrus* can be heard in the claim that he and his friend "completely held the reins of each other's desires," and knew one another so well ("our souls were yoked together in such unity") and "contemplated each other with so ardent an affection, and with the same affection revealed each other down to the very entrails, that not only did I know his mind as well as I knew my own but I would have entrusted myself to him with greater assurance than to myself" (213). Trying to find the exact words for this true friendship, Montaigne struggles on until he represents it as a complete merger of selves. He could tell his friend anything because he was telling it "to him who is not another: he is me" (215). A modern reader almost certainly hears Freud talking of mourning and melancholia here. Melancholy results when a very strong identification with a loved person ends and instead of a process of mourning the person, the emotional cathexis reverts back onto a continuing identification independent of any relationship because part of the ego is now wholly identified with the lost other. Freud believed that melancholy usually resulted from a relationship that was already narcissistic (he was me) rather than erotic, so that the loss of the person creates an inassimilable confusion. Blaser's self-conscious citation of Montaigne plays several themes at once therefore. He takes up the disavowed homoeroticism of Montaigne's melancholic elegy on friendship and plays it alongside the poetics of subjectivity, so that he ends with a poignant sense of the erotic and politic costs of a subjectless writing.

Our rush to Freud may be premature or perhaps too belated. The Renaissance historian, Natalie Zemon Davis, best known for her scholarship on the story of Martin Guerre, shows us how we might be wrong to read Montaigne entirely as a melancholic, by arguing that in a period when selves were not nearly so individuated as they are now, and "the boundary around the conceptual self and the bodily self was not always firm and closed," that people could explore their selves by doing so in and through relationships. "One could get inside other people and receive other people within oneself, and not just during sexual intercourse or when a child was in the womb" (56) and in that faraway world "it was not always certain where one person ended and another began" (59). Davis points out that although Montaigne talks of his friend as someone with whom he had the kind of mutuality never possible between family members like father and son, he does actually locate much of his discussion within his relations with his own father and his own son Leonor, as the field of intersubjectivity in which friendship is manifested. Davis does not say, but it seems implicit in her argument, that Montaigne's total identification with his friend may be described as one of these strategies for exploring the possibilities of autonomy in a culture in which the self is so closely part of the family, the father or other kin, that its distinctness is not evident to a strictly psychoanalytic discourse. The seeming self-erasure of "he is me" might be better understood as a form of specular self-consciousness otherwise hard to achieve in this milieu of partially merged subjectivities in the immediate world of kin. This prompts a further speculation. Maybe this strategy is not so pre-modern after all, and our growing cast list of phantoms, maximuses, fallen men, absent friends, vegetation gods, and poets may all have a common dramaturgy.

Blaser's essay finds other allies beside Montaigne for its elegiac strategies, most notably in Claude Lefort's moving introduction to Merleau-Ponty's *The Visible and the Invisible*. Merleau-Ponty died in 1961 leaving only some contradictory schema and a few working notes for Lefort to work from. Lefort's preface begins in an unashamedly elegiac tone: "However, expected it may sometimes be, the death of a relative or a friend opens an abyss before us" (xi). The opening paragraph continues with a strong statement of the individual and collective loss of someone who appeared "to have always spoken and to be destined to speak always." Lefort then goes on to speculate about the ontological change in a text when its author dies, and this would have underlined similarities between his situation and Blaser's position as literary editor of his friend's work, as well as lending support for the poetics which Blaser proposes as his reading of Spicer. Lefort's articulation of loss must have expressed much of what Blaser himself felt about his own role, notably the sense of "the sad privilege of entering the room where the writer worked, of measuring with his gaze the abandoned labor, the notes, the plans, the drafts which bear everywhere the palpable trace of a thought in effervescence, on the verge of finding its form" (xv). As well as a precedent for his own knot of personal and literary mourning, Blaser found other arguments that would have helped clarify his approach to the problem of writing an essay on a poet and friend. According to Lefort, the actual death of an author suddenly confronts those who knew their author with works from which the "writer has disappeared," and these authorless texts have to be read all over again as a making visible of the absence of a subject. While the writer is alive, both writer and reader-friend are "subject to the same rhythm of the world" (xii), as if to live in the world as friends is to share a poem, but once the author is dead the work is no longer simply trying to "render intelligible the reality before which it takes its form" (xiii), because it has now become a part of that reality itself as an object. "The work therefore lives on the outside. Like things of nature, like facts of history, it is a being of the outside, awakening the same astonishment, requiring the same attention, the same exploration of the gaze, promising by its sole presence a meaning of an order other than the significations contained in its statements" (xiii). One metaphor stands out, an imagined Adamic privilege of taking the "risk of naming what in the present had no name" which the text supported by a living author could do. After the death of the author the text cannot perform this Adamic role now that it has fallen into the world it once named, and therefore has no special privileged standpoint from which to articulate what is other to it. This is why it is "outside." Lefort's account might have been written to demonstrate Derrida's diagnosis of logocentrism, especially when he distinguishes between the living speech of a text coeval with a living author and the writing of someone who has died—"the interrupted conversation abandons us" (xi), and so by implication the work becomes writing in the author's absence. When Lefort implies that reading is always mourning for a lost conversational presence, he might be unmasking himself as the anonymous interlocutor in *The Archaeology of Knowledge.*

This grief struck essay gives Blaser a precedent for an extrapolation of individual loss into a generalized condition of language and textuality, which then enables him to construct his own chiasmus within his reading of Foucault, who as I said earlier, provided a replacement imagery for the pastoralism of elegy. Foucault offers a "philosophical laugh" in the face of what he depicts as the humanist lament for the self, represented rhetorically as the disappearance or "death" of "man," yet Blaser generously allows a grieving actuality to these tropes that paradoxically rediscovers something that Foucault's work has often been interpreted to elide. Judith Butler, for example, interprets Foucault's discussion of the relations between the soul and the body in *Discipline and Punish* to mean that the soul or self is an effect of discourses that are practiced upon the body. Its peculiar ontology as inwardness depends upon an absence that is actually a function of the way discourses act upon the body.

> The figure of the interior soul understood as "within" the body is signified through its inscription *on* the body, even though its primary mode of signification is through its absence, its potent invisibility, for it is through that invisibility that the effect of a structuring inner space is produced. The soul is precisely what

the body lacks; hence, that lack produces the body as its other
and as its means of expression. In this sense, then, the soul is a
surface signification that contests and displaces the inner/outer
distinction itself, a figure of interior psychic space inscribed on
the body as a social signification that perpetually renounces itself
as such. (335)

Blaser's essay is about the "outside" that results from such a renunci-
ation, as his comment that Foucault's epitaph for "man" should also
be "the laughter of poetry" shows, but Blaser's elegiac concern with
an actual loss makes his rhetoric consider the inverse of Butler's
proposition. It is through the invisibility of the author that a structur-
ing outside space of public scale is produced, and so he asks whether
the death of the author is a ritual sacrifice made in order to ensure a
new season of political growth? Blaser describes his friend's poetic
strategy as dangerous because "it removes the manhood or the image
of it, which the settled discourse gathered and held together in a
stoppage or finitude that spoke only of himself" (280). What Spicer
did was effectively to make the soul's invisibility visible, with all the
potential consequences for himself, for friendship, for poetry, and
even politics, that this might entail.

A POETICS OF PERFORMANCE

Translating the universal category "man" into "manhood" may seem
a small change. It is not. Its effect is to insist on the material histories
of loss implicated in any history of the death of man in a modern
thought already awe-struck by the affective dynamics of loss. It is a
certain kind of masculinity and its heterosexual diremption of the
field of genders that is disappearing. The literalization of Foucault's
historical metaphor of the death of "man" as the death of his friend
enables Blaser to produce a remarkable resolution of the conflict
between the two literary constellations. The epistemological ambitions of the New American poets, and the linguistic reflexivity of
the Language Writers are shown to be mutually negotiable without
setting aside one or the other in his concept of a "performance of the
real." Spicer attributed his poetic impetus to that Yeatsian apparatus
of "dictation," with a certain knowing irony about the overstrained

beliefs in metaphysical entities that such a claim usually entails. He
was more interested in the attempts to provide an image and an
ontology for the attributed origin of writing than in one or another
belief system itself, and this enables Blaser to gloss dictation as
a deictic for the "unknown, or the outside," so bringing Spicer's
terminology into a zone conceptualizable with the help of Lefort and
Merleau-Ponty. Poetry should make possible a "performance of the
real," and can do this by letting "the unknown, the Other, the outside
in again as a voice in the language" (276). This sounds Heideggerian,
and Blaser allows Heidegger to make a brief and not altogether
convincing guest appearance, with the idea of art as a disclosure or
"exhibition of world." So far this all sounds perfectly compatible with
Olson's poetics. Blaser, however, has a different diagnosis of political
ills to Olson, who believed in the renewal of democracy by a redis-
covery of individual responsibility for history and its determinations,
and presented this as possible through collective and singular acts of
will. Blaser is more cautious, having learned the lessons of ideology
from homosexual culture and from his French philosophical men-
tors. He believes that the closure of the public sphere by a public
discourse which naturalizes meaning as a fixed structure can prevent
any realization of its social construction, or what Blaser calls in an
earlier terminology, its "composition." Hence Olson's project might
be halted. It is not far from this point to Ron Silliman's insistence
in an essay first published in 1977, and widely reprinted,
"Disappearance of the Word, Appearance of the World," that a new
poetry should be the "philosophy of practice in language" (17) in
order to challenge the "commoditization of language" (12): "under
the sway of the commodity fetish, language itself appears to become
transparent, a mere vessel for the transfer of ostensibly autonomous
referents" (11). Blaser had already drawn the connection between
transparency of language and the restoration of discourse in his citations from Foucault, especially Foucault's argument in the opening
section of *The Order of Things*, that twentieth-century literature has
made sure that "through literature, the being of language shines once
more on the frontiers of Western culture" (44). This passage probably
caught Blaser's eye because it is part of a surprisingly nostalgic
passage about a pre-enlightenment relation to language, when the

writing was primary and when, as Foucault expresses it in poetic imagery close to Merleau-Ponty, "the seen and the read, the visible and the expressible, were endlessly interwoven" (43). Foucault could be implying that his recent predecessor was really an anachronistic throwback, whose phenomenology was really just a reheated Renaissance ideology.

This convergence may remind some readers that Blaser's essay preceded almost all the essays by Language Writers and must surely have influenced some (Bernstein actually studied with Blaser in the very early seventies). The Blaser essay also moves in another direction however, by arguing that we lack images of the political sphere adequate for cognition of the processes at work, in a manner which anticipates many much more recent arguments about the loss of images for the social world. Benedict Anderson's argument about nationalism depends on the claim that modern communities cannot construct their commonality on empirical bases because of the sheer size and complexity of states, and substitute the emotional cathexes of imagined nationalisms. One anthropologist, Marilyn Strathern, argues that in Western societies "we have potentially abolished the particular relationships on which our symbolic capacity for relational imagery was grounded" (152), and this avoidance of the pervasively elegiac rhetoric of a lost *subject* by the use of the term *relationship* as a primary site of loss, points in the direction of Blaser's own argument. It depends on the recognition of a modernity which, as Anderson shows at a much greater level of detail, has experienced a massive expansion of the political realm with the extension of the franchise, growth of population, extension of education and the sharing of power beyond a small, internally recognized elite. Blaser begins by recalling us to the humanity of politicians.

> The men themselves, when one could see them in their acts, were horizons. Their acts remain in language where we join them. When the language breaks up into disbelief, their images disappear and we are, as now, invisible to one another. Left alone inside our needs and desires. We may all be the same there, but it is a leveling and a disappearance into an invisibility called necessity. The curious thing about language is that it holds and makes visible. It performs one's manhood. But it is so much older than oneself, so much a speaking beyond and outside one-

> self, that a man's entrance to it becomes at once new and old,
> spoken and speaking, a self and some other. The hierarchies of
> thought were found in combat and became quietnesses. (290)

This is a social condition, a "large and cultural extremity in which
meanings fall to be remade again," as well as a "disappearance of
manhood" (322). Blaser is ambitious enough to say that a new poetics
of performance could help restore the diminished symbolic capacity.
Once again performance is central to its possibilities.

The most prominent concept in Blaser's entire essay is the idea of
a "performance of the real." This apparent oxymoron might seem to
a social constructionist to talk of the "real" in an alarmingly positivist
manner, despite the allusion to constructedness, as if any mention at
all of the "real" were to rely on the belief that some reality prior to
representation were then represented by the ritual itself, but Blaser's
careful formulation allows a coexistence of two different ontologies.
Blaser is not scared into scare quotes. His duck/rabbit clause,
"performance of the real," has a second meaning, that the reality
effect is generated by the performance of the artwork. "Performance"
does similar work in Merleau-Ponty's concept of "flesh" and
Foucault's multi-purpose conceptual vehicle "discourse," because it
instantiates the chiasmus of subject and world through the insistence
that both world and language are activities, and not conditions,
entities or systems. Blaser almost paints us into the same corner as the
poststructuralists when he says we are inside language, but then
opens a door by saying that this interior is itself a performance, and
like certain rituals, there are only performers within its ambit: "Jack
knew we were inside a performance of language." The absent man's
knowledge validates the proposition. A terminological instability in
Blaser's essay's use of the term "discourse" creates some interference,
jamming the sideband on which he explains that discourse is the
deployment of language as system: "a discourse is the language
system in which one lives—the use of language each of us agrees to."
This neatly modulates certain waves of poststructuralism which have
too readily repeated Saussure's thesis that "language is a system of
differences" as if it were a natural law rather than heuristic method.

Systematicity in language is only one area that Blaser's undevel-
oped concept of performance challenges. In her recent study of hate

speech, Judith Butler, the theorist of performativity in gender and politics, explains that even hate speech does not originate from the subject who utters the words, because

> that subject is produced in language through a prior performa-
> tive exercise of speech: interpellation. . . . The legal effort to curb
> injurious speech tends to isolate the "speaker" as the culpable
> agent, as if the speaker were at the origin of such speech. The
> responsibility of the speaker is thus misconstrued. The speaker
> assumes responsibility precisely through the citational character
> of speech. The speaker renews the linguistic tokens of a com-
> munity, reissuing and reinvigorating such speech. Responsibility
> is thus linked with speech as repetition, not as origination.
>
> (*ES* 39)

This political and legal theorization of the performativity of language arrives at a point similar to Blaser's when it argues that performance is the creation of sociality, but sadly it can only do this by denying *poiesis* again. Blaser uses the concept of performance to counter three tendencies that determine the reception of contemporary poetry: "Naive realism, the reduction of experience, and the idealism of a certain poetics" (314). Neither a materialist positivism, nor a psychology of the subject as the origin of the poem, nor an idealist celebration of the poem as an autonomous act of imagination, are adequate to describe the practices of the most innovative contemporary poetries. In a sense Blaser arrives at the concept of per-formance for exactly the same reasons as Butler does—performance encompasses both innovation and repetition. What he retains is the possibility that a poetic performance of the real can be a creation of new knowledge as significant as that produced by science and other intellectual disciplines, and so answers Robert Duncan's concern that poets simply play alongside the discourses of fact and belief. Blaser also helped make possible a long revolution in the way poets understand performance, signaled by the recent emergence of performance writing in the United Kingdom, and the growing consciousness of the history of poetry performance in both North America and the United Kingdom. A longer history of the way performance in the arts since Dada, and earlier perhaps Cubism, has found methodologies of practice that are not simulations of science, nor gatecrashers into everyday life, but a complex form of enquiry which lacks an adequate symbolization still.

"The Practice of Outside" has other frequencies too, on which it rehabilitates Romanticism, on which it discusses the role of belief and disbelief in poetry, and on which it reflects on the conditions necessary for a contemporary language of the sacred, which I shall not discuss here. Blaser's brilliant essay continues to be important for the way it anticipated and still provides guidance for so many subsequent dilemmas in poetics. I think its most remarkable achievement, however, is the way it identifies the prematurely elegiac tone of poststructuralist thought and composes an elegy for that tone. The essay points out a route not yet followed by poststructuralist theory in literary and cultural studies. It indicates a space for the work of writing as a performance in itself, neither a communication nor a text ready deconstructed for perceptive readers to find. By shifting from man to manhood, Blaser introduces not only a male erotics of language, he also allows the possibility of rescuing the ideals of humanism from its tendency to oppressive essentialism, by reconfiguring them as a gendered and sexualized intersubjectivity that is always in performance. This disappearance of man which Foucault laughs at as a necessary development in modern culture, Blaser questions by placing the dying Spicer at the conclusion of the essay, saying *"My vocabulary did this to me. Your love will let you go on"* (325; emphasis in original).

The emotional necessities of a tribute and the analytical assessments of a critical essay might have gridlocked argument in what was intended as an afterword. Oppositions between public and private, objective and subjective, encomium and judgment, intimacy and history could have become part of a chopped dialectic, but instead the essay transposes these pressures onto the concepts borrowed largely from contemporary French theory, so that the concepts themselves are marked by this impossible task, twisted, fractured and riven with these demands. The deeply felt need both to acknowledge Spicer's homosexuality and yet not to speak of it in any familiar or sociological manner adds further force to this refashioning of concepts. By setting up a contrast between the idea of a poetry as a "discourse true only to itself" and Jack Spicer's conviction that poetry is "an act or event of the real," and then treating this as a fugal performance of poststructuralism and phenomenology to be resolved in the reiterated phrase, "performance of the real," Blaser makes it possible to reconsider the cognitive ambitions of New American Poetry. Instead of treating its self-reflexive methodologies of history and other forms of contemporary knowledge as opposed to the rigorous explorations of the linguistic condition found in Language Writing, it might be possible to treat both as a "performance of the real" and to rethink the complex historical antecedents and affinites of both literary movements. He did this out of a deeply felt sense of loss which compelled him to make visible the widespread elegiacs of recent theory and poetics, and to measure these speculative revolutions in discourse with a comic metapoetics of Spicer and the tragic loss of creative intelligence in his performance of a poet's career. The result is an enduring essay, which stands alongside the best of Robin Blaser's own poetry.

WORKS CITED

Anderson, Benedict. *Imagined Communities*. London: Verso, 1983.

Andrews, Bruce. "Constitution/Writing, Politics, Language, the Body." *L=A=N=G=U=A=G=E*. Vol. 4. Ed. Bruce Andrews and Charles Bernstein. 1982. 154-65.

_____. "Poetry as Explanation, Poetry as Praxis." *The Politics of Poetic Form: Poetry and Public Policy*. Ed. Charles Bernstein. New York: Roof, 1990. 23-43.

Bernstein, Charles. "Writing and Method." *Poetics Journal* 3 (1983): 6-16.

Blaser, Robin. "The Practice of Outside." *The Collected Books of Jack Spicer*. Ed. Robin Blaser. Los Angeles: Black Sparrow, 1975. 271-329.

Butler, Judith. *Excitable Speech: A Politics of Performance*. New York: Routledge, 1997.

_____. "Gender Trouble, Feminist Theory, and Psychoanalytic Discourse." *Feminist/Postmodernism*. Ed. Linda J. Nicholson. London and New York: Routledge, 1990. 324-40.

Davis, Natalie Zemon. "Boundaries and the Sense of Self in Sixteenth Century France." *Reconstructing Individualism: Autonomy, Individuality and the Self in Western Thought*. Ed. Thomas C. Heller, Morton Sosna, and David E. Wellbery. Stanford: Stanford UP, 1986. 53-63.

Foucault, Michel. *The Archeology of Knowledge*. Trans. A. M. Sheridan Smith. London: Tavistock, 1972.

_____. *The Order of Things: An Archeology of the Human Sciences*. London: Tavistock, 1970.

Merleau-Ponty, Maurice. *The Visible and the Invisible.* Ed. Claude Lefort. Trans. Alphonso Lingis. Evanston: Northwestern UP, 1968.

Montaigne, Michel. "On Affectionate Relationships." *The Complete Essays.* Trans. M. A. Screech. London: Penguin, 1991.

Olson, Charles. "Human Universe." *Charles Olson: Selected Writings.* Ed. Robert Creeley. New York: New Directions, 1966.

————————. *The Special View of History.* Ed. Ann Charters. Berkeley: Oyez, 1970.

Perelman, Bob. "Plotless Prose." *Poetics Journal* 1 (1982): 25-34.

Ross, Andrew. *The Failure of Modernism: Symptoms of American Poetry.* New York: Columbia UP, 1986.

Sacks, Peter. *The English Elegy: Studies in the Genre from Spenser to Yeats.* Baltimore: Johns Hopkins UP, 1985.

Silliman, Ron. "Disappearance of the Word, Appearance of the World." *The New Sentence.* New York: Roof, 1987. 7-18.

Strathern, Marilyn. *After Nature: English Kinship in the Late Twentieth Century.* Cambridge: Cambridge UP, 1992.

Taussig, Michael. *A Particular History of the Senses.* New York and London: Routledge, 1993.

Von Hallberg, Robert. *Charles Olson: The Scholar's Art.* Cambridge, Mass.: Harvard UP, 1978.

Whalen, Philip. *Self-Portrait from Another Direction.* San Francisco: Auerhahn, 1959. n.p.

MUSIC AT THE HEART OF THINKING

Fred Wah

MHT#110

With the shade of an alibi this land haunts its
thought with voice the word repeats (though
thinking can't) the shadow of a broken Kachina
doll one ear lost to the yellow of the dandelion,
green wants in, to return, this Pueblo in exchange
for an icefield, yet who's frightened by the ghosts of
repetition, the level of the lake inside history, that's
the spirit.

MHT#111

The purety of spelling rests in the bole of a
cottonwood tree out of the way of those musk-ox-
like syllables in the distance with their potent loads
on their backs each letter a nameless squirrel all
eyes and spasm chittering deep under the
encephalo roof.

MHT#112

Citation that close is a way to deflect being full of
yourself or if such gesture will be the history of
everything then an epigraph to our century could
be *a* [big] *voice lost from the person it did belong to*
suddenly stopped, look, listen, then follow the
emptiness around any big tree nearby just to get out
beyond the last street, the city limits anyplace
anywhere but get lost, those were Christ's
strawberries, so to be not full is to be full.

MHT #113

The signature in parenthesis *sans souci*
the body of authority contained for shipping (with string
attached) for example local movements include
Lake Frank O'Hara fossilized or broken Frank Slide
better not *call it politics*
but keep an eye on Turtle Mtn's sliding signifier
sidelined in the moment yet repeatedly
folding fault until touched into action
mind winding down the list, ah!
there the *fine(d) nature of bodily sensation*
being carried is pretty good.

MHT#114

That's the drawer of poetry, closed to keep the lake from flooding. *it is probably the secret of syntax itself.* Indefinite junktures of the hyphenated -eme-clutter posing in wait for a synapse or quilt of meaning. Nothing's wrong, in other words. *a humming sound, of bees perhaps.* Just throw it into the drawer (twisted threads); mess is poetry's mass.

MHT#115

THE LAUGH'S LAUGH
it nothing does to holler
there are and it is is outside this

it nothing does arguing crows
instead of to distance oneself behind
this, that's *a cal lamb of tea*
          Opal might say, 'the near
          is too close'—which is
          her feels

Lars Porsena flies to the top of an old fir
Whiteley whispers, "Bring it all closer
Together"
he caws, "Truth gives no news,"
then swoops into a black signature,
"meet me in Albion,"
since distance is presence

          (w/ Opal Whiteley and Blanchot

MHT #116

Postpone the ladder but remember to discuss the
number of steps since they are but mounds
swimming, up against the particles which deflect
into the cant of shore the ultra violet climate, the
lean-to for the potential snow storm, falling for the
tilt edge of bed the clinic of the night and
disappearing weak spot of forgetfullness's why the
poem lists north or stars fell on slopes

MHT#117

one time when Roy Kiyooka and I are driving west
across the Burrard St. bridge we see a harvest moon
over the armory, huge and bulbous along the top of
the Molson clock. The two O's in the sign are
missing. M_ls_n. "I feel the cutting edge," Roy said,
"of an un named neon stalking my vernacular.
Such forkt bedevilments of the Owl bespeak this
midden dialect with which I paint the taint."

MHT#118

That huckleberry patch is Pauline's secret white
wheat, *her katha,* the answer that is the
question.

MHT#119

finding along the shore of the lake   submerged
maps, heart-clock diaphragmed into two pears of
iron filings, rock terra surfacing the prevailing
thorn, such deep purple, not chinoiserie but gene
pool highways and mountain rangers   edge of of
the old bearded lapis man, hunched miniature and
reappearing through the mist, teahouse,
cartographer's green, jade route   could it lock
origin?   when you push against whose gods
doesn't it set up junctions? missing engines   a
half-breed, that has possibility, even beauty   a
ringing at the door of the poem, floor tilting   a
frame unplumbed, mitre missed, never a road not
taken, demystification's new mystery further
studies, the day is the place Paris France's brief to
Butterick 7/29/88 unless cut this vetch will dry up
and go to seed Calypso Lille, Frank Slide Harebell,
Clematis Creek Humming, The Proof of the Crocus,
Zattar for my bread and cheese, Idaho is a
panhandle she said   driving it north of the Bitter
Root conscious it's a secondary road   darker green
this valley   *have TV breath   old boy piss. . . . retiring
to his Connecticut pasture, some alumnus to be the
rector of the poetry   to play some tennis* Rodefer said
today it'll be over thirty the scotch broom still
yellow and Thel's Eagle ask's the Mole "what is in
the pit?" the root within the secret air of fading?
Lily of the Valley, Cloud, Clod of Clay, and Worm?
"Why a little curtain of flesh on the bed of our
desire?" What if dying means you are dead already?

Note to MHT's 110-119
(Opal Whiteley, Maurice Blanchot, Blaser's *Syntax*, Giorgio Agamben, and
others mentioned)

STILL, AND DESPITE

Paul Kelley

To the memory of Gillian Rose

> *"Let me then be destroyed. For that is the*
> *only way I may have a chance of surviving."*
> –Love's Work

(Today matters are become somewhat different. This now is each memory's silent, distant future tense. It departs from— it reverses—the dull and dulling, fate of days; now they are lifted from that tiring, tireless accumulation. Today time, escaped from its storehouse, reaches and disperses us: a moment stands still. Its plentitudes, unnoticed, having travelled invisible paths, stop at us, stop with us. The crunch of separation, long among the forgotten sounds, breathes through us: a shudder, shapeless, turned inside-out. Outer interiority is ejected, all possessions turned loose, unmasking every image, every semblance, every moment. All through whom the thread of time runs are pulled apart by it.)

If one who, upon making an examination of Robin Blaser's poem "The Iceberg,"[1] sought to begin by attempting to indicate, if only silently, that which marked the uniqueness of such an experience, he or she might be very hard-pressed for words, as is only to be expected in the events we gather under the word "significant." That single word is often called upon to do duty for all the others that do not come easily, and sometimes, if truth be told, "come" not at all. Yet, in the difficulty of speaking of an experience—especially when it is the experience of a poem—is to be found a paradoxical truth. The poem "The Iceberg" has the effect of removing to a puzzlingly remote distance the usual array of words and practices employed to render comprehensible and communicable the reader's experience. That inaccessibility is, in fact, at the heart of the experience of *this* poem, perhaps the heart of all experience. It is immune to all summons. Hence it dislodges and sets awry the orders of the one who seeks to order it. In this sense, one could say that the experience of the poem is nothing less than a certain *dis*-engagement, a rupture, or a severing of self from all a self is held to be—knowledge, ego, desire—and equally, from all that is commonly called upon in support of that self—societal institutions, the past, the future, language, culture itself. Certainly one finds oneself in a somewhat bewildering predicament! One has, it could be said, been gifted with a certain impoverishment that is the equal of the—startling—freedom it conveys.

These two words—impoverishment and freedom—are not, admittedly, customarily paired. To bring them into such tense proximity here is not intended as yet another attempt to ennoble the former through contact with the latter. To the contrary, the intention is to gather light and warmth from the sparks set off by their salutary, abrasive contact. As treasures of culture, poetry and philosophy are said to enrich. Surely. But poetry, especially modern poetry, does not recommend. Philosophy recommends. It argues and urges, even when it appears not to do so. But in the encounter of philosophy with poetry, is it not wise for philosophy (and literary criticism, too, to the extent that it relies on or appeals to philosophy) to abdicate recommendation in favor of exploration, one that can proceed, perhaps, only by interrogation and self-interrogation? That is, only by its own poverty? It is never really a matter of making a "choice" between them, between that is, one mode of thinking over another. Equally, it is not a matter of equating them, of asserting that poetry is a form of philosophy or that philosophy is a form of poetry. The terms of both the choice and the equation are misleading and tiresome. A better way of perceiving each is to see that they are in relationship with an unacknowledged Third which is the source of their differences: responsibility. For, before all loyalty to their respective discourses and their respective histories, each must respond, without disfiguring it or abstracting it, to a demand—perhaps a beseeching—that nevertheless remains outside, beyond both. In this, both poetry and philoso-phy seek, in the best sense, a deepening of experience's complexities, recognizing therein their transformation into reflection never absolved of unpleasant, unwanted questioning.

The gift of impoverishment—a gift of "Nothing"—permits one time enough and breath enough to find (even to find again) thought's fidelities rather than oaths of allegiance. Such a sentiment, in as much as it seems not only to have arrived at limits but also bristles to push beyond them, is not only the legacy of Nietzsche; it is also to be found in Kant, as Heidegger and Foucault have shown.[2] The experi-ence of having arrived at the limits of reason and of language is noth-ing very recent. It is in this situation that Heidegger speaks of under-going "an experience with language" in which we are overwhelmed and transformed (*OWL* 57). That overwhelming and transforming is, according to Gadamer, the true nature of experience. It means that the occurrence of an experience is always an intervention, and by just such intervention we are prevented from going on as we did before.[3] Poetry, to the degree that it is a certain dis-ordering of language, allows us to behold something of the nature of experience itself, for poetry disrupts and dislodges not only one's customary relation to experience; it also disrupts one's customary experience of language itself. Moreover, the two are indissociable. The intervention in one's experience and in one's experience of language demonstrates that poetry is not a "second-order experience," the proof of which is affirmed by the loss of language in which, or by which, to grasp expe-rience. (Consider what happens when we fall in love, for example, and can find no words to do justice to the intensity, the uniqueness, and the turbulence of feeling and thought.)

At the same time, however, despite the profound disclosures of the discussion of experience and language offered by Heidegger and Gadamer, it is difficult not to have the intuition that something seems to be missing: the experience of language itself. Language, too, undergoes experience. It, too, is caught short of breath and trans-formed by historical events through which it lives, the events which stamp it and age it. "Words get tired and worn out just as human beings do," Gabriel Marcel has observed (199). Language experi-ences its own hollowing, its stupefaction.[4] Such a stupefaction, a

falling silent of language, would, of course, have severe consequences
for poets. Equally, as that through which and in which understanding occurs, the falling silent of language would have severe consequences for any and all experience itself. Something of a "poverty of
experience"⁵ would be a result, a condition that could be opened to
understanding only by exploring the very particulars of which it is
made.

* * *

> By homely gift and hindered Words
> The human heart is told
> Of Nothing—
> "Nothing" is the force
> That renovates the world—
> —Emily Dickinson (#1563)

If it is the case that in the poems that reach us, we encounter a language neither we nor anyone else could speak, it is this thought that
reminds us that the fact of speech can never be accepted as merely
given. The poem, especially the lyric poem, carries within itself
silence, even, perhaps, silences—not only those in which it has been
composed, but also those *with* which it has been composed. Just as it
is the case that a poem is not simply another "order" of language or
of discourse, so, too, is it the case that silences are not "orders" of an
all-encompassing or primal or original silence. Each silence, as each
word, is, in the poem, final. The words and the silences compose a
time of stops and starts. This is what each poem worthy of the name
imparts—or rather brings to awareness. Such a silence, because absolute, partakes in memory (the past) and anticipation (the future); partakes, that is, in history, at the same time as it cannot be restricted to
temporality, if the latter is understood as the occupation of a point
upon an imaginary line supposed to signify advance or progress, a
motion of development—time's "direction." If it can be said that a
poem is obviously composed of silences as much as words, it is then
also the case that silences, like the words, cannot be separated from
history, from their histories. These silences, too, are brought into the
poem where they are encountered. Thus, if it is the case—and surely

it is—that a poem seeks to give utterance to (a) truth, that truth is to be heard in the silences in equal measure as it is to be heard in the words. Therefore, the poem's silences are not for nothing; nor are they merely formal; nor are they strictly a sign of a word's absence. Silence in a poem is not analogous to the background in a photograph or a painting against which the *figurae* are foregrounded or brought into relief. In the poem, silence does not "serve" to bring the words forth. Thus, silence does not constitute a condition (a muteness) which the words overcome, issue from, or over which they "triumph" as over a personal incoherence, out of which they, perhaps defiantly, rise, only to sink in or return to once they have done their work. Such a description may, of course, be applied to certain poems, but they are not the poems that speak to us despite their authors' mistaken insistence upon their "speaking" as of the highest value. Our daily experiences are full of people and devices that want to "speak" to us, "say something" to us. The recognition of that fact may be enough to begin to provide a new measure for poetry—for the best of poets (and prose writers) are deeply aware of and especially sensitive to the difficulty of "speaking" to us. Even more: they are aware of the extreme difficulty of speaking at all. Hence, the apparent irony that the poems that best "speak" to us do so not by overriding, denying, or negating silence—by, in other words, talking it out of existence—but by admitting it as a constituent of experience, thus transforming it in the act of poetic composition. Which is to say that such "speaking" as this is accomplished by the poets not speaking at all, by their refraining from speech, by withholding it. The silence everywhere drowned by the relentless proliferation of words, "messages," and speeches that inundate our everyday lives does not find or make a home in the poem, but returns, transformed, by way of it. The poem carries silence toward us. The words of the poem, then, do not emerge from that silence; rather, they preserve it, preserving thereby all that exists prior to language, on its other side. The poem carries this particular silence toward us.

Thus the historical, this-worldly character of silence, in contradistinction to its theological or religious character, becomes discernible. The changing character of sound and of speech makes it so. Which is to say that silence, too, is produced—as the inverse of the noise of

the world of men and women and their devices, delights, horrors, vio-
lences. To perceive and to apprehend silence in a manner that does
not render it merely the abstract negation of speech entails taking this
historical dimension of silence into account. For every poetry confronts—must confront—silence as a reality, as a particular silence
occurring at a particular time and in a particular place. To begin to
understand silence in this way means to begin to understand that it
is multiform. The multiple forms of silence render it polysemic, one
might even say multiguous.

To consider the social-historical actuality of any silence, its being
produced or made, poses particular difficulties. Not only is it the case
that silences are always contextual and situational; it is also true that
a discussion of any of the diverse manifestations of silence will necessarily contain one or more of them. Be that as it may, some attention to manifestations of silence in relation to speech and language,
in so far as these relate to poetry, seems called for. Perhaps the most
ostentatious form of silence is that which takes the form of a vow one
makes to oneself not to speak, or not to speak of certain matters.
Silence is, here, an exercise of will, a self-censorship the motivation
of which, except in the case of legal prosecution (actual or potential)
where admissibility of guilt is at stake, remains completely unknown.
At the same time, such a will-to-silence may also be directed at others, for the one who resorts to such a self-protecting silence does so
not only as an attempt to shelter him or herself in it but also out of an
unwillingness to hear or to listen. Thus the refusal to speak may carry
an order, unmistakable despite its implicit character, to another to do
likewise—to be silent. The silence of the prohibition, however, is a
thoroughly public silence, although the weight of its interdiction is
felt privately and personally. This mandated silence, oppressive, omi-
nous, and terroristic because secured through the legal mechanisms
of the power of the state to exact punishment for its violation, suggests
the finality and violence of death. To break this silence imposed as
the equivalent of a death sentence is to risk actual, physical death.
Such a silence, because unambiguously political, makes of speaking
a "speaking up"—a political act. But perhaps the most common,
because ubiquitous, form of silence is that of the noise of many speaking at once. Here speech's sound produces the noise of its self-

destruction. Speech consumed by this noise, is unheard, ignored, and made "background," hence "naturalized." When the sounds that constitute this form of silence manage to be heard, most commonly through the increase in volume needed to "rise above" the surrounding din, they are often little more than a nuisance. But this is not to say that they "make no sense"; to the contrary, they always make ready sense, pre-known, pre-explained, thoroughly familiar.

The silence of poetry, no less social-historical, is of a different sort than these altogether. The silence of poetry is thoroughly multiguous. The distinctive feature of the silence of poetry is that of having to be created and composed in order to be heard at all. To do this is to create a kind of counter-silence, one that releases from silence its significations. The authoring of this counter-silence in "The Iceberg" is nothing less than a double emancipation: of silence, and of the words sedimented and forgotten within. Silence and language work on each other and un-work each other. The poem, knowing that all that is "put into words" cannot rest there, withdraws from discourse and the traffic noise of words. The creation of silence sets free the no-longer heard, the unheard, in each word. Thus, the poem incorporates silence as a condition of and as an element of its composition. Only through the silence it incorporates and brings to audibility can a word be made, a making that releases a freedom beyond choice. In this sense, the silence of the poetic word has a particular power to release a possibility absent from every other silence—and from every word. This is its intimacy, inseparable from its truth: the poetic word speaks with its silence not only *of* an experience but *out of* that experience itself, in all its stunned complexity: all this it strives to convey.

This is, in every way, a thoroughly questionable process, a questionability which separates from all other occasions of language the experience of reading a poem. For not only is the creation of the poetic word exclusive from the making of a choice, identified socially and politically as an index of freedom; it proceeds by means of releasing the question of itself each word contains. Such questioning releases from the word the alterity which renders the word and the language to which it belongs foreign, even when or perhaps especially when, that language is one's own "native language." Thus, despite the fact that the poem may be addressed, it evidences the signs of a dialogue that does not occur, an impossible dialogue, and to this degree, it constitutes a critique of the concept of dialogue. Dialogue—rather, dialogues—happen *in* the poem (as well as between poems): between the words and, importantly, *within* each word. To such dialogue the poem, the poetic word, attends. The auditors, no matter how small in number, likewise follow this questioning. Hearing the poem means hearing its questioning, and questioning, through their encounter with the poem, not only the poem itself, but also themselves. Such questioning is both crucial and critical at once. For to assume such radical questioning is to confront not only otherness in the poem; it is also, by means of the power of its critique and self-critique, to confront one's own otherness.

In poetry, the critical attitude which finds its origin in the silence imposed on crises everywhere denied as the normal state of things— the denial and obfuscation of crisis (of being, speaking, doing)—is, even if only indirectly, presented. That poetry remains in this crisis concerned with it makes it the accursed of speech: all that speech neglects, ignores, disfigures, mutilates into the order of normalcy. Poetry, by remaining on this side of speech, shows that what is often nearest retains the immeasurable distance of what is most other. Poetry, which often sounds as if it consisted almost wholly of words which have strayed from the orientations, the referential compasses of meaning, as if made wholly of words forsaken by these orientations, gets lost, wanders into the indeterminate, uncircumscribed area of the other, a territory where speech cannot proceed, will not enter, should not penetrate, threatened by the finality of the stupefaction on the verge of which it is, with very placement of its feet, always poised—close to catastrophe that continues to occur.

The silence of the poem, critical, not merely formal, means not only that everything is not sayable but also that some things are not worth saying in the manners and in the words which the culture provides. In this sense, the silence indissociable from the poetic word can be understood not only as a lack of words but also as a critique of words' lacks, of their insufficiencies. The apparent impoverishment for which silence, identified as a *sine qua non* of social and political privation, has come to stand is at the same time an indictment of the poverty of words, which are proliferated in insane quantities. The degradation of silence is accomplished only at the cost of the degradation of the words enlisted to castigate it and supplant it. The devalorization of silence is accomplished by the compensatory move, that is, the over-valorization of speech, which, like currency, becomes inflated. The hustle of business and the bustle of speech meet on the shared ground of the ideology of success. Where silence is a sign of failure (the failure to utter is failure at its uttermost) logic decrees that speech, therefore, rings with the sounds of success. Where speech is equated wholly with freedom, it cannot avoid being mediated by the market, the various aspects and sectors of which are said by the experts to "communicate" with each other. Where autonomy comes to be defined as exercising the right to speak, of giving oneself permission to speak, a certain form of terrorism has all but been perfected. The right to speak makes sense only in connection with the right to silence. To have nothing to say, to say nothing, to exercise the right to silence—this is at times, perhaps, a relief, but more, it is also a chance to discover that which might be worth the effort of saying it. Admittedly, this may not sound very pleasurable or satisfying. One could say, with Adorno, that it is *"presque rien"*—"almost nothing."[6] But the point is to keep open that "almost."

* * *

The Iceberg

I want no summer to melt you
I want no tip to disappear where
I find you—and the largeness
out there, wanders, incomplete,
a constant creation to leap into . . .

Wholly in keeping with the direct address to the object, which immediately calls to mind Shelley's "Ode to the West Wind," or "To a Skylark," or Keats's "Ode: To Autumn" (which offer a treble honoring—to the object, to the reader, and to the tradition itself into which the honorees are absorbed and enfolded), the unsettling effect of the surprise of beholding this iceberg is brought into the poem, not through description of this state, nor through description of the iceberg itself, but rather through the unsettling of the address itself, from which the poem breaks off to follow an as-yet unknown course in an as-yet unknown, unanticipated, direction. The reader expecting a representation of an iceberg will, therefore, be disappointed. The tradition of *ekphrasis*, according to which one is gifted with a word-picture of a phenomenon, intending to make available to experience the phenomenon's invisible meanings, rendering it more real, more of a subject in its own right, is quickly departed from.[7] The object is, simply, not delivered. A desire aroused by the promise of *ekphrasis* for a fuller possession of the phenomenon is, as it were, left hanging. This iceberg can be no such gift. This aposiopesis means that the iceberg, always going toward its own absence, remains unrepresented and uncircumscribed. Thus it is as much a matter of what the poem does not say, what it does not do, as what it does say and do. The gift of the poem consists of a certain mis-giving. As the iceberg has "wandered" into view, so too has the poet, and as the poet's vision wanders from the iceberg, after having frozen it forever in the poem, the poem itself "wanders." Neither the iceberg, nor the poet, then, is the true subject of the poem: neither of them can ever be found again occupying the same space as when each was first noticed or beheld—when their presences were first "felt." Each is, however, *of* the subject. The "subject" of the poem is this particular kind of wandering that cannot be understood as anything but the action of thinking—without direction—which is to say, in all possible directions; without voice—which is to say, in the polyphony of possible, yet unvoiced voices; without goal—which is to say, without final answers to the questions shuddering in each word.

* * *

Such wandering has, in fact, already begun; it began with the title which strikingly brings together those examples of the "absolutely great" which Kant finds in nature and designates as "sublime": the solidity of the mountain and the ceaseless, restless motion of the sea. At the same time, however, these two are never quite easily united as the name "iceberg" might suggest. A hybrid-name, originating in Danish or Norwegian, it is composed of the literal "ice" yoked to the metaphorical or analogous "berg." But an iceberg, an "ice mountain" or "mountain of ice," is no "berg" at all. A gigantic chunk of ice, it has the countenance, the shape, the appearance only, of a mountain: it *reminds* of a mountain: a mountain dis-placed, out of its element. Thus, the two words, one literal, the other metaphorical, which are joined to make this compound name, nevertheless are already separated by their different semantic and topographical registers, a separation the compound word, made of two separate registers, nevertheless and quite paradoxically contains. Separation is, of course, that which marks the origin, the "birth" (the technical term is "calving"!) of an iceberg, its cleaving from a glacier or glacial field and the beginning of the suspended temporality of its watery travels along and against currents and courses both visible and invisible. Having broken off from a glacier, an iceberg, its grandeur notwithstanding, is already and always a fragment, an incomplete part of an absent whole never to be re-attained.

This incompletion, this presence of the fragment, which implies the absence of, and the loss of unity, is just that which the poet seeks to preserve in the prayer-like address of the opening verses—an address itself broken, interrupted. "I want no summer to melt you / I want no tip to disappear where / I find you. . . ." Though asserted with all the boldness associated with the formula "I want. . .," there is, nonetheless, a beseeching, almost plaintive tone to these lines, inseparable from the impossible desire—desire for the impossible—they express. That desire, a selfless seeking of the preservation of the irreducible other, constitutes absolute hope—hope in spite of everything. The entwinement of hope and desire—desire-in-hope and hope-in-desire—are, because the desire of all desire, their *contra naturam*, the counter-temporality that belongs to all prayer. This is the case even when the prayer does not beseech but apparently commands, as in, for example, the words "O, Lord, hear my prayer," in which the supplication, the plea, is unvoiced, yet the statement itself is such a plea, a request. This means: O, Lord, I pray that you hear my prayer. Which is to say, every prayer contains the prior prayer that it be heard. Thus every prayer contains a painful question of its own possibility. Prayer, then, is a particular order of language wholly oriented to a *now* released from time's inexorable flow. In such a *now* is

the relentless tick of time—which amounts to its loss—arrested, interrupted in such a way that another, already forgotten time, its *nunc
stans*, may occur and be fulfilled. Therefore, even when it is found as
the subject of a statement, the I is the I who beseeches, who, in a state
of lack makes a request, one, moreover, that may not be heard. The
request of the prayer is thus joined to the passive activity of waiting,
which establishes a time-out-of-time, a little eternity, a time frozen
yet full of motion, as the experience of anyone who has ever waited
for the arrival of a hoped-for word, or the presence of a beloved, can
no doubt attest. This *now* bears all the characteristics that exempt it
from identitary time, that is, progress and development. At a stand-
still, this now-time, so full of movements, is nonetheless cut off from
the movement of chronological (identitary) time, those qualities
which make time measurable, give it dates, a destination, a purpose,
and a finality from which it can be recounted, as the *"Finis"* that
marks the end of every narrative marks the point at which that narrative began and its *raison d'être*.

Once separated from notions of development, the movements contained in the time-of-the-now cannot be understood by means of continuity. The principle of continuity is turned into its opposite. From
the point of view of continuity, however, actions which are discontinuous, which is to say dis-organized, are already lost—without goal,
purpose, direction—and, to the extent that these qualities determine
meaning, such actions are held to be mere flutter, meaningless.
Nonetheless, only in the interruption of chronological time and its
suspension in the time-of-the-now can the critique of history as
progress, that is, the forward movement of time, where "forward"
means amelioration, be undertaken. In the fissures, the hesitations,
the separations—the blanks—are the pain and the sufferings of history, which history ever busily conceals, brought out, made audible,
discernible. Only the arresting of time-as-progress provides, paradoxically, that which progress promises: the attainment of the moment
when human beings are allowed to breathe easily and freely.

*   *   *

The self, the subject, is likewise turned inside-out by the eversion of
history-as-progress. The suspension of continuity which that notion

contains effectively demolishes the self-certainty of the subject, its unity, its becoming, by arresting it in temporal stand-still. In time's arrest, the subject, too, is suspended and its fragmentedness exposed. From the point of view of chronometrics, such a suspension is equivalent to a catastrophic breach, a massive *disorganization*. The immobilization of time does not result, however, in a state of affairs that might be equated with, or considered, homogeneous but one of an altogether different sort. Time at a stand-still is not a syncretic gathering up of the separate moments which, when compounded, compose a continuum. Rather, the opposite holds true: it results from the stunning of the continuum into moments no longer capable of easy summation, moments which are divided against each other, even as they are considered (by identitary time-consciousness) to form a unity which over-rides its heterogeneous components by absorbing them under a single, conceptual organizational principle, thereby transmuting the heterogeneous into the homogeneous. The cessation of such a conceptually unified time breaks it open, allowing all it had contained to spill out, as it were, revealing much which the concept had concealed. The disruption of homogeneous time is marked in language by the use of the subjunctive mood. The expression of wishfulness, of desire, accomplishes far more than a mere indication of a problem to be rectified. The subjunctive mood indicates a subject and a state of affairs which are lacking. In this sense, it is the incompletion of the subject which the use of the subjunctive manifests. When, in the opening verses, the poet writes, "I want no summer to melt you / I want no tip to disappear where / I find you. . .," these apparent declarations front, as it were, a request muted in their assertions. When the *appeal* of these words is heard, the assertion of the "I" is utterly transformed into the very absence of self-assertiveness: the lack, rather than the plenitude, is manifest. That these words seem to have no clear addressee, though they are obviously addressed, renders them devoid of intention: they exemplify language removed from intention, action, and utility—and, therefore removed equally from the thrum of the circuitry of "communication." Without destination, adrift, these lines contain the not-yet words, the silent under-words of speech. A momentary hush in the midst of the world's clamor.

✳   ✳   ✳

The not-yet words, the inaudible murmurings of wishes that bring a halt to time, have the effect of rendering space itself blank. The territory of the under-word is the *no-where* from which it seems to emerge and to which it goes, having no path, no definite road to travel, no destination, or *telos*—without where, without why, without how. It is precisely here, in the not-yet and the nowhere, that we find ourselves on the outside of, and prior to, the orders of language, discourse, communication, knowledge, unbound by the dullness of definition. On the outside, with no fixed address—this is the location of the "I," and this "I" cannot be comprehended by regularities and expectations and assumptions of any discourse(s). Such an "I," neither grammatical nor empirical, is the pronoun that marks—perhaps *only* marks—the place of a subject which, far from emulating the completeness that marks the subject, cognitively and discursively, is that in which a past and a not-yet coincide. The subjectivity here presented is one composed of the scars and cracks of its history as well as the longings which, unsatisfied, make of history a history of such dissatisfactions, stirring relentless, unformed, unsettled. The "I" of the poem, then, betokens a subjectivity wholly out of keeping with, and removed from, normal—and normative—ways of speaking, thinking, acting, and being. In fact, it can be said that this "poetic subject," incapable of such confirmation and conformity has departed from such a discursive, cognitive subject, allowing the observation to be made that the poetic subject marks a place for subjectivity yet to be realized because its true place is beyond the markers of the self-identical subject, the imaginary unity of which occludes or mystifies the subject's self-diremption (into the one who knows and the one who knows that it knows). If the split in this subject is not resolved by regression to an imaginary unity, part of the subject's dividedness becomes recoverable for a relation not determined by that of cognition in which the knowing subject stands over against the known object. The split inherent in self-consciousness, if conceived outside a cognitive relation, is freed to a wholly other relation. The "I," in a state of *distraction* from itself (and from the spatio-temporal co-ordinates by which it is situated and determined) encounters an object likewise estranged, disconnected from its pre-established identity. In this relation, the absence of a self-identical subject is co-equivalent and equiprimordial with the absence of a self-identical object. The poetic "I" reflects upon its "object" and reflects upon itself *via* that object, producing itself, creating itself, through that relation, from which it is inseparable and unabstractable. In this creative relation, which Hölderlin names "transreflexive," the otherness of the subject no less than that of the object is released. The singular, the unique, the irreducible—the extraordinary in the ordinary—shows itself: the condition of creation.[8] That creation is one of *exposure*. To speak as a subject is to be deprived of the language that nonetheless fills the mouth and chokes the throat, an inescapable fact that turns every apparently gilt-wrapped utterance to lead soon enough. The self that seeks, does so only haltingly, gaggingly, half-forgotten by the language of which it is supposed to be the master. The blank words of its silence affirm, thus, only its own incompletion. Which is to say, within the wandering question that is "The Iceberg" are enfolded the twin troublemakers: memory and longing.

*   *   *

> Lorsque la mémoire nous sera rendue,
> l'amour connaître son âge
> —Edmond Jabès

History begins at the moment of the experience of separation, a moment with which any life is replete. History is, to put it simply, an accumulation of discontinuities which the word "change" renders anemic and incorporeal, smothering it under the weight and the opacity of a "natural law"—the coldest, the most automatic, the most thoughtless: the *summa potestas* of impartiality, under which any rupture in continuity is understood as part of a continuous process. The notion of change, therefore, is one of ex-change: the past exchanged for a present which supplants it and fulfills it and renders it mute. But even more, that notion renders the present, because, as supercession of the past, it is the new-and-improved, just as quiet as the muted past out of which it issues. History understood under the principle of change, itself pseudo-natural, is, therefore, the infinition of the same in which any substantial difference that might obtain is erased, all separation abstractly united in the concept. This "history," in so far as

it evacuates experience and renders it superfluous, is but a disguised
metaphysics to the degree that it raises "change" to an immutable law
that operates far above the heads—and the bodies—of human beings.
Yet when such "history" is brought into contact with that otherness
which is unabashedly and inescapably metaphysically riddled, i.e.,
"Love," is it pulled down, like a kite, from celestial empyrean heights,
for which it may nonetheless yearn, and brought into the hands of a
physical being whom it may have thought to have left far below. The
sheer physicality, hence mortality, of love, apart from which it is
inconceivable, operates on history as something like a reality principle, detranscendentalizing it, making it, therefore, actual, experi-
ence-able, memorable—and destructible. Only, in fact, when love is
understood in this way is its critical aspect recognized: for only love's
otherness can, literally, preserve the very differences, the distinctions
which "history" writ large demolishes and forgets—forgetting the
demolition of those differences thereby. History is the history of such
destruction. It stupefies love in so far as its self-generated amnesiac
forwardness stupefies memory. If the muted request of the poem
which throbs as a secular prayer is heard as historical, then the aim
of this plea is the emptying of the self of the amnesia of "history"
itself, and hence to reveal it as the emptiness and destructiveness it
denies, in order to initiate the unspeakable "leap," the break in the
syntax, which "creation" involves: the history "history" effaces.
Through this "leap," appearances, terms, thoughts, and all that is
excluded by the logic and grammar of choice, come into relations
previously prohibited. Freedom is released—from a teleological
never-never land and from its formalized procedures, to become
actualized in the "leap" that is simultaneously a "leaping clear" and
a "leaping into."

*   *   *

'Love' wanders, the speechless
mind of it, all that cost of the
flowers and statues—all that
city of delighted streets and
whimpers   O, the locked heaven
whose gate jangles   I wonder
at the steep of it

That "'Love'" appears suddenly and wearing quotation marks at once reveals a truth about it: although unpredictable, it has always and everywhere already been spoken. Moreover, its having been spoken does not diminish by a jot the force of its arrival, its presence. Nonetheless, having been spoken, it has a history. It has opened lips and welcomed mouths all of which have felt it but none of which has ever held it firm. It remains no one's property, and hence perpetually—"constantly"—turned into a kind of outlaw—contradictory, nullifying every calculated choice. Its originary condition, like that of history and freedom, is separation. As freedom's truth is to be found in its continually freeing itself from that which limits or contains it, love's truth is impossible to comprehend apart from freedom's actualization, apart from its activity. This is not to say that love's task is that of ceaselessly stitching up unities torn by freedom's activity. The attempt to form unity, or community, out of parced-out social particularities first known in the "bindingness" of religion (the *religare* of Christianity) could not, under contemporary conditions, perform any but compensatory duties—and rather domestic, menial ones, at that, in order to ensure the smooth operation of the household and all its inhabitants. When love is brought, as it were, into constellation with freedom, its *historical* face emerges, an emergence which in no way eliminates love's transcendental or metaphysical dimensions but rather enhances them. At the same time, such a constellation does bring love closer—perhaps uncomfortably—to reason, which, even if it does not operate in quite the manner Hegel thought, is nevertheless bound inextricably into history. Only when love is understood historically can history's forgetfulness be made plainly visible—and hence can that which was forgotten be awakened from the death-like slumber, the oblivion, to which history had consigned it. Love's "reason" is, then, anamnestic: it "keeps track," as Johann Christian Metz has said, of history's "forgetting" (191). That is to say, not only of the forgotten history but also of the forgetfulness of history itself. Love, when perceived to be historically constituted, then, is free of the myths and the dogmas of its ahistorical fulfillment—either primally, as pre-history, or finally, as post-history—traces of which, inasmuch as such myths and dogmas suggest happiness to the fullest degree, they nevertheless contain. The anamnestic reason of love,

however, continually encounters guilt and culpability, failure and dis-
figured hopes—in a word, suffering. That alone is enough to make it
very unpleasant. In the claim of every "advance," in the heralding of
every "achievement," and in the declaration of every "improvement,"
the anamnestic reason of love hears "alibi, alibi, alibi." Only in the
recognition of failures, cruelties, and culpabilities, the currency of
suffering past, present, and future, to which the anamnestic reason of
love is thoroughly attentive, can the capacity for freedom achieve the
dignity it already pretends to have secured for itself.

* * *

The body of love is breath. "'Love's'" appearance in quotation marks
also sets that word loose to wander speechlessly. To wander means to
have no destination, whereas to be "lost" is altogether different. To be
lost means to be separated from one's destination and the way that
leads to it. As in traveling, so in thinking: the destination determines
the line. Without a destination, linearity (of thinking, of discourse, of
temporality, of poetry) is not. The absence of destination, of the place
of arrival, suspends the unity and singularity of a journey, its *cursus*,
and shatters it. The "line" of such a journey (abstract to be sure) can
now be defined only by its splittings, its deviations from linearity: that
line is a *broken* line. Without destination, or future, the line can be
known only by its past, from the silences and absences of which it
ceaselessly "comes." In this way, that which wanders moves beyond
itself, away from itself, for its past neither determines it nor propels it.
Rather, it is that which is left behind. At the other extreme, its desti-
nationlessness equals a purposelessness—the freedom of drift that it
is to "wander," a word which signifies a condition known only nega-
tively. "Wander," not retreat, is the negation of "advance." Moreover,
though it suggests activity, or action, it is essentially passive—a passivity from which it is nonetheless grammatically barred. "Wander" is
a verb without a passive voice. Yet its activity, without goal, will, deci-
sion—without all the attributes of action—confers upon it a rather
special condition, one in which activity and passivity are inextricably
enfolded. The activity, informed, so to speak, by the absence of anything that resembles action, is passive, while the passivity, inasmuch

as it is in motion, is informed by activity. "Wander," then, is a passive activity and an active passivity. It suggests both restlessness and peacefulness while holding each in contiguous tension. If its restlessness suggests that there exists no peace or tranquillity, its peacefulness suggests the futility of endless, unsatisfied activity. And the tension between them suggests that peacefulness can never be achieved without the restless dream of its restfulness, its "resting," being finally attained, paradoxically, in its dissolution.

* * *

If poetry appears to have grown tired of the subject of love, that may be due to the fact that it is now concerned with matters that seem more pressing. No matter. For love has fled to the airwaves and the media, where it forms the inexhaustible fodder of country-western songs, TV sitcoms and talk shows, and self-help books of the sort written by the likes of John Bradley, Leo Busaglia, and Marianne Williamson. This market for love is not, however, mere testimony to love's degradation, for the market's liking for love is far from new. Nonetheless, when love is trafficked in the market in this way, its consolational force, which it provided *against* the conditions concentrated in the market, emerges clearly as an attribute of the market itself. As something like a salve for the brutalities that the market normalizes, the marketeering of love serves to reinforce those self-same conditions, strengthening the very market in which the hurt and the balm are produced. The love industry, which includes the love-talk industry, is, then, the metaphysical machine *par excellence*.

If lyric poetry has ceded or abandoned "love" to this market, that cannot be considered yet another triumph of capitalism; it cannot be understood in terms of market forces alone. Rather, the love of lyric poetry may have, on examination, elements which render it, even in a small, uncertain way, incompatible with, if not hostile to, the current apparatuses of the love factory. At the risk of over-generalizing, it is nevertheless possible to claim that the love of which lyric poetry has sought understanding is a far more complex matter than the current consolational model offered across the counters and over the airwaves. This complexity is to be found in lyric poetry beginning with

Sappho and continuing forward, but obviously not in a straight, or unbroken line of development. And for good reason. For in such poetry, as it is concerned with the *experience of love*, is to be found an aspect which consolational love must keep out if it is to preserve its perfect commodity status: the destructive character of love. This aspect of love, not just "hearts and flowers," is treated by the lyric poets through the ages. It undoes those who experience it, destroying the ego and shattering both the self and the certainty of self-certainty. In short, it ruins all that which the industry and the administration of love seeks to maintain—self-improvement, self-affirmation, self-help. Thus it is the vulnerability of the self, incorrigible and insuperable, which the lyric poets give us, and of which they remind us in their swoons, their agonies, their heartbreaks—the doubly-inscribed losses: of the assumed self and of the love that broke and refashioned that self as its troubling gift, larger and more powerful than the life in which it lives, as Rilke observed in *Letters to a Young Poet*. From the viewpoint of the market, this type of love is an item bewitched by instability, unpredictability, and unmanageability; it is a product with no future, a failed product because a product no right-thinking consumer would want. It just will not sell.

If the quotation marks on both sides of "love" can be understood as the wrapping in which, like *bon-bon*, pill, or prophylactic, it is delivered up, no longer "larger than life," but now rendered small enough to fit into purse, pocket, or wallet, that packaging is the jail-house or the asylum from which it "wanders," erring, so to speak, if not free, at least on the loose.

Perhaps there is a simpler (but not "simple") truth to be seen and heard here: love is a word that is always quoted, even as it is subjectivized; in fact, its subjectivization is always a quotation. If it is difficult not to hear an ironic tone in the quotation "love," that irony owes perhaps to the insight that poetry never decked love out in kid gloves. Putting gloves on love has been the achievement of capitalism—to keep it warm and safe and ever-young—and, in accordance with consumer protection, to guarantee safety *from* love. At the same time, these quotation marks also indicate that love has a history, as do lovers. Like them, love, too, ages. The aging of love lies in greater nearness to the negative, destructive qualities that Sappho relates than can be acknowledged in the facile de-historicization of love, its ever-youthful glow, which dominates the current epoch of history, and from which love, especially in its erotic form, was never very far. For of all experience, the experience of love brings with it the recognition of one's own aging, the withdrawal of the self from the surface of the skin. In these marks on either side of love can be seen its scars and its wrinkles, the feet on which it walks, and even hobbles; can be felt the breath with which it is taken into the lungs and expelled from them; the hands that caress hands, faces; the lips through which it passes, out and in; the tongues that it conjoins and mingles—continuing all that, "repeating" it, reversing us, for that reversal is nothing other than experience. Love's absence from poetry, poetry's self-imposed silence on love, is not just a sign of a failure to understand or to present that experience; it is also a mute accusation against a world which increasingly deforms, disfigures, and truncates that experience. Yet, against love that world founders and sinks away, repeatedly.

✳ ✳ ✳

Every utterance of "love" is a quotation and every quotation is a sign of the distance in time and space of that which is quoted—of its elsewhere and of its having been. That which, by means of quotations, is drawn into the here-and-now of the present also lifts that present out of itself, away from its familiar and familiarizing co-ordinates. That "love" is memorialized, even commemorated, then, in its having been spoken, if only with inward accents, holds no real surprise, yet it most likely contributes to its poignancy. Love greatly needs objectivation, not merely as proof of its existence, but of its having been— and proof, too, of its possibilities having been. Its life, therefore, is not only that which admits the past but which is also, in every moment, passing; which is to say, turning into the past. Love, an always unanticipated isolation, is always passing. Each of its objectivations is also its *memento mori*. The continuity of love is to be found, paradoxically, in its brevity and its mortality, both of which every monument, every token, not only proves in its objectivation but arrests there as well. The *memento mori* is also a *memento vitae* and a *memento vivendi*—a remembering in two directions. In the objectivations of memory—in literature, or in the flowers placed against hard, cold stones in every cemetery, for example—are manifest the tendency of love to outlive its lovers. "Love" has a particular affinity for memory, by which it returns—and turns the one who remembers away from the habits and cares of the self, from the inexorable flow of things and events in which the present is only a step toward a future. For the "I" that remembers confronts, in the act of memory itself, an act of awareness of absence, otherness—not only that of the Loved One but also that of the self. In memory, the otherness of the self, not merely its past, is made manifest. The "I" that remembers designates nothing that can be seen, and the invisibility of the "I" that remembers allows us to understand that this pronoun is essentially and cognitively empty. Only when spoken in a specific utterance—which is to say only when it is filled by that which it offers in any particular saying—does it come into any visibility, even to itself. In this sense, the pronoun "I" also wears quotation marks, occupying a point between a repeatable system of the entirety of language and the unique, unrepeatable speaker. To be able to say "I," an entire language is required. Without hesitation, one could add "an entire memory"—an *alien memory*—which, like language and in language, precedes and shapes the speaking "I." Where the pronoun "I" occurs at the contact of the general and the particular, a homology is revealed with the word "love" which, though always containing something of the general and the abstract is nevertheless wholly specific in one's experience: no matter how common or general love might be said to be, it is always different when it comes to *you*. Love, then, is not merely quoted by the "I"; love also quotes the "I"; the speaking subject does not merely, or one-sidedly, appropriate language, but language, equally, appropriates such a subject. In the experience that is love, this is especially true. For it is not only that the "I" wants to say certain words; it is also that these words want to be said, to be spoken, to another, and they want to be spoken by the one they have singled out, at a particular moment, to speak them. Only thus, by being delivered up to a speaker, does language acquire a voice, and an "I" become I. The Beloved of language is the Lover. The entanglement of love and lovers, language and experience, comes to the fore in memory, a site preserved in poetry, where all that is said lasts beyond, while at the same time is suffused with, the particular moment in which it is spoken.

*   *   *

If it is by virtue of love that "I" can be said to participate in a "we," the generation of that first person plural pronoun forms the subject as well as the subject-matter of all politics, most especially all politics in which democracy has pride of place. Yet the uneasiness of the relation of love to politics emerges quite clearly when they are declined in the inverted genitive of *chiasmus*: "the politics of love" implies something equal in scurrilousness to "the love of politics." The tensions in the relationship of the two words do not owe, however, to the attribution of "otherworldly" or "ethereal" to love while politics is held to consist of the "real" or "pragmatic" affairs of the world—an attribution that merely re-plays the gulf between the transcendental *civitas dei* and the practical *civitas terrena*. Nor is such a tension to be understood through the retention of the duality of a private sphere that exists in a simple, though necessarily complementary contradistinction to a public sphere. Nor is it a matter of seeking to resolve that dilemma by announcing the mutual interpenetration of these spheres, hence making one a version of the other, identifying them as really one and the same. Rather than rehearse once again the old and the new formulae, it might be more illuminating to attempt an understanding of these apparently irreconcilable dualisms by examining the point at which they draw near each other, as if from opposite sides of a two-way mirror. That point is ethics.

This can be stated rather straightforwardly: politics devoid of ethics is, at best, mere formal proceduralism; at worst, disguised oppression. On the other hand, love without ethics is mere *sexus*, one-sided or reciprocal instrumentalization. In other words, the presence of ethics, in so far as it reduces the autonomy of both the theory and practice of these activities, disturbs them thoroughly. Without the self-criticism which ethics affords and requires, politics loses sight of its *telos*—the establishment of a true universal freedom and equality—to become not only a *perpetuum mobile*, but a *mobile* the goal of which is simply its own self-perpetuation. Without ethics politics has no measure of judgment but that of instrumentality, thus inverting means and ends: the end is quite simply the perpetuation and expansion of the means. Only ethics, oriented toward an order more worthy and more befitting human beings, is able to suggest a dimension and quality of life not wholly reduced or reducible to the order of politics. The utopian possibilities for which ethics *qua* ethics stands, though suspended or largely ignored in the present age for which all politics is a version of *realpolitik*, is all that is able to resist the reduction and debasement of this form of thought and action—as Marx openly acknowledged when he wrote that the end, or goal, of politics was the end, that is, the cancellation of the necessity, of politics. Ethics simply cannot accept the self-sufficiency of politics; for politics judges itself according to its own standards of calculation, especially today, when "society," local *and* global, is decidedly and frighteningly Hobbesian: the triumph of a terroristic logic according to which each person, antic and fearful by turns, is coerced into coercing others in multitudinous ways, and each is another's—or one's own—instrument.

Alienated from ethics, love is merely another *quid pro quo*, one more act of sale-and-consumption, subject, therefore, to the market forces that shape and permeate it. The exclusion of ethics from love that is *sexus* renders it a marketable, functional, manageable commodity. *Sexus* is eros punished, pre-disciplined by the principle of exchange, in the same manner as fantasy is dream degraded—mutilated and distorted by the absorption of the interdictions against it. If *sexus* can be reproduced endlessly, its manufacture obscures, beneath the sheer sparkle and glitter of its surfaces, eros's dull, irreplaceable shock: that shock is the shock of ethics. "To spend the whole night with someone is *agape*: it is ethical," Gillian Rose has written (65). Eros and ethics can be sundered only at great cost: objects call themselves subjects but, nonetheless, suspect themselves and each other of merely maintaining, and being maintained by, appearances—the facades behind which the subject, unable to come into its own, is caged. Ethics, here identified with *agape*, enables subjects to be released, that is, to become subjects.

Perhaps the clearest distinction to be drawn concerning the apparent incommensurability of love and politics is that of the relationship each bears to power. For, while politics retains the assumption of formal equality, it is dedicated to the pursuit and attainment of power. Thus equality is determined according to the measure of power. The proof of politics is to be found in the calibrated, quantitative securing of power, as evidenced in the formulation "power-sharing." Love, however, is concerned not with the attainment, the securing, the exercise, or the "sharing" of power, but with its surrender in responsibility. In a relationship that includes ethics, equality, to the degree it can be said to exist at all, cannot be achieved through formal procedures and their presuppositions but rather through mercy, which may be offered or withheld. Democracy, and the equality essential to it, cannot form the basis of the love relation. In a love relation, the power and the vulnerability of those involved cannot but be considered absolute and non-negotiable. Such inequality is, at the same time, however, the precondition for the experience of freedom and equality that such a relation can not only make possible but actualize. For while neither freedom nor equality can be claimed *a priori*, these are nonetheless produced by love's particular form of labor. Kindness, generosity, mercy, honesty, responsibility—the exercise of these qualities and abilities, their embodiment and reciprocity, form the substance of love's freedom—the fruit of its labors, which involve nothing less, as Rosa Luxemburg observed, than the shaping of the human beings who bring love itself into being.[9] In ethics is freedom fostered and created, not preserved as abstraction or concept, but enacted and embodied, undertaken specifically and mutually. That, and only that, comprises the substance of the equality that emerges from it. From the point of view of that which is referred to as "everyday reality," ethics is considered largely to be an inconvenient intrusion, if not an outright nuisance. If it is considered at all, it is usually endowed with something of a religious halo first—the better to put it in its place and confine it there, where it can be easily ignored or forgotten. Consigned to, in the words of the poem, a "locked heaven" (a phrase that brings to mind Blake's *The Marriage of Heaven and Hell*), it is removed from where it doesn't belong and deposited in the vaulted necropolis of stored ideals, a strong box which, by virtue of its steep remoteness, could be thought of as safe and secure only by those who observe themselves and their desires from too short a distance. To this savings account mentality of potential and progressively deferred riches, ethics delivers a shock—

by which the depository is lost but the saver, released from the true hellishness of the locked-down, unwavering empty time of numbing routine, is saved.

* * *

I wonder
at the steep of it

Wonder, even had Aristotle never esteemed it as the origin of philosophy, is worth thinking about. It is another of those verbs, not only intransitive but indicative of no discernible action at all. The verb "wonder" is identically twinned with its noun form, its action a condition of non-action. "To wonder" is to be in "a state of wonder." Yet this non-action, too, is devoid of a passive voice. To wonder already contains in its invisible, indiscernible activity the condition it names. Its similarity to "wander" (as in the ditty "I wonder as I wander"), while it may induce a wry smile, has more than a small share of truth, for wondering is a kind of mental traveling but without appointed goal or destination. Though wondering can be brought to a halt, it knows no end.

Perhaps it is just this quality of its endlessness without anxiety that has brought about its restriction to the province of childhood. Children are permitted to wonder. With children it is the innocence, the naïveté that colors their fledgling mentation, the endlessness of their questions. At the same time, it is, because endless (an end in itself), that which does not qualify to be considered "thinking." Not at all teleological, it is a most free form of play: one that not only has no goal, no appointed purpose, but one that follows no established rules or laws. In this regard, the activity and the state designated by wonder are completely and radically autonomous. Wonder, as a condition and an activity, is permitted to children in the same measure as it is denied to, and forfeited by, adults. Adults do not have time to wonder, do not have "time for" it. Nothing—nothing pragmatic, at any rate—comes of it. It leads not to solutions to problems but rather, if only with respect to the quantum of time it seems to evaporate, pesters the adult's life even more. The wonder apportioned to the "pre-thinking" or the "not-yet-thinking" characteristic of and desirable in children is, when indulged by an adult, considered to be just that: an indulgence, a self-indulgence, a reversion to childhood. From the point of view of adulthood, wondering—thinking without end or purpose—is a kind of shameful squandering of time. Thus, for an adult to wonder is not only to reject the seriousness and sobriety of thought oriented to an articulated purpose but also to deny that a boundary separating the child from the adult has been crossed, a denial which is described as "childish." Perhaps this occurs because those who express their wonder do so in a manner that is not readily or easily translatable into words, not subject to control by words or by their speaker. For, to be in a state of wonder is to have relinquished, without will, the control over language and over the self that the communication of purposeful thought and the performance of action require. Because incapable of analytic reflection without destroying itself, the language of wonder often sounds pre- or even post-linguistic. Discourse fails, overtaken by monosyllabic exclamation, the sound of breath taken away and restored: pure immediacy. Communication, to the degree that it occurs at all, becomes contagion.

The relinquishment of control over language, or the sudden loss of the ability to control it, entails a corresponding relinquishment of control over the self. What is the I that wonders, but an I distracted, distanced from itself? In wonder, the I is led away from itself, beyond its barriers and boundaries: dis-oriented, de-centered, as un-de-limited and amorphous as the anything—the unforeseen something—to which it responds, which evokes it. Boundless and mortal at once, and therefore, not, obviously a matter of volition, of self-direction, wonder is beyond will. If the I who wonders cannot find the terms to convey or describe that condition of experience, perhaps this is because wonder itself is without terminus. And perhaps it is precisely this quality that gives to it its alarming indiscretion. The self of wonder has entered relations incomprehensible according to the standard coordinates of subject-object; indeed, the abolition of such coordinates is indissociable from wonder itself, from the composition of its unnamable "'it" to the "steep" of which the wonderer is brought. This is not to say, however, that wonder simply carries out, behind its own back, as it were, something of a conceptual synthesis. It does not assemble or combine the separate and the discrete into a new unity. Rather, it simply does not undertake an analysis in accord with knowledge's taxonomies and regulative procedures. Thereby, wonder preserves, in all its moments, their suspension, their discontinuity: a simultaneous plurality of uniquenesses rather than customary hierarchies. Thus, the overwhelming sense of the uncanny that is the source of new experience. In distinction to a relation in which a subject of knowledge stands over against an object (or set of objects), wonder holds in tensile relationship all that with which it does not interfere. For wonder is just this non-interference, an emancipatory mode of thinking in which the object, free and spontaneous, is joined inextricably to a subject itself absorbed and dissolved in the "it" of the encounter. Wonder suspends the mastering gesture. The subject, dis-positioned and de-privileged, has no single vantage point, no spatio-temporal perspective that can be named, and justified, as such. The here-and-now of wonder sets adrift both time and space. Wonder transverses them.

If wonder can be considered an uprooted and non-directed self-surpassing of thought, an opening to new experience brought about by an unforseeable it," a "whatever,"[10] the uncanniness of that "whatever" also has the power to render old experience—the past—alien as well. All that is far draws near. The passings of which the past is formed present themselves in the present. And they are delivered by way of a questioning: for the past poses to the present the questions of what it is and how it has come to be what it is. To respond to such questions entails the recognition of the past's incompletion, entails the recognition that the past is composed by incompletenesses that have been forgotten. Such is its silence, its obscurity. The past, as an other of time's present, shows up; it catches up: one is caught up in it and by it. The past, it could be said, after Proust, awaits patiently. Its release to the present reverses time's movement by instilling that waiting that is attention itself.

> I wonder
> at the steep of it
> then wait, astonished that
> the sweet heart grows in some
> root or depth—and turns
> into ceremonies   there are

the losses of the heartland, light,
sleepless forms against themselves
I repeat you endlessly—

Waiting, scorned as a passivity to which one is forced, by circumstances, to comply, amounts to a breach in the continuity of time,
displacing activity with an emptiness made all the more unendurable
by its unfillability. The discomfort of waiting consists in its apparent
interminable issuelessness, its total uselessness. It can only be broken
off by summons or distraction. Hence, its destruction, always wished-
for, is that on which it depends, that for which it exists: waiting exists
to be destroyed. Until delivery from it, those who wait endure time's
mere passing, an endurance achieved by withdrawal. As anyone who
has spent time where waiting goes on—bank queues, the reception
room of doctors' offices, airports, railway stations, bus terminals—
waiting involves a withdrawal from the place and the time in which
one happens to be. If a somewhat haunting—or haunted—quality
attaches to waiting, it is the degree of the inclination for self-absence
it seems to instill. To the question, Of what does waiting consist?, all
that is signified by "memory" and "anticipation" presents itself. In
waiting, one is inescapably alone with one's own aging. Behind the
skin, the self decomposes into a temporality riddled through with
memories and hopes from which anxiety is never distant. Perhaps this
allows for consideration of the vacant expressions on the faces of
those who inhabit fully this timeless time and spaceless space, for
"memory" and "anticipation" name absences in two directions,
absences joined in the ineluctable duration called waiting. In fact,
such a pervasiveness of absences confers upon those who wait an
unmistakable and common anonymity: the anonymity of the "one"
who, on the surface, is nothing but waiting, shows nothing but its
emptiness, nothing but the presence of non-presence: a presence
made wholly of absences, and the (final) absence that awaits.

It is in the sense that it is possible to understand both wonder and
waiting as factors contributing to a state of exposure. In wonder, one
is opened to otherness; in waiting, the past, unmastered, dissolves, in
its own otherness, the development from it which the present claims
as its achievement, an achievement that effectively seals each from
the other. The past's otherness sets atremble the solid lines of self-

certainty in the present. Waiting is attending to the otherness of the past. It *is* this attention, entwined within which are memory and anticipation—both unforeseeable. The dis-positioning effected by both wonder and waiting, as a transversal of time and space, reveals history in such a manner that the hiddenness of the past is exposed and made present. So, too, are the hopes of the past, hopes by which a future (not, perhaps, this one) was once imagined. In fact, it might be said that history remains only obscured as long as the hopes of the past, the hopes *in* the past, go unattended. To attend to those hopes, to perceive in them their counter-finality, requires, even presupposes, an uncommon practice of freedom: one directed in opposition to the supposed direction of freedom—straight ahead over the horizon where the future stands waiting. Where freedom is defined exclusively—even primarily—through a fidelity to an idealized future (always "new" and always "improved"), attention to the past and to its hopes, amounts to "rubbing history against the grain," in Walter Benjamin's well-known formulation. Attention to finitude—and finitude is most strongly presented by that to which the word "past" is affixed—chastens any confidence in freedom's progressive evolution. Past hopes, consigned to oblivion as waste products of history, still contain, despite their unachieved contraversion of the world to which they responded and to which they opposed themselves, the breath that inspired them. Freedom's attentions, indivisible from ethics, rightly belong to finitude, to the passage of every living, concrete moment.

❉   ❉   ❉

The poet is first a listener *par excellence*. He or she hears history in a word, hears the breaths with which it was taken in and expelled, and hears in the word itself that inhale and exhale of the lives that gave it the life sedimented and concentrated in it. In the poet, history finds words—because words are, in the poem composed through such attentions, united with their histories. These words the poet takes up again, seemingly in repetition for the umpteenth time. The poet's retracing, by ear, the lost traces of a past through words—a past that preserves traces of itself in words—risks in this "repetition" the loss of utterance itself. The twin dangers of babble-like stammering, on the one hand, and silence, on the other, are ever present. Poets proceed along the sharp edge against which both are counterbalanced. Writing is vigilant: it is a waiting, the unfulfillable desire poised on a vacant point of time. This vacancy gives to the time of waiting its especial strangeness. For waiting is not merely a matter of remembering, or recapitulating the past, of repeating it in thought; waiting also offers a discovery of the past. Equally, and contradictorily, waiting contains the sense that it offers, somehow, a future repetition: this endless moment of time's mere passing will be, one day, experienced in the future, when it will be cited (and "sited" and "sighted"). Waiting seems like endless repetition of the past and the future alike, a time contaminated by both. Waiting is the gap in time that cleaves together all its separate moments.

"I repeat you, endlessly" the poet writes. A statement of four words, each a question and each question made of other questions. An "I" that repeats a "you," and does so "endlessly"? Do these words not refer to the situation of dialogue, one in which an "I" *addresses* a "you," dialogue as that without which neither "I" nor "you" exist? For is dialogue not the calling of the other, the you, that also calls the I forth? And are not these two little pronouns, the very foundation of dialogue, perhaps the most oft-repeated? But what sort of dialogue would be that in which "I" repeated "you"—and "endlessly"? Would not that kind of repetition, a mere duplication of the other, because nothing but an echolalia, founder? Would it not be dialogue's impossibility? Would not the interchangeability of I and you enacted as a repeat suspend them both? Would an "I" that merely repeats a "you" not present an extreme image, perhaps even a caricature, of a language speaking itself only to itself? More questions. Would it not be the case that an "I" that repeats "you" is an I lacking, an I at a disadvantage? Does such an I not lack even the capability to speak or to respond? Is this I not such that it lacks that which would make it an I? Is it not, then, an I that lacks a you? Is its condition of lack not one of asking? Of asking for a you? And is it not the case that to ask is to seek? Is the repetition the I performs not, then, an asking for, a seeking for, the you that allows it to be? "I repeat you endlessly" means "I search for you endlessly." It is a seeking that "commons" us

and "sorrows" us and "olds" us—and from the first it has its inclination to tip us, to tip us over, to tip us out, toward another, endlessly.

                           *   *   *

              Something that can go, ungreeting
              as all that is turned to heart
              is coming.
                              –Paul Celan

In one of his stronger assertions, Walter Benjamin—no stranger to
forceful assertion—wrote in the preface to his translation of
Baudelaire's *Tableaux Parisiens,* "No poem is intended for the reader
. . ." ("Task" 69). That statement still has about it more than a little of
the feel of provocation, perhaps moreso today than at the time, more
than sixty years ago, it was written. For its categorical negation denies
poetry, and hence the language of which a poem is made, any actuality in the sphere of communication. Moreover, it seems to deny to
the poem the quality of "humanness" that attaches to the notion of
communication. Further still, it seems to extend such a denial to
both author and reader alike. The identity of the author, while never
a matter of indifference, is here not the question. That question,
rather, is: who, or what, is the reader for whom a poem is not,
as Benjamin writes, "intended"? Better still perhaps, to phrase this
question in the conditional voice: who *could* the "reader" *be?* That
question, in so far as it departs from the empirical, even the
hypothetical, givenness of any particular reader, opens a way to the
understanding of poetry that cannot be encompassed by any form of
"communication" for which there is always an *intended* recipient
who, *qua* recipient, is always determined by the function he, she, or
it serves within a closed, anonymous system.
    The uniquely ostentatious form of language that is a poem has a
direct bearing upon the act of, the experience of, reading. This statement seems to say no more than the obvious: that one reads different
texts differently. One does not, for instance read a novel in the same
way as one might read a newspaper or a report. But there is more at
issue here. The paradox of the intimate relation of word (language)
and silence that a poem imparts (if only quietly) meets its counterpart

in the paradox of reading it. For this reading contains its own interruption. The act of reading a poem contains the very interruption
and cessation of that act. A poem makes no demands. *Any* notion of
compulsion simply does not apply to the reading of poetry. Equally,
for the reader, a poem does not simply stop or conclude. The reader
of a poem does not simply finish it—or finish with it. The *discipline*
of reading a poem paradoxically involves the averting of the eyes from
the page. Reading consists of a mesh of attentions, and such attentions involve a mesh of interruptions. If reading interrupts living,
it also extends it; equally, and just as paradoxically, the living that
interrupts the poem also extends the latter. Such interruptions inter-
penetrate each other. Reading, too, has its gaps, its silences. Thus, the
poem makes of the person reading more than, other than, merely a
person reading, releasing the reader from its page, from the book,
from the table supporting the book, from the room around the
table. It invites, it calls for and toward, just this freedom, a freedom
beyond thought. As nothing forbids the poem to dream, to think, to
remember, just so with the experience of the reader. The nowhere of
the experience that is reading begins here, at the threshold of the
nowhere of the poem, its U-topia. In such experience is a double
displacement: lost to the everyday demands, expectations, pleasures,
satisfactions, and conformities that pass for responsibilities, the reader, ejected from the self such activities and attitudes shape, is lost in
the uncircumscribed space the encounter with the poem has opened.
Reading released from words, reading beyond the page, beyond the
book and the books of pages—what is this form of reading unrestrict-
ed by, unconfined by, unconfined to, the text but distance? The
poem gives distance, the distance it has created, into which the
reader wanders, attentively. From this distance, the reader is able to
observe not only the space or the terrain of the poem. The distance
the poem realizes allows the reader a special vantage on the world,
the society of women and men that he or she inhabits. And the poem
allows one to see oneself, the self that has been left behind, on the
other side of the poem. Just this observation and self-observation,
undertaken from the vanishing point of the poem, places the self, its
society, its world in quotation marks, and places it, all of it, therefore,
in question. That self, that society, that world—that allness—is pre-

cisely that from which the experience of reading a poem can be said to desist by *indirection*, by a wandering that is both a wandering away and a wandering through—a seeking at once an attention, an attention at once a freedom, a freedom at once a responsibility.

NOTES

1. In *Pell Mell*, 25. The poem also appears in *The Holy Forest*, 223, where it is dedicated to Michael Ondaatje.
2. See Martin Heidegger, *Kant and the Problem of Metaphysics*, and Michel Foucault, "What is Enlightenment?" 32-50, esp. 33-37.
3. See *Truth and Method*, esp. 346ff.
4. The aging, not to say the poisoning, of language is an abiding concern of Paul Celan. See, for example, his "Edgar Jené and the Dream about the Dream" in *Collected Prose*, 4-5. Walter Benjamin, too, discusses "the maturing process of . . . language" in connection to translation. See "The Task of the Translator," 73.
5. The phrase is from Walter Benjamin's essay "Erfahrung und Armut," in his *Gessamelte Schriften* II,1: 213-16. My translation.
6. T. W. Adorno, *Negative Dialectics*, 407. When this essay was almost completed, I discovered Simon Critchley's *Very Little . . . Almost Nothing*. Critchley quotes Adorno's phrase, 20.
7. See W. J. T. Mitchell, *Picture Theory*, 165ff.
8. See the admirable discussion of Hölderlin's reflections on the subject in Andrew Bowie's *Aesthetics and Subjectivity from Kant to Nietzsche*, 67-72. Bowie writes: "Hölderlin wishes to make the dividedness of self-consciousness part of its own creative potential, which strives to show in aesthetic production what it would be to overcome the division without regressing into an imaginary unity" (71). Bowie, to his credit, observes the political relevance of this exploration of the subject incapable of being objectively grounded: "There is. . . in the fate of Hölderlin and that of not a few other artists of his age, a warning. . . . [A]ttempts creatively to explore the I which are not backed up by vital social and political advances will lead to disaster" (72), a recognition to be found through the works of Adorno and Benjamin, as well, both of whom were attentive readers of Hölderlin. See Friedrich Hölderlin, "On the Operations of the Poetic Spirit." Cornelius Castoriadis has examined this relation with respect to differing registers of temporality in "Time and Creation," 38-64.
9. See *Comrade and Lover: Rosa Luxemburg's Letters to Leo Jogishches*, esp. 104-5: ". . . a task like ours: to shape a *human being* out of each other. . . . It means we keep changing and growing, and this creates an inner dissociation, an imbalance, a disharmony between some parts of our souls and others. Therefore, the inner self must be constantly, re-examined, readjusted, harmonised. One must constantly work on oneself . . ." (Emphasis in original).
10. See Giorgio Agamben, *The Coming Community*, 1-2.

WORKS CITED

Adorno, T. W. *Negative Dialectics.* Trans. E. B. Ashton. New York: Continuum, 1973.

Agamben, Giorgio. *The Coming Community.* Trans. Michael Hardt. Minneapolis: U of Minnesota P, 1993.

Benjamin, Walter. *"Erfahrung und Armut."* *Gessamelte Schriften.* Frankfurt a.m: Suhrkamp, 1982.

———————— *"*The Task of the Translator.*"* Trans. Harry Zohn. *Illuminations.* New York: Schocken, 1977.

Bowie, Andrew. *Aesthetics and Subjectivity from Kant to Nietzsche.* Manchester: Manchester UP, 1990.

Castoriadis, Cornelius. *Chronotypes: The Construction of Time.* Stanford: Stanford UP, 1991.

Celan, Paul. *Collected Prose.* Trans. Rosmarie Waldrop. London: Carcanet, 1986.

Critchley, Simon. *Very Little . . . Almost Nothing.* New York: Routledge, 1997.

Dickinson, Emily. *The Complete Poems of Emily Dickinson.* Ed. Thomas H. Johnson. Boston, Toronto, London: Little, Brown, 1951; rpt. n.d.

Foucault, Michel. "What is Enlightenment?" Trans. Catherine Porter. *The Foucault Reader.* Ed. Paul Rabinow. New York: Pantheon, 1984.

Gadamer, Hans-Georg. *Truth and Method.* 2nd Rev. Ed. Trans. Joel Weinsheimer and Donald G. Marshall. New York: Crossroad, 1990.

Heidegger, Martin. *Kant and the Problem of Metaphysics.* Trans. James Churchill. Bloomington: U of Indiana P, 1962.

————————. *On the Way to Language.* Trans. Peter D. Hertz. New York: Harper and Row, 1971.

Hölderlin, Friedrich. *Essays and Letters on Theory.* Trans. and ed. Thomas Pfau. Albany: SUNY Press, 1988.

Jabès, Edmond. *Je bâtis ma demeure.* Paris: Editions Gallimard, 1959.

Luxemburg, Rosa. *Comrade and Lover: Rosa Luxemburg's Letters to Leo Jogishches.* Ed. and trans. Elzbieta Ettinger. London: Pluto Press, 1981.

Marcel, Gabriel. "Toward a Tragic Wisdom and Beyond." *Tragic Wisdom and Beyond.* Trans. Stephen Jolin and Peter McCormick. Evanston: Northwestern UP, 1973.

Metz, Johann Christian. "Anamnestic Reason: A Theologian's Remarks on the Crisis in the Geisteswissenshaften." Trans. Barbara Fultner. *Cultural-Political Interventions in the Unfinished Project of Enlightenment.* Ed. Axel Honneth, Thomas McCarthy, Claus Offe, and Albrecht Wellmer. Cambridge: MIT, 1992.

Mitchell, W.J.T. *Picture Theory.* Chicago: U of Chicago P, 1994.

Rilke, Rainer Maria. *Letters to a Young Poet.* Trans. M. D. Herter Norton. New York: Norton, 1954.

Rose, Gillian. *Love's Work.* London: Chatto and Windus, 1995.

Robin Blaser as Theseus in Euripides's *Hippolytus*, performed at
Simon Fraser University, early 1970s

ARCHIVES

Jess Collins, Madeleine Gleason, Robert Duncan, Robin Blaser, and Jimmy
Broughton at Madeleine Gleason's apartment, c. 1952–53

Blaser acting in a masque by Robert Duncan (unpublished)
at Duncan's San Francisco apartment, c. 1951

DIALOGUE OF EASTERN AND WESTERN POETRY, BOSTON, 1956

Robin Blaser and Jack Spicer

Annotated by Robert Duncan
Edited and Introduced by Kevin Killian

"THE CARDS"

An inch-thick stack of lined index cards, 3 by 5, bound by a pair of flimsy rubber bands, sitting at the bottom of a sturdy banker's box among the Robert Duncan papers at the Bancroft Library at Berkeley. I picked up these cards long ago, and riffled through them like a flipbook, noting the jumbled numbers in the top right hand corners. I recognized the handwritings: Robert Duncan's plummy, slightly florid script; Robin Blaser's scratchy, readable diagonals, Jack Spicer's childish scrawl—a fifth grader's. Then I popped off the rubber bands and dealt the cards. That's what I called them—the "cards," like a fortuneteller or Tarot reader, or indeed, like a seasoned Vegas habitué. Then my textual nightmare began.

Robin Blaser and Jack Spicer were young—each had just turned 30—when they wrote the following "dialogue on Eastern and Western poetry," in Boston, late in 1956. For Spicer, Boston represented a kind of dead end; after a brilliant beginning at the University of California in Berkeley in the years immediately following World War II, he had come to the East Coast to seek fame and fortune in New York, but after six miserable months there, he had repaired to Boston, where his Berkeley friend Blaser had found him a library job. Spicer had cut a brilliant swath through the poetic circles of Berkeley, but found life after college a depressing swamp of disappointments and dashed dreams. He had nearly ceased writing poetry, though he continued to consider himself a poet.

Blaser's case was rather different. His own poetic career was just beginning. Although he had written poetry for many years, he was shy about exposing it to the world, and labored steadily and quietly in the shadow of gabbier, showier friends. Sensitive, brilliant, intellectually curious, Blaser was working as a librarian in Harvard's Widener Library while his boyfriend—I guess the word then was just plain "friend"—James Felts, worked at nearby Tufts University. Blaser's great personal beauty won him many admirers, whereas Spicer's looks caused him great pain—he had earlier written a poem comparing himself to a "dancing ape" who must dance alone while other animals couple off. Abrasive, cutting, often unkempt, Spicer made an odd contrast, almost a foil, to Blaser's elegance and charm.[1] Their year together in Boston, thrown together, far from the Berkeley bohemia that had nourished them, became a turning point for both men.

Blaser and Spicer remained very much conscious of a third poetic presence, always looming psychically nearby, one that informed or contextualized every word they wrote: a ghostly ear, listening in. This was Robert Duncan, whom both men had met as students in Berkeley. Six years their elder, Duncan seemed already to have lived an incredibly rich and full life—he had known Anais Nin, Henry Miller, Paul Goodman, Pavel Tchelitchev—and had already "come out" as a homosexual, in the pages of the magazine *Politics* in 1944. In Berkeley his furious energy and his enormous enthusiasm for the then-untaught moderns (Williams, Pound, Loy, H.D.) was an education all by itself, and Spicer and Blaser fell under his spell at once.

The overwhelming mode of the Berkeley poets was, for various reasons, the elegiac, and had been so for ten years: the ultimate fruit of this mode was Spicer's grand long poem "Imaginary Elegies," in which every element—music, image, line—is subordinated to a long slow discourse of absence, loss, utopia. The wartime elegies of T. S. Eliot, Dylan Thomas, Allen Tate, John Crowe Ransom, Edith Sitwell, Rexroth, Auden and H.D. were largely responsible for this post-war turn to melancholy and slow music, while the depth and richness of Berkeley's homosexual culture had converted this strain to a poetry of lost love—what Blaser, in this dialogue, calls "the personal parade." Now, in 1956, this Boston moment was to change radically the direction of the Berkeley Renaissance, as Blaser and Spicer found themselves under new influence, new pressures.

Robert Duncan, as usual, began it, when in the very early fifties he encountered the poetry of Charles Olson, Robert Creeley, and Denise Levertov, poets of the so-called "Black Mountain School" and quite Eastern—two Harvard men and an Englishwoman. To Spicer's astonishment, Duncan declared himself impressed by this new poetry—declared it to be not only equal to, but better than, the poetry being written in the Bay Area. Spicer dug in his heels and refused to acknowledge Duncan's conversion, while Blaser, who moved more quietly, began to study it with utmost seriousness. All around Spicer and Blaser, Boston was bursting with the poetic activity of those who had studied with Olson and Creeley at Black Mountain College: of particular promise were two very young writers, John Wieners and Joe Dunn. Another seminal figure was the black poet Stephen Jonas, who although never formally connected with Black Mountain shared many traits of the new spirit. These Boston poets showed the Berkeley refugees a new bohemia, one based on anarchy, drugs, cool jazz, midnight parties, broken syntax, and a vision of the page as an open field in which form is never more than an extension of content. The Berkeley bohemia, "literary and University centred" (to echo Duncan), with its beliefs in ordered ideals of purity and hierarchy, was never like this. Spicer was entranced by this Boston underground—if Berkeley had been an elegiac Billy Strayhorn arrangement, Boston soared into the uncharted cool realms of Charlie "Bird" Parker. In Spicer's case, a new kind of poetry followed the *coup de foudre* that attended him the moment the young Joe Dunn bought him a drink at a bar by Harvard Gardens—as another poet crudely commented of Spicer, he "wrote with his dick." Elsewhere I have discussed how, in Boston, first Blaser's, then Spicer's poetry broke from its elegiac limits into new and exciting fields: the sites of their future masterworks.[2] Poems like "Letter to Freud" (RB) and "A Poem to the Reader of the Poem" (Spicer) could not have been written in Berkeley; okay, they could have been, but they would have been very different texts.

It was in this spirit, and under these conflicting systems of influence and alliance, that the "Dialogue" began to unfold. Blaser adopts a placid, reasonable tone—exactly the tone guaranteed to provoke Spicer into ever more desperate and amusing casuistry. Spicer, well-versed in Surrealism—at least in the Marx Brothers' free translation—delights in being argued into a corner: it allows him to escape the horizontal, go vertical. I imagine this "Dialogue" began out of the fatal desire to capture the brilliance of table talk (and, of course, to give surcease from irksome library chores). Yet underneath, the purpose was deadly serious—a reconfiguration of American poetry, one which would alter the map to make Berkeley its center. As the index cards continued to mount, the insult comedy (itself a 50s innovation, one at which Spicer excelled) wavers from the Oscar Wilde level to the *bon mots* of Addison De Witt battling wits with Eve Harrington (*All About Eve*, 1950). The difficulty was staging this remap in Boston itself. Spicer's and Blaser's was not the Boston of the official histories of poetry—the Cambridge Peter Davison celebrates in his memoir *The Fading Smile*, in which chapters apiece deal with W. S. Merwin, Adrienne Rich, Sylvia Plath, Richard Wilbur, etc., while Blaser, Spicer, Dunn, Jonas, all go unmentioned.[3] (Note Spicer's uncertainty as to which generation Lowell belongs to: the two men would not meet for another 18 months, in San Francisco.) This "Dialogue" looks at Eastern poetry from the outsider's point of view; it's acerbic, unfair, arch and high with malice. Spicer made plans to send the piece to Robert Creeley for *The Black Mountain Review*. Would Creeley have published it had not the magazine (and the College) folded during its composition? Perhaps. But hearing the news of Black Mountain's collapse, Spicer and Blaser instead mailed the cards to Robert Duncan for his input, with the results noted below.

In its truncated form, "Dialogue" reminds me of the snappy, inspired repartee you find sometimes on today's Internet—a version of thought moving faster than words. This "spontaneous bop prosody," when combined with Robert Duncan's slower, more measured and judgmental commentary, written at greater leisure, gives the project an element of hypertext, thus to negotiate it seriously requires of the reader a double response. The three voices, moving in and out of one another like living systems, give us an eerie sense of poetic thought as it existed in 1956 among a small subgroup of homosexual men. The saddest thing is to see Duncan, while comparing Spicer's strategy to that of Shylock, referring so uninflectedly to "the Kike of Venice." What's up with that? Slip of the tongue? 50s ironic iconoclastic cool? Ezra Pound once more exerting powerful paternal racist influence? Private joke, jab at Jack Spicer's own anti-Semitism? I apologize for offending readers with this slur, but, wow, there it is and how could I elide it?

But back to my textual nightmare! A few cards were obviously lost or misplaced; different cards sport the same numeral; some of the links between thoughts seem so tenuous I'm afraid I'm missing a beat or two. Happily the handwriting of the three participants can be easily distinguished, and their casual approach to spelling provides no real confusion. A tougher obstacle to understanding by present-day readers might be the level of private reference shared by these poets. "You begin to sound a little like Mark Shorer who always tells the seniors that," complains Blaser to Spicer, and the reader may ask, who is Mark Shorer [sic; actually "Schorer"]? The American fiction writer and biographer was a fixture of the Berkeley English Department; among the poets his name was a synonym for dumb homophobia, pompousness, unearned pride. To use this reference, as Blaser does, implies a chatty, near-libelous familiarity all around; it also illustrates the degree to which, ten years later, these writers were still living amid a host of California ghosts. It's instructive to remember that while Spicer, Blaser and Duncan were all away from Berkeley, during this one eighteen month period, they had surrendered the Bay Area to the mass publicity of the Beat Invasion — the famous "Six Gallery" reading occurred in October, 1956 in San Francisco. Soon all would return to defend their turf from the Trojan invaders.

But meanwhile, freed from Berkeley gravitas, Blaser and Spicer's collaborations grew increasingly imaginative and playful. At the Bancroft, "the cards" are mixed among similar cards from a simultaneous Boston project—the so-called *Playboys of the Last Frontier*, a compendious tome, to be liberally illustrated with period documents and reproductions of paintings, which Blaser and Spicer planned as their intellectual, spiritual, and sexual autobiography—a cross between Cyril Connolly's *Enemies of Promise* and Robert Graves's and Alan Hodge's *The Lost Weekend*. In this book, old scores would be paid, rivalries rehashed, boys toasted, and the great poems of the period analyzed and put into cultural context. This project was never realized, but the truncated "Dialogue" is scribbled over with notes for it, "flying, crawling, swimming, burning / Vacant with beauty. / Hear them whisper."[5] And so are passages Spicer picked up out of John Donne's sermons and letters, using the cards as a commonplace book: passages which evoke distance, proportion, the loss of Paradise with cool metaphysical irony. I hope I've separated the wheat from the chaff—though the chaff's pretty darn provocative too.

—Kevin Killian

* * *

We have read in the natural story, of some floating islands, that swim and move from place to place, and in them a man may sew in one place and reap in another.
—John Donne, Sermons, CXXXI, 344, V

1
    Spicer: Eastern poetry—there isn't any Eastern poetry—and besides, too many people read it.
    [S. takes out a large red handkerchief and blows his nose.]

On reverse of above:
    Duncan: I have the advantage in entering the "conversation" of not being until after the fact a "present" voice. As some kind of fair play, in commenting I shall not choose to read ahead of the current speakers—; tho each time making my say as a third speaker rather than butting in after each one and two.

3
    Spicer: Look doll, this is supposed to be a dialogue, not a manifesto. Don't talk out of too many sides of your mouth at once. What I mean is that while poetry is an imaginary garden with real toads in it, that stuff published in Eastern magazines that they call poetry is an imaginary crossword puzzle with real rhymes in it. It has about as much to do with poetry as Scrabble does.

4

Blaser:

Nearly everything has to do with poetry. Just the desire to write a poem is in a sense a poem. Eastern poets, as we see them in *Poetry*, *Partisan*, *Hudson*, have chosen a kind of table manners of poetry. They set a problem for themselves, a rhyme scheme, a metrical pattern: what results is a well-baked cake with real icing. They use the tools of poetry brilliantly.

On reverse of above:

[Duncan:] Jack is always betting that others in the conversation will be as ignorant of what is going on as he is. Unfortunately since I am only vaguely informd about conventional, literary poetry I can offer no rebuttal. And it is interesting to compare Jack's "I dare you to show me one literary poem that is about anything at all" with Graves (who can afford to put money

[Unnumbered Card]

on the board) who in attacking the experimentalists (from Yeats to Dylan Thomas) dared his imaginary antagonist to show him any line that was about anything at all.

This is a disgraceful diversion.

On reverse of above:

[Duncan:] But one has only to compare Auden with Pound, or Tate with Hart Crane, or Louise Bogan with Marianne Moore, to doubt that the literary poets are to be distinguished from the vitalists by their brilliance.

5

Spicer: You mix your metaphors with Dylanesque obstinacy—table manners produce cake! Table manners are useless if there's nothing to eat. Poetry has to have passion for its food—either passion cooked up in tranquility or tranquility cooked up in passion. Eastern "poetry" has neither. We wait politely at the table and are served nothing but silverware.

Blaser:
(I have every intention of editing the mixed metaphor out of this tale.) Poetry is not limited to a passion of events or even to a vision of events. Passion is an easy way to make a poem necessary to oneself. There is nothing that cannot become a poem—a filthy story, the sexual act, a walk on Times Square, skating in Boston Public Gardens. Passion is a part of the poet's strategy, not a necessity of poetry.

On reverse of above:
[Duncan:] Spicer seems to be saying that "Western" poetry is vitalist "real toads"; and "Eastern" poetry conventionalist "crossword puzzles with real rhymes." But conventionalist poets Winters (and school); Horan, Schevill, Elliott, Emerson (who thinks Williams has provided a new literary form), Miles, Stacton, Roethke are all Western.
   Vitalists Wheelwright, Goodman, Zukovsky, Olson, Creeley, Blackburn

[Unnumbered Card]
   [Duncan:] are all Eastern.
   The greatest figures in the conventionalist army: Graves, Auden, Herbert Read, are British "Western Europeans."
   The greatest figures of the vitalists—some of them—are Continental European—René Char, Perse, H.D., Astrid Claes.
   The only active "Center" for publishing the second group is Eastern—*Black Mt. Review* and *Origin* (out of Boston).

On reverse of above:
[Duncan:] The most steady Reviews are all by the nature of finance & steadiness literary and University centred: *Partisan, Kenyon, Hudson*. It is interesting, as Blaser notes, that they set problems (as professors by trade are problem lecturers & examiners)—not only in rhyme & metrics but also problems of liberal or conservative social, political, psychological interpretation.

7
   Spicer: I said Passion cooked up by Tranquility or Tranquillity

cooked up by Passion. If your walk in Times Square is Tranquillity cooked up by Tranquillity or your sexual act is Passion cooked up by Passion, then your poem isn't worth writing. It belongs in a letter or a diary. I challenge you [S. takes off his pants and waves them to denote challenge] to name one poem that is an exception to this.

[Unnumbered Card]
　[Duncan:] We are trapped if we answer Jack at all: I cannot accept that the "passion" he is talking about here, or the "tranquility" are exchangeable terms for "passion" (which might mean the passions of our Lord for instance) or "tranquility" as I would mean. Like the "Eastern" magazines Jack is presenting an approach for a lecturer (however eccentric) and

On reverse of above:
　[Duncan:] not a concern of the "Life in poetry."

8⁵
Blaser:
　You're simply saying that the poet and the poem aren't the same thing. It seems to me that a tranquil poet's passionate poem (or put it the other way around) will be no less a poem than a passionate poet's passionate poem. You set up a kind of opposition between the poet's personality & his poem. Again, this may or may not be the case. Or do you mean that poems are always written after the event?

On reverse of above:
　[Duncan:] Blaser is quite right that a poem cannot be defined by its having any of these particulars—passion or instruction, literary quality or pathos.
　Is there any thing illuminated in trying to establish in place of kinds of poetry an orthodoxy of true poetry and a hinterland of fake poetry? Decidedly I think not. It is mere contension in the absence of and in

[Unnumbered Card]
　[Duncan:] default of interest.

9
    Spicer [putting on his pants]: You missed my point. Passion and Tranquility are capitalized. They represent moods of the *poet* and not moods of the poem. If Duncan's Strawberries in the Snow had been cooked up in Tranquillity it would be an Eastern "poem" fit only for a diary. If my Diogenes poem had been cooked up in Passion, it would be merely embarrassing.

On reverse of above:
    [Duncan:] Here Jack seems to switch positions—vitalist Dylan Thomas (perhaps because he was adored and licked up by conventionalists in U.S. Universities; but Tate was Hart Crane's sponsor; and Parkinson got his degree on Yeats) is reproved for "mixing metaphors": a very literary nicety!
    But as a vitalist—I agree with Jack poetry is preferred with passion.

10[6]
Blaser:
    You'll pardon me, Socrates, for being so stupid. Your statement still comes to the same thing. Only this time, the poet's mood and the poem's manner are in opposition. Again, possible poems, but hardly a necessity. This way WCW's little red wagon aren't poems, Moore's fishes, clearly seen, aren't poems. Too much poetry disappears.

On reverse of above:
    Duncan: The most important distinction to be made is between poetry written in order to participate in *Literature*: this is mainly produced by Professor-Poets of the Universitys; and poetry written in order to live passionately. The first group where it seeks mastery of *form* conceives of form as conventional and tends to interpret "romanticism" or "modernism: as being experimental:

11
    Spicer: No. They are being passionate about the clarity of the image. There are days that you can see an ocean or a blade of glass so clearly that they can break your heart.

On reverse of above:
[Duncan:] i.e. the lab work preparatory for new conventions in literature.

The second general "group" conceive of form as process, ritual, organism or emblem of experience: as a means of poetic experience.

Very good poet, for instance, who is of neither group is Frost. Ransom, Lowell, Josephine Miles all show that the conventional poet has a wide range.

In the second group are Pound or Cummings, but also as vast a range

[Unnumbered Card]
[Duncan:] of incompetants as is to be found in the first group. Certainly there are as many tricks, taking tricks to mean what I think Blaser means — "gimmicks" in uninformd organic poetry as there is in uninformd {conventional/literary} poetry.

Poets in the vitalist group are also distingishd from poets of the

On reverse of above:
[Duncan:] literary school because they are given to anti-conventional mysteries (Yeats is a theosophist; Eliot is in a secret cult of the Anglo-Catholic gnosticism; Pound actually has seen and heard Artemis and the animals of Zagreus; Rexroth practises Yoga and is an anarchist; etc.) (Stevens — angels)

Poets of the first group have conventional problems of belief, liberal or Regionalist social attitudes etc.

12
Blaser: Quite right. But that isn't quite what you said when you thought nobody else was listening. Besides, you begin to sound a little like Mark Shorer who always tells the seniors that. What you really mean is that the poet has to feel strongly & precisely & these Eastern poets don't. Table manners with not our cooked Hamburger.

On reverse of above:
[Duncan:] Thomas had passion but lackd intelligence. Auden has a "liberal" intelligence but lacks intellectual passion. Your choice.

However passion has many disguises and Spicer I think speaks truly when he indicates that it is his impression that it is to be "cookd up." This is just as truly not my impression.

13
Spicer: So I'm a hypocrite! [He grimaces disclosing a toupee on his tonsils] What I mean is that if the Poet (not the person) feels strongly he has to write precisely. And if he feels precisely he has to write strongly and the Eastern poets don't do either. But I like the words Tranquility and Passion because they're more mystical and therefore much truer.

[Unnumbered Card]
[Duncan:] Now Jack is pulling a swift one. After two offers of a counterfeit dollar he hopes to upset the set-up with the real McCoy.
Williams has said that he meant the *Wheelbarrow* as a passion. This *is* the so-much-depends. The "so-much-depends" of literary poets is whether the poem is good or not.

On reverse of above:
[Duncan:] Jack often is a confidence-man and uses the ploy "So I'm a hypocrite" or the Kike of Venice approach. Yet after being demasked he states the vitalist conviction very well. I too would like Tranquility and Passion because they are mysteries (but *mystical* to Jack) and truer to my feel.

14
Blaser:
I think St. Theresa might have done better and been truer, but I'll ignore the fact that you like to bait us Romans. But I'm more interested in what these Eastern poets—what we really mean is all these poets who appear in magazines published in the East & the Middle East (Chicago & Denver)—do do.

15
Spicer: There's not one that's under forty that does anything. They just rhyme and pick their noses.
I'm assuming Lowell is over forty.

16
<u>Blaser</u>:
  Your Passion and Tranquility offer what seems to be a good strategy for writing poems. What disturbs me is that such strategy leads
to a kind of sameness in the poetry. What Eastern poets do allow is
a poetry in which there is no demand for any special categories of
experience. Anything at all is subject for poetry.

17
  Spicer: You'd better give an example of a poem by an Eastern
writer under 40 that is about "anything at all" that you'd be willing to
read more than once, not an immortal poem, not even a good poem,
just one that you'd be willing to read more than once. I don't think
you can find one in all your magazines and books.

18
  <u>Blaser</u>: (It took 2 days to find one.) My point is that Jack Spicer's
poems are nearly always about love, and I don't think that subject any
more poetic than any other. I'm guilty too. The poems one really
noticed are James Merrill's "Orfeo" & "The Bed," Cid Corman's
"The Bearer," Jean Garrigue's "Cantabile," V. R. Lang's "25 Years."
Love

18a
  [Blaser:] poems. Nemerov's "Truth"—a mood poem. Can't a poem
be less charged, more direct, dependent upon precision of speech &
directness of sight? Much as I like the personal parade, much as I'm
guilty of it, that western poets make poems of, can't a good poem be
made at a distance from the personal tribulations of the poet? Take
Ann

18b
  [Blaser:] Ridler's "Choosing a Name" (Not an Easterner and better
than most of them.) Joe Miles, a Westerner, writes this way and the
East publishes her. See "The Campaign." Or take Louis Simpson's
West.

19

Spicer: It's curious that the only poem you can quote to prove your point is a poem with a California landscape. Time is a perfectly proper subject for passion and therefore for poetry and the poem isn't a bad one. So—I still challenge you! I won't comment on the first part of your statement since you're trying to change the subject and I don't want to change it.

19

Blaser:

Okay . . . Well take a poem which I refuse to say is good, but a poem which that mouthpiece of serious poetry, as Vernon Watkins calls it, *Poetry*, sees fit to print. What is it that recommends O'Hara's "The Eyelid Has its Stains" to Rago et al? Is this a poem in your sense or just in Rago's sense?

20

Spicer: I gather that you accept my point. As for the O'Hara thing, I don't understand it, don't like it, and see no reason even to discuss it. Third hand Rimbaud. But third-hand Rimbaud is better than third-hand Emily Dickinson which is what most of *Hudson* contains.

[Unnumbered Card]

[Duncan:] My viewpoint shld be clear. It is the attitude of the "literary" lecturer that there is third-rate Rimbaud or that there is third-rate Emily Dickinson. It is the conventionalist who thinks there is first-rate Rimbaud; and who asks to see a good poem.

Then the vitalist can answer nothing. Or rather this one can answer nothing. I do not, except by error, presume that all the meaningless

On reverse of above:

[Duncan:] conventions of Auden are bad poetry. Nor am I capable of seeing that it is good even with the expert guidance of Marianne Moore.

This "Eastern"/"Western" business is almost prohibitive anyway to any clear ideas.

21
  Blaser: Third Hand Rimbaud hell. Rimbaud illumines, and I don't mean to take his word for it. I'm not accepting your point, not yet, because I don't accept its product, which is not to say the product isn't good. What we need to do is suspend your position a moment and ask what recommends this poem or that one. Try Wm. Meredith's "The Fish-Vendors."

22
  Spicer: A "Talk of the Town" item in *The New Yorker* obscured a little and indented as poetry. It might have been two sentences of good prose.

Here is a new mathematics; without change of elevation or parallax, I that live in this climate, and stand under this meridian, look up and fix myself upon God, and they that are under my feet, look up to that place, which is above them, and as divers, as contrary as our places area, we all fix at once upon one God, and meet in one centre; when we do not so upon one syn, nor upon one constellation, or configuration in the heavens; when we see it, those antipodes do not; but they and we see God at once.
                                    –Donne, *Sermons, LXVII, III, 205-206*

ADDENDUM: MISCELLANEOUS CARDS

4-D
Chapter Landscape

1. Duncan's poem.
2. Imaginary garden with real toads in it.
3. Where people come from
4. Imaginary poets.
5. Imaginary enemies.
6. Wilson (on obverse: Wilson—Boys in the Back Room."
    Pacific ocean is dull

Too much scenery
No seasons. Spender, Thurlow, Connolly.

7.   What landscape meant to us.
8.   Suicide in Sandiago
9.   Weakness in the landscape—
     people from the landscape.
     Types of landscape—
     Sur—more like the Riviera than the Riviera

3
10.   Landscape (Removed)
      North Coast—
      Big Sur—Jeffers—
Energy of the   Treesbark—Sebastopol
Landscape.   Mary & Ham Tyler—
      Southern Calif—Desert—Bakersfield
      Moon-like Mojave.
      South Coast. beach landscape.
      Oasis landranges. Orange belt—Redlands
      Joshua trees—oranges on the trees.
4-D
On reverse of above:
                         "growne [illegible]
To such vastness as, if unmanacled
From Greece, Morea were, and that by some
Earthquake uprooted, loose Morea swoone
Or seas from Africks body had severed
And torn the hopefull Promontories heads"
                    —Progresse of Soules XXXI
                         p. 265

4
10.   Lost Valley—mountain area.
      LaBrea Tar pits—where nobody's
           dream comes true.
      Gilmore Island.

(Coachella Valley—cotton?)
Jefferson Dunes and Camels—from
       Egypt—
Bakersfield—
Tehachape
Santa Barbara

6
On reverse of above:
       "My verse, the strict map of my misery."
                              —To Mr. T.W.
                                   p. 173

5
       Central valley—Selma. Wm. Everson.
       Chinese Towns in upper valley.
       Owens Valley—MulHullen.
              Raped—water—
                     H. suicide.
                     canyon of beer.
       Hollywood . . .hills—Hollywood land signs
       Berkeley hills

3-C
On reverse of above:
       "We say the world is made of sea and land, as though they were
equal; but we know there is more sea in the Western than in the eastern hemisphere."
                              —D.EO. XIII, 555

6
       San Francisco—Golden Gate
              Park—hills instead
              of mountain—
       San Simeon—Hearst Castle—
       Pismo Beach
       Carmel & Monterey

Malibou beach—Ringe railroad
Valley of the Moon Eugene O'Neill,
          St. Helena; Jack London.
On reverse of above—   10
"That unripe side of earth, that heavy clime
That gives us man up now, like Adams time
Before he ate; mans shape, that would yet bee
(Know they not it, and fear'd beasts companie)
So naked at this day, as though man there
From Paradise so great a distance were,
As yet the newes could not arrived bee
Of Adams tasting the forbidden tree;
Deprived of that free state which they were in
And wanting the reward, yet beare the sinne."
                    –To the Countess of Huntingdon p.149

7-E

"A man may sail so at sea, as that he shall have laid the north pole
flat, that shall be fallen out of sight, and yet he shall not have raised
that south pole, he shall not see that; so there are things in which a
man may go beyond his reason, and yet not meet with faith neither."
                              –Ser LXXVI, III, 385

On reverse of above:
                                        in dim
          way to imagine what a real
          landscape looks like

                                                      1-E

                        *   *   *

NOTES

1. I'm simplifying, thus falsifying, the picture a bit here. Blaser, from a tiny town in Idaho, preferred to act out the city mouse while Spicer, who hailed from downtown Los Angeles, could play the country mouse, Will Rogers, "show me" naïf to perfection. Characteristically, the urban Spicer chooses his metaphors from the world of nature ("days when you can see an ocean or a blade of glass so clearly that they can break your heart") while farmboy Blaser deconstructs table manners. But we can also see this as a difference between two homosexualities, queer narratives that contain superbly their own contradictions, as Spicer's use of Walt Whitman's visionary discourse invariably stands Whitman on his head, while Blaser puts on his fey, effeminate act in order to allow genuine perceptions of the mystic and divine to shine through.

2. Killian, "Under the Influence: Jack Spicer, Robin Blaser and the Revision of 'Imaginary Elegies,' 1957," *Exact Change Year Book* #1 (Boston, MA), 1995, pp. 133-34.

3. Peter Davison, *The Fading Smile: Poets in Boston, from Robert Frost to Robert Lowell to Sylvia Plath, 1955-1960* (New York: Alfred A. Knopf), 1994. On page 26 Davison dismisses Wieners as "the sweetly demented poet."

4. Jack Spicer, "Imaginary Elegy #2"

5. Confusingly there's a second card marked "8," which may or may not have been a false start on Blaser's part, but it's one I don't want to miss: "Let me return to table manners. The difference between eating with silver or with the fingers, is like that of eating on a table or on the floor. To be without a table is a kind of deprivation."

6. On a second card numbered "10," Blaser interjects, "While you've talked on—I've found an example. Apply your argument to Pound's Vilanelle: the Psychological Hour." If the argument was applied at this time, the card's missing from the Bancroft; but three years later Spicer's thoughts on Pound found expression in "Fifteen False Propositions against God."

(Above) Blaser at
home, Vancouver,
British Columbia,
c. 1970s

(Right) Blaser and
Karen Tallman
(daughter of Warren
Tallman) en route
to the Acropolis,
Athens, 1972

Excerpts from

ASTONISHMENTS*

Robin Blaser

Editor's Note: I have removed many of the truncated or repetitive starts, stops, and conversational noises in translating these tapes from oral to written. I have also taken out some passages where the phrasing is confusing or the sentences seem to disintegrate in a tangle of phrases and mixed constructions; these elisions are indicated with ellipses in square brackets. However, I have tried to keep the rhythm of speech in this transcription and have punctuated sentence breaks and grammatical incompletions with dashes.

In attendance at these talks were Robin Blaser, Warren Tallman, Daphne Marlatt, Angela Bowering, Martina Kuharic, and Dwight Gardiner. Where voices are difficult to identify, I have used "Question" to denote a question or remark.

–Miriam Nichols

[Story VI, Side 19 (May 1974)]

TALLMAN: OK, well what are we getting tonight, Robin Blaser?
BLASER: I've got some notes. I wanted to stick with them for awhile at any rate because this is folding back and trying to make up for some slips and a bunch of other things and also trying to start a movement. The chapter's entitled "Dante Was My Best Fuck," which is— [*laughter*] . . . It shows the bitterness of my—yes, of my sexual life— and as a further point, it's true: he's a much better fuck than anybody else I was ever around. So that I wanted to fold it back in and then we'll see—at the end I want to ask you some questions about it because maybe I haven't gone far enough this time. Anyway I did want to just take up at the beginning, that I really have been having

*Text Preparation: Maureen Donatelli. Copy Editor and Advisor: Irene Niechoda.

a hell of a time with these occasions. . . . It seemed to me part of [it] was that my methodology was being challenged and I wanted to go at that a little bit right off the bat. In a very profound sense I always read, listen to and think with another man in order to discover a methodology because to me the method is actually the heart, this is the stance. Olson's stance is actually methodology, the way one stands and so on is method, so as a consequence the methodology I call a *techne*, and a *techne* is a way of knowing, and for me this would be a poetic knowledge. And then I also translate the whole job of poetry into the task of knowledge. The narration of that task is what I'm trying to get into the story, so that I build a landscape and the landscape that's built is, yes, the desert. I'm going to do that tonight: the unfinished water landscape that was to match that which not only polarizes the landscape from which I came but it actually is the unknown landscape. Water becomes the unknown for me. So I wanted to do that and get all that folding back going again.

Now "astonishment," as I've taken the word from Ernst Bloch to name these conversations, is the very source or origin of the world itself, an aspect of what the serial form can hold and present, and I'll come back to that when I do the serial form and the Orphic stuff, Angela. "[Astonishment] is the very source and origin of the world itself, ever at work and ever hidden away within the darkness of the lived instant, a source which becomes aware of itself for the first time in the signatures of its own estuaries as it resolves itself into them."[1] This is the pool in the center of the forest, the *"lago del cor,"* "lake of the heart," as Dante says it. In other words, I want to move from the simple geography, the limited geography of my own place and my own time where at the point of the meeting with Kantorowicz and Jack, I then fall into history—into time on a completely different level so that my present flows backward towards origins, primary thought, and begins to join the major movement of modern—of poetic thought in the twentieth-century, with Pound going backwards. They don't go back to traditions, they're going back to primary thoughtful condition and the condition of original feeling. Melville called this "original character." To have an original character means you . . . break the grid down, you knock it out, you go—you may go backwards, and you almost always have [to] in order to know that you

were present at all because the future form is something else and that
comes up later on. So I want a sacred geography to come out of this
book, and the sacred geography won't be there unless I can have the
clarity of the companionships which tend to be my only method of
being alive. The first astonishment, so to speak, is Jack [Spicer]. . . .
Now the next one is Dante—Kantorowicz, Dante—I mean these
runs of people. And these people are all in my view angels. I mean
even Robert Duncan, God help me. Angels are not always brightnesses in your life, [to] put it bluntly. But he is angelic.
QUESTION: Or they're brightnesses that fall.
BLASER: What?
QUESTION: Or they're brightnesses that fall.
BLASER: They're, yes—"brightness falls from the air," to quote a
marvelous line.² The sacred geography thing, with this unknown
water as a landscape that's not quite there for the original landscape
that I started [to] describe is for me an interrogation of death. I think
all serious thought is an interrogation of death. Jack, for example, met
his own death on Polk Street in San Francisco three years before he
died and brought the image that he met to me: a dark shadow . . . he's
walking toward to meet on Polk Street, and met it, and then it turned
out to be himself as the shadow—himself—literally seeing his death
this way. Now the interrogation of that informs Jack's work all the way
through. But then I think all serious thought even among those people who do not mention the word very often, that ultimately that's
what one is doing. The interrogation of death is why I want the Dante
in here because it's Dante who manages to let one move in a certain
direction and it's Kantorowicz that gave the Dante that wasn't the
baby-book Dante. OK?

Now, the issue then for me and that has been caught in an awful
lot of trouble is—well one is—and it has nearly stopped these sessions
at times—the Idaho kid didn't know that the manhood was dead. So
that now when I say that the manhood is dead that's something I did-
n't know, but now know in another way: that the manhood had died
into itself as closed form and thought, closed into his need, into his
grief, into himself as measure, his will then imposing upon all things
and turning them into a human image, losing the actual interaction
between himself and the world. The Idaho kid did not know that, the

later kid is going to go through a whole bunch of stuff that tells him about this and that's why those companions—the Nerval, the Mallarmé, the Marquis de Sade—the whole thing then becomes horizonals. They pull me out to where I don't know, and I go with them when they do that. As a consequence, they are as much a part of my biography as anything else I do—the trip on the bus from Idaho, or the father and mother, any of that. All these people have that same intimacy for me.

TALLMAN: Robin, go right back through that again because that's important.

BLASER: The Idaho kid didn't know that the manhood, his manhood, or the manhood of all of us—because finally my view is that we are all dead, and cannot see one another; our visibility to one another as men has closed and we now really do no longer see one another. We have no public space and our poetry—we can go on writing in our living rooms and reading it to our coterie groups the rest of our lives. It has no public range. The interchange between the world and the manhood, the world in me was destroyed. But then when I find out that it seems . . . that's true for everybody, then I wind up into the mysterious thing that our lives are invaded by the unknown. The moment that the known becomes the definition of the manhood by itself as though it closed, it killed God, it closed the universe, it made up a psychology that said only men did the thinking. It lost the very polarization of his world and man, *face à face*, and having to, as a consequence, build an action. Later in these remarks I put it that we are visible there for the sake of the action; we are actually only the visibilities, the images of an action larger than ourselves. I'm playing with Aristotle when I do that, but we are there for the sake of the action and not vice versa.

TALLMAN: OK, now when you say "manhood" is that a kind of a sexual term like "malehood" or do you mean "humanhood"?

BLASER: Human, human, *humanitas* itself. And the reason for bringing this up now will turn up when I get to Dante, because the extravagant thing that I learned from Dante was about the *humanitas* itself, in which he winds up a heretic and they ban his books after his death. [They] would have burned him I guess if he'd been still above the grave. So the Idaho kid didn't know that until the Idaho kid tried to join the world and found it absent—the world itself, and all the images in the world. So the visibility, the manhood as *humanitas* or whatever you want to call it, the human element is no longer a visibility in the world at all, but a closure of relationships, interrelationships, a lyric voice that speaks only of itself and closes into itself, no longer narrates the world and the actual astonishment of the world. OK, that absence is for me the unrecognized disaster of a world devoured into the human form, rather than a world disclosed in which we are images of an action, visibilities of an action, an action which otherwise is invisible, larger, older, and other than ourselves. We are very beautiful bits and pieces there as in a comedy or a tragedy for the sake of the action, and not vice versa. The greatest need of the intellect is the unknown. Just there, the body becomes the companion of the intellect, a limit that is on the face of that limit, that on the face of it gives visibility to the invisibility of our unlimited form. To have dropped out of the active astonishment before the world—either as a singular small man, as a cultural grid, or as a whole nation—is to remain in the limit of what I am whether that be poor and broken or rich son of a bitch. The quotation that I like to use at the drop of a hat for this comes from one of my beloved French companions, Victor Hugo, and I'll put it in here:

> Every man has in him his Patmos. He is free to go or not to go onto that terrifying promontory of thought from which darkness is perceived. If he does not go there he remains . . . in ordinary consciousness, in ordinary virtue, in ordinary faith or ordinary doubt; and it is just as well. For interior peace it is obviously better. If he goes on that peak he is caught. The profound waves of the marvelous have appeared to him. . . . A certain quantity of him now belongs to darkness. (Bays 116-7)[3]

In these conversations I want "the profound waves of the marvelous" to roll over us. For me this astonishment, these marvels, have come to me by way of companionship out of the desert into the sea like a water baby. My meeting with Jack was an astonishment. He was an astonishment himself. His early poems are the—my first thought actually—the sea beyond that sea of the cat's eyes that I described in an earlier session. And just put those early poems on the block here. These are coming from 1947.

After the ocean, shattering with equinox
Has cast the last of creatures on its shore
After the final tidal wave has turned
And churned remaining rock to sandy vestiges
Ebbing, it leaves its tide pools in our skulls
Amorphous and amphibious, we gasp
And grasp the call and rasp of all recall,
The fishly odor when a mermaid dies. (Spicer 6)

* * *

4 A.M.

The many clanging bell peals loud.
The pulsing, driving sound
Falls groundwards, spent of tone.
Unbound.
I see,
Mind bent around the inner ear,
The long unfeelingness of things
Beyond all sound. (14)

* * *

CHINOISERIE

Sea lions bark, betray the rocks,
Define the jagged edges of this night;
Everything echoes.
Contorted conch shells strew this shore —
My share of that desiring
And that aching, slapping sound of a hundred waves. (6)

TALLMAN: Robin, just for the text would you identify those poems?
BLASER: Those were published, and never republished, in *Contour*
magazine in Berkeley, April 1947.[4] Some of the poems come from
'46, which is the year that Jack and I met. Here I've tried first for a
geography: the desert, the people, and the language a map. I wanted
to be speaking rather than to have been spoken. One voice of the
map is muffled, changed, and changing. Another voice remains,
holds, here in the words and in the poems, the language as a permanence. This is bringing forward the view—and again it's discovered

in Dante and it's discovered with Jack and Duncan—that the only thing [. . .] scientifically speaking, the only thing that is permanent is the mind. And then if you sit over that mind-boggling phrase very long and try to figure out what it can mean, it only can mean Language, and this is a capital "L" Language. It means language in a broad spectrum of language—this would include movies, this would include painting, and so on. But it is the way in which we speak, and it is the mind, and it is the only permanence. The body is not permanent and the mind as we think and theorize all the time only has public space, viable form, when it goes into the language in one form or the other. And that language is—that's why there's so much power. Also why the poets feel so much grief that their poetry really is only read to a coterie, and also why people such as myself are cranks about the lyrical poem, that [it] is only the expression of one's self. Jack's beautiful letter to me in "Admonitions" in which he says that he's broken into another poetic where he no longer speaks in— well his failures in love, and his griefs and desires—that he now has to move into something else. And when we get to the Boston session I'll go through what that meant with some documents to show the way it was, because Jack moved. Well, I'll do "The Hunger of Sound," too, because the Dante image turns up that's behind this. And like it's what?—ten years later—that it turns up in that poem. But Jack makes that move to break from the lyrical form quite a long time before I do.

So those childish books I brought: I wanted them here to show how the desert met the sea, the sea as the unknown and unseen except here in the books and in the cat's eyes. Now these books were the first companions and they did include Dante, which I'll come to in a minute. The *Inferno* one you've seen, but the *Paradiso* is almost twice the size. And you have to think of a three- or four-year-old boy turning pages of a book that seems enormous, I mean unbelievably enormous. . . .

TALLMAN: This is the Doré isn't it?

BLASER: This is the Doré, and it's years before I discovered the Blake and the Botticelli but these were findings, with the Satan frozen in the ice, and then if you go back to the memory of that—because as Dante approaches he first thinks it's a windmill that's there, and then he thinks of it as a cross that's there. And the whole reversed form of the *Inferno* is in that image. The stunning one, for example, of Ulysses, and . . . the guide that lifts them down into the lowest pit of Hell, the giant, and the marvelous one here where they're all frozen in the ice and Virgil says to Dante, "Watch your steps, you're going to kick people in the head." [. . .] Ice right up to the eyebrows. Oh I love those images and they were, of course, coming through the pictures. . . . I also had the great fairy book, and as I told Dwight, there were not so many books, there were marvelous ones but we were poor, and we were in the desert, and there weren't libraries. So the rarity of the book, in a way, the great fairy book was one. But if you looked through it you'd find carefully colored illustrations . . . unbelievable how meticulous I was. But that's where I first move into the relationship with painting which is a major aspect of the way I move in the arts. It always [has] to be attached to painting. Duncan, of course, does that magnificently and in his own life has a marvelous painter with him. One of the wonderful things in companionship with Duncan was that all this children's books stuff came forward all over again with [him] because these books all begin to be part of the conversation. Often the conversation would be in these realms for the whole twenty years that we were talking.

QUESTION: [Does] that mean that Duncan has very much the same kind of background as you?

BLASER: Very much the same background. What Duncan taught me was that instead of growing up and dumping this stuff, that this was the literal ground of the imagination. So we continued, and we got on big book tours buying more children's books and things we'd never read and discovering. I had many of them in the house with notes from Duncan saying, "I found this and thought of you . . ."—many children's books. The greatest addition to all of our books that—I had never heard of him until Duncan turned it all up—was George MacDonald. *Back of the North Wind* and *The Princess and Curdie*. . . . I mean that was like one of the gifts of all time. [. . .]

My point here is that in peopling landscape and in doing it this way to get those companions to come forward, they're the binding form for me—the binding form of the world. And I cannot substitute myself in these conversations for these enlargements anymore than I can substitute sensation for form. My hostility to that whole incredible mess, especially evident here on the west coast it seems to me, is that the real evil [is] the substitution of sensation for form. You know, you read a poem and if they don't get it then goose 'em and they really got a thrill out of that fucking poem. That's the substitution of sensation for form and separating the mind from the body. Anyway, years later among those people, 1962 when she dies, here is that grandmother that you heard so much about, Sophia Nichols.

Sophia Nichols

the wind hits and returns   it is easy to personify
a new place and language,   but the new body stings

these men with green eyelids, drawing their worth,
it was rumoured, from Egypt, knew

the work is part of it   a power arrived at the
same thirst

he borrowed a head for a day

but which head   the phrases tremble in the other
mouth   it is true and false   the veil of her face,

an old porcelain, not for the same hand to comfort   she
moved beyond the sop one gave for affection   'My

success has been to keep duty and love alive'   she said
her hand waved with the power of disease   Sophia

Nichols of the orchards, the deserts, the flooded
ponds and games wherein the moon sought our feet

died with a mouth full of tumour   it is true and
false   the moon flowers (that is Blake talking)

tonight it is the half blossom and the stars too
above this mud are from the other mouth   this city

untouched   the streets, Hotel Lyric have a foreignness,
a place outside a window   a sound of bees pulling

the lilac   above cement this wonder (the other mouth)
that crickets were men once who so loved the muses they

.   forgot to eat   now fed on thistles, the language must
sting   the flesh turn to a dew (the other mouth) the

loss,   some glistening blood on the leaves of the mirror
plant   Sophia Nichols of the story, the golden rod,
of the snake that entered the cage and ate the captured
sparrows, the telegraph keys, pale yellow paper,   of

the Odyssey and the homing stories of the soul,   the sea
imaginary, light and foaming green on the rocks dark

further out as the eyes of the cat

                                                      if she would be
free from words, she would free me   even in the night

there are birds summoned by words[5]

"The other mouth" is borrowed from the fairy tales where you keep changing heads and the heads keep speaking different stories in the fairy tale.

TALLMAN: Does she ever invade your life, dreams, or?

BLASER: Oh yes, I speak to her every day, every morning. And in that poem that's a total invasion. . . . I only caught this by accident . . . but this is the edition of the *Hawthorne Wonderbook For Girls and Boys* which is just a marvel of the Gorgon's head and the Chimera and all that stuff. I brought the Maxfield Parrish last time, because I'd so loved that—my taste for kitsch as Duncan calls it—and I love that edition. I don't know whether I told you but when I started to bring it over here I had to cut the pages because I discovered, after forty years or something, I had carefully cut only the pages to look at the pictures. . . . I was going through it today, reminding myself of what was in it, when lo and behold in the story of the three golden apples in the gardens of the Hesperides I find—and that's what she was doing when she put me on the pond in a tin tub with a shingle to go across—[6]. . . . Hercules arrives at the edge of Africa to go off into the southern sea, the unknown sea, and he can't get across. And suddenly he sees this glimmering on the ocean and up comes this enormous

cup and he winds up down there talking with Atlas, where he pulls a
dirty trick on Atlas, or Atlas pulls a dirty trick on him. Atlas gets him
to put the world on his shoulders and then is going to go off and have
a good time and he says, "Oh, but it hurts my head, it's rubbing. I've
got to take my tiger skin off and put it on my head so the world won't
rub my head raw." So that stupid Atlas puts the world back on his
head while Hercules is supposed to be putting his tiger skin up there
and of course Hercules says "So long," you know, "thank God."
Anyway that's where she [Sophia Nichols] got that.
TALLMAN: Yeah.
BLASER: And it was amazing—this I discovered today. I had no
memory of this. The Maxfield Parrish doesn't have—
TALLMAN: That's the tub.
BLASER: That's the tub. That's where she [Sophia Nichols] picked
up the notion, where she's translated out the Hesperides. But who
cares how she did it. Now the babies story, *The Water Babies*, was a
book that I really, really loved. It's the most amazing kooky book. It's
the water landscape and I wanted to throw in at least some aspects of
it. It is a fairy tale book and it's about a boy borrowed from Blake.
Years later I found out, because I had no Blake until years later, it's
Tom the chimney sweep. [. . .] Tom is a chimney sweep and he's
treated terribly by this guy that runs his life—the unwanted little
boy who's sold to the chimney sweep so to speak, and crawls up the
chimneys to clean them out. It's Tom from Blake's great poem and
Mr. Grimes is the son-of-a-bitch that runs his life. And so Tom goes
into the mansion to crawl up all the chimneys to clean, gets into a
room upstairs and sees the most beautiful little girl in white, that he's
ever seen. He has never seen anybody so clean ever, and here she is
and then he turns around and sees this hideous, dirty, black little nut,
just a monstrous looking thing, and it's in the mirror and it's himself.
Well he then knocks something over and makes a terrible noise—the
andirons or something—trying to get back up the chimney where he
belongs—wakes her up, she screams and he goes up and they all
begin to chase him. So he runs over valley and dale and winds up
with a mysterious Irish lady behind him, who keeps following him.
And she keeps going but he doesn't see her and she follows and
follows and finally he winds up down by a stream where suddenly

he's transformed, right out of an Ovid kind of story. He's going to clean himself—he's seen this beautiful lady, girl—he's going to clean himself up. He gets in the water and he shrinks to a tiny thing and he has gills on either side of his neck, which he pulls before he realizes what they are and he's a water baby. He's been transformed from the land to the sea and then the story starts. And it is absolutely—I really love the story. Well, the passage for example, on what they eat I love so I'll give you just a few little passages here: "And what did he live on? Water-cresses perhaps; or perhaps water gruel and water milk; too many land babies do so likewise. But we do not know what one-tenth of the water things eat; so we are not answerable for the water babies" (Kingsley 88). That is the end of that. [*laughter*]

Water forests are really marvelous. He's swimming around trying to discover himself . . . and it turns out he's quite naughty. He's brought his land habits with him so he tortures the trout, and he . . . tries to get a hold of things. And the dragonfly section . . . do you know what a dragonfly is? Great elongated body with magnificent wings, blue or green, very long, a strange awkward thing. Well anyway, he goes swimming around trying to figure this out and then sometimes he comes to a deep, still reach and there he sees the water forests . . .

[Tape change: Side 20]

BLASER: . . . now think of being in the desert. This is what you're reading, in the midst of the desert. It was enough to—I think Jack always said that his destiny was to be an alcoholic and mine was insanity, and maybe this is where it starts, I don't know:

> They would have looked to you only little weeds: but Tom, you must remember, was so little that everything looked a hundred times as big to him as it does to you, just as things do to a minnow, who sees and catches the little water-creatures which you can only see in a microscope.
>
> And in the water-forest he saw the water-monkeys and water-squirrels (they had all six legs, though; everything almost has six legs in the water, except efts and water-babies); and nimbly enough they ran among the branches. There were water-flowers there too, in thousands; and Tom tried to pick them: but as soon as he touched them, they drew themselves in and turned into

knots of jelly; and then Tom saw that they were all alive—bells,
and stars, and wheels, and flowers, of all beautiful shapes and
colours; and all alive and busy, just as Tom was. So now he found
that there was a great deal more in the world than he had fancied
at first sight. (89-90)

Now he moves around through this world and we kind of lose sight
of him as he discovers the world. And we suddenly find the beautiful
young lady at the seashore where she has been taken by a professor
named Ptthmllnsprts, you spell it—
TALLMAN: Oh, I've met him many times.
BLASER: P-t-t-h-m-l-l-n-s-p-r-t-s.
QUESTION: There isn't a single—vowel.
BLASER: There's not a single vowel. The language problem in this
book is among the most maddening in the world, as you will see.
Anyway, we have great problems because Professor Pth is an expert in
the problem of the apes, whether the apes have a certain thing called
the hippopotamus, and if they do—because we have a hippopotamus
in our brain—if the apes have them we are really apes. But of course
we are not apes, so the ape must not have a whatever. . . . I began to
remember the number of times I had to go to the dictionary in this
book, it was just a maddening book to read. "But if a hippopotamus
major is ever discovered in one single ape's brain, nothing will save
your great-great-great-great-great-great-great-great-great-great-great-
greater-greatest grandmother from having been an ape too" (153).
[*laughter*] Absolutely mind-boggling. So he goes on. They're standing
at the seashore and the professor is quarreling with the little girl Ellie,
the beautiful little girl, because she sees a water-baby. And guess who
it is; it's our Tom. And he gets in Professor Ptthmllnsprts's net and
Ptthmllnsprts will not admit that this is the case. So the fairies
punish him for all of this [and] the professor finally winds up—he's
gone very far indeed says the book

for he had read at the British Association at Melbourne,
Australia, in the year 1999, a paper which assured everyone who
found himself the better or wiser for the news, that there were
not, never had been, and could not be, any rational or half-ratio-
nal beings except men anywhere, anywhen, or anyhow; that,
nymphs, satyrs, fauns, inui, dwarfs, trolls, elves, gnomes, fairies,

> brownies, nixies, wilis, kobalds, leprechaunes, cluricaunes, ban-
> shees, will-o'-the-wisps, follets, lutins, magots, goblins, afrits,
> marids, jinns, ghouls, peris, deevs, angels, archangels, imps,
> bogies, or worse, were nothing at all, and pure bosh and wind.
> And he had to get up very early in the morning to prove that, and
> to eat his breakfast overnight; but he did it at least to his own sat-
> isfaction. (153-54)

Now he winds up somewhat punished for this because when he's
arguing—it's a marvelous line, it's unforgettable—he's arguing with
little Ellie that there aren't water-babies, he finally is so exasperated
he says—She says, "'Why are there not water babies?'"

> I trust and hope that it was because the professor trod at that
> moment on the edge of a very sharp mussel, and hurt one of his
> corns sadly, that he answered quite sharply, forgetting that he
> was a scientific man, and therefore ought to have known that
> he couldn't know; and that he was a logician, and therefore
> ought to have known that he could not prove a universal nega-
> tive—I say, I trust and hope it was because the mussel hurt his
> corn, that the professor answered quite sharply:
> "Because there ain't!" (155)

TALLMAN: You know what this is reminding me of? I'm reading
Gertrude Stein right now—
BLASER: Oh, I think yes.
QUESTION: Yeah, the kind of language.
BLASER: He really gets into a terrible mental condition, the Professor does, because the little girl falls down and dies you see, in a
magical way, and she too winds up a water-baby. So they had to take
him in hand, "and she filled his head with things as they are not, to
try if he would like them better, and because he did not choose to
believe in a water-baby when he saw it, she made him"—the fairy, the
Irish fairy—"made him believe in worse things than water-babies—
in *unicorns, fire-drakes, manticoras, baselisks, amphisbaenas, griffins,
phoenixes, rocs, orcs, dog-headed men, three-headed dogs, three-bodied
geryons,* and other pleasant creatures which folk think never existed
yet" and so on (161). The doctor is finally called in and the cure,
when we finally get the cure, they go through—they give him everything, poor man—and so finally we wind up with this: they decided

they would go through the possibilities at the end of the trail of what to do with this poor Professor Ptthmllnsprts. As the discussion goes on they take

> As successfully employed by the old inquisitors to cure the mal-
> ady of thought, and now by the Persian Mollahs to cure that of
> rheumatism.
>> *Geopathy, or burying him.*
>> *Atmopathy, or steaming him.*
>> *Sympathy, after the method of Basil Valentine his Triumph*
>>> *of Antimony, and Kenelm Digby his Weapon salve,*
>>> *which some call a hair of the dog that bit him.*
>> *Hermopathy, or pouring mercury down his throat to move*
>>> *the animal spirits.*
>> *Meterapathy, or going up to the moon to look for his lost wits. . .*
>> *Antipathy, or using him like "a man and a brother."*
>> *Apathy, or doing nothing at all.* (168)

The final cure's for him. So then you meet other people called Mrs. Doasyouwouldbedoneby and Mrs. Bedonebyasyoudid and Mrs. Bedonebyasyoudid is really quite awkward to deal with because we start hunting for a land called the other end of nowhere and looking for the other end of nowhere you get little messages like "children are living poems" and so on, which gives you a little hope as a child. But on the other hand, the other end of nowhere's very difficult and Mrs. Bedonebyasyoudid is very difficult to get along with. So then he comes to a place called "Stop" where he stops and he receives—

TALLMAN: Very sensible man.

BLASER: Very sensible, and he receives a marvelous examination. I don't know whether I can find the examination or not quickly, but he receives a marvelous examination there just—

TALLMAN: Robin, identify something for me. Are you reading this to yourself as a child or is Sophia reading this to you?

BLASER: Sophia would be reading this one to me because—

TALLMAN: At what age? Got any idea?

BLASER: Oh boy, this would be six, seven-y maybe, five, six, seven-y, somewhere in there. It's when I can read but the book's too hard in many ways.

TALLMAN: Because it's so tricky.

BLASER: Oh, just incredible.

GARDINER: Not enough vowels in it.

BLASER: No vowels, and the language thing just driving one up the wall. And then things like the examination: where the examination starts out there are no toys allowed. You come to a place and it's like Dante's Hell. There's a sign that says "No Toys Allowed," and that's the end of that. And suddenly you're in there and here are all the little kids. Oh, there's a turnip speaking too—he's quite a funny character, I love the turnip:

> "I can't learn my lesson; do come and help me!" And one cried, "Can you show me how to extract this square root?"
> And another, "Can you tell me the distance between α Lyrae and β Camelopardis?"
> And another, "What is the latitude and longitude of Snooksville, in Norman's County, Oregon, U.S.?"
> And another, "What was the name of Mutius Scaevola's thirteenth cousin's grandmother's maid's cat?"
> And another, "How long would it take a school-inspector of average activity to tumble head over heels from London to York?"
> And another, "Can you tell me the name of a place that nobody ever heard of, where nothing ever happened, in a country which has not been discovered yet?" (300)

QUESTION: Yeah, I can see why it would get hard. [*laughter*]

BLASER: Well, you'd just—the book is just—it had to be six or seven because I know I'm in school. It's after I'm in school but it's still too hard.

TALLMAN: Do you remember this, Angela?

BOWERING: Oh, yeah, yeah.

BLASER:

> Then he came to a very quiet place called Leaveheavenalone. And there the sun was drawing water out of the sea to make steam-threads, and the wind was twisting them up to make cloud-patterns, till they had worked between them the loveliest wedding veil of Chantilly lace, and hung it up in their own Crystal Palace for anyone to buy who could afford it; while the good old sea never grudged, for she knew they would pay her back honestly. So the sun span, and the winds wove and all went well with the great steam-loom; as is likely, considering—and

considering—and considering—
  And at last, after innumerable adventures, each more wonderful than the last, he saw before him a huge building, much bigger and—what is most surprising—a little uglier than a certain
new lunatic asylum, but not built quite of the same materials.
None of it, at least—or, indeed, for ought that I ever saw, any part
of any other building whatsoever—is cased with nine-inch brick
inside and out, and filled up with rubble between the walls, in
order that any gentleman who has been confined during Her
Majesty's pleasure may be unconfined during his own pleasure,
and take a walk in the neighbouring park to improve his spirits,
after an hour's light and wholesome labour. . . . (309-10)

So we move through this and finally it turns out—the lovely imagery
of the sea weaving which stayed in my mind all the time and is part
of that not-known sea—in order to get there you come to a place
where you may go up the back stairs. That stairs is a way to get up
there cheap and easy, but oh you get in trouble with the back stairs
and so when we get to the back stairs finally he gets some help, Tom
does, and winds up back with Ellie. But first of all we have to go to
the back stairs. And they blindfold him and let him go up because he
mustn't see that he's done this, but they had the key to the back stairs
here.

For thousands of years we've been paying, and petting, and obey-
ing, and worshipping quacks who told us they had the key of the
backstairs, and could smuggle us up them; and in spite of all our
disappointments we will honour, and glorify, and adore, and
beatify, and translate, and apotheosize you likewise, on the
chance of your knowing something about the backstairs, that we
may all go on pilgrimage to it; and even if we cannot get up it,
lie at the foot of it, and cry—
  'Oh backstairs,
  precious backstairs,   *comfortable backstairs,*
  invaluable backstairs,   *humane backstairs,*
  requisite backstairs,   *reasonable backstairs,*
  necessary backstairs,   *long-sought backstairs,*
  good-natured backstairs,   *coveted backstairs,*
  cosmopolitan backstairs,   *aristocratic backstairs,*
  comprehensive backstairs,   *respectable backstairs,*
  accommodating backstairs,   *gentlemanlike backstairs,*
  well-bred backstairs,   *ladylike backstairs,*

commercial backstairs,	*orthodox backstairs,*
economical backstairs,	*probable backstairs,*
practical backstairs,	*credible backstairs,*
logical backstairs,	*demonstrable backstairs,*
deductive backstairs,	*irrefragable backstairs,*

potent backstairs,
all-but-omnipotent backstairs,
etc.
Save us from the consequences of our own actions and from the
cruel fairy, Mrs. Bedonebyasyoudid!' (322)

[laughter]

MARLATT: Oh, this is lovely at any age.

TALLMAN: Oh, I never read that book, my God.

BOWERING: I remember being utterly, utterly terrified by Mrs.
Doandbedoneby.

BLASER: Oh she does—she catches you. You get caught in back, and
when they do let him go up the backstairs I remember the thrill
because he wasn't crying all those terrible words, some of which you
had to look up: "irrefragable backstairs." Let's turn it off for a minute
after all that.

[Recorder switched on and off]

BLASER: The other Hawthorne story that I wanted to draw attention
to is read to me very, very early on and fascinates me almost my whole
life. It's Hawthorne's "Artist of the Beautiful." You know that story?
"The Artist of the Beautiful." This business of what beauty is I hope
will turn up . . . because Warren accuses me of—that what I want in
the poems is beauty, and I really don't object, because I think that's
really what I'm after and it's also laughter. . . . Oh incidently, later on
I'll tell you one of the reasons I was so unhappy at the trivialization
that went on when [Frank] Davey was here, when I was asked, for
instance, to criticize Jack that evening. I have an area in which I can
criticize Jack. It's going to turn up at the end here in the Dante on
the nature of the soul, whether it's a duo or a trio . . . and that stuff
on the soul will come back later on. But that's where I think there's
some trouble, and my sense that ultimately what is so really almost
painful to me is that I think that art ultimately should be laughter.

That's the real pathway. Jack seems to me to be among the few American poets who can laugh in his poems. I'd really have great difficulty with that and yet Jack did not take the laughter as a vision of some kind, but something else, and we'll get back at it. [. . .]

BOWERING: Tell me right now what it was, the laughter that wasn't—

BLASER: Jack refuses to accept the laughter as a vision, an actual vision of the world.

BOWERING: So then what is it?

GARDINER: . . . talking in terms of disgust or something like that.

BLASER: Yeah, well as a matter of fact Duncan says Jack taught him disgust. And I think there's no question. It may turn up because the Boston poems reflect the word disgust in my poems repeatedly and I'm sure this is something I'm learning from Jack also, the disgust element. And then it became so bad, what Jack called the fix, that he did not see the world as moving forward as laughter, but would even sometimes move to the edge where he heard a hideous laughter rather than the other. [. . .] That night, I said Jack has done it for us; we don't have to do the same thing that—God help us if we do. And I noticed the blank faces when I said the whole business of style as personality—style is the man, is bullshit. It is the most poisonous English professor's crap. Style is not the personality of the poet but the distance he has moved in the language and that is the reason that a young poet cannot pick up a great poet whose work is accomplished and copy his style. He also is forced toward his stance. This is why we have so much trouble with people attacking Olson here in town, because the moment they try to copy that style they can't pull a fuck-ing thing. It's the literal distance he's moved in the language. Then they're pulled to the stance and then they don't like that—that's like, you know, getting your chest up against a big chest. That's pretty hard to handle. In fact most of us are tall enough to get our chests at his belly. [*laughter*] Anyway, "The Artist of the Beautiful."

TALLMAN: Yeah, but just one second. Laughter, then, does that mean a non-tragic universe?

BLASER: A non-tragic universe. And that will come back and attach to the theme that I think we are all dead, so that I wind up with actually a non-tragic movement that's beyond the edge of that which has been going on for so very long, and will turn up in Nerval—well in Marquis de Sade first and then in Nerval, in the way I'm doing the narrative. And I also want to go at that whole business of the substitution of sensation for form because that issue has been played out by a great writer, Artaud, who spends half his poetic life in reversals between a duplicity of the spiritual separated completely from the body on the one hand, and then a reversal that will turn it all into the body, and we get the theatre of cruelty out of that. And then Jack's realm inside all those major issues because the thing about the word "soul" and the world—this is coming to Dante—the word "soul" and the word "God," "ghost," a whole series of these, they're all broken words. They've fallen because they belong to a hierarchy of some kind, a world vision. The world vision fell, the words still are there and they float and haunt us, "ghost" in particular haunts us. When Jack and I are entering college you could not [respectably] use the word "spirit" [or] "soul," in any writing though you are reading poetry that is jammed with it, and as a consequence unless you were a pretty fancy-footed kid—we both were—you wouldn't even be able to handle the content of those words. And one notices that the moment that the words dump out of their images, the hierarchy had the image of God as the old bearded daddy in the sky, a fully humanized figure, the soul with the very definite range of—well, there are even images attached to the nature of the soul. But certainly it was [confused] by its relation to intellect. As they fall down, the words all re-open and they re-open into their contents. One notices immediately that the moment that you know that the unknown is at the very edge of the known, and you can take the known to be you at whatever limit you're in at the moment—the unknown, that the moment you've hit that, you've also hit one of the contents that was inside the word "God." [. . .]

"The Artist of the Beautiful," though was a story—you'll see in a minute why that fascinated so much. It is a story about a watchmaker, and the watchmaker is in love with the beautiful young girl and he's loved her, you know, all his life. It's one of those—they're meant somehow for one another. Her beauty—he adores her and he's a watchmaker, and he's worked all his life at this and it's rather mysterious, that he's there working. She marries another man who's really a great big practical guy, you know. He doesn't do this funny stuff over here fixing the clocks and working with things like that.

TALLMAN: He kicks the gong.

BLASER: He kicks the gong and fucks the girl and they have a baby. And here's the watchmaker, still devoted and [he] visits them. He decides he wants to make something for her and for her child, something so exquisite, so perfect. He works secretly: you walk down the little town street at night and you see his light on and he's in there leaning over this and he's working. And finally he comes with a beautiful box that he's made and presents his gift and it is a mechanical butterfly and it's taken years to make. And he opens it up and the butterfly all by itself lifts and glitters and fills the room with all of these lights like a prism, and flies around the room—

TALLMAN: —and all of America.

BLASER: All of America and my heart. I was in agony because they wouldn't send me to Bowdoin College where Hawthorne had gone to school and that's coming, I'm six years old, I wanted to—you ask me why I wanted to go to college. I wanted to go to college because Hawthorne went to college, that's why I wanted to go to college. I don't know any other good reason to go. It had to be Bowdoin College, and we couldn't afford it. So anyway, the butterfly—exquisite. I used to dream about it. I would go to sleep and think about it. It goes round, and as it gets over towards her husband it pales and then it goes towards her and brightens up and then it moves around the room a little more, still unsettled, and flies down and the little boy of course is looking up with wonder, this marvelous little boy, and he has his hand out and the butterfly comes down all a-glitter, almost like a flame, lands in the palm and the little boy closes his hand and crushes it. Especially Hawthorne's vision. Perhaps part of mine. According to Robert Duncan, Jack's and mine are both owed to Hawthorne. It is actually Poe behind it. But that story and then the Dante. . . . That business of the little boy opening the big Dante book. So the beauty thing will come back.

But anyway, at this point, this is moving us forward into '47 and '48 where the Jack poems are—where the importance of Kantorowicz was actually putting one in time. I don't think it was just because I was coming from a provincial range, either, but you came in not in time. You came into things not in time [in] some way and it was

Kantorowicz who put you into time. The thirteenth-century course, among all the courses we took, was the one of greatest importance, to me at any rate. That was because Frederick the Second is the center of that century—dies in 1250—he is the last of the great emperors of the Holy Roman Empire, the last of [a] vision of a world with an emperor figure who would hold it as one world, a political realm, the practice of human life as the entire world under one figure held together. Now that was Frederick the Second at the center of the century. Dante is born in 1265, writing *The Comedy* around 1310, with its action taking place in 1300 and Dante is taking on the entire breakdown of the world image. In American terms, *Mont-Saint-Michel and Chartres* (1904), by Henry Adams, is a perfect American—almost so intellectualized it's unfair—but it is almost tearful; it is elegiac about the lost vision of the thirteenth-century virgin. Those of you who've read the book, its power and beauty—he wrote a marvelous poem called "The Virgin and the Dynamo" which should be read along with the book, but you can get a sense of the magic. Dante's taking on the whole broken world image and my point in wanting Dante here is that not only at this end of the stick—now where I am—but then Dante was the whole issue of the missing world image. The world is absent.

I've come out of a Catholic world, I've done everything: I've studied my medieval Latin and/or Church Latin in order to be a priest; I've knelt before the virgin for hours; I've gone through everything in the book; and I wind up in Berkeley and there you are—the world image is absent. And Dante suddenly, by the gift of Kantorowicz, putting it in time. [. . .] It not only means a great deal to me, but Jack's *Heads of the Town Up to the Aether* will not be read right without some sense of Dante. Because, well Jack himself has said it but it is simply true: Hell, Purgatory, and the Paradiso are the structure of that poem. Duncan's work I do not think has the Paradiso in it yet. I think that the work that he will end with is a Paradiso, 'cause Dante is extraordinarily important to Duncan. All three of us are tied at this point because the structure—and it is the world image that's involved—it's broken, it's lost. And Dante is the one who takes it on.

KUHARIC: Do you read Dante in Italian or do you read it in English?

BLASER: I use a bilingual. I have enough Italian and I've read it for so many years and there is an edition now that is so stunning. It's not complete, it's going to be six volumes. The one that everybody's used is the Temple edition, the little ones. They're in my suitcase: if I go on a trip I always have the six volume Temple edition. But this one is brand new, by Singleton, and it's got the Italian text, a prose translation, extremely careful, and there's a volume of commentary on each section of the *Comedy*. It's just magnificent. It's just out and the *Paradiso's* not done yet, just the *Inferno* and the other. Marvelous thing. Since I have some Latin training—and that may lead to an amusing story about my Latin class and E. M. Forster and Robert Duncan at another time—I have enough Latin to handle Italian. With the aid of the bilingual, I can get an awful long way, and hear it, which is important. Anyway so what we're doing is heading into one of those great companions and this is another companionship of Dante different from the one the little boy would have in the picture book.

TALLMAN: Now, now—and Kantorowicz is your corridor—

BLASER: He's the guide, the corridor, the master. It's amazing because reading Dante, inside of all this is the very shady realm that literature is something invented—Jack was later to say [he] invented nothing—that literature was the imagination different from the real. At the same time there's a shadow, even in the water-babies book, that it is somehow part of the composition of the real. There is something very peculiar about it. You wind up in Dante and the whole world image is at stake in *The Divine Comedy*. The poetry takes on the task of knowledge itself, begins to argue about the nature of the intellect. It also argues something that fascinated all of us, and it couldn't fail to fascinate somebody close to Jack when he says "Evil is the king of the world." Because you open the *Comedy* with the trip to Hell which is full of evil—and it is full of evil. That image of Hell is special and important. Now when I started on the Kantorowicz thing, I did quote from Kantorowicz's own teacher, Friedrich Gundolf, those passages on the difference in vision of manhood between Dante and Petrarch. And what I keep trying to say is, this stuff really isn't snazzy. It's just that once it's there it's so absolute and one had no sense of how crucial this thing of the thirteenth-century was, that the world image is disappearing then and Dante takes it on to battle and quarrel for the nature of the world image, whether it would be God-given or man-given. And this is stunning, the point where what does the manhood do that Dante argues. . . . Dante on the one hand, with the manhood within a hierarchy and which he then tries to hold with extraordinary tension; Petrarch who lets it entirely go. Petrarch's *Triomphe* is a marvelous thing that goes back and looks all the way through for ancient men—is after character. He re-opens the manhood. Dante will see man as having done something that has eternal viability, eternal truth to it; you look to that person's action as something whole and there permanently. Petrarch, just after him, comes in [and it's] no longer that at all. Between the two of them, when you watch Dante and Petrarch—and this is part of what you were getting out of Kantorowicz—is that, it is [the] thirteenth-century that for the first time discloses history as a process, the first time, so that when we get to our period and have to quarrel through Marxist views of history and all of that we are literally, for my mind, doing something that I discover through Dante first with comfort and with astonishment: history as a process rather than history as an eternal form. It also happens that history as process has a closer, more intimate relation in its particulars as far as experience goes, to the ancient world. Then when you get to Pound, Olson, all the rest of us who do all this it tells you something about what it means. Why do we make ourselves alive by going backward, so far back?

[Tape change; Side 21]

QUESTION: [. . .] What are you saying that Dante is doing?
BLASER: Dante's taking on the issue and arguing for what can remain permanent. And argues the nature of the intellect finally in a way that frankly makes him, well, pre-heterodox. He's outside the range of what the Church could accept and has quarreled with in his own time, that is, they knew that he was up to no good. It is Dante who, in my experience, it's the first time that I know of, learned anything about the human collectivity—and this is a word that belongs to Dante. He means a totality of the human that is beyond the individual and we now come all the way back into this in modern thought in other terms, among people who pay no attention of course

to this. One of the things that was fascinating [. . .] [is] the structure of the *Inferno*, the *Purgatorio*, and the *Paradiso*, and one notices obvious things, really lovely things. Maybe I'll just quote the lines as we go on. At the end of each of the three sections the word "stella" comes, the stars return each time, holding it together so that the constellated form that is the sky tied to the earth begins the central issue of the structure of the whole of *The Divine Comedy*. You also enter in a wood, a dark wood and a wild wood, in the middle way in the beginning. You then, at the end of the *Purgatorio*, are in another wood except it is the lovely one, with speckled light and the light filtering through the trees—a completely different forest wood.

TALLMAN: "In the midway of this my mortal life I found me in a leafy wood alone."

BLASER: Alone. That's the opening of the *Inferno*. You wind up in the other great wood. One of my reasons for wanting to say why it is so important to have these companions: when Charles Olson and I meet in Gloucester, Massachusetts, yes I spent the afternoon having him read poems I always wanted to hear and so on but what did we talk about? It wasn't gossip about Robert Duncan or anybody else. We sat down at the table having lobster, which Charles loved, and Charles looked at me straight in the eye, smiling, beaming, telling me how much he loved "Hymn to Christ the Son" . . . and the next thing I know, a little compliment over with, he says, "Who is Mathilda?" Well, I can tell you a little about Mathilda tonight. Mathilda is the first lady that you see as we enter the *Paradiso*, the terrestrial paradise at the top of the *Purgatory*. She's a very special figure and I don't think my answer to that question was adequate in those days. [*laughter*] It drove me quite crazy trying to figure out who's Mathilda? I still don't know why she's called Mathilda.

TALLMAN: Yeah. "Waltzing Mathilda.'"

BLASER: That poem, yeah, unfortunately that's a later song. But now the *Inferno* . . . this is going back to my remark that all serious thought seems to be an interrogation of death. There is no one alive in the entire . . . *Divine Comedy*, except Dante. Everyone else in all three books is a shade, or an angelic form, a power of some sort or another. He is the only one. In the lovely line when suddenly someone sees him there in *Purgatory* and one of them says, frightened, "Why are

the sunbeams broken by his form?" And no one else—of course . . .
the light has poured through them and if—

TALLMAN: Can you digress into when Ulysses goes into the underworld? Is this the same or is this—?

BLASER: I'm going to even read that passage when we . . . he's
[Dante is] using it, he's taking it, but he's taking the underworld—of
course there's Christ going under the world too, but he's really using
Virgil's—in the *Aeneid* is the pattern, because Dante doesn't know
Homer directly. His information is coming via other sources and he
gets similar material out of Virgil and out of Ovid because he knows
a great deal of both of those, but he does not know Homer. [. . .] He
knows Homer by way of them, not directly. Homer, you won't get for
another century as something you can read in Europe. But the
Inferno is a book in which, and it's spectacularly so, you notice immediately that everyone, all condemnation is due to the way you lived,
acted, practiced your life; the argument is that your mental condition, your condition in terms of feeling and thought at the moment
of death, is your eternal condition. I think one of the most fearsome
notions in the world, and it's only in the modern period when they
have refused to think in oppositions, [is] if you think of time without
an opposite you simply—you have resolved into the worst kind of—
well, an inadequate thought. It's like taking the body and forgetting
there's a mind or something, the way some people like to do too.
You can't read Blake or anybody else without having to think about
eternity. "Eternity" is so filled with contemporary hostility towards
religious thought that they will not think of it as actually that which
is other than time. And so when you die, that moment of feeling and
thought are your eternal condition. This is literally the plot of what it
is that brings you into Hell, if you have made the earth here Hell.
When you enter the Inferno there's a group of people who wander
around rather dazed and so on and I always—I was absolutely
knocked out by them. This is before you hit Limbo.

TALLMAN: They're your water-babies.

BLASER: They're not. They're worse than water-babies. They are the
men and women who did nothing. They can't get down into Hell or
Paradise. They're simple non-entities, beyond the entrance to Hell.
Then you begin going down and down into the circles until you see

Satan at the bottom frozen in ice. And Dante first thinks he's a wind-mill, and then thinks he's a cross, and you find him as the reversal—the absolute reverse and opposition of the cross as Christ—and, as a consequence, get the proposal that Hell is only the outside of Heaven, as though you had turned it backwards. What is its other? But it is the action in the life that brings one into Hell. Now the Purgatory—it fascinates me because there's a whole incredibly marvelous—I was watching Charlie Chaplin the other night. Sunday night for ten weeks now they're going to have Charlie Chaplin, and don't miss *The Kid* whatever you do when that one comes on.

TALLMAN: That's the great one.

BLASER: But there's one—I'm sure the first camouflage war movie ever turned up—and here's Charlie running around and he's dressed as a tree. Well, instead of having it just speckled, he's a whole fuck-ing tree stump and he's running around. And suddenly, you know, the Germans are after him and so he goes like this, and he literally disappears into the landscape. And if they get too close one limb goes bong and he's knocked out a German officer, and so on and so on. Anyway, he winds up even stealing the seats of the Kaiser's car and a lot of other things. It's a terrific story. But it reminded me immedi-ately of the suicide section in Dante, because the suicides have turned into trees and the hounds rush through the trees knocking the limbs off. In Dante's magnificent words, when the limb breaks off what issues are words and blood. The suicides inside the tree have been so against nature they are now in a metamorphosis that puts them back into a natural form. Yet when you break the limbs, what you hear are words mixed with blood. Think of Hell: you're going down in Hell in a cone that is the exact opposite of the hierarchy of the cone in Yeats's *The Vision*. That's where those cones are really coming from. The double cone is coming out of this realm of thought: the Paradise is at the top of the point, Satan's at the bottom, and the oppositions are set. They're made in images so you will think and experience these polarities. . . . The pretension that there's nothing called evil—and we have to have a gorgeous book by Hannah Arendt, *The Banality of Evil*, the Eichmann book, to even tell us that evil is present these days when it's there. But inbetween it is a realm, the Purgatorio. Now the *Purgatorio*, in the way I read it, is the place given. It is so like the earth, it turns out it is on the earth. It's in the southern seas, a place we've not seen in this geography, but it is terrestrial and has the Paradise to which you may return. You return to that by moral and intellectual concern and thought. It's a completely human effort to get to the terrestrial Paradise. And when you come out of Hell, which is non-light, the whole realm of Hell has no light, it is light which casts no light . . . suddenly the burst of natural imagery in Purgatory. There's a guardian of *Purgatorio*, and we've come out of the suicides and the rest of them, and who should be sitting there guarding the Paradise but Cato Uticensis, Cato the Younger, who is a suicide in the pagan world. He is the guardian of Purgatory and he committed suicide, in Dante's reading of his life out of Cicero, for political freedom—and we wind up in the entire moral act of manhood as the nature of Purgatory. It is also the realm in which you are given the possibility of re-learning love—any range of your life that has not known love, understood it—been able to act in it since it is an action and nothing else, but an action that will then finally return you to yourself. The Purgatory is where you re-learn love and then finally the Paradiso—and if you want me to I can do a brief thing another evening on it, because that's based on the tradition of light and it works by images in such a way that one is literally carried.[7] Dante talks in the Can Grande [della Scalla] letter about the literalism, what he means by the literal experience of image. By light images we are raised finally to that point of light that is the origin of the world and the vision of the rose, what Olson calls that "longest lasting rose."

TALLMAN: OK now Robin, you've written a little essay called "The Fire." Now where's the heat in here and the light?

BLASER: The heat would be Purgatory and the light—I mean I'm taking this as kind of a metaphorical way of doing it—and the light then is the rec-, the total recognition moments, the heat being the movement, the effort both of thought and feeling, of change, transformation to the point where one then is in a new realm of recognition each time.

KUHARIC: But isn't it also Hell?

BLASER: No, Purgatory is outside Hell.

KUHARIC: No, the fire.

BLASER: Oh fire, yes, you're burned by it. But there's another fire. You see, light is different from fire.

TALLMAN: To me, Blake's great correction of the Christian notion of light was that Blake said that heat has to be there too. That the sun gives its heat and gives its light. That both have to be there. And it seems to me that Charles was constantly saying you've got to have the heat before you can have the light.

BLASER: Well, he says that you've got to have the heat and forget wisdom.

TALLMAN: And that's the marriage of Heaven and Hell isn't it? Or is it, of the burning, that the Christian pushed Hell down there, the fire was down there with Satan and the light was up there with Christ and that split was what Blake was complaining about.

BLASER: But that's the split of the soul dividing the body and all immaterial form, soul and intellect, in two parts. It's Augustinian. St. Augustine pulls this off in his arguments, the Protestants pick it up and it is the western tradition of Christianity as we know it, reflected by Irish Catholicism, but not by all the European Catholic thought. And certainly not by Dante, because the opposition to the—see that would be a polarization, if properly thought and felt, of material and immaterial, body with soul, intellect over here. So intellect's a pretty strange combination of things to throw together. All you've done is, without ever saying [it], you've lost the ability to think properly and you've said that soul and intellect are the same thing because they're both immaterial, we can't see them. And we live in this space still. This is where Kantorowicz brings the gift. You can read this in that gorgeous chapter, "Man-Centred Universe" at the end of the *King's Two Bodies* where this is going on. Dante, who knows the whole range of this argument, decides to throw it back into a trichotomy, into a triadic experience which is to say body, soul, and spirit. Body, intellect, and soul are three different things and you must work with a triad. The intellect then begins to be what Dante calls the good of the intellect and he talks about those who have lost the good of the intellect, a line that always just drives me up the wall, because that intermediary point is the way in which you keep the action of body and soul going. And it is so important that you keep the triad rather than what we live in where material and immaterial forms—and all

you do is reverse back and forth. You're either a theosophist—spiritu-
alist—or you're a materialist, and both of you seem stupid to me.
TALLMAN: OK, but now give me some reference points. Like it's fairly clear to me that you're taking Dante as kind of the chief intellect
of the western world.
BLASER: I do.
TALLMAN: Now where do you set Shakespeare? Like how does
Shakespeare figure? How does Chaucer figure? How do the other
great intellects figure?
BLASER: . . . One of the great texts that belongs in all this stuff—
except it seems to me like I want to do everything—is *Anthony and
Cleopatra,* because this is, it seems to me, the greatest play in the
world. You know how I like to make pretentious remarks like that.
But to me it is the glorious—Yeats calls them holy books, so does
Blake, and I think that's a holy book, *Anthony and Cleopatra.* It's in
the same range where the world image is at stake. It's also the same
range that Dante is repeatedly working with and has to work with in
terms of the whole narrative structure of *The Divine Comedy.* It's the
issue of where do you give the world up for love?
TALLMAN: All right, but do you see Shakespeare as profound as
Dante, or in a different realm than Dante, say because all of us can
understand Shakespeare because we grew up on it, you know, and
most of us did not grow up on Dante. You were lucky: you had access
to Dante via Kantorowicz.
BLASER: Well, thank God for Kantorowicz, yeah. But I think
[Shakespeare[8]] is by that time in a completely humanized universe. .
. . If you take that Edith Cobb essay, "The Ecology of Imagination,"[9]
that I like so much, where she says, "I'm going to oppose most contemporary psychological views of the world that the child looks for a
self because I've taken the autobiographies of something like 1,500
artists of all kinds and every one of them tells me one story; that
they're looking for a world in which they find themselves." And she
said surely we must take this seriously—I mean seriously. It's the
absolute point. It's driven the poets crazy while they had to listen to
all this tremendous reversal of where the self was to be found. And
Shakespeare seems to be an extremely humanized universe. This
does not fault Shakespeare but it makes it a very different tension

because Dante's world is so consistently tensed to what is Other than the human. Yes, God is present always, the Christian God, in Dante's thought. But one of the things that you find out by way of reading *De Monarchia* and the *Convivio*, *La Vita Nuova* and so on, that is once you've found out what a grandy he is, then you go back and read everything like we always do with great authors. You then suddenly see [what] he has made in this human collectivity thing that Kantorowicz talks about. The collective manhood does something that individual men cannot do, he argues, and the terrestrial Paradise is the job of the collective, the manhood. He says that one must include all: the pagan, the non-Christians. It's absolutely a mind-blower in terms of what one thinks of as the Christian side—then the Christian illumination is an illumination beyond death. It is a further illumination. The terrestrial Paradise is a man's job and may be done. In fact I have it here because the four cardinal virtues, temperance, justice, and so forth—it's the intellectual stuff, that man may himself manage the terrestrial Paradise. These, he says, belong to the manhood. We may do this, all the human world may do this. Our Paradise, our world image on the earth. The illumination beyond that is Christian, is something else. That's another entire realm beyond the edge of death. . . . That world is given to you by the divinely infused ones—faith, hope, and charity—which Jack does so marvelously when he takes the streets of Los Angeles and they keep changing—faith, hope, and charity. [. . .]

TALLMAN: . . . Where's the Beatrice figure, since most men I've known, myself included, tend to take human women as love objects. And now how does Beatrice figure here?

BLASER: The true story of Beatrice as the scholars have doped it all out, of course, seems to be rather against what we get in the vast structure of Dante's thought. That is, he doesn't make the time elements quite the same way. He meets her when he's nine years old and falls in love with her and she dies, so he never—I mean it never becomes an earthly love. Then the job that goes on, the new life, the new recognition, is how does one continue a love which isn't earthly? You then already get the doubleness of a love which isn't simply earthly, and Beatrice throughout *The Divine Comedy* is, of course, in heaven. She's the one who's arranged it so Dante has the power—mind-

boggling choice that he makes a pagan, Virgil, take him down into
Hell and all the way to the terrestrial Paradise, at the end of
Purgatory—to meet Beatrice. In fact Virgil only disappears—and he
disappears without—well he says one thing which I'll bring up—well
no. I'm just going to drop my notes now the way this is going. Virgil
leaves him. . . . This great chariot with a griffin—the griffin is Christ
with wings that go all the way up to Heaven, if you look at Blake's
illustration—it comes sweeping in and there are figures of all kinds
standing for the books of the Old Testament, the books of the New,
and the very strange, sad old man in back who is St. John of the
Revelation, and everything else. And here in the center is Beatrice in
the chariot. At the moment she appears, Virgil turns to Dante and
says, "*per ch'io te sovra te corono e mitrio*" ("I crown and mitre you
over yourself") and [he] disappears. This is the third, the last of the
Cantos. In the three cantos it takes to get Beatrice, he's already said
the old feeling had come back to me, as he knows who it is that's
there. Yet he bows his head to weep and that's when Beatrice first
speaks and says, "Don't weep," and draws his attention up so that he
keeps going further into the imagery, where finally it will take St.
Bernard, because there are no words, for beyond what he can see in
the eternal rose, the yellow rose. He can see no more. The curiosity
is that the whole of the Comedy works because the earthly love is
missing and then he wants to find a love that lasts and is permanent.
And then that love, the imagery by way of Beatrice . . . guides and
leads him finally to Paradise, the Paradise that is beyond the earthly.

TALLMAN: OK now, now shift to Shakespeare's *Anthony and
Cleopatra*.

BLASER: Well, that of course is entirely giving the world up for love.
Both of them lose the world for love. Dante makes a specific point, in
fact, puts two great lovers into Hell because they gave the world up
for love.

TALLMAN: But do you see them as human or as Gods?

BLASER: I see them as human and having lost the Gods. I adore
them for it . . . but one sees their love as that, and that perhaps it was
worth it, but everything is lost. I mean, that's one of the extraordinary
aspects of that play: the world is lost, and their lives.

TALLMAN: They believe in love more than they believe in the world.

BLASER: More than they believe in the world, and Dante would say this is—

TALLMAN: They don't believe in Caesar.

BLASER: They don't believe in Caesar. Of course Cato gets out of Hell because he refused to submit to Caesar and commits suicide for political freedom, and as a consequence is the guardian of those actions which will allow you to enter the earthly paradise.

TALLMAN: But what a strange thing it is that Caesar was an actual living man who provoked these legends.

BLASER: Well, he not only provoked them, but Napoleon is still acting on them post-French Revolution—once the French Revolution is lost, which was in ten days.

TALLMAN: So Napoleon and Josephine are—but they're pale figures.

BLASER: They're pale but they are still reflecting upon a world image that may be drawn together in one political figure who will hold the world together: the terrestrial paradise.

[*Here follows some conversation about whether Elizabeth Taylor and Richard Burton might fit in to this discussion of love and world image. Blaser continues to argue a distinction between love of a person and love of the collective.*]

BLASER: Well yeah, but what I'm saying [is] we are diminished. That's where I started: we have no world image. We're so diminished we have ourselves left and now we've disappeared. Like we've got nothing left but our sleazy little egos, and the poets keep fighting through this. Olson's whole range in the first *Maximus* poems is how to act in this world: go out and do the fishing; his bibliography's for everybody; learn your locus. . . . It's like Dante's love of Florence: the only way he can see that you make the world again is that you so tie yourself to the order of a place that you begin to put order around yourself there with your action, and then maybe the world image will reappear. Of course in the later *Maximus* he goes into those magnificent images. The *imago mundi* does come back in Charles's work. I was just trying to think—that marvelous Canadian artist, painter, movie maker Michael Snow in that, what is that called?

GARDINER: *La Région Centrale.*

BLASER: Yeah, *La Région Centrale*. Not only is it major art, but it seemed to me, this is world image. And the thing that was incredible about that—you know they bought a whole bunch of stuff and they took the goddamn computers up there in the Quebec backwoods. There are no human beings, and this camera is working, this thing going around and it always goes by horizons. The horizons, horizontally, but the horizons vertically as well. And they keep turning around, and it's all world image and there are no human beings in it. I'm going to have the movie brought back and I'll ask you all to come because I'll make the university pay for it.

TALLMAN: I've never seen it.

BLASER: It's unbelievable. It takes three hours and you just take your cigarettes and sit there and don't leave, because it's just absolutely beyond. I want to write on it because I think it's a major event in modern art, but in terms of Canadian stuff it's fantastic. It seems to me to move to be a point at which he not only sees what is absent, but then this is the point where the world as landscape comes back in, and there's not even a man there—and the silence. Yet the turns as the whole thing shifts, extraordinary thing. I would like to write about it. Let's turn this off.

[Recorder switched on and off.]

BLASER: The business about language that is not an emptying out: the two terms I've adapted from two different philosophers—the term *Gerade* in Heidegger's German means—

TALLMAN: Speech.

BLASER: Speech—but empty talk, it means just talk. We use speech to empty out so much and I'm trying to say we have speech—language—which we close into ourselves, making it ourselves. Philosophy's based on this: we only wind up in a range of thought that will leave us speaking, us thinking, and we even suspect the reality of that and all that goop. *Gerade* is then the emptying stuff we use. Our only word we have near it is "gossip." It's not, it doesn't have the strength. In French it's *"parole vide,"* "empty word," because they have both *parole* and *langue,* and so they have real distinctions, where we just have a terrible time. We've got language which goes splattering off every place, and we don't understand capitalizing it. Our word "word" is strange—and if we capitalize it, you can't, and so on. [It] becomes very complex. . . .

[Tape change; Side 22]

BLASER: And that business of the language which empties or the language which closes in contrast to the language which discloses and composes is the issue of poetic language, and as a consequence poetic language has never stopped doing this. This is no news to a poet—none—but why it has to be news to the whole fucking culture while they leave us off talking to ourselves all the time I don't know. I'm well . . . so I could do a little bit on the tradition of life, if you want.

TALLMAN: Pound in the Cavalcanti essay—Pound goes into the whole theory of life which is absolutely crucial, evidently—

BLASER: It's crucial.

TALLMAN: Cavalcanti to Dante to the whole—

QUESTION: Whole world.

TALLMAN: I get the sense that it's a very scientific, mystical appre-hension of the nature of life . . .

BLASER: Well, yeah, it is actually medieval science, and he wanted that rather than this Christian religious tradition of life. Then when it turns out they're really the same thing—later on Pound doesn't bother to correct it. His crankiness with Dante and of course his debt to Dante is enormous.

TALLMAN: But I'm still curious because I always had the perhaps naive feeling that the first guy who broke through the Christian light theory was Blake with his heat theory. That's why Blake says well, Satan is Christ: that is the heat. You've got to have that heat joined to that light. . . . Did Cavalcanti and those guys, did they count for heat too, or?

BLASER: Well, Cavalcanti would wind up in Hell because Cavalcanti is willing to give everything to the earthly love, in Dante's view. So yes, in fact I think you could probably just go through and pluck the images of heat out of Cavalcanti and out of the whole courtly love tradition which goes on in Cavalcanti. Dante's actually belongs to the tradition called the *"fedeli d'amore"* rather than courtly love and quarrels with giving the world up for one's love. When he quarrels he means to quarrel on the level that you know what you are doing, because the loss, the complete giving up of the world, is something you don't have the right to do—it must be close to despair. To so give it up into one's own realm means that you've lost the image of the world which is, well in Dante's view, the God-given. But in anybody's view—when you run into Mathilda for example, the reason she's there is that it's a pastoral scene. We've suddenly come to the earthly paradise. Oh God, when Dante comes across that way, across the beating, beating seas, and winds up there to go and meet Cato, and Cato turns to Virgil and says, "wash his face and put rushes around his head." The rushes are the only thing that will grow in the beating sea. So Virgil pulls the rushes from the sea, walks over, a little out of the sunlight where the shade still is and takes his hand and picks the dew out of the grass and rubs it across Dante's face and the light returns to his thought and to his feeling. Move then all the way through the incredible imagery of doves and fireflies. I mean you just have to watch what Dante's doing. Then you get up there and here's Mathilda. Well, the tradition is this is a pastoral scene: here we come, thumpty-thump, and all poems about pastorals have got a shepherdess to go along with the shepherd. So here she is, you know, diddly-dee, picking flowers. But do you know who she is? And Dante tells: she's Persephone—oh God, she's marvelous. And then it turns out that she's singing a song which tells us that she must love the world. The point of the passage as I read it is that, for this figure which belongs to the tradition of the girl one loves and the lust and the rape and everything that belongs to her, Persephone, there is also the realm in which she must love the world, that which is beyond. And Dante must recognize her as such and then she's the one who tells him how to get across the stream, Lethe—in fact bathes him in Lethe and takes him across to the procession of the chariot, and the griffin, and the seven candles.

TALLMAN: Did Kantorowicz ever talk about Milton?

BLASER: No, I don't think he would have known a lot about Milton. He could have mastered him in a hurry, but he wouldn't have much interest in that. He never taught the Reformation. He did Renaissance but he never got to the Reformation. My sense is that there was a very funny kind of personal impatience with Calvin and Luther. He never offered it and the material I got was from a very drab man. He was not of the same intellectual quality. So I'm getting Luther and Calvin from Jack, who's reading them voluminously. And I must say you have to read a hundred volumes. With Jack I wasn't sure that he didn't somehow read two or three volumes and have the whole thing. TALLMAN: You know Robin, I can't help telling you this. My favorite cartoon: it's Adam and Eve being pushed out of paradise, and their heads are bowed and they're going out the gates, and they're obviously doing terribly and they're whispering to one another. Eve is leaning over to Adam and the little balloon says, "Don't tell him about the oranges."

[*laughter*]

BLASER: He did this for the apple for fuck's sake. Dante's marvelous point is—he's trying to go at the nature of original sin. If Adam and Eve could hold the collective business of a fall—a sin, an improper action, something that you've broken—if one man and woman can hold that, then the collectivity of mankind can reverse that and go back to the original Adam in the terrestrial paradise. Yeah, I want that on the tape. [. . .]

Dante's absolutely into the collectivity of manhood. *Humanitas* itself may reverse and go back to what was the collectivity of the Adam before and terrestrial by intellect. Dennis Wheeler arrives over in the middle of my preparation for this evening and he's going into the really deep radical stuff among the local Indians here, magnificent stuff. And he was telling me a scene in which the young Indians will not listen to anybody except their elders, and he described the scene in one tribe where this old man came in and he had the stick which is the stick of the world with feathers on it. The old man comes in and when he puts it down it is the human— This isn't the human will which we're so used to, that imposes on the world and then devours it. This is the human, the mind and the heart in its bind to the world, that finds a place there. And when the stick goes down, it is in the world and it is that symbol of man who stands there with his place. . . . That's Dante.

[*Here the session breaks into chat. Blaser comments on Jo[sephine] Miles, a professor who taught Blaser, Spicer, and Duncan at Berkeley; a Chaucer professor; Ed[ward] Dorn, eating quahogs with Olson at Provincetown; and an interview with Gregory Corso, Allen Ginsberg, and Peter Orlovsky at Harvard but these topics are not developed. At one point, Warren Tallman seems to be initiating a separate conversation about Margaret Atwood, but this is not developed either. The tape ends with Blaser saying, "Oh yeah, I loved Gregory [Corso]." Over the next several sessions, consisting of four tapes, eight sides (23-30), Blaser picks up this talk on Dante to discuss the "metaphysics of light," a tradition in which substance is understood as light. The heart of these sessions has been transcribed and edited by Daphne Marlatt, and published in* The Capilano Review *(see my introductory essay for the citation). The following session, which I have chosen to juxtapose to the above discussion of Blaser's companions in poetry and the poet as maker of a world image is a session that circles around and around James Joyce. Blaser sees in Joyce the writer who best offers a modern response to the tradition represented in Dante.*]

* * *

[*Story IX, Side 31*]

BLASER: . . . oh here they are.

TALLMAN: We've got plenty [of tapes]. We can go for 30, 60, 30, 60, 30, 60, 30, 60—we can go for four hours if you want.

BLASER: Well, we don't need to go that long. Also there's trouble, because on the way over here—it's such a quiet day—I opened both windows in the car and a gust of wind came and blew my notes out the window and—

TALLMAN: You've got to be kidding.

BLASER: No. They blew out, just—

TALLMAN: Robin I don't believe this.

BLASER: It's true.

TALLMAN: You mean you opened the window and threw your notes out the window and you're telling us—

BLASER: I think—

TALLMAN: —that a gust of wind came and blew the notes out.

BLASER: I think what I wanted to do was throw them out the window 'cause I have had trouble concentrating. But when they went out the window, I felt a little like that famous Chinese poet, the princess. There are no poems. She's supposed to be a tremendous poet but she threw all of her poems in the river as she wrote them, and that's a little the way I felt. Anyway, my house is full of peonies and the perfume of the peonies has been disturbing my mind. I went out into the garden to get away from that and the foxglove is taller than I am and it's all full of bees, and somehow I don't think my notes came up to that. So the wind took them away from me. It was very strange 'cause it's so still today.

TALLMAN: OK, in view of that fact, what would you like to do?

BLASER: Well, I'll try to reconstruct a little bit of it.

TALLMAN: Is it a message to you?

BLASER: I hope this isn't going to be a downer from last time.

TALLMAN: Is it a message to you that maybe you didn't want to use those notes but maybe you wanted to use something else.

BLASER: Well it may be, I'm trying to figure that out. I feel better if I've sort of formulated a little more, a little better what I wanted to say and then let it run from there. But I'll try to reconstruct it a little bit. I wanted to call this evening and the next two evenings "The Knowledge of the Poet" and start moving on that, because from where we were leaving off we'd gotten into all that Dante stuff and headed for the companions, as I call them. But I suddenly realized that moving out of the angelology—I had an absolutely literal belief in angels, and my whole language trip now is to find the way to bring the imagery of the angels in. The angels in my view are the literal images of the intellect. That's why I went on about the tradition of light—I belong to that too—and pick that up later on with the Arabic stuff and with a lot of other things.

But I first wanted to get the disturbance. What seemed to me very strange was where did contemporary poetry, modern thought, enter all of this? So that's really where the notes were going: where does contemporary thought come into this? It turns out in my memory of the events back there then, it is Joyce. It's Joyce for all of us. Joyce is Duncan's gift. I did want to at least point out certain aspects of what

it was that Joyce was doing, but in terms of the modern thought thing
I'm back with my concern. Angela brought it up to me the other
night when she said the one thing that struck her about what I was
doing was my tentativeness. This was in the midst of your drunken-
ness, dear. And I wondered about that phrase, 'cause I listened very
carefully and then I quarreled with it. I quarreled with it in the sense
that "tentative" I didn't like, Angela, and I didn't want that to be the
sense of what was happening. What I really keep trying to do—number one, I want the form of this book, as I worked for the form of the
poetry, to do something to the people who read it. And I want the
moment of the book to do something for me. . . . I also worked since
the period that we're talking about in a sense of lack of power. I come
to do this book at the end of seven years of silence. Now that seven
years of silence sounds funny to people because I talk all the time at
the university. I make my living that way: they bought my ass and I
do my best to earn that stipend. But I have been really pretty much
silent seven years—that seven years is since Jack's death. That's a
mind-blower for me. On the one hand the challenge of the language
that leads you that way; on the other hand, my companions and
masters who went in the same direction. Nerval, who as I've said
hanged himself on the lamp post. We have to go into what it means
when you enter such language, the death of God thing which I've
said is a linguistic danger, the cosmological . . . that I take to mean
actually a conscious mode of life that ties you to everything that is
other than yourself. As a consequence, then by way of the light tradition I manage to make an equivalence, an analogical equivalence.
That's why I brought analogy up and we'll go back to analogy in a
minute, because Jack was a master of it—an analogical equivalence
between love and light: light is the actual substance of the world
then, and as a consequence, intelligence, recognition, consciousness.
I think of the poet as a master of consciousness most of all and of language as the performance of manhood in the world and the only
place in which it's performed. I do not think that work performs our
place in the world: it performs ourselves and our necessities. I don't
think that radical thought begins even to face this because no twentieth-century radical thought knows anything about public space and
public space can only be maintained by the . . . imagery, in fact the

vision of manhood in the language. In other words, it can only be done by art; it is not done by the State.

TALLMAN: Is it done by the newspapers then or not?

BLASER: Newspapers?

TALLMAN: Yeah, public space you said . . .

BLASER: Newspapers aren't public space. Newspapers are simply news of something that's going on that may affect you. But public space as that which we share in terms of intelligence and love has to be what by way of a language that performs the presence of the manhood in that which is other than himself. And the language is the seat and throne of the Other. When I went into that angelology stuff, my notes went out the window, so I don't have it all now and I won't try to go into it. But I had the angels all listed from the seraphim, the cherubim, all the way through them—all thrones, dominations, powers and all that—so you got into the business of where the intelligence actually recognizes the order of the world and is bound to it, and that's what angels are. They're not supersititions at all. They have an absolute reality, providing language has a reality. If language doesn't have a reality, it's always transparent to the real or transcendent to the real. Then we may disbelieve it and remove ourselves from it, or we fall out of the grid and so on. We thought everybody had a cosmology earlier and I said well, the way I want to use the word, since it meant harmony, I used it in a large sense. I thought we had no cosmology at all and that, in my view, is what's been taken on by some of the major poets—not all. But some of them—

TALLMAN: But don't rush now, Robin. By angels do you mean invisible presences or do you mean that there are individuals who are angels?

BLASER: Well, I find individuals as angels—and angels, remember, are both good and bad. There are dark and light angels. I mean like, I'm not losing that at all: there are both dark and light ones. In my original notes, I had stuff on Byron's *Cain* because I wanted to draw that forward, and that's because of Joyce. Because what I'm doing now is to go all the way back into 1947 and it's Duncan and Throckmorton. It's before *The Venice Poem*, moving towards *The Venice Poem*. [. . .] None of us could tolerate the way in which the university handled contemporary literature, poetry, modern. I mean

like in those days, Joyce to me was supposedly alive. . . . *Stephen Hero*
had been published in '44, that's to say the year I'm arriving in
Berkeley and a year before Jack arrives. And in '47 Joyce of course
meant nothing to me. The problem of the "Chinese Nightingale"[10]
as I used that poem as a kind of basic mode of the poetics that seem
to be alive and beyond, well, beyond Longfellow, beyond you know,
beyond the kind of ordinary rhyme that one thinks of—that somehow
that was moving into another realm. Curiously, that is nostalgia, and
one thing that does fascinate me about the whole Berkeley period is
the way in which it went into nostalgia. In other words, everything is
elegiac. The greatest poems of this period are Duncan's *Medieval
Scenes*, the *Domestic Scenes*, and *The Venice Poem*. They are simply
beautiful, but they are elegies. All three are elegies. Now it's not that
Duncan taught us elegy, it's that Duncan is the central focus of elegy.
Then that elegiac tends to be something like the absence of a landscape, the absence of a place, the determination to let one's life fall
and rise upon love itself, and love itself then bringing an order that
passes all the time and all the poems indicate this. I think of Jack's
marvelous poem, "We Find the Body Difficult to Speak," which is
there then. But by the time I begin at this point—and I'm trying to
watch these moves I make like, what were you doing in the sense of
things then and then what do you do now? Now when I look at that
nostalgia I see what enormous intelligence that nostalgia has,
because what it does is throw all of us, and in this instance I have to
say myself, into the realm of not what T. S. Eliot, say, is doing—irony
about the modern condition—but an actual grief and tears of the
modern condition. If you go through Duncan's *Medieval Scenes* for
the marvel that that poem is—and it is in spite of the arguments with
Duncan—it is a serial poem. It is for Jack and me the first serial
poem. We find other serial poems later, but it is the first one. If you
look at that poem it is grief of the world and not simply the grief of
the voice of the poet. It's making a move and it's throwing us into the
realm, the wooded, the forest, the unsettled landscape, the mystery of
the missing landscape. . . . It's double all the time. *Medieval Scenes* is
full of the voices of the people who were then present. They can all
be identified somewhere, directly identified like Leonard Woolf in
the "Goliath" poem and so on. But at the same time, they're thrown

back into the total tapestry from the *Medieval Scenes*. Well, the same pattern actually is working in a very different form in *The Venice Poem*, where *The Venice Poem* is made out of an enormous amount of Robert's interest in the Renaissance and in the history of Venice which moves back with the Renaissance, and backward and forward. The whole interest in this is a kind of iconography from that period which then begins to tie and bind to the grief of the world. His image is adultery and the scene of the poem is set because there's an analogy between the poet and his grief—Othello's grief—and that occurred in the city of Venice. And then you begin to move through those doubles and layers, and the layers are really fantastic. But that nostalgia really, really begins to fascinate me.

Well, I then began to think this thing really is where modern thought is, because the first time you had a sense of a contemporary poet it was Duncan. And I think this is true for Jack, too. Then I tried to think, well, where does modern thought as such begin to come in instead of its being traditional something, where you're literally facing the thought of another writer and that writer becomes directed and aimed. That's James Joyce and this is at Throckmorton in '47 when Duncan pulls off the first "free university," and he organizes the evenings I mentioned before. He was doing *Finnegans Wake*, and others did Lorca, and there was Baudelaire and, well, there were others, but those were the main ones. I mean those at least stick in my memory and certainly [were] the ones that stuck in Jack's memory, those three. Joyce is interesting where Jack's concerned because Jack didn't like *Ulysses*. He thinks it's the world's most boring book. I never joined Jack in this, I still don't join Jack in this. But the books that were important were the way in which we try to save ourselves from the absolute horror—and I speak here for myself as Jack did not ever, tell me directly that he felt horror, but he was trying to go through *Finnegans Wake*. There were over twenty people attending that occasion with Duncan reading it and reading it beautifully. He had a simulated Irish accent and would read it, and then we would work at it and it took twenty people with every little bit and piece of information each person had to get through anything. As I remember the only thing I ever had to offer was some knowledge of the Bible which I'd paid attention to but at that point nothing else seemed to

be very helpful. My Latin, at that point at least, I didn't seem to have
any assurance that I could use it. So my sense was horror. That book
was so unbelievably beyond anything I could imagine, in fact, it broke
my imagination, and not in a bad sense but in a good one. I had no
idea how you could work in language this way, the words smeared. In
fact, it took me several occasions at that evening of Duncan's before
I knew that we were in realms of pun and laughter. And now coming
here at this point in my life I turned back to that great book with the
sense of our inside laughter as I've never had it before, but that's, so
to speak, after the fact. Now, Warren you wanted to—

TALLMAN: Yeah, what were the mechanics of it? I'm just curious.
Was it every Sunday night or every—?

BLASER: It was week nights, as I remember, Wednesdays for the
Finnegan, 'cause they changed nights.

TALLMAN: And what would happen? Would Duncan read it for a
certain period of time?

BLASER: Duncan would read. Each week we were assigned a chapter and then Duncan would read it and he gave broad indications
at the beginning the way in which it circles on itself, which was a
mind-blower and still remains a mind-blower. And it gets more so as
I go on with a fascination in poems that no longer are willing to deal
in a linear narrative but in narratives that turn round in circles. The
greatest examples of these that I [can] think of off the spot are Blake's
Urizen, which I knew nothing of then, and *Finnegans Wake.* He
would read and so on and then we would go word by word, line by
line trying to pull out what were the base English words and then you
also tried to pull in enough information to get what the story was,
what the referential stories were, what the analogies were, and then
what the puns of sound were. Of course, it was very laborious and we
never managed to finish it. You had to finish the job on your own and
it was before the key was published so there was no help—none—
and it was a marvel. I don't think we were any of us competent but it
didn't matter, because it was the playfulness and the extraordinary
intelligence of it, not available in the university. What it did was
throw both Jack and me into a range on Joyce, and I think Joyce
really the greatest challenge at that point. What are we at that point—
twenty-one, two? It threw us back so what you did was turn to Joyce's

earlier work to see what was going on, because even then we had a sense that there could be, there would be development in an author's work.

Today now my impatience, my anger and horror at the universities that they set up a methodology of survey courses where you read a piece of something or a single poem, and are not conscious of the fact that they have literally been teaching something about the nature of language and the nature of art without ever telling what it is they are saying and it is a lie from beginning to end, and a disaster for the great artists of the twentieth century. We won't worry about Homer, Dante and the rest of the big-shots, but for the twentieth century it's become a disaster. Pound is unstudied and of course will remain unstudied in universities as long as I'm alive because they can't, they won't change it. It costs too much in their view. Anyway, it was Duncan's proposal in Throckmorton and that we would move into ranges of this kind of work. Behind it all was of course Duncan's plot to write a novel of his own which was very much patterned on *Finnegan* and as complicated and he had, I suppose he has the notes. I've searched and I don't have them. I think they were never given to me. We sat eating chocolate doughnuts at the Kingpin while he would draw maps showing me what the novel was going to look like and very little of it I think was ever written. Out of the same period comes the story "Love" which isn't in this range of difficulty at all.

Anyway, Jack and I turned backward to—well to see what's going on. Now they had just published *Stephen Hero* in '44 which is a year before, well the year I'm arriving and the year before Jack and I meet and two, three years before this starts going. So we turned back to *Stephen Hero* with that funny kind of—oh what do you call it, I don't know—the nit-picky that both Jack and I had as part of our personalities. You would go back and look at a manuscript that was behind *A Portrait of the Artist* kind of thing, and we began to move. Now what happens and what I'm trying to draw attention to is that if you keep the Dante in mind simultaneously [as] the Joyce is going on, Joyce amounts to not only the admission of and the confrontation of that entire tradition, but it begins to take on the whole terror and breakdown of the contemporary world. The whole tradition begins to fall. It's breaking and it's falling and in *Stephen Hero* you can get that very,

very clearly. Now Easter Sunday 1947, Duncan and Leonard Woolf
and I are sitting at Blake's restaurant having strawberry sundaes—
TALLMAN: Which is a famous Berkeley—
BLASER: Hangout. And we are having strawberry sundaes and the ice
cream was lovely and great big strawberries on it, and Leonard Woolf
leaned over—Duncan and I are sitting on the same side of the booth
facing Leonard—Leonard leaned over, he's the one [in] "Goliath," in
the amazing "Goliath." He now writes poems in Yiddish and teaches
at San Francisco State College and he wrote a book called, what?
Oh, I can't think of what the name of the book was, but anyway the
leading poem is "I am hamadryad hunted, none so fair," I can
remember that. That was published shortly after Duncan's *Heavenly
City, Earthly City.* Anyway he leaned over as we were eating the
strawberry sundaes and he said, "These are the wounds of Christ,"
and took a great glob and stuck it in his mouth. And Duncan took a
spoonful and went "mmmmm," with, you know the way Duncan
loves to sound things out. I burst into tears. At which point I would
like to stop for a moment.

[Recorder turned on and off.]

BLASER: Well anyway, Robert ran out on the street to get me and so
on.
TALLMAN: What did he say to you when he—? Can you remember?
BLASER: Yes, I remember very well what he said. He said, "I didn't
know. I just didn't know." He didn't—there was nothing else to say,
he just didn't know. And at that point I had held onto this entire
tradition with bare hands, so to speak. It's also the tradition that's
coming from the sacred heart and all that stuff moving from the
youngest period. I mean the "Chinese Nightingale" is no challenge
to this, and in the meantime I've not yet faced what was going to be
the ultimate challenge, and that was Joyce.
TALLMAN: But Leonard Woolf said, "These are the wounds of
Christ?"
BLASER: "These are the wounds of Christ" and took a big—I've
never forgotten, a big ice cream spoon and stuck this strawberry with
ice cream in his mouth and chewed it with a kind of, you know, a

ravenous aspect to his mouth, and Duncan then took his spoon and then made sounds with it "yum, yum, yum, shhlp."

TALLMAN: Slurp, slurp.

BLASER: At which point all I did was burst into tears because it was an ultimate image for me.

TALLMAN: You left.

BLASER: I left, yes I left, well, I was ashamed of crying—

TALLMAN: And Robert came out.

BLASER: And Robert followed me and he said "I didn't know," that's all he said.

TALLMAN: And did you have a sense that he understood why you had burst into tears?

BLASER: Well, I take it in saying "I didn't know," that he was saying "I understand." I mean this was Easter Sunday, and I'd already been going through the business—I don't know whether you know what Newman clubs are or not, but having been at one point semi-trained in medieval Latin and so on and so on for possible priesthood, the Catholic Church followed me wherever I went. When I was at Northwestern, there would be calls on me. When I got to Berkeley, the Newman club sent up, and so on and so on. So there was a constant edge to this. Actually, what was happening, was the edge of belief versus disbelief and I find now my impatience with the people who instead of recognizing the realm of disbelief as an actual realm of methodology, who now simply want to not think at all of what these terms are. And yet our greatest art has taken on the whole issue of what it is to fall out of these realms of assurance and explanation and ultimateness. That you drop into a kind of pseudo-positivism, positivism without even a theoretical basis. I'm interested in this fall and I will be for the first time lecturing on Joyce. I want to see what the young do now when they see the extravagance of this realm? What happens when they face onto a book that says the absolute is dead? What happens when the horror of what the Church has been in countries where it has political power, as in Ireland, what happens when the Church begins to be the definition of the dead? How much this can carry over, since I find Canada very much the realm of the dead. I want to see can they recognize that this is actually the issue they're in and it is not to return to something, but it is literally to know what the commotion is. And I return to my sense there of the poet as "commoter"—that they know at least what this is and the peculiar anguish. A *Portrait of the Artist*, for example, is a book of anguish and if you watch him you get an entire poetics out of Joyce. The early books are particularly fascinating because he's working out at the same age we were, that is, he's twenty, he's at college, he's doing something to St. Thomas Aquinas that is utterly amazing. There are several fascinating things about Aquinas. Number one, he says in the *Summa*—and I can even give you the references if you want that stuff, where to look for it—he says flatly—how I think of Jack in one of the Vancouver lectures where he uses St. Thomas Aquinas and he says [there] couldn't be anybody with less imagination than that, and it's quite true. St. Thomas stops writing the *Summa* at the end of his life, that's true—and then there's a great occultist, alchemical text that is thought to be Aquinas. For those people who want to go in for that kind of history you can sort of fix Aquinas. But anyway, Aquinas says that poetry is the lowest kind of knowledge. By implication, it is primary but then he has a hierarchy of knowledge, and it is the lowest. He then goes into the untruths of its analogies even though they are like to or aping the analogies in theology, the four-level readings of theology, and he—well, it's just generally an attack on poetry.

TALLMAN: But then he places theology over poetry.

BLASER: Oh way over, yes. Well, theology's the queen of science, the queen of knowledge, and poetry is the lowest level of any kind of knowledge. It is dangerous and so on. If you want to get the modern line on this—and it's fairly fascinating to read, both Jack and I read it and I'm sure Duncan read it too, because one of Duncan's charges against me on the *Chimères* was "you lousy Catholics"—at the point where that's no longer even a possible charge. But part of the information by which he gets clarity about this is Jacques Maritain in a book called *Creative Intuition in Poetry and the Arts*. It's a Bollingen book. It's interesting to watch that book, a very good book. The book that Jack liked of his is a book on scholasticism, which will tell you a lot about this. Anyway, just one more point on Aquinas I mustn't forget.

TALLMAN: Maritain is one of the few Catholic theorists, right?

BLASER: He and [Étienne] Gilson, the great Dante man, would be good examples of twentieth-century Aquinian thought. In that book he delineates in detail—and this is going to become important in awhile, Angela, for your question about Orphism because I have to turn to a whole Cocteau evening fairly soon—he begins to beat on the whole business of what the poet knows in that book, and takes on his whole aspect as a knower because knowing should belong to theology and the poet may not know in this sense and it is delineated with an attack upon Rimbaud in particular. It's a very important book if you like lining things up like this. And I think they're useful to line up because the knowing of poetry is the very thing that's in question, what kind of knowing it is. . . .

Oh, the other thing about Aquinas: Aquinas has a notion of language that needs to be paid attention to, and he still argues language as the principle of participation in the world. Aquinas is really almost the last of those big overwhelming systematizers, almost the last, who is very clear that language is the mode of participation in the world. . . . That the world speaks into the language, the older and Other than what we are, that it is a real speaking of the world. And then as we join it there's the middle mode called participation. This is discussed beautifully by a man named Owen Barfield.

[Tape change, Side 32]

BLASER: So Joyce takes the Aquinian thing and makes a poetry of an extraordinary high realm. This is going to become a real crack-up in the San Francisco scene that I'm talking about ultimately. I'm not going to take on what that crack-up is 'cause I have to move through the arguments more carefully later on, but he does adopt the Aquinian view that the work of art should deal with wholeness, with harmony, and radiance. I think those are the words that Joyce himself uses and any critic brings up those three. It's in A *Portrait of the Artist as a Young Man*. The thing to notice about A *Portrait of the Artist as a Young Man*—again nothing original with me, it's been pointed out—one of the great games in the book is that the word "God" is so much in question. That's the way to put it: Joyce is the first interrogative writer that I read and since I think of interrogation as central to contemporary poetics, I won't differentiate Joyce from poetry. I see no differentiation in his work from poetry. I do in a lot of prose: I think prose is a real flatulence in a great part. I don't mean always, but very often it's just simply pissing around. . . . I've forgotten now what my point was—well, it didn't matter.

If you look at *Stephen Hero*, it's only a little piece of *A Portrait of the Artist as a Young Man* in what would have been its first version, but it gives all kinds of very head-on details and so many of them remind me of Jack. Early on in the book you get a whole considered interest in language and the peculiar way in which—oh I know what it was, I'll go back to the God word in a minute; God after all is a word and boy do you get to do things with that when you get into this sensitization of language. Early on in *Stephen Hero* you'll find Joyce going over Skeat. Now among Jack's books and he left very few, [William Edward Hartpole] Lecky's *History of European Morals* [*from Augustus to Charlemagne*] or whatever that thing is because the prose style he adored, and Jack's prose is beautiful, unlike Duncan's and mine. He really [had] a superb clarity in that prose and liveness that he had. Anyway, Jack left the etymological dictionary along with some books on chess and bridge, and a whole bunch of mystery and fantasy stories. There was Skeat and it is a Skeat very like the one Joyce must have used, so that you get the whole etymological base.

TALLMAN: OK, so identify Skeat just for the hell of it.

BLASER: [He was] a great linguistic scholar of the late nineteenth-century and still [is] the standard etymological dictionary. There are new ones. I've not checked it out enough to really know what's up, whether, for example, the [*Oxford*] *Etymological Dictionary of the English Language* has improved it. I can't afford to buy it and I've been too lazy to go to the library to spend hours with my Skeat alongside that. In my last essay I used a business of disaster for example.[11] In Skeat if you look up the word "disaster" you'll find "aster" (Gk. αστηρ), is star, and dis is to turn away from the stars. And I wind up in that essay talking about "dis-stars" and so on. [. . .]

Well, this is the kind of thing that Joyce goes at. He's also fascinated by puns, and in *Stephen Hero* and *A Portrait of the Artist as a Young Man*, they're not really quite as clear. You have to look at the way in which he expects the mind to take one thing and tie it to another. One of the organizing principles in *A Portrait of the Artist as a Young Man*: you've got to notice that "God," if you look at it in a mirror, spells "dog" and one critic, I think it's [William York] Tindall has said that that's where Dylan Thomas gets his "Portrait of the Artist as a Young Dog"—from Joyce and in the play of God and dog. And then you begin—you play with words in this way. Reminds me of that beautiful example here in Vancouver that Jack used that last year when he said that puns were terribly important. He said there's this guy in this forty-two story building and he decided he was going to jump. I mean life is just too much, so he jumps. Well, there's a guy on the eighteenth story, leans out the window and he said, "Have you got vertigo?" And the guy said, "Yes, seventeen stories." And Jack said it tells us something about death. The profundity of that of course is what Joyce knew only too well. This is what *Finnegan* is about: the nature of death. There is no escape from the business that death is inside the language. That's where it is and that's what we're dealing with all the time. And as a consequence of the death of the modern world, the death of God and so on, all has to be worked in terms of the sensitization to language, the consciousness of language. This is why contemporary poetry talks about itself all the time.

TALLMAN: OK now Robin, just let me interrupt you. I've heard the death of God many times. What does that mean in your mind?

BLASER: Well, it literally means the death of God and, oh all right—

TALLMAN: But what does it mean happened? What happened in the society or the universe that has produced this?

BLASER: OK. . . . The Christian God requires a cosmology. Take the word "God" and give it an equivalence to the word "world," but be very careful of that. . . . You cannot think without others and as a consequence these discriminations are terribly important, one doesn't get sloppy about it. God and world, the notion of a total explanation of the world, one in which I know where I am, my self then begins to play in an assured and ordered way with the world—will come up smack against God in all of western tradition. And I think probably by the very nature of language it will come up against God because it so happens that Indo-European languages do not let us escape him. At the end of Alfred North Whitehead's superb *Process and Reality*, in the next to the last chapter, he says, "all right we've reached the point where if you want to put the word God in here, it's here, that's where

it is, this is the unknown." So now I've got another equivalent with
the unknown. He takes a Goddess in one of the most beautiful
passages in that very great and important book, which is a book that
only comes into the scene many years later by way of Olson. God-
world; God-unknown. In the Christian tradition God is what is Other
than yourself, but God is always Other than the world—he's outside
the world. And in Dante, who is the last great author in whose work
we will find this, the absolute knowing methodology of what it is to
work in a world that is created by that [which] is Other than itself,
that is the entire universe other than God and God outside it [and] as
a consequence unknowable, to be experienced in light imagery at a
point in the *Paradiso*, but other. [. . .]

[In] Greek mythology—and the whole funny range where Joyce
gets involved in this, all of us do—the Greek mythology and the
Egyptian mythology and Chinese mythologies: the Gods are always
the world in its movement. . . . The Christian makes a very difficult
thing because the unknowability and the Otherness is even beyond
what the world is and all the others are the movements of the world.
Now the death of God in the west, in western terms as far as I can tell,
becomes a very funny thing and the best thing in the world to read
on this I think is, and again this is very late, Nietzsche. I mean just
begin with Nietzsche 'cause he's it as far as the thought of this is concerned. His methodology's philological: what he knew at the very
base of everything was that when you tried to hold on to the world,
tried to think about it, tried to think with it, tried to think in it,
tried to hold it together between you and any other person, that the
language was the mode. And what does the language do? What he
noticed was that all the thought moving from the eighteenth century
forward was beginning to close the world into a manhood and that
God was absent from it. Now earlier, Warren, when we were talking
and I was really using Foucault's information, I said the basic
methodology of our thought—and I've denounced it in my latest
essay ["Stadium of the Mirror"], as best I can at this point—[is]
anthropology, sociology, and psychology, which all can tell you a very
great deal about the human being, but none of them has any methodology for dealing with this polar alive truth—that is, myself and
all that is other than myself. Nor can they speak of love except as

instinct, as desire, and love is none of those things. Marxist thought cannot even speak of love, for example—the major sociology of our time, brilliant. I'm going to be in Marxism, as I've told Dwight, because I feel like I've got to take it on because anything in the contemporary world is my business. We wind up at the point where the world closes into ourselves and this can be traced by the methodology of what thought is able to do. We even wind up with philosophies— the two great examples would be Husserl and Wittgenstein—in which we either talk about, in the latter case, [a] kind of logic—Wittgenstein in the famous phrase, "we won't talk about what we cannot find in logic"—or, in Husserl who brings us, following from Kant through, you get to the point where you have a world that is only thought by men—and we then fall into every possible cosmological problem in the world. You wind up with animals without souls, which is all built into Christianity because the intelligence is consistently moving in western thought into the realm that it is man alone who thinks.

Now the thought that proposes that there is a double world that goes on and it is literally something speaking into the language—this is Jack's dictation I'm headed for—and that one moves then into the language—is a mode so contrary to that. In fact all of poetry of any distinction is in opposition to this. The visionary aspect of Duncan's work is one great example of the effort to make the imagination hold and order as part of the real. So the real does not consistently close and you wind up then killing God, and what Nietzsche said ultimately was that it was not God who was dead, but man was dead. And Foucault says in the most marvelous of—what do you want [to] call it—a conundrum, a paradox, whatever it is—that what we must notice in this thought is that the murderer and the murder are the same act. If the world is an action then that is one thing: the murder and the murderer. And that's where my thought moves. It is also the despair of it, it is also part of my silence and so on. Now have I answered your question? [. . .]

All those examples I've used of modern methodology for dealing with the real, with literature, with the world and so on, all close and tend to humanize, those are all anthropomorphisms in the most extreme form. They are in my view only like some kind of tag end of the anthropomorphism that turns into Blake's Mr. Nobodaddy, that turns into God that looks like manhood when one knows that God can't be a manhood. And yet then we have to go back and reconstruct the manhood that Dante will see at the end of the *Paradiso*, where looking at the blinding, endless point of light suddenly he can also there see the human figure. I can't even speak of that image in these evenings yet, perhaps because of my own difficulty—but at least the narrative of this book doesn't allow me to move the manhood through such a range of the universe. This is a correspondence between the world and man that works and it is in some way lost and that correspondential is major to Jack. It's argued in *Admonitions*. It's major from Baudelaire onwards and one gets it in Dante and Blake, in particular, and of course it's a major proposition in the twentieth-century. It comes from Yeats and that whole business of the way in which they correspond. Jack with the lovely "my lemon must speak to your lemon"—Lorca's—and it's a Spanish lemon speaking to a California lemon, it's a dead lemon speaking to a living lemon. The correspondential is the analogical that I was talking about before and this again was in *Stephen Hero* and in *A Portrait of the Artist as a Young Man* for us in 1947.

TALLMAN: OK, now let me ask you another question. Blake is one of my great heroes. Blake said the universe has a human form. Now I don't understand the "God is dead" in that ethos. Like I can read that equation either way, either the universe has a human form, or man has a universal form, or God is alive for Blake.

BLASER: Oh, God is alive for Blake, and Blake's saying it's all gone wrong. That's why he hates Newton. . . . First he says, it's language when he makes all the holy writ literature in imagination; then he says the imagination is what is real; and then by way of the imagination's power one may then find the manhood with its place in the divine, in the eternal, in the permanent, in the lasting. When I have taught Blake—and I have done so repeatedly, and at least at Simon Fraser I was the first one to do that out there—I found it extremely difficult to articulate that aspect of the manhood. Not that I didn't believe in it, but because I speak to an age in which the pleasure of Blake and the genius of Blake may very well be in danger, that we will simplify that into a humanism. Blake's whole point is that one must not take the limit of what we know there, the five senses, which he

attacks repeatedly almost like a Tibetan Buddhist in the five infer-
ences. [. . .]

I've adored these poets. They're my angels. That's the reason that
I've adored them and the reason I suppose in part that I've been
silent—not tentative, Angela, but silent.

TALLMAN: We're back to *Stephen Hero* again?

BLASER: On *Stephen Hero*. . . . I'll just go down these since I've left
my notes behind.

TALLMAN: Out in the wind.

BLASER: Out in the wind someplace blowing around like the Tarot
cards. If you let them loose they'll get you.

TALLMAN: Maybe if I open the window they'll come back in.

BLASER: They'll get you somehow.

GARDINER: Somebody might be reading them in the Cecil right
now.[12]

BLASER: Oh, maybe so.

TALLMAN: They'll all [say], so that's what Blaser thinks, eh?

BLASER: If you watch this little book [*Stephen Hero*] carefully you'll
find him talking about Blake and Rimbaud, you'll find out his interest in the business of the value of the letter. Then you also find him
making very sharp remarks about isolation, the isolation of the poet.
And one, I think, of the most important aspects that I get from him is
the whole issue about playful exile—the whole business of the exile,
the isolation of the poet—in other words, the re-placing of the self so
that it becomes alive again to the outward and all the strategy and
task of knowing begins to fall in that movement between poet and
outside. He has a flat statement that the poem is made not born. This
must be the earliest example that I know of, of the attack upon inspiration that's gone on in the whole twentieth century. The greatest
voice of it is in Valéry, of all people—a man that Jack liked very much,
never been a great favorite of mine—but that the whole business that
it is made not born, that it requires a special consciousness is what one
gets from that. Now I had an example here of a little passage where he
flashes his antlers, and I so loved the image I remembered it for years:

> In spite of his surroundings Stephen continued his labours of
> research and all the more ardently since he imagined they had
> been <put under ban>. It was part of the ineradicable egoism

which he was afterwards to call redeemer that he conceived con-
verging to him the deeds and thoughts of his microcosm. Is the
mind of youth medieval that it is so divining of intrigue? Field-
sports (or their equivalent in the world of mentality) are perhaps
the most effective cure and Anglo-Saxon educators favour rather
a system of hearty brutality. But for this fantastic idealist, eluding
the grunting, booted apparition with a bound, the mimic warfare
was no less ludicrous than unequal in a ground chosen to his disadvantage. Behind the rapidly indurating shield the sensitive
answered: Let the pack of enmities come tumbling and sniffing
to my highlands after their game. There was his ground and he
flung them disdain from flashing antlers. (34-35)

I hope my last book will be called "Flashing Antlers." Now the editor
of this does a nice job because he noticed and remembered that from
a poem called "The Holy Office," a very funny poem of Joyce's that
comes out in a different form. And I'll read the note he put in
because I wanted to just [look] at one of Jack's first poems—it must
be from when he's a teenager. The section that has those antlers in it
is different from the marvel of that up there:

> 'So distantly I turn to view
> The shamblings of that motley crew,
> Those souls that hate the strength that mine has
> Steeled in the school of old Aquinas.
> Where they have crouched and crawled and prayed
> I stand, the self doomed, unafraid,
> Unfellowed, friendless and alone,
> Indifferent as the herring-bone,
> Firm as the mountain-ridges where
> I flash my antlers on the air.' (35-36)

And that reminded me of a lovely little passage Jack once gave me,
written in his handwriting, ancient stuff in which I found the lovely
imagination of him. This must be a teenage poem and it's called
"English Work, A Compending Compendium of the Best of My
Writings by Jack Spicer III. Rights for Albanian translation held by
the author." No! This is absolutely—
TALLMAN: He had his drollness from the first.
BLASER: From that, this poem "Wings" is corrected in red pencil by
the school teacher:

Wings on a butterfly are not as sound
As are a bird's, and often in the rain
The moth is driven, flightless to the ground
To die without the dignity of pain.
But birds are heavy and ungainly things,
They fly too far and do not sleep at dusk.
In birds the voice and not the color sings,
They never dream of violets and musk.

Wings of a man are sounder substance yet;
Their colors are of rich and solid hues;
They carry loads that no one can forget.
So if, by chance, that you are asked to choose
The soundest wings which break the air's still breath,
You can but choose the wings of the man and death.[13]

[There is some discussion about Spicer's age at the time of "Wings." In 1974, Blaser dated the poem at age 14. He dates it now as simply "teenaged."]

BLASER: . . . What's going on here with notes on reading *The Holy Grail* and stuff, quite funny the way he does that, and he has a whole passage on safety rules. There are a whole marvel of things. Anyway, I thought that poem an interesting one and—
TALLMAN: Yeah, well to say the very least.
BLASER: —and that it ought to be on the books someplace or another.
TALLMAN: He beat Keats by four years.
BLASER: Take that poem that I just read, and then the thing I told you that Jack's mother informed me about his belonging to a Methodist study group just the year at the University of Redlands before he came to Berkeley. I got none of that from him. So his condition was very similar to mine when I burst into tears. [. . .] Jack's condition sometimes must have been very much like mine, and we may be among the last authors who moved to that range. You see Duncan's theosophy is very different in its cosmology from this and will become of considerable interest to me, at any rate, if an annoyance to Jack in many ways. But it is still returning to a grid of ancient thought, a wisdom and revelation that is there and both Jack and I must enter this range. And perhaps as I say we may be the last of the authors who entered the range where the extravagant anguish of not

holding that, where all realms of that belief turn into disbelief and
then you have to reconstruct the vital form of belief and disbelief as
actually being companions of the nature of the world.

TALLMAN: Now, now just a second. Was Duncan doing that for you
or seemed to do that for you in certain poems?

BLASER: Oh Duncan didn't do this at all, Duncan. . . . No, no, no,
no, no. The story I told about eating the strawberries was simply to
differentiate the tonality of our minds from one another and the
extravagance of the image of the strawberry sundae.

This passage is where Stephen is talking to his mother and his
mother's been hearing about things that he's been doing and what
he's been reading and this will lead me to two other texts that I want
to draw some attention to tonight of importance for all three of us. So
she says, while she is nicely folding the handkerchief she's ironing,
she says:

> —What does Ibsen write, Stephen?
> —Plays.
> —I never heard of his name before. Is he alive at present?
> —Yes he is. But, you know, in Ireland people don't know
> much about what is going on out in Europe.
> —He must be a great writer from what you say of him.
> —Would you like to read some of his plays, mother? I have
> some.
> —Yes. I would like to read the best one. What is the best one?
> —I don't know . . . but do you really want to read Ibsen?
> —I do, really.
> —To see whether I am reading dangerous authors or not, is
> that why?
> —No, Stephen, answered his mother with a brave prevarica-
> tion. I think you're old enough now to know what is right and
> what is wrong without my dictating to you what you are to read.
> —I think so too . . . But I'm surprised to hear you ask about
> Ibsen. I didn't imagine you took the least interest in these mat-
> ters.
> Mrs. Daedelus pushed her iron smoothly over a white petti-
> coat <in time to the current of the memory.>
> —Well, of course, I don't speak about it but I'm not so indif-
> ferent. . . . Before I married your father I used to read a great
> deal. I used to take an interest in all kinds of new plays.
> —But since you married neither of you so much as bought a
> single book!

—Well, you see, Stephen, your father is not like you: he takes
no interest in that sort of thing. . . . When he was young he told
me he used to spend all his time out after the hounds or rowing
on the Lee. He went in for athletics.

—I suspect what he went in for, said Stephen irreverently. I
know he doesn't care a jack straw about what I think or what I
write.

—He wants to see you make your way, get on in life, said his
mother defensively. That's his ambition. You shouldn't blame
him for that.

—No, no, no. But it may not be my ambition. That kind of life
I often loathe: I find it ugly and cowardly.

—Of course life isn't what I used to think it was when I was a
young girl. That's why I would like to read some great writer, to
see what ideal of life he has—amn't I right in saying "ideal"?

—Yes but . . .

—Because sometimes—not that I grumble at the lot Almighty
God has given me and I have more or less a happy life with your
father—but sometimes I feel that I want to leave this actual life
and enter another—for a time.

—But that is wrong: that is the great mistake everyone makes.
Art is not an escape from life!

—No?

—You evidently weren't listening to what I said or else you
didn't understand what I said. Art is not an escape from life. It's
just the very opposite. Art, on the contrary, is the very central
expression of life. An artist is not a fellow who dangles a mechanical heaven before the public. The priest does that. The artist
affirms out of the fulness of his own life, he creates . . . Do you
understand?

And so on. A day or two afterwards Stephen gave his mother a
few of the plays to read. She read them with great interest. . . .
(84-86)

And so forth. She liked *The Wild Duck* it turns out, especially so.

> —Of course you know Stephen

she says after she's read some of it,

> he treats of subjects . . . of which I know very little myself . . .
> subjects . . .
> —Subjects which, you think, should never be talked about?

—Well, that was the old people's idea but I don't know if it was
right. I don't know if it is good for people to be entirely ignorant.
. . .
—Then why not treat them openly? (86-87)

And she goes on. I'm sorry I've, with my notes gone I've missed—well
I suppose we can fix this up if I found—

[Tape change, Side 33]

BLASER: [There's an] absolutely splendid passage which I'm going
to quote badly if I try to do it from memory at this point . . .
TALLMAN: What are you driving at, Robin?
BLASER: In this?
TALLMAN: Yeah.
BLASER: Well, I'm trying to get to two more books about the relation
of poetry to life at the moment, but I also am trying to get at Joyce's
attack on God. Let's turn it off for a minute and I'll see if I can find it.

[Recorder turned off and on]

BLASER: . . . That movement between belief and disbelief is such
that Jack will even . . . re-situate the question. That is the name of
Saint Anselm's great book *Cur Deus Homo*, because Jack will immediately then along with that *credo quia absurdum*, which I quoted last
time . . . he will also put the question all over again. *Cur Deus Homo*:
how could God become man and you're back in, the movement of
belief—

[cassette glitch]

BLASER: *[Responding to question, garbled on the tape]*
No, no but that would be a lie. You see he can't, he's not polar, he
can't polarize, he's trying to stop it, he wants—in other words he's
trying to get a total vision. What he doesn't know in these methodologies, he wants a total vision and a total vision means you've got to
reduce it to the human being and his desires, his needs, his trip. As I
say it's like going on a sociology that doesn't know there's love.

[*At this point, the talk veers when Angela Bowering introduces a prob-lem with a speaker in a class at the university (SFU). Most of the remainder of the session, with the exception of some isolated passages, has to do with chat about the university, about Spicer and Duncan, and about Blaser's consulting of the Kenkyusha*[14] *before his move to Canada. Blaser returns to the issues raised by his reading of Joyce in the next session. This session has been catalogued as Story X, but is actually a continuation of Story IX that segues into new material on Yeats , Lorca and other moderns.*]

✻   ✻   ✻

[*Story X, Side 35*]

BLASER: We're still at the run called "The Knowlege of the Poet" in which I'm after something. In the last conversation we ended with the reversal of words, "God" and "dog" as Joyce plays it. These rever-sals of words—sometimes a nonsense like "poet," "teop," or a freezing cold like "dog" are reversals of language. The words reverse into a directness and unease of language that is a movement close to the reversal of language into experience. A density and binding of thought, a re-tied heart that is only the other face of the untied heart. It may be full of blasphemy and praise simultaneously, as if they were the same condition. These are broken words whose meanings do not hold. High poetry works in this condition always, because the high, the sublime, which is the shining form of what is held composed and performed in the public space, is also always primary. To begin a life is to think. The feeling is held in the medium as a suddenness, image, a movement, and gathering out of the imageless. The form is the vital movement of image out of the imageless. Language is itself a first movement of form, a binding *rhythmos* or form of the mind. One of the oldest meanings of the word *rhythmos* is "form," and it should tell us something since we use it to mean simply something close to meter or something slightly larger than meter. But the beat of the movement and actually, of course, it is the restlessness of form. *Rhythmos*, then, I think of as the first movement of form as having the restlessness of hell—translating the body of each of us into what is

other than itself. My continuous argument in these conversations—
that the poet has a particular task in the work of the Other—should
not be taken as simple mysticism. This mystery lacks the *unio mysti-
ca* as Nerval did, as Jack did, though the mystery of the commotion
in language is the presence of the unknown as it invades the known
of our manhood. In contemporary thought where the poet has a
primary task, the peculiar consciousness of the Other faces us everywhere. We are articulated into labor, life and language, the three
great modes of the Other. Here I'm adapting, using, and misusing
Foucault. The modes of these so other than the suddenness of
ourselves may remain unconscious where consciousness is only my
reason, or a narrative may reopen that will account for labor, life, and
language, as in Jack's sense, that puns tell us something about death.
We are bound to history by the older and Other than ourselves.
Labor, whose forms stretch backward, move about us and push
beyond any momentary present, so with biology and language which
are not ourselves. In the turn of the Gods towards us or away from us
they are the words of a narrative of this Otherness and they return by
silence and by speech. Why it is that in my own thought there is
laughter in all this and yet in my speaking poems I hear sadness—I
think it is that I have not yet mastered the narrative. For me this narrative is commanding, even a compulsion.

   In the recent silliness and melodrama of my life as it stands, as it
stood, stupidly and silently and suddenly apart from the real, another
trap in the piled up stories of my love of young men, I wanted in that
silent way to die. It just wasn't worth it. Two months with nearly no
sleep. A loss of thirty pounds weight on a man not very heavy anyway.
The body broke out in hemorrhages. Was the blood flow then
too close to the surface? The body's SOS's were real. Friends moved
forward at—and they literally moved forward, Colin Stewart being
the best example in the most extreme evening of all—arrived as
though he were in a trance at the back door. But he was there to stop
something that he didn't know he was stopping. I literally believe in
that message. And right now I'm away, Angela I'm responding to—
when I said to you about Jamie Reid that I continued to respect him
because his moving into the Marxist realm, however much I found
that a resolution and a destruction of the real as he works at it, I also

found that what his movement was about and I was talking with you, Dwight, the two of you together, that I felt it was his move into the Other and that I had to respect that. Then I now am responding to George's remark that that was my mystifying—that I was mystifying what Jamie was after and I do not agree and that's what I've tried to point out here, that the three great modes of the Other in our lives are labor, life, and language, and Jamie has chosen labor. What he knows about life, I doubt very much that I need to respect: number one, Marxist thought has lacked a respectable biology because Marx lacked a respectable biology. It has also, of course, lacked a respectable language because Marx was an eighteenth-century intelligence who thought that language was transparent to the real and as a consequence I'm now trying to say, no I'm not mystifying.

Yes, I'm talking about a mystery, and yes, I'm talking about the absolute invasion and the peculiar task of poetry to perform in public the Otherness of these huge realms. The presence of God in these will turn up more clearly—I know my language gets funny and people begin to respond—will turn up when I get to the Nietszche thing because the condition of the Other is such that the narrative and vocabulary immediately returns the Gods and you get into all the events of the Gods as they turn away from you or turn toward you, and that is our condition. As a consequence, the poets are absolutely inside that again. I think of years later in New York, when Don Allen and Frank O'Hara and Vincent and John Ashbery and a bunch of us [were] together, and Frank said joking, "Let's have a meeting and decide we're all going to use mythology in our poems." Well, Frank was a marvelous poet and so on but he was really camping up this trip on mythology. What had happened of course around this was the realm of Pound-Olson who'd already recognized that the narrative of the Gods was literally of a presencing for which there is no other vocabulary.

TALLMAN: Now, Robin, let me ask you one question. As you say these things, do you consider these things in complete consonance with Jack's concept of language? Or have you yourself, since Jack died in 1965 which is almost ten years ago now, have you moved into a different concept of language? Or is that a question you don't want to deal with?

BLASER: No, I don't mind dealing with it, but I think it'll come up in a more formal way than this, because, no, I don't think the articulation of this is such that Jack would entirely agree with it because Jack wanted to keep entirely within the mystery of it and I keep wanting to move towards the radiance of it. And I can only do that because I have Jack as my companion, as the angel of that thought, and the commotion of his thought was such, as I tried to face it and spent seven years as a matter of fact facing it after he died that is, that then I could only move from that. So in part I move from it, but it's always from it, and yet I don't think that I am in any way untrue to what Jack meant by the unknown.

WT: So his concept is a kind of a baseline that you push out from.

BLASER: That I push out from.

WT: His baselines still make sense to you, sort of.

BLASER: Yeah. We don't have to repeat Jack's cost. We may have costs of our own, but we don't have to repeat Jack's cost. It doesn't seem to me that we need to. And I think of that as a cost. I don't think of that as in that incredible little footnote in the attack on me by Duncan on the *Chimères* where there's a footnote, "a warning to all poets, Jack chose death over life" which shows—well I don't care what it shows. I think it's so obvious that any comment on that is contemptible. Anyway what finally stopped that silliness as I, in my own life, stopped that, what reopened was the narrative, a command and a task in the midst of my ability to crap on the world I worked in. I remembered *melo* meant song, radically changing the melodrama. I thought of Artaud's effort, madly flinging philological discipline aside to make the word drama. He tries to attach it to "rama," the acting out of a God's name. He rightly knew it is the narrative of a mental condition. I began to play in the song of the language again: "there is no not being, something red is a green not being, there is nothing red." And there I'm playing a game with the syllogism . . . but I'm also bringing forward one of the courses Jack and I took in this period, '48 and '49 . . . in which we were shown how to make syllogisms to prove that there really are unicorns and so on, and so on. But here I'm playing a game with what?—how it is to make the red of the blood disappear so that "there is no not being, something red is a green not being, there is, therefore, nothing red." What that did to the color of blood was absolutely funny.

So the broken words in the mirror, words—if we write them backwards the mirror straightens them out; if we write them straight
forward the mirror turns them backwards. Jack smeared words into
their pure sounds, which he called "Martian." This removed the
established sureness of the combining vowels and consonants, the
words then became mystery and laughter. Sitting in Gino and Carlo's
listening to Martian was not always comfortable. Thinking this
evening out, I took a card of notes on the soul as language, on the
logos as language to the bathroom mirror and watched the disappearance of what I thought, my longing turned into a peril of the mirror,
not through the looking glass but at the edge of it, standing without
the gloves of the dead[15] to get through, to cleave the shimmering
mystery of what was there, God-dog. I placed an exclamation point
following the word to force the word to stand still, not reverse,
then added another exclamation point in front of the word. The only
unreversed element was the sound "O." If you do that before a mirror
it's quite extraordinary because I was so disturbed as I watched this,
God turning into dog in the mirror, that I went out the back into the
kitchen and got out my pen and put an exclamation point at the end
of "God" so I had it and then when I put it in the mirror it did tend to
at least disturb the mirror's power. And then I thought well, that's
unfair, so I went back again to the kitchen table and put another
exclamation before the word "God" and then, of course, what I had
was one unchanging letter "O" in the centre of them going back and
forth. My mind wandered back to a childhood language and that
language I thought made words secret. It's one I think you may know
because I think it's [a] standard childhood trick. It was hard to handle
with words of more than two syllables. [*Here Blaser performs a few
lines of* OpEnglopish.] All you're doing is to every vowel system adding
"op." Could you hear what I was saying? I mean you could hear,
"I don't know what I want to say to you in this conversation, an
autobiography indeed" [. . .]

TALLMAN: But getting into childhood, was this a language you used
in childhood?

BLASER: I spoke it incessantly, to the point where I was spanked
for it.

TALLMAN: But were other children involved?

BLASER: No, I did it by myself in order to keep the other little shits out of there. [. . .] I had one friend, Bill Haley, who shared this with me. We had an atlas, we divided the world and we had a terrible war. I was the Duc d'Orleans, naturally, so I got France and I very much wanted Africa and China. But he wanted to fight for China, and I let him have England—I had that hostility going even then.

TALLMAN: And you didn't know he got Chaucer into the bargain until you stole it back from him.

BLASER: That's right. Now this one is what I call a mo*pind*-blo*powoper*—a mind-blower:

> In the vale of resteles mynde
> I soghte in mountayne and in meed
> Trustying a trew-love for-to fynde.
> Upon an hil than took I hede;
> A vois I herde (and neer I yede
> In greet dolour compleynyng tho:
> "See, dere soule, my sides blede,
>   *Quia amore langueo.*"
>
> Upon this mount I fond a tree;
> Under this tree a man sittying.
> From hed to foot wounded was he,
> His herte blood I saw bledying;
> A seemly man to ben a kyng,
> A gracious face to loke unto.
> I axed him how he hadde peynyng:
> He sayde, "*Quia amore langueo.*

And it's these images I wanted you to hear:

> "Loke unto myne hondes, man!
> Thise gloves were yeven me whan I hire soghte.
> They ben not white, but rede and wan;
> Embrouded wyth blood my spouse hem boghte.
> They wol not offe; I leve hem noght;

[Blaser]:

> Look unto mine hands, man!
> These gloves were given me when I her sought.

They be not white, but red and wan
Embroidered with blood my spouse them brought.
They will not off, I leave them not.

And now this passage, which I just adore. These languages are all
going on at the same time. We're back in '48, '49.

> "In my side I have made hir nest.
> Loke in, how wide a wounde is heer:
> This is hir chambre, heer shal she reste,
> That she and I mowen slepe in fere.
> Heer may she wasshe if any filthe were;
> Heer is socour for al hir wo.
> Come if she wyl, she shal have chere,
>   *Quia amore langueo.* (Stevick 88-90)

[Blaser]:

> "In my side I have made her nest.
> Look in, how wide a wound is here:
> This is her chamber, here shall she rest,
> That she and I may sleep together.

And all of this because I languish in love. And so on. This is a stunning poem, contemporary with Chaucer.
QUESTION: Who is it?
BLASER: Anonymous. But it came to mind so suddenly in the middle of this, mind-blower, in the middle of these funny languages and
Chaucer's language is change. And yet we go in love and all that stuff,
because it's "in the veil of restless mind I sought in mountain and in
meed trusting a true love for to find" and so on. And then of course
when he finds this man on the mountain and the man begins to talk
and says "I am true love that first was never, my sister, mon soeur,
I loved her thus because I would in no wise deserve her, I left my
kingdom glorious." Really it's an absolutely glorious poem.
TALLMAN: Name the book.
QUESTION: *One Hundred Middle English Lyrics.*
BLASER: *One Hundred Middle English Lyrics.* I had it from another
source when I was back there then, but that's an easily convenient
paperback.

TALLMAN: And who's the editor of this?

BOWERING: Stevick, or something like that, Robert Stevick.

BLASER: Robert Stevick, yeah, and it's that Bobbs-Merrill Library of Literature. [It] is [a] standard kind of textbook that the UBC bookstore would have and certainly Simon Fraser does.

O*pearlo*pier, which means earlier—

TALLMAN: Old lop ear? Sounds to me more like Briar Rabbit. Old lop ears.

BLASER: In earlier language, "*Introibo ad alterae Dei. Je m'approcherai de l'autel de dieu.*" Those are the opening words of the mass. "I would enter before the altar of God" and in the two languages that I was learning them in other than in the one that I speak. Up through the stairwell to the top of the tower looking out to sea, a mirror laid over the shavingbowl, quote: "For this, O dearly beloved is the genuine Christine: body and soul and blood and ouns. Slow music please. Shut your eyes gents. One moment. A little trouble about those white corpuscles" (*Ulysses* 9). "*I am the boy / That can enjoy / Invisibility*" (16). And so back to Joyce. Those are taken from the opening sections of *Ulysses* and so back to Joyce.

I have so far begun to weave the strands of the story. I want the record of my belief that I've spent my time with the finest thinkers of that time: Jack, Olson, and Duncan among them. Kantorowicz taught me to think always at an edge in a large movement; Hannah Arendt to discriminate in words. I want to speak of the peril in the lyric voice, that crying, singing center of the mode of the poem as it meets the gathering storm of the language. This I see most clearly in the gathering storm of Jack's work, and here in a meandering way, like the river that word "meandering" comes from, try to follow the vocabulary of it, the works of it, the *wild logos* of it, to adapt a term from Merleau-Ponty—*logos*, that difficult word. All the problems of it begin for us in Heraclitus and I suggest looking at—why I remember things like this—[Geoffrey Stephen] Kirk's edition of *Cosmic Fragments* pages 37-40. I can't even forget them because they run down all we mean by that word and this is developed into Plato's foolish glossary of the degrees of the real . . . so that we have a permanently abstract real and all other language can then be an imitation of that permanence and so on.

This will finally come folding back in because I have to go at Olson's attack on Plato and what that's about. *Logos* means word or speech and in Jack's work, or in mine, and I think equally in Duncan's but I don't want to be aggressive about that. The hidden text is Saint John's, the theory of witnessing. As a matter of fact, as I made these notes, I realized that the greatest conversation I ever had on the nature of "I, John saw" as the witnessing is with Duncan and is coming from this period. And that aspect of Duncan's work remains absolute. In *The Opening of the Field*, for example, the beautiful bells on the bushes poem thing and then where the ground gives way, that stunning poem. That's the witnessing mode in Duncan's work, which is the mode that I hang onto for dear life.

TALLMAN: When did this conversation with Duncan take place?

BLASER: That conversation with Duncan would take place some-place around 1949 because it's close to the time of *The Venice Poem*, in which the question of what he was witnessing in that is brought up. I turn back into that because that's what Jack is actually questioning in the poem: the range of the witnessing and the way in which it's resolved in *The Venice Poem*.

TALLMAN: Jack wasn't in on this conversation with you and Duncan?

BLASER: No, this is between Duncan and me, and I'd like that at least in this thing as a major conversation about the witnessing. The poet stands as witness which is one of how many thousand terms for the witness 'cause I also want to call him the transmogrifier and the word "transmogrify" means to change and to change so extremely that it's really absurd. The word itself is an absurd coinage: according to the dictionary, "transmogrify" is utterly to change to the point of the absurd. . . . Jack actually knows about transmogrifying . . . whether it comes from the Carroll, whatever it is, it's the condition of the work. Anyway, that element of witnessing comes out of a great text, a great voice as of a trumpet and, so I wanted to simply get this little text [in] which so many of you will know but anyway it needs to be there:

> . . . I am Alpha and Omega, the first and the last: and What thou seest write in the book, and send it unto the seven churches which are in Asia; unto Ephesus, and unto Smyrna, and unto Pergamos, and unto Thyatria, and unto Sardis, and unto Philadelphia, and unto Laodicea.

And I turned to see the voice that spake with me. And being
turned, I saw seven golden candlesticks;
And in the midst of the seven candlesticks one like unto the
Son of man, clothed with a garment down to the foot, and girt
about the paps with a golden girdle.
His head and his hairs were white like wool, as white as snow;
and his eyes were as a flame of fire;
And his feet like unto fine brass, as if they burned in a furnace;
and his voice as the sound of many waters.
And he had in his right hand seven stars: and out of his mouth
went a sharp two-edged sword: and his countenance was as the
sun shineth in his strength.
And when I saw him, I fell at his feet as dead. And he laid his
right hand upon me, saying unto me, Fear not; I am the first and
the last: (*Revelations* I: 11-17)

I want that there, if only because the Tarot cards will have to come
out. But in the meantime, it's for the witnessing. In those passages
from Joyce last time, in *Stephen Hero*, I wanted to get at the disbelief
and the rebellion against a grid of meaning, this piece of a very young
book that stands behind *A Portrait of the Artist*, where an Aquinian theory of art will argue the beauty and stillness of art as a completion. The
beautiful there is the radiating quality of truth. Joyce by a peculiar twist
not really clear in either book will refuse to separate art from life, will
not leave it as a transcendence. . . . One phrase does that: "I will not
serve that in which I no longer believe." *Stephen Hero* is jammed with
the stuff that will involve the work of Jack, Duncan and myself:
Swedenborgian thought, Byron's *Cain*, Bruno, Skeat. He read Blake
and Rimbaud in a passage that I find really quite interesting. He wrote:

He read Blake and Rimbaud and the values of letters and even
permuted and combined the five vowels to construct cries for
primitive emotions. To none of his former fervours had he given
himself with such a whole heart as to this fervour; < the monk
now seemed to him no more than half the artist. He persuaded
himself that it is necessary for an artist to labour incessantly at his
art if he wishes to express completely even the simplest conception and he believed that every moment of inspiration must be
paid for in advance. He was not convinced of the truth of the saying [*Poeta nascitur, non fit*] "The poet is born, not made" but he
was quite sure> of <the truth of this at least: [*Poema Fit, Non
Nascitur*] 'The poem is made not born.' The burgher notion of

the poet Byron in undress pouring out verses [like] just as a city
fountain pours out water seemed to him characteristic of most
popular judgments on esthetic matters and he combated the
notion at its root < by saying solemnly to Maurice—Isolation is
the first principle of artistic economy.> (32)

Jack's argument in his later poetry, that the loneliness of the poet is
an absolute necessity, is grounded in this learning. It is part of the
isolation of the first principle of artistic economy. The implied attack
upon inspiration is fascinating for us . . . because we not only
believed in inspiration as the ground and that left you in a very
strange realm and the figure drawn to that is Valéry. The figure that
comes in—because the major figure to attack inspiration as poetic
doctrine in the twentieth-century is Valéry and that's where Jack's
attraction went: that inspiration was not adequate, that, in other
words we are gnostics. We are in a kind of *gnosis* and what Jack calls
"spiritual discipline" becomes the discipline of something that is not
inspirational, so that you see you're moving the center of the poet.
The moment you attack inspiration you're moving the center of the
poet, you're endangering him and attacking him.

Now how conscious we were exactly of those I'm not going to argue.
All I know is that the way we read, all of us, was such that those things
hit and they hit very, very hard. The stuff with Yeats, with Joyce, is so
stunning a blow. I never heard Jack express himself as blown by Joyce.
I can't believe he was not, I don't believe that Duncan was not. I think
that it was a mind-blower and for me it was stunning. *Finnegan* was
simply a mystery beyond belief, and the work of finding laughter in it
was there, but the other thing was that we were reading all this other
Joyce to get through and it was jammed with what I've said is the stuff
that would involve the work of all of us. Ibsen is going to return in a
bit and has been important to all three of us, and in addition, there
was Yeats. I think that it is Joyce actually that brings Yeats forward to
Jack's mind and becomes Jack's major master in it. . . .

*[The tape trails off here with a few more remarks about Yeats. Side 36
picks up the reference to Yeats with some discussion of "The Tables of
the Law," circuitously returns to* Stephen Hero, *and then on to other
topics.]*

*   *   *

NOTES

1. This English translation of Bloch's definition of astonishment is cited in Fredric Jameson's *Marxism and Form*, 122. Blaser cites the same passage to announce *Astonishments* in his biographical summary at the back of *The Collected Books of Jack Spicer* (n.pag.). In conversation, September 3, 1999, Blaser informed me that he took the passage from Jameson.

2. This line comes from the *Imaginary Letters* of Mary Butts. Blaser provided an afterword for a 1978 Talonbooks edition of the letters. The line occurs in a couplet that is repeated at points throughout the text:

> *Brightness falls from the air,*
> *Queens have died, young and fair.*

3. The citation is from Victor Hugo's *William Shakespeare*, as it appears in Gwendolyn Bays's *The Orphic Vision*, pp. 116-17. In conversation, September 3, 1999, Blaser told me that he took the quotation from Bays's text.

4. These Spicer poems have now been published in *One Night Stand and Other Poems* (1980).

5. "Sophia Nichols" appears in *The Holy Forest* (99).

6. Blaser here refers to a story about Sophia Nichols putting him in a tub in order to cross a small, storm-created pond and get to the commissary. The story is told in "Image-Nation 24 ('oh pshaw,'" published in *The Holy Forest* (353-63).

7. See "The Metaphysics of Light," in *The Capilano Review* (Fall 1974): 35-59.

8. Blaser actually says "Dante" here, but the context suggests that he meant "Shakespeare."

9. Blaser also refers to Edith Cobb in "The Fire" (in *The Poetics of the New American Poetry*, 239).

10. "The Chinese Nightingale" is the title poem from a collection by Vachel Lindsay, *The Chinese Nightingale and Other Poems* (New York: Macmillan, 1917).

11. Here is the passage on the etymology of disaster from "The Stadium of the Mirror":

> The Sublime, the Beautiful, the Terror are not exactly human (Arendt), and that is the reason the Image-nations are not devoted to my logic of desire, but to a nation invaded by what is other than itself—a continuous forming. An original precision of meaning may then enter the word desire: 'Perhaps (like considerare) allied to sidus, a star, as if to turn the eyes from the stars' (Skeat). The body in the suddenness of its form stands there like the period at the end of a sentence. This off-spring of the universe then refurls. Dis-aster—the reversal of an act—dis—to turn from aster—star. Dis-stars. (57)

12. The Cecil was a "poet's bar" in Vancouver—a hang-out for local writers.
13. Unpublished manuscript, in the collection of Robin Blaser.
14. The "Kenkyusha" as it is called, is the second edition of a Japanese-English Dictionary, published by a firm called Kenkyusha. This edition (and this edition only) is used for divination.
15. Blaser's reference to the gloves of the dead comes from Cocteau's *Orpheus*. In this film, Death and her entourage move back and forth between this world and that of the dead through mirrors. With the help of magical gloves, they can open a mirror with their hands and pass through, as if it were water.

WORKS CITED

Bays, Gwendolyn. *The Orphic Vision.* Lincoln: U of Nebraska P, 1964.

Blaser, Robin. "The Stadium of the Mirror." *Image-Nation 12 and the Stadium of the Mirror.* London: Ferry, 1974. 53-67.

Butts, Mary. *Imaginary Letters.* With an afterword by Robin Blaser. Vancouver: Talonbooks, 1978.

Jameson, Fredric. *Marxism and Form.* Princeton: Princeton UP, 1971.

Joyce, James. *Stephen Hero.* Ed. Theodore Spencer. New York: New Directions, 1944.

_____. *Ulysses.* London: The Bodley Head, 1960; rpt. Penguin, 1975.

Kingsley, Charles. *The Water-Babies: A Fairy Tale for a Land-Baby.* London: Macmillan, 1892.

Spicer, Jack. *One Night Stand & Other Poems.* Ed. Donald Allen. Preface by Robert Duncan. San Francisco: Grey Fox, 1980.

Stevick, Robert D., Ed. *One Hundred Middle English Lyrics.* Indianapolis: Bobbs-Merrill, 1964.

Robin Blaser at Brown
University, 1994

Robin Blaser and David Farwell, at home in Vancouver, 2001

INTERVIEW WITH ROBIN BLASER

Miriam Nichols

Like all the conversations I have had with Robin Blaser, this taped one starts and stops, but doesn't begin or end. I arrived on his doorstep in Kitsilano as arranged, on a Friday afternoon at one o'clock, and we began to talk. I told him that I had several groups of questions prepared, although I knew these would probably change in the course of the interview. I was going to ask him, I said, about what the post-war push into the postmodern looked liked from a distance of several decades and many social changes. I also had some questions about the serial poem as lyric and then a few more about the politics of his poetics. Somewhere in the course of my preliminaries, the interview began and I turned on the tape. We talked through the afternoon, stopping for cigarette breaks, and a trip to the post office before it closed to pick up Michael Davidson's book, Ghostlier Demarcations. *Toward the end of the afternoon, when both our energies began to flag, I started to listen for a good stopping place, some summing-up witticism, but one thing always lead to the next and so on and on and on, as Robin says. Finally, I just stopped the tape. On the way out, I commented on a really good cast-concrete dragon sitting on the stair railing, all scales and coils. "Birthday present," he said, "from the Avant Gardener. I liked his folds."*

In transcribing this interview, I have followed the same editorial procedure as with Astonishments: *I have taken out repetitions and false starts, and elided phrases that are confusing or incidental. I have punctuated sentence breaks with dashes and my elisions with ellipses. However, I have not tried to standardize the tenses or pronouns; the grammatical instability I take as a form of parataxis that is not separable from Blaser's speech rhythms.*

–Miriam Nichols

*   *   *

NICHOLS: July 30th—

BLASER: July 30th, oh yes—

NICHOLS: 1999.

BLASER: Oh God!

NICHOLS: It's 1:40 in the afternoon, and I'm sitting in Robin Blaser's kitchen. We're going to start an interview that has, I think, already started about half an hour ago.

BLASER: Oh!

NICHOLS: I'll just ask one of my questions, Robin, and then we'll see where it goes. This first one is about Berkeley, because you've often been introduced in reviews and at readings through your participation in the poetry scene at Berkeley in the 1940s and 50s, and you talk about the importance of that period for the *Astonishments*. I also notice that in "The Practice of Outside" you mention Duncan's remark about the three of you making a poetry up out of whole cloth out there, and I wonder if you could talk a bit about—how do you tell that project to yourself now?

BLASER: [*laughs*] Well, I mean I tell myself that project because I'm extremely grateful to that project and to those meetings. My earlier remarks about, you know, nobody's in the twentieth-century, I mean until you get someplace and run into the twentieth-century—and quite frankly, in Berkeley, running into the twentieth-century meant Robert Duncan. I suppose you could say it was because Duncan was seven years older than I was and seven years older than Jack,[1] because Jack himself, though he was a sophisticated LA-an, he too wasn't in the twentieth-century *that* way. You know Duncan had been to New York and met the surrealists and so on and so on and so on and it went on and on and on. And he was all full of these various things and a writer, I think, of considerable accomplishment then. I mean Jack's work postdates that too—I'm talking about 1945. It would be the very beginning of it all. And then there was the University of California which then, at that time, was said to be one of the three greatest universities in the world, and I think it was. I mean it had as many mediocrities as any other university always has, but it also had the Ernst Kantorowiczes—Kantorowicz and a wonderful man named Schafer, too, who was also in medieval studies, and it had Josephine Miles. Duncan didn't like her, but both Jack and I did, and learned a very great deal from her, a poet herself. And it had Hannah Arendt there for a brief period of time. She hated California it turns out, when I read her biography, and that's too bad. But it was a rich commotion that one suddenly ran into. It gave you some sense that you weren't somehow in an eternity that was always behind you, which is I think very much what Idaho would think the world is—an eternity that is somehow behind you. And it's the viciousness of religion that they continue to teach that—that you are always in this universality and so on that excludes more than it includes.

Anyway, so when you get to university you begin to do things, and also what would be called modern poetry, twentieth-century poetry turns up first, there. I had had the nearest of the great poets insofar as the twentieth-century personality recognizes them—it was Whitman. I picked that up in Twin Falls, from a wonderful, wonderful teacher named Mercedes Paul. She's the one that fixed it up so that I got to Northwestern and stuff in '43, before I went on to Berkeley. There was another one named Helen White. I don't remember all these people, because there were such magnificent people in that funny little place in Twin Falls. Push that off for a minute. I just want to show you something.

[*I turn the tape off, and Robin brings out the August 2, 1999 edition of the* New Yorker *to show me an announcement in "The Movies" section of a film called* Twin Falls Idaho. *The brief announcement says that the movie is about "the lives of two conjoined twins." There is also a picture advertising the film and this is what Robin wants me to see. It is hilariously dreary. Two identical chalk-faced, black-suited expressionless men sit in a single armchair in an ill-lit livingroom, while a woman of equally depressing appearance dozes in another. The caption says "Opening July 30, Michael Polish's 'Twin Falls Idaho.'"*]

NICHOLS: [reading] Twin Falls, Idaho, Michael Polish's *Twin Falls Idaho . . .*

BLASER: [*laughs*] This week's *New Yorker*—it's apparently a movie, by a small company, and it's about two twins who are tied together at the hip [*laughs*]. And the . . . *New Yorker's* little shot in that depressed livingroom reminds me very much of Twin Falls. [*laughter*] They made no explanation. I'll have to go to the movie when I get a chance, to see what in the hell they're doing in Twin Falls. This is the August 2, 1999 issue. Crazy *New Yorker*. But of course Twin Falls still means so much to me that if it turns up anywhere it'll pop out of even small print.

But the business of coming into poetry, then you began to— well Whitman is another matter, but the recognition of Whitman is so, well, for American poets it's so twentieth-century. Everybody has to face him one way or another. I think I was overwhelmed, in all of my seventeen years, I was overwhelmed by it, and wrote quite, I would say vicariously, and perhaps even a little, well borrowing too much and so on. I mean even the leaves of the trees began to look different after reading Whitman.

NICHOLS: As a teenager.

BLASER: As a teenager. But I was very beaten up for that in Northwestern, by a woman who is in *The Moth Poem*.

NICHOLS: Mrs. Arpan.

BLASER: Yeah, Mrs. Arpan, yes.

NICHOLS: [*laughs*] Was she an instructor at Northwestern?

BLASER: Yes, she was an instructor at Northwestern, and I had to use the phrase "simple, separate souls" which she claimed was a plagiarism. Well, it's certainly very close to a line of Whitman, but it wasn't a plagiarism, it was just a—and the rest of it was that she obviously didn't like [the poems]. I think I destroyed them all, I think they were all pretty soft in the [*laughs*]—in the head. So anyway, when I had to make my living by teaching all these years, I just noticed that nobody that came into the classes, mine and I presume others as well, was in the twentieth century. Always someplace else. The wars are being forgotten. The greatest heartbreak of the century, the holocaust, is not even something of concern. Of course we can blame that on the way in which the churches were implicated if only by their having not done anything about it, or having recognized from what place fascism comes and stuff. But you have to be in the twentieth-century even to ask these questions, even to become concerned about what the body is, and so on. And now we have to live through all this commotion, you know, Freud's dead. My ass he's dead. Thought doesn't work that way, never has worked that way. Nor does a great poet like Charles Olson wind up simply to be dismissed, in the name of some ideology. You always check them for their ideologies, all those people, and they have been—the British have been particularly uneven and unable to read their own twentieth-century poets, let alone any of the American bunch. A few get through, but not very many.

Peter Quartermain has just done this new anthology, which I hope you've seen, called *Other*. He did it with another fellow. It is on the other poetry in Britain. Well, that was going on in Vancouver's consciousness, because of Bunting's presence at UBC back when Creeley was at UBC[2] and this all made that commotion around the 1963 conference and the TISH poets because it meant a big move, which is still a difficulty in Canada, I think, for everybody. What was the latest attack I heard on the greatest of our poets, bpNichol—[that] *The Martyrology* is a religious poem? When I was in Buffalo to give the tenth anniversary lecture of Olson's death, both Steve McCaffery and bpNichol came down for the occasion and did some things of their own, and we were on a panel together, and I've not forgotten bp looking up at me across the table, and saying you know I'm thinking more about God lately. [*laughter*] And it was a rather stunning thing to say in that circumstance, but it also was that deeply serious side of bpNichol, and so on. And you've got to be a pretty strong, it seems to me, a pretty strong twentieth-century current—that is your own training of yourself, and so on—to be able to follow bpNichol in that, the great venture that [the] *Martyrology* is. And Steve McCaffery's incredible work. Those two are, in my mind, stars.

Anyway, back to Berkeley. Very generally, it was that way. The wildness—I was there nine years. I never called for a degree until I left the joint, and I gave up—there were three PhD proposals that I made, two of which—[I] was politely asked not to. One was

on Burton, and the other was on John Addington Symons, and
both of those were considered not exactly the thing one should
work on. So I then—

NICHOLS: What was the Burton? What were they about, Robin?
The Burton was to be—was that *Anatomy of Melancholy*?

BLASER: No no no no no, oh no no no no no. [*laughter*] Later one,
the adventurer in Africa. And these were not respectable. They
[supervisors at Berkeley] did it very kindly, but then I did exactly
what was a kind of summary of my behavior throughout university, and for that matter, Duncan, who never took a single degree
from anything, and then [went] wandering around through
everything—I decided, well all right then, I'll write on the poetic
drama from *The Borderers*, Wordsworth, all the way through into
Hardy's *The Dynasts* and the Yeats, and of course this is far too
big for any one PhD dissertation, but it made for splendid reading. [*laughter*] And I took all of my exams, language exams and
stuff and so on and so forth, and then just dipped out. Mark
Schorer was then head of the department, and I went in to tell
him I just had to leave. Irving Howe had written a thing in
Partisan Review on conformity—this was the 50s, you know—and
I believed every word of it. That's the way I felt too.

All these attacks on the 60s are so absurdly ideological, because
of course the 60s was exactly the attack on the very thing they're
trying to bring back, that is total discipline and formality, and if
we tear those pieces together we know exactly what we're going
to get. But anyway, I said that I had to have a leave, and Mark
Schorer was very kind. He said, now Robin, I'm going to tell you,
you can have two years, but I'm also trying to tell you by that, that
if you don't come back in two years you never will. And he was
right. Jack took his leave too of the PhD project because Berkeley
was a place in which you actually—for all of the discouragement
of certain things I wanted to do, it was a place where you could
have done that, I think. This is long before Buffalo where you
could go, as Peter Gizzi did, and he had this, you know, Charles
Bernstein and Robert Creeley and Susan Howe. And I said, well
I'm going to go back and finish too. [*laughter*] I want the same
[committee]. [*laughter*] I'm going to go right back there now. You

know, what would I be doing that [for] at 74 heading for 75.

But anyway, Berkeley was a marvelously rich place, and it was full of everything else. I mean we found out that John Cage came there and gave performances, if you were interested in new music, and in the meantime the city, Berkeley, San Francisco [was] building up, and there was a thing called—in the early 60s, there was the Tape Music Center, to which the really good dance groups came. [Morton] Subotnick was there [at the California Institute for the Arts], and on and on and on. In the meantime Mills College, which was still all women, was over there with [Darius] Milhaud, and hiring people like Subotnick, and it just went into riches upon riches upon riches. The Music Department in Berkeley was a marvel. It was one of the very great ones at that time, and it probably still is. You could walk out of your apartment, back onto the campus at night, and just drop in to a whole evening of Schubert. [*laughter*] It was like, why it was like, you know it was like being civilized, becoming civilized. [*laughter*] It was really quite nice. And all my gratitude to Twin Falls and the time that they tolerated me there. But my goodness, I mean when one went *there* [to Berkeley], there was a kind of richness of personalities. The place was filled, since it's a university city. Canadians have so little experience with that, at least here in Vancouver because they are all commuter universities, both UBC and Simon Fraser. But that was a little city, Berkeley was a city. The joke, you've heard me name them before, they were called the *wiederstudenten,* the always students, they never stopped. Rosario Jimenez, a wonder of wonders. She was this extraordinary person who couldn't ever get her job done. I've told these anecdotes before, so I won't repeat them, about my relations with her. But she was a superb classicist. She hid the fact that she came from Puerto Rico. Well, we got García Lorca from her. At the University of California in the English Department you couldn't really study twentieth-century stuff. You had the New Criticism that could read T. S. Eliot perhaps, but it could not read anything else. It certainly couldn't read Pound, so you got beautiful passages if you went to a course in Pound. William Carlos Williams you didn't deal with. So Duncan lived in this place on Telegraph Avenue called Throckmorton and there he set up a thing and it included an enormous number of people. There would be thirty or so. We read *Finnegans Wake* there, each of the thirty people having to feed in information so we could get through because this predates even the key to *Finnegans Wake* and stuff that came out a couple of years later. I mean there was nothing that you could do with it. And also *The Cantos*, we did *The Cantos*, we had Mallarmé, we had García Lorca. I'm sure that's the first time that Duncan—

NICHOLS: Mallarmé came in then in the 40s?

BLASER: Yes, yes, ummhmm—

NICHOLS: Right at the beginning?

BLASER: Yeah, way back, with stunning difficulty. [*laughs*] What in the hell's this! So that it was lovely, all those many years later for me to leave Simon Fraser University with a Mallarmé course. It was supposed to be a gift to the students, because they were taking on all this theory stuff and none of them knew anything about Mallarmé, and all of that theory stuff is profoundly indebted to Mallarmé. Even Derrida has to give footnotes to Mallarmé. And I have good things to say about Derrida. I'm standing against all of these people that have lost their way, in my view. But it was a marvelous kind of thing. It went all the way back to 194— that would be 1947, I think, and here I was in 1986, yes, '86 about to leave Simon Fraser in high dungeon at what they were doing to the university, and so I was taking off early, and I got Jery Zaslove—he is the best mind in Vancouver—that is, Jery Zaslove is simply a star in my mind and a companion of an order that I can't do without. And he was the one—he was head—and he allowed me to do that. The French Department nodded its head, yes, as well, so everything went on all right and it worked very well as a bilingual course on both levels. So it was quite a thrill to do this. But I'm trying to say that you moved into what amounted to a kind of puzzle—what do you call those puzzles that come in many pieces? Jigsaw. The jigsaw—it was like in a jigsaw puzzle— which was exactly what the twentieth-century seemed to me.

I had been refused, in Twin Falls, the draft, for reasons that they never gave me except that I was—and then later on when

Korea started they tried again but by that time I knew how to fight back.

NICHOLS: Do you think it was gay discrimination at that time?

BLASER: Oh well, it was certainly that they suspected that, they could hardly—I would hardly have known what to say about that, other than desire [*laughter*]—and desire is such a marvelous thing. But what was it I was just reading in—well, we'll come back to Cyril Connelly at some point or another, because this is an important event too. There we are in the middle of the war. Now Duncan had been in the army and got dumped. Jack wasn't on for obvious reasons because he had all kinds of physical disabilities, and there I was a 4F. And so there we all were, in the midst of this war and then politically moving in all kinds of directions and trying to do all [kinds of] things, and Berkeley is just this hotbed of what's going on. And the atom bomb and everything else. He [Oppenheimer] was a member of the faculty, the big one that they like to make charges against, and we were able to hear him.[3] We joined Trotskyite groups, and I think I've told this on the tapes [*Astonishments*], this story about the Trotskyite group that threw me out because I said I was papal *nuncio*. [*laughter*] Well, they were trying to—they made a motion—there were not as many as eighteen people at this meeting and they were going to pass a motion to ban supernaturalist religions. [*laughter*] So I punched Jack and said, "I'm going to say I'm papal *nuncio*." And so he said, "do it!" So I did. [*laughter*] I was thrown out—they moved their meetings.

NICHOLS: The papal *denuncio*. [*laughter*]

BLASER: And then I ran into the man who was head of it, his name was Robin Bauer, as I recall, of this Trotskyite group, and he explained to me, that when the revolution came I would hang on a fence post.

NICHOLS: Oh, *that* revolution.

BLASER: *That* revolution, yes. I believe that has a strong relation to all religions. [*laughs*] But it was the richness of all of this. And one was going through the [Henry] Wallace movement,[4] the whole thing, and fighting over their—[I forget] their names, who were executed for treason—the Jewish couple [the Rosenbergs].

What am I doing with their names? They are two famous instances of executions which we were all pretty much opposed to, but in those days we couldn't be sure they knew what they were talking about either. We still wouldn't have supported the death sentence. But ah, that'll turn up—they'll come to my mind another time and I can fill it in if you need information. Anyway, so much I suppose for Berkeley [except] in terms of details about what happened to one's sense of history say, by working so long in courses with Kantorowicz.

It was astonishing because it went from the very beginning— the Byzantine background of the western world including Christianity and all the difficulties—all those snazzy things around the word *ousia* and so on, for substance—and I can go through that list for you sometime, just to be pissy I suppose. Anyway, you went all the way through those, and then a course in the thirteenth-century which led us directly to Dante. And I remember the midterm question on that one. Should Innocent III be called "great." Well, now just think about it. On a *midterm*. What do you think the word "great" means? I mean I just sat there—I don't know how I wrote anything on that. I was so terribly—absolutely astonished by the question. 'Cause Innocent III is extraordinary as a pope, and we had gone through all this stuff and we were all headed for Dante and then on—I mean all this stuff goes on. And Schafer was giving more medieval things and then we got it all because Kantorowicz had connections that fascinated us, with the George circle in Germany—he had been part of that circle. And it is not true that George accepted the position that Hitler offered him. He left for Switzerland.

NICHOLS: Stefan George?

BLASER: Stefan George, yeah. I was supposed to do a translation job with a friend down there whose name is not coming to me at the moment either, but he's still alive—he had such good German and he wanted me to work with him. We were going to do a translation of George. But he [Kantorowicz] had that, and he brought us all down to [Friedrich] Gundolf, *The Mantle of Caesar*, which is a very important book for Duncan, for Jack, and for me. Part of that was the whole business of watching the Roman coming all

the way down into the twentieth-century. And then the constitutional—that was two terms—the constitutional history of
England, which moved all the way . . . down through the kings
and *The King's Two Bodies*, that book you've seen, which gives a
record of pretty much of what we were doing. But it was the
richness of that marvelous sense of history that became very
important to one's intellectual efforts. And it also opens into that
range in which Josephine Miles would unpleasantly call
us the museum poets because you began doing what for me
is Dantesque—that Dante would always talk to all the other
discourses. I mean that's how it works, you can include them and
quarrel with them and use them and do everything else. Pound
got it from Dante, I got it from Dante, Duncan got it, and Jack,
in some part too, though Jack remained freer of that kind of thing
than either of us.

NICHOLS: I want to go back to your comment about being in the
twentieth-century and a remark that Jery Zaslove made in an
essay in the collection that was brought out after the conference
on *The Holy Forest*—a remark that—

[At this point David Farwell arrives home and we stop for greetings.]

NICHOLS: The remark was that there was a project going on in the
50s that was truncated, and I wondered if you could comment on
your remark about being in the twentieth century and on something going on there [at mid-century] that has not been fully
brought out yet.

BLASER: I should go back and look at Jery's piece there too, because
that would be a great companion to this. But yes, I think there
was a project going on in the—this would be the late 50s—
because it took the 50s some little while to even begin to turn
back to look at what had happened in '45. There had been an
enormous war and it wasn't over yet. And Korea was coming up,
so you had all of that—the interesting aspect that they always tied
the American to the European world so much, and the Asian
world. And you had all of the problems of the farm and there's a
real commotion of mind going on. Also what was the war really

about? The holocaust, it seemed to me, was quickly shuttled under—it wasn't thought about. It was a long time before we had to—before, well, the talk at Harvard, when they had me doing all the holocaust stuff because women shouldn't see such horrors, when I came—that's still, that's 50s still—anyway, turn it off for a minute, so we can greet this gentleman [David].

[I turn the tape off and we talk to David for a few minutes.]

NICHOLS: So you said it was the Rosenbergs that were—

BLASER: —that were executed for treason because they gave . . . secrets away—Ethel and Julius Rosenberg. This was a big campus commotion. Those who were—well, I mean look at the question, what the question is doing is putting to you your relationship to your country. Does the country have the right to execute treason on this matter? And of course you have all the communists—and then you have the sort of pacificists, I suppose would be more where I would lie in terms of that. There was a very important group of pacificists around Dick Moore to whom Spicer dedicates a poem. [Moore] is one of the founders of KPFA, which is the founding of public radio—it first was in Berkeley. . . . Rexroth had a program to review books. It was the secret of his great library—as he got all his marvelous, unbelievable books, which he reviewed. And Spicer had a program on folksongs and stuff.

NICHOLS: On what?

BLASER: Folksongs and ballads. And Jim Herndon, the lovely Jim Herndon was his guitarist for that and he [Spicer] was always trying to get him [Jim] to change the words so they'd be slightly dirty. Which Jim didn't like to do, but he [Spicer] could get him to sing labor songs, the favourite one being "God Damn Their Eyes." *[laughter]* It's a great labor song. Spicer claimed his father had connections with the Wobblies—Rosa Luxemburg and all that stuff, way back. But I mean the commotion of it all—as a project it's very, very interesting, because when I say that people aren't in the twentieth-century I don't mean just that they've not read the writers or looked at the painting or the architecture and so on, of the twentieth-century, though that's of course the voice of it. But I mean that they've not even stopped to figure out whether or not there's a question about the twentieth-century. So when you come into it, as a very young man, and you're coming out of a place where they absolutely want everything to remain perfectly still, as in Twin Falls, Idaho, and your family doesn't want to let you loose ever either, which is one of the ghastly parts—

[*Tape change*]

BLASER: —one of the ghastly parts of going back to that "stone" is that they not only want it to stay very still, but they don't—as though the war never happened. And of course my father wasn't in the war, and so on. The connection with the war is very strange because it is my step-grandfather Auer who was involved from the first World War and received a considerable punish-ment—the stories I've told in the poem ["Image-Nation 24 ('oh, pshaw'"], and so on, about the house being painted yellow and so forth. And then of course with the second World War since I wasn't there—my brother went—the brother next to me, Gus— went into the navy. Jimmy was too young, so he didn't. And then I don't think any of us wound up in the Korean draft, at all, though I had—I actually went through a psychiatrist because I couldn't figure—they made me 4F and then look what they were doing now. Now when you were made 4F back there in 1943, just turning eighteen, it really is a crush of some kind on you, because you are tied to your country in some way. I mean recently when Charles Bernstein had me write a piece on nationalism for that *Boundary* that just came out . . . I had to answer no, that writing didn't attach to a nation.[5] That I don't know how to do it. And then I went into a big fluff about governments. They are manip-ulators, and democracy has been lost everywhere, most danger-ously, I think, in the United States. Challenged at least, at this point, by what has happened in bringing the religiosity back in— this extraordinary, endless, endless turn to religion, which is part of the stillness that goes on all the time.

But there were two projects. Modernism itself was a project. Every period is modern to itself and every century has that, and

you can find it wherever you read, that there's a kind of modernity and that it's ahead of the past in some way. And there is even
an aspect of modernism that is apocalyptic. I've always found the
apocalyptic, since a very young man, as being really a pretty
phony notion because it's all tied in—well, even philosophy ties
you in with the end of time—and you've got Fukuyama and that
thing where the end of time means you are all American liberals
and so on and so forth. It's an extraordinary argument and it's
another matter when you're going back and trying to reconstruct
it in terms of say Hegel or even Marx. But then this ability to read
the future, which is their way of saying an end of time—they
might [be] better off if they'd go back to what was the original
Hebraic sense of time which is certainly what the sense of time
was in the Christian testament. I'm quite determined that we talk
now—there's a Hebrew testament, a Christian testament, and a
Muslim testament. The new and old and all that stuff really is
fundamentally condescending to people, I think. But in the
Hebrew testament, which was the only one available, and so on,
the sense of time was [that] the past is behind you and it is what
is known. The future is ahead of you and it is what is unknown.

   Now I think that this business of the projects of the twentieth-
century with modernism where the great excitements of say,
Dada, Jarry, and the *Ubu Roi*, and Duncan doing his version of
the *Ubu Roi*—all these wonderful things that were just part of the
wildness of the place. That's the reason when I found Merleau-
Ponty's phrase "wild logos," I thought that was perfection—the
way my mind works, and I thought it was sort of the way the
whole shebang works—was wild logos, which was what I thought
Merleau-Ponty meant also. But you had *Ubu*, you had the anti-
art thing, you had surrealism, which was proposing a different
kind of move completely. It wasn't anti-art, but it had some
obvious limits—it's really a continuous project, actually, it's still
continuing in a very fascinating way. The whole anti-art thing,
which was originally Dada's gift to breaking apart something—
and then you have to figure out what was being broken down.
What was it that got so hard hit by this? What did they wish to tear
down? It's certainly not a matter of tearing down a style, but it was
tearing down and saying something about what the world was—

and so we would tear it down in order to open it up again. And it goes on and on and on and on—all these instructions that kept moving forward. Modernism—if you were interested in painting for example, you'd take the 1913 Armory Show—it is America finding out that something was going on and it never changed. I mean . . . not leaving Victorian morals, that wasn't the fundamental issue. The fundamental issue was that an entire tradition had become untrue for millions of lives. And at some point or another, when you get into both modernism and into postmodernism—and the postmodernism includes structuralism, they are not separate—there is a constant area in which you've decided that some question has to be asked. And one of the most interesting ones is the question of singularity. When can singularity and particularity begin to have a place of honor. Now that's fundamentally a democratic question. And most of the world works, did work, against the democratic and still works against the democratic. The democratic is the least understood political form that one could possibly imagine. It is certainly not Fukuyama's American liberalism . . . that's globalization which is quite a different thing.

NICHOLS: The globalization of trends.

BLASER: Yes, and it's fundamentally very anti-singularity and particularity. It's dangerous—but that jumps one all the way up to very recent years. So modernism itself set a project that the second World War stopped, truncated. Curiously, the arts went right on with it. You could wipe out, in places like Italy, all of Italian philosophy, for example. Then when you get people like Giorgio Agamben suddenly coming up, it's like a renewal of something that didn't get a chance under *that* fascism. In Germany, you saw them try to destroy almost everything that was not a kind of—I would put it that they were after a kind of realism—it was their realism that was an ideology, and an ideology is an idea, not a realism. But they destroyed as much art as they could, they did all this and so on and so on. But the war itself was an enormous shock, I think, to everybody.

You know, one way to translate that is that it was a triumph of the west, and certainly marvelous things happened—the Marshall plan and the rebuilding of Europe and all that stuff which now is having to be re-patterned in the Balkans all over again, and on and on and on. But I think the war was an enormous question, about what it was. And then when Truman, who was a popular president, and a courageous one in many ways—a disaster on art—he stopped a whole show of paintings being sent to Europe because it was disgraceful to show America in that guise. And of course I think most of the stuff was abstract expressionism at that point. Poor Truman. But in the meantime, he dropped the bomb, you know. . . . We as students—it was really something we had to decide whether that should have happened or not. San Francisco was very interesting in that instance, of V-J Day. The ships had come in and they had let all the sailors loose in San Francisco. This is still not written about, and I'm told that—well, I suppose now they can get the material about it—the Freedom of Information Acts and so on—but the city blew up. The sailors came in and turned into riot. They attacked. They threw civilians through plate glass windows, they turned over the streetcars on Market Street, they set them on fire. It was one of the most hideous riots, and it was not written up. There may be a book now, I haven't checked recently, but for a long time there wasn't even research on what it was about. But now if you're living there you know that it's about something. As a matter of fact, I can still feel the policeman's hand on my back, pushing us, because they got as many cops out in San Francisco as possible, and then they got every civilian they could find. We were all down in this big celebration. Chinatown was marvelous. I had to cover my head with my topcoat and it was burned through with the firecrackers that were being tossed from the balconies and— that wasn't meant, it was just what happened. And anyway so we all went down, we were going to Market Street—this big thing, and so on—and there we all were and then this started. This absolutely enraged, mainly naval personnel, as far as I can remember it, that we saw, and the police were in there 'cause I remember being pushed personally—the cop's hand pushing us back up, to get us back up the hills, off of Market Street and headed back up, well, Russian Hill, in the direction I was being pushed in. And it was an astonishing moment, but once again these are things that one stops over. This was supposed to be a celebration of victory.

NICHOLS: And there was so much anger?

BLASER: Anger out—just unleashed, against all the civilians who'd been there and not lived through what was the horror of that. We're reaping the harvest of that at some point or another now, because I really sometimes wonder if they could talk a whole population into a war of that kind again.

NICHOLS: On that scale?

BLASER: Yeah, and that's one reason that they've developed all these—

NICHOLS: Small wars—

BLASER: . . . these, well, small wars, and also weapons—that you can do it all through distance, so to speak, like Mr. Bush's attacks on Iraq.

NICHOLS: His surgical strikes.

BLASER: Yes, the new world order. But anyway, so there was a project. Modernism was a project that I think was very much attached to a kind of democracy—at least no longer willing to let the arts stay where they were—and so it was a kind of wreckage and then one fascinating part of that is to watch the way in which Breton and the surrealists tried to make some kind of connection with the Marxists and they were, of course, flatly refused. Marxists ain't going to bring any of this unconscious stuff into their view of the future. And so modernism itself is a great project, and then if you watch the poets that one reads, all of them, including T. S. Eliot, are actually quite radical. Eliot is trying to see what can be saved spiritually, not entirely unlike the *Ancient Mariner* where Coleridge is desperately trying to see what can be saved too, and has a hell of a time doing that. And Pound with that marvelous moment when he gives Dante a good eye and finds out that Dante saw hell as being really in the shape of what your own bad life had been in one way or another, so he takes it on and does this incredibly, wildly ridiculous satire on his own contemporary London as hell itself, and all the years later when I did my Dante piece I find this Italian reporter [in] Dante's town, saying "hell is here. . . ."[6] So what is postmodernism doing in all of this? [*laughs*]

NICHOLS: When do you date [it]?

BLASER: Well, I date it, and I also give the term to Olson, 'cause Olson called it—what he said [was] 'we are post the modern.' And that was the first time I ever ran into the term in Olson. I think he's moving from the second World War. It's fundamentally what can be done and Olson—the thing that is so held against him—is that he saw it as building an entire new *mythos*, so that when you get to the second part and third parts of *Maximus* you're into a realm in which you have to be able to read mythological language, which is done by trying to weave it back and then forward. . . . And then the black chrysanthemum is still trying to do it, where he's using—adapting Jung—I don't like to say he's using Jung, because he had reservations on Jung, which Charles Stein doesn't discuss in that book on the black chrysanthemum. Oh,what would I say that postmodernity is trying to do? My first response, tied as I was to a late arrival in modernism, in the twentieth-century, was great hostility to the term itself. And I wouldn't use it at first. I date it to the [second] World War and it was only by the time I kind of went back to Olson's 'we are post the modern' that I began—that was the way I opened the door into the postmodern, because there is that apocalyptic side of postmodernism, that modernism is all over and here we are, and this is all going to be right—

NICHOLS: And now the postmodern is over and—

BLASER: Yes, oh yes, and oh boy that was mainly brought to an end by English Departments that couldn't read Derrida right at all— got it all wrong—and Derrida let them get away with this adoption of him, and as a consequence has wrecked his reputation. He's one of the grandees of the whole postmodern project which was to be able to see through something. Now, I'm not sympathetic with that notion that theory replaces the text and all of that, but I don't myself think that's really what Derrida is saying at all. But he—that's at least the way it came out and you couldn't do it, I mean, in some sense Derrida is France's James Joyce, if you look at books like *Glas*. France didn't get a Joyce. But anyway, he's a philosopher of great distinction and yes, now it's all over. Well,what is over is not postmodernism or the project of postmodernism, which was fundamentally no more than, but certainly not less than, a correction of modernism. Because modernism could let fly the most ghastly anti-Semitisms, it could let fly all kinds of reactionary elements, as though somehow those were part of having escaped a past.

NICHOLS: Would it be the problem of trying to invest authority in the State instead of in the religious order that was perceived as having fallen apart?

BLASER: I think that's one of Pound's difficulties, but then that was Marx's difficulty. And as it turns out, it was Hegel's difficulty. They had no idea that there was anything possible except the State, and then when—the vulgar way of putting it—when Marx decides he can just reverse Hegel, and we wind up with a materialism and you're in the same—it's like atheism, which is one of the most ridiculous ideas the world ever ran into. It's nothing but the other side of the same thing. [*laughter*] And they just keep going on and on and on and on and on. . . . And so there we are, and we're going to get a perfected humanity. I read this book by some guy, what was his name—Penguin published it—it was a book by an East German who was explaining that if people would just come along and do all of this stuff this way there would be a perfected humanity and everybody would be a poet. Well, number one, not everybody will ever be a poet, and number two, perfected humanity is a profound question inside all of this move. It's a very, very interesting issue about what it is. And human vileness is the central issue out of the holocaust. Whose is it? Where is it now? Is it really just German? I doubt that. I doubt that very much. I am interested that a whole population can participate in human vileness.

But the project itself fundamentally and repeatedly returns the answers to the arts. Now one reason for postmodernism was to correct all kinds of difficulties in modernism that were either dead-ending or whatever. Because style will dead-end, can't handle content that goes another way, and so on and so forth. It doesn't mean it's not art anymore, but on the other hand, art isn't eternity either, and art doesn't want to be eternity. That was one aspect of the New Criticism. They literally did believe in Coleridge's primary and secondary imaginations, and so there was, you know—it was a neat way to save art, because if it somehow answered to God's primary imagination then of course it was grand, it was very grand indeed. Well, grandeur is a subject apart, and you'll figure out there are not very many grand poets. There are some marvelous poets, but there are not many that—and you don't worry about that—that isn't what you—you don't sit here and say I'm going to write a *grand* poem today, and I do hope posterity sees this is *grand*. [*laughter*] So that it was an absurd notion that New Criticism broke on, because New Criticism has a modernity and a saving device in many ways, for the arts, [but] couldn't read most of the twentieth-century writing. They were hopeless in the face of Pound. They could get Eliot, but then Eliot was in a very different—and I think in some ways—I tend to want to think of him nicely now. I always thought that return to religion was—at one point of my younger life I thought of it as—oh well, for heaven's sake, you know, because I so loved *The Waste Land* and then, I don't know afterwards. He was radical in a wonderful way. It doesn't work. I wouldn't go there for love nor money. What does Cyril Connelly say? He loved money, and he loved money and sex. [*laughter*] Those are great subjects for poetry.

So the postmodern project began to be a way in which to try to read the arts, to read them well and to find out what it was they were really doing. That threw things into a kind of materiality that we had not really had before, and that was the materiality of language, the materiality of mode, the materiality of means, and out of this we get the distinction of the very best of the language poets, but we also get a real sensitization of the relationship to whatever it is the work of art is trying to do . . . I mean it's very interesting because the Derridean project—to let him stand for one thing—the Derridean project consistently goes back to art. If you read somebody like Giorgio Agamben he'll take you all the way. That *Infancy and History* book is just a stunner of a book, and everybody needs to know that there's a point at which the infant is something that can't speak and so that there's the issue of that. But at the end of it, we have to turn this over to poetry, he says. Well, specifically—and it is to poetry, it isn't to anything else.

If you go over, which I hope one day to do—just got a postcard from Fran Herndon. Darling Fran. She discovered the manuscript which they didn't remember they had, and so they never found it for me when I was doing the collected books of *The Holy Grail* [by Jack Spicer]. So I received a phone call about this, and I said, well, of course it's Fran's. He left it there, it's hers. She should get as much money for it as possible, and I'd like it to go to Berkeley, so see what they'll do. It's Berkeley, it's gone to Berkeley—so she can go back to France. So I got a postcard from her in French and she's gone all the way over the Pyrenees to Bilbao to see this Guggenheim in Bilbao, which is one of the great, great examples of what modern art can do.[7] It requires computers to figure out whether you can do these whorls and ziggles and zaggles and so on. [Frank] Gehry is one of the—if you haven't looked into this you must because I think it is one of the great things that the century's got, and I even sent Harrison Birtwistle a copy of the Guggenheim catalogue because I wanted him to enjoy the sense of this as much as I did and I think he did. But she [Fran] went all the way over there to this great example of where art will finally take you, even in buildings. It's more like sculpture, and Adrienne Clarkson [CBC host] did that thing on television with him, which she did very well. She says compared to Frank Lloyd Wright—he said yes, that's flattering, but you know he didn't like painting. [*laughter*] But he comes out of painting and sculpture—you must look at it, just go in a bookstore. . . . Gehry is the architect's name, and the Guggenheim put up—I keep saying it's because they didn't have room in New York for the stuff that they're showing—and they gave the money for Guggenheim in Bilbao. It's worth a side trip. . . . But anyway—so I got off on one of my tangents.

NICHOLS: Talking about the postmodern—

BLASER: The postmodern, yeah. So if you're trying to test out the postmodern I think you have to look at what they were trying to do. To what degree, the fundamental speech of it is so often the analysis of an art work of some kind. It can be poetry, it can be a text of some kind, but it is constantly looking at the way in which language can do something. Now modernism didn't do that.

Modernism assumed the power of language. Postmodernism assumes that there is some difficulty with that power. And as a consequence much of what [the] postmodern did, a great part of it is extremely useful stuff. But now where is the world. OK? Postmodernism never did ignore the world. It's just that nobody is paying any attention to these guys that are helping with this. And I don't think poets are really at ease with that business of cosmos or world or whatever you want to call it, without some companionship.

NICHOLS: From the other discourses.

BLASER: From the other discourses. That's me, and I'm somewhat alone in it. But it's fascinating to watch the poets that I so adore who don't fool around with this stuff, but they have another way that is world. Creeley is one of the greatest world poets that I know about. He knows how to get the present so that it's the world itself. And I envy that. It's very difficult for me. It is just grand. But what they have done—they are not paying attention, especially this anti—the postmodern is over with stuff—they're not reading Michel Serres, they're not reading Giorgio Agamben, Deleuze—Guattari and Deleuze—I mean to include that whole run of books—Jean-Luc Nancy to name only the most obvious people who are voices that repeatedly know that art is one of the wedges of their own concern. Every single one of those, and they are philosophers. It's true, they're moving from a different range. I mean suddenly Henri Bergson is back here of some interest . . . not because he is the last word on anything, but he was one of the great modernist voices, especially after the first World War. When I did the American Philosophical Association show at the Widener Library, I had cases running the relationships with Bergson, all the way through until you hit Santayana and Whitehead where there were more cases. Well, I think we should stop.

[I turn the tape off, and we step outside where Robin can smoke. During the break, I ask him what he thinks of the critiques that have come out about the postmodern, specifically the postcolonial complaint that postmodernism is Eurocentric and complicit with imperial-

ism, and the Marxist critique of the postmodern as quietist (ahistorical, incapable of macrostructural analysis, individualistic, politically impotent). The conversation picks up from this question when we head back to the kitchen and turn the tape on.]

NICHOLS: OK, we're talking now about the post-

BLASER: Did you get that last one? The business about Serres—

NICHOLS: Yes, Michel Serres and—

BLASER: I wanted just to add Alphonso Lingis to that. . . . Because [Lingis] is not Eurocentric at all. I first ran into him as the translator of Merleau-Ponty's *Visible and the Invisible,* and then here when he gave that talk which nobody seemed to be able to follow, which I thought was mainly because they had not—you know—you should do a little preparation. Don't go into a lecture like it's all going to be clear.

NICHOLS: You're talking about Lingis's visit to Vancouver. That was a couple of years ago.

BLASER: Yeah, you went to that didn't you?

NICHOLS: No, I wasn't able to go. You gave me hell afterwards too.

BLASER: Oh yes, for not going. Because I thought it was a great event. . . . But he belongs [with] these and he's certainly not Eurocentric. First off, one has to say, we cannot dismiss Marx. I'm not talking about Marxisms. Their record of practice in the twentieth-century has put a question to Marxism that not one of them has answered. There may be a start of an answer in Jameson's [*Political Unconscious* and *Cultural Turn*].[8] I was even going to write him about it—I was going to call them mash notes. Because both Eagleton and Jameson have been important to me, but I've been very angry that we go on and on and on with Marxism, and Marxism never says what went wrong in its prac-tice. And it's time for the whole bunch of them to sit down and start talking about what went wrong and not going on with this. Now that is not to dismiss Marx. In fact, I've threatened repeat-edly to call all my favorites back—I'll offer a seminar . . . and [we'll] reread Marx together, because Marx is our last great thinker of social justice. You go back and look at that. Marx is not a Bible. That was their problem, that they didn't know the Bible

disappeared when they put another one in its place and went on
with the futurism. They all became fortune tellers which is a
Hegelian mistake and it was one that Marx didn't protect them
from presumably. But to reread Marx together would, I think,
be a marvelous thing to do. So that, all right we're not going to
quarrel with Marx, but we will say that it's time for you guys to
talk a bit about— Also when Marxism falls into the east what
aspect of Europe goes over there and turns into killing fields? I
mean that's an old Yeatsian point, speaking of an old reactionary,
that dear old poet there. He was, you know [speaking of] when
the east falls into the west and the west falls into the east, and
when the west fell into the east, my lord, look at the problems of
it. And I'm not talking about the fact that those movements were
involved in freeing from previous, terrible political systems. But
then when you're released, what do you get, you know? And also
the business of the sacrificial which Marxism has not lost. It
belongs to their sense of the future, in the practice of it, and the
sacrificial is the one thing we'd better start worrying about. And
here postmodernism is one of the major areas in which to look
[for] help. . . .

NICHOLS: You sacrifice the present for a future agenda?

BLASER: So you can kill anybody—kill 'em all, and it'll be perfect
tomorrow. I'm sorry, but that doesn't work. You've lost singularity, particularity. You've lost everything, and you don't know
anything about what it is to be perfect. And so, no. They must
talk, that's all. And we'll stop that one. Now as for the others. I
could go through in very many places in Michel Serres where I
will find . . . the issue of the political going on. In Levi-Strauss,
those last chapters of *Triste Tropique*—we're not talking
Eurocentrism, we're talking about how to see life in a different
way. And isn't it a major, major effort in philosophical terms to
look at and reconsider what it is that has brought the western
philosophical tradition and western metaphysics, including its
constantly returning religion, to find out what it is that does
not make a decent society and certainly not a democratic one?
So, does every single thinker have to answer the same question?
No, not every single thinker has to be Marxist, either. And on

and on we go. This great kerfuffle about the *Specters of Marx*, of Derrida's. Well, I think you'd better start taking another look, you guys. Derrida was extremely interesting in all of this, because Derrida is the one that everybody is going to blame and especially the English Departments.

If anybody wrecked postmodernism it was the English Departments because they turned everything into theory. They didn't read the stuff that they were supposed to read. They couldn't even teach it. They just went on in theory. . . . And you don't talk about poetry when you don't know anything about it. Now it seemed to me very curious with somebody like Deleuze, not to be interested in the degree to which there's actually a repeated political question that goes on throughout. The fact that he's insistent on reading the world in a different way—that you read it as though you came out of a root. That he's insisted upon that doesn't mean that he hasn't said something that is political. When he talks about the American poetry being the most important twentieth-century poetry, it's a very interesting issue. Who does he choose to quote? Bob Dylan! Not a bad choice either. The choice there was specifically because it had political possibility that he used to [provoke] dialogue. These [dismissals] are vulgarities, and also I watch them like a hawk because . . . I'm running into an ideologue. I've been with them, and you know they are all of them mixed up in divinity fudge, even when they don't know it, and it's simply got to stop. [*laughter*] Thought doesn't work this way. These people are thinking—the fact that they've not given them a blueprint—well, did Marx give a blueprint—I mean Marxism, give a blueprint for a new society, a just society? Who has? If you read Eagleton, for example, I can sit and read Eagleton with great pleasure and nod my head with agreement throughout, and throughout, and throughout and then when I get through I want to know how come we ran into this wall. . . . I suppose these people would say Hegel said nothing about politics. Well, he certainly did. There's a whole theory of the State there, but there's not one that understands what the State is. That's a problem—a nineteenth-century problem, which in some sense is one of Hegel's limits. The thing with Marx is the same—that he doesn't have that—he didn't know to warn on that. The whole notion that you replace the present structure with another one, simply leaves the next structure in danger of more atrocities, and they're all full of atrocities.

NICHOLS: As opposed to holding open—you were speaking about the Hebraic notion of time—as opposed to holding open a future where there could be deliberation?[9]

BLASER: Yeah, yeah. And with a great Jewish thinker behind them, a very great one, Marx, then they ought to sit back and think about what that is, what it proposed to do and wherever it had a weakness. There are people to read along with that I'm very interested in and attracted to, and I may, if I get too hot under the collar, just get my graduate course together and we'll all sit here and read Marx together. Because it's a very good project and a very poetic one, if you go about it in the right way. . . . Now there was one difficulty with Marxist thought, and that is the notion that language—this is our means of getting to the world—it actually is even the way we create the world. It is very directly related to our singularity and the song of our singularity. And all of that kind of thing. But the Marxists don't see it that way. Language was something that floated in the air as though it were really a free form of some kind of power and [you] used it then to push the world around. This is not what postmodernism has been saying over and over and over. And the beginning of it was in structuralism, which also then became, I would say, super-structure, which is the way in which it too then had to be given a critique. And the postmodern thing is not over—it's not over except in English Departments where I hope they do what they should have done in the first place. They're such dumb asses that they should go back to the old-fashioned close reading and sit there with the students and read closely. And that's all they have to do. I'll give them a PhD from my university—[laughter]— which is called the White Rabbit University. We will go down the hole and give them their fucking degrees all over again. Go back and do that, because that's all you know how to do, and the rest of this, you better leave it alone until you get some brains. And that brain matter is entirely dependent upon what it has concerned itself with. It is a matter of attention. Attention is the gift you give to the world. That is all you've got. It ain't your love, it ain't your sex, it ain't your this, it ain't your that. It's your attention, and I would just be very firm that, number one, that you have not read postmodernism broadly. They have instead taken up that move toward the theorist of the text and let that stand as if that were the postmodern project. It is not alone the postmodern project, it's only one page of it.

NICHOLS: Robin, you've talked about singularity a couple of times. Could you say a bit more about singularity? How does one write the singular?

BLASER: Well, the lyric is the mode of the singular and the lyric— that's why lyric is so marvelous and I—Lord, don't give it up— don't give up rhyme. Don't give up—you could hope to be blessed by a language like Italian, where as, was it Mandelstam said? It was in my Dante piece. It was Mandelstam, wasn't it, that I was quoting? No! That every vowel rings and rhymes—a wonderful passage. I mix—sometimes when I get so fussed, I mix these things up. Anyway, it's in the Dante piece. It's a wonder. It takes a whole quotation, too, 'cause all the vowels ask to be included—[*laughs*]—that wonderful sense that he had of trying to learn Italian. You could be blessed in that way. But I mean the lyric itself, and this is, of course, what is so disappointing about what I would call the redundancy of lyric. If you think there's nothing else but yourself in the lyric, then you can get—what?— about two poems out of it—one of them in which you talk entire-ly about yourself and how much you love somebody, and the reader of the poem can't ever see "somebody." And the other one is to project upon vegetables and things. [*laughter*] It's not lyric. Lyric is the song element. . . . Lyric itself . . . is the thing which I think a poet has to protect. It is that intimacy with the sound that is constantly a kind of song. And it can have long lines, short lines, single words—and you're always weaving the sound with something. It can be a person, it can be an object, it can be anything. It might be very big—it can be cosmos or, you know, my lover likes bacon, so that's what I'm makin'. [*laughter*]

NICHOLS: I remember you saying a while ago—a long time ago— that a poem will begin for you with sound or rhythm, rather than words.

BLASER: Yes, yes, that's a long time ago. Yeah, I remember that. Was [it] at the Western Front, or was that over at Cap[ilano] College?

NICHOLS: I don't remember.

BLASER: I remember saying that too. . . . I even used to carry an instrument around. I wound up loaning them and they never returned those instruments. But yes, I usually do hear sound first when I know it's there, and that's what's with the libretto for example, where it's being very complicated because the real sound's the music and I don't have anything to do with that— and then I move in as best I can, trying to keep the line working. And so often Harry [Birtwistle] will say to me, well, it's so text-centered, by which he means that it's too dense, I think, in imagery or something. And so it's been an experience to do it in such a way that you are always leaving yourself open to some-thing that will be set in sound [and] at the same time, have it so that it is sounding.

NICHOLS: This is coming into the project that you're working on right now?

BLASER: Yeah.

NICHOLS: —with Sir Harrison Birtwistle. Do you want to talk a little bit about that? Is it called *The Last Supper*?

BLASER: Yes, it's called *The Last Supper*. Well you know, I mean it gets involved in all of this turn to religion. That's the reason right now I'm reading this book, *Philosophy and the Turn to Religion*. [The title is] so carefully worded because the turn to religion happens over and over and over again, even when you're talking of Hegel and Marx, you're mixed up in it. And it keeps coming back. And then if we're here, it's especially strong in the United States and seeps into Canada all the time. The turn to religion is just everywhere. It's endlessly so, and it's so because it's headed for politics, not for religion at all. That isn't what they're interest-ed in, they're interested in power. And of course that power then is defined as a moral power. And the moral power will then become an imposed morality, and then people have very great difficulty thinking about what it means to be a virtuous person, if all you're talking about is a moral person. Family values, for example—well, listen to that phrase. It's such an interesting phrase because it gives a definition of what the body is. It lays an enormous burden upon women and then it says what the body can't do and what it shouldn't do. The Roman Catholic tradition was such that you weren't even supposed to enjoy fucking unless you were trying to have a baby. And then that wasn't enjoying it, it was trying to have—etc. etc. etc. etc. But it's a very dangerous area.

The Last Supper is calling the twelve apostles. We don't reach the crucifixion because that comes after the supper. You're calling the twelve disciples and Christ back. And I had two problems immediately when I agreed to do this. I flew from Venice— that wonderful trip to do the Dante thing—because I got word of Harrison's—Harry's—interest in this. I flew from Venice to London—David and I went there and had dinner, and this came up—and that was the subject proposed. And I said yes. Well, the first problem that I had when I came back to think about it was, well, one, you had the last supper, and Harry's doing marvelously interesting things in stage work because you go backwards. There'll be tableaux of the crucifixion appear before you get to the supper and so on, so you've got to go backwards. The opera itself ends with everyone leaving the stage to go walk among the olives in the garden and talk of happiness.

But the first problem was there were no women. And so I brought this up and this seemed to me impossible, and I wasn't going to bring the Marys on and have them wait on table, my dear. It didn't seem quite the way I have ever looked at women or that I thought they would care to look at them[selves] on stage. So I created a figure called Ghost. Harry said it's really you, isn't it? And I said yes it is, and I'm going to audition for the part. And there was silence at the other end. Anyway, she actually runs the show and he's cast her as a mezzosoprano, which is wonderful, just wonderful. And then Harry said—'cause he's still worrying about this—he said what if I give you a chorus of all women? And I said, that's marvelous. So the chorus is to be below the proscenium and the designer, this marvelous woman is giving them halos, so that you can see their halos all the way through. Well, then the next thing was, could I put everything they say in

Latin. After some few—I would say what do you call it when you
start having various facial tics and so on—I said yes, we would fix
it in Latin. So they sing in Latin. It's a very interesting thing to
do. And so there they are. Now you've got the twelve disciples to
be brought on stage, identifying themselves in one way or another, and waiting for Christ to appear and so on and so on. It is a
major paradigm of western thought that you're dealing with. And
it should be dealt with with respect and care—and love. And so
you bring them in and there's the foot washing scene, which I
mentioned to you before, where Christ is going to wash the dust
of twenty centuries off their feet. And then you're at the very
moment where the table itself is still Passover, not yet Eucharist.
That's in the libretto as well. Because Christ is free to [go].

NICHOLS: And that dust of twenty centuries is the practice of
Christianity?

BLASER: And that comes right into twentieth-century practice,
belief, and so on. And that is not to be treated as a diatribe
against, or something, because it's there and very much there,
and it's also in western philosophy in all of that notion of
completion, of absolutes. All of those [absolutes] belong to the
same tradition Platonized as it is very often in philosophy, and so
on. So I just became very interested in—to leave the libretto now
with problems which remain, such as an aria for Christ, which I
have still to do. And I've used Emily Dickinson for Ghost's last
thing, but I think maybe that's too easy for me to do. I should do
something else.

But anyway I've got very interested in—to return to Derrida. If
they want to go through all this stuff about the political, and
about possible political action, if we're not going to turn always
into the same thing, which is into an enormous violence, then it
seems to me you've got to figure out where the violence is coming from, and one of the places that it comes from is from
religion. Which is one of the most violent aspects of our lives. It
is a violation repeatedly of many people's sense of the body, and
so on. Now this Hent de Vries has written a very good book,
Philosophy and the Turn to Religion. . . . It is deeply indebted to a
piece by Derrida which is called "Faith and Knowledge" [in
Religion, edited by Derrida and Gianni Vattimo]. . . . He's gone

through talking about, in French *"la pire violence"*—worst violence—is this one. I'll just kind of summarize I guess—the worst violence . . . is an abstraction of abstraction, over and over again. Now look at the future—

NICHOLS: This is where the singularity would come in.

BLASER: Yes.

NICHOLS: The refusal to abstract, which is the refusal to foreclose the future.

BLASER: And there is the lyric voice, by its beautiful self. I'm going to quote just a bit from Hent de Vries on Derrida:

> For Derrida . . . *la pire violence* first of all means abstraction *ad absurdam*, looking away from every singularity that is other or belongs to the other, and, by the same token, the abstraction from the general and *a fortiori* from universality, called for by the 'democracy to come.' (20)

He puts "democracy to come" into italics now. Before I ever ran into this, I wrote a poem called "As If By Chance" in which I talk about democracy—how new it is, how little understood it is, how un-Periclean, un-Athenian, etc. . . . OK. So what shows up then in the worst violence, shows up in the body politic's obsession with a limited conception of the body—in other words, with a sexual politics that exerts its violence to no small degree as a . . . mutilation or at least a denial of possible sexual identities. Now that's a major political analysis, in brief—too brief, probably. . . . It also takes me back to the question which hovered over my mind throughout my care with this *Last Supper*. I wanted to know where Christianity was in relation to the violence of large numbers . . . in something like the holocaust. . . . I won't be able to do this in the libretto, but I am moving in my own work to talk about a kind of violence, because I felt strongly that it was time for Christianity to say, if it had either been a part of such a structure—social structure—or that it could not do anything to abet such a social structure—either is the same answer. I have a very, very deep sense that somewhere inside this constant and ever recurring religious mess—this is not atheism, this has nothing to do with that. . . .

NICHOLS: And I would take it that much of [the religious mess] is secular?

BLASER: —that there is a violence that—it can become secular and you just put a different name on it. And it is a violence that is taught almost from the cradle. I mean rock-a-bye-baby does fall out of that tree. Or at least that's what I thought when I was a child. I was always rather frightened by "Rock-a-bye-baby, in the treetops."

[Tape change]

BLASER: . . .[Christ] didn't make any of this stuff that we have to worry about so much. Most of it is much later. I did research up to my whatevers and I'm surprised I haven't gone bald with some of the stuff I'm reading. But to figure out what it was that was there before they began theologizing and turning it into the power system where Paul is a major figure in turning it all over into the Roman.

NICHOLS: Robin, what do you think about the Lacanian line, that there's a fault line in the social. It's a being-out-of-phase.[10] Some of the new Lacanians like Žižek have taken that into the social as well as the psychoanalytical.

BLASER: But I think that's why Lacan is still so very important. There was a while there when they dismissed Lacan too, you know, I mean for biographical reasons. . . . I've read quite a bit of Lacan. Lacan, actually, in the recognition of him, he's marvelous. . . . But Lacan actually belongs to the postmodern, and as we saw it at Simon Fraser with that fellow—what's his name?

NICHOLS: Anthony Wilden.

BLASER: Anthony Wilden, yeah, his book was so important to me . . . just [at] the beginning of the *Image-Nations*.

NICHOLS: It comes into your essay, "The Stadium of the Mirror"— Lacan comes in there.

BLASER: I don't know what he's doing with Lacan anymore because they had some kind of falling out, and he said to me once . . . the main interest is in the metaphors and so on. I'm not sure that's— well, that isn't where I stand. If I'm told things like that I go check that all out to see what's going on. But still on the postmodern thing, I would say, you see, the postmodern is very much involved exactly in trying to let some of this stuff come out in the open, and they're not all going to be sitting there telling you that you're going to be doing this in a political form or that you're doing that. . . . Lingis is particularly good on that kind of thing where the imagery—what is happening to you when you have an image that isn't the same as yours, and so on and so on—that he falls in love with what's happening and I would prefer to be that way myself. But then I've never had this. My father was anti-Semitic, very nastily so, and I think it meant the wandering Jew in his life. [He] was very unhappy when I was running around in high school, very briefly, with . . . Janet Pink, wonderful name. . . . And wonderfully beautiful young woman—just wonderfully beautiful. And I'm sure they [her parents] disapproved as much as he did. But that experience which is—that's too awful. Where is that coming from? You don't even have to have met a Jew to have an anti-Semitism going.

NICHOLS: This is the violence that you're talking about.

BLASER: It's the violence and of course it's a violence that somehow works itself very well, even without an object. And then if you can get an entire structure . . . [and break] it down to open it, then you can go get 'em. Somehow murder and sacrifice belong awfully close together. In the libretto, I have a moment when Christ says the holocaust broke my heart. And I mean by that line it broke all our hearts. It took some years before I got far enough in knowledge about it that I could—and in part that was the gift of that awful job I had to do at Harvard.[11] I had a staff for the Arabic and a staff for the Hebrew and assembled all this stuff and so on—oh the joy of what was going on with their aid, those wonderful people. But the holocaust, the stuff that came through my hands would just make me shake. When David and I went to Washington last, we went to the new Jewish museum there and I just began to shake. We got out, we had to leave. . . .

It endlessly returns—and then with the treatment of blacks— I suppose I was fortunate in some way, I don't know, maybe it was also escaping from certain aspects of my family that made me sort

382 *Even on Sunday*

of—that isn't where I want to go. That I couldn't imagine this treatment that one learns of. Well, I remember in St. Louis—that was that little fellowship to Northwestern and we went by way of St. Louis and then on up. I had met a priest on the train in the dining car who had asked me to visit the Archbishop's monastery and stuff out there—very beautiful part of St. Louis. Hot, oh my God, it was just—I couldn't believe the way that heat moved right down the river and all that. Anyway I got on a street car—this is shortly after that great woman made all the kerfuffle and won—that she didn't have to sit in the back of the bus anymore. So I got in the street car and it was practically empty—and sat down, not too far from the driver—a black driver—because I wanted to be sure that I could hear when I had to get off for this visit with the Arch—I met the Archbishop and fell on the floor instead of properly genuflecting and kissing his ring—I fell down. [*laughter*] Anyway, all was forgiven and so on. . . . But anyway I sat down and I was all by myself—the place practically empty— and a very, very big black man got on and sat down beside me and hit me with his arm, so hard that I actually went out for a minute or two. I mean, it was—well, I was terrified, absolutely terrified. But my response was very peculiar. I knew immediately why he did it. So finally I got enough courage to get up and get out from around him, 'cause he was on the aisle, and that was when the stop came. The driver called the stop and I got out to go where I was going. But I knew exactly at that moment why he had done that. It scared me.

But I just didn't have it. I mean I don't have that in me. I don't have that. I suppose it's my business of singularity—that every singularity is a deliciousness. . . . But no, this business of the racial—the work of that is not [the] work of a theorist, it's [the] work of a social body who will do something about it. That's social justice. That's where Marx could be valuable.

And also this growing difference between the rich and the poor which is more and more and more so. Well, it's covered up. They're off the wall on what the postmodern project has tried to do. Jery Zaslove is one of the really grand thinkers in our town in this range—so here's another one and I would think of him

as a postmodern thinker. And I'd love it [if he would] collect his
essays in a volume. . . . He's over there now in Prague teaching
Kafka. . . . He sent me Kafka's house, a card, from which I took—
well, he was interested in that thing that I did as a tenth year of
the Kootenay School thing, where I took up the business of what
human form you have . . . and I used two different pieces. I used
one from Borges and one from Kafka where the human form is
not there anymore and as a consequence—and of course
with the Kafka I like it because it comes like a spool, something's
unthreading—the thread is coming off of what the human form
is. You're not going to get this from religion—they don't know
anything about the human form. The only reality of theirs—this
is where the reality really has a problem to it—the only reality is
in the other world, the immortality. That [was] D. H. Lawrence's
marvelous point in that superb book called *Apocalypse*. It's a
wonderful prose book in which he finally says, well, the real mistake they made was to give it all over to immortality. . . .

NICHOLS: This would go back to the stillness in Twin Falls, right?
Where you don't want anything to move, you want a transparent
relationship with the world.

BLASER: Always.

NICHOLS: And have it stay the same.

BLASER: And then your comfort [comes] from the mass, and of
course I come up from the period in which the mass is still in
Latin. That's why I learned it in French and Latin and English.
That was very valuable to me because one, it gave you a sense of
languages, but two, it gave you some historical sense that I could
make use of when I got to read *Finnegans Wake*, with inadequate
knowledge there in Throckmorton, but also to work with
Kantorowicz's courses. . . . I mean I even got exorcised. [*laughter*]
I didn't know anything about the Masons, but I had an uncle that
got me—he was up to no good, obviously, but he got me to go to
Masons and I think he thought I knew what DeMolay was all
about and stuff. Well, I [hadn't] figured it out at all, and anyway
I became a big shot in it. I got my picture in the local paper in
Twin Falls in full regalia, and so on. And the phone rang, and it
was Monseigneur O'Tool. He didn't even identify himself. He
said you come to the sacristy immediately. And I went over there

and I learned who the Masons were [*laughter*]—and who DeMolay was—and so on and so on. And then in full Latin I left the sacristy sopping wet with holy water. [*laughter*] And I'm still shaking [it off]. . . .

[*I turn the tape off for a break, and a trip to the post office.*]

NICHOLS: OK, we're back after a break, and I just wanted to go back to the idea of the lyric and singularity, Robin, if you could talk a bit about that in relation to the serial poem, maybe?

BLASER: Hmm. Singularity in relation to the serial poem. Well, the serial poem fundamentally in my practice and insofar as Duncan wrote poems in series, and certainly with Jack, maintains the lyric form throughout and I think that's on purpose and it's also of course an aspect of this singularity of the person. But the serial itself allows for the realm of chance, the realm of astonishment, the realm of sudden discovery, excitement, and the realm of question—that one might call mystery or mysterious or whatever, and even elements that one would think of perhaps as a kind of mysticism. The serial poem allows all of those to play, because in terms of singularity, all of those have a tendency to correct themselves. Not mysticism that floats toward the heavenlies and you never come back, but anything that might be named a mysticism is one in which the singularity is questioned by what? Something mysterious. Everything puts a question to it, and of course in my own way of doing it, the serial poem lent itself to a travel poem, trying to find your way home, because you weren't at home ever, and as a consequence all aspects of where you are not at home come to be present in the series. And not being at home, doesn't mean you're ever going to finally get home, because maybe you're one of those singularities that's simply homeless, and I think that's not really, also—

NICHOLS: Such a bad place to be?

BLASER: —bad place to be. I have not, in my own [serial] actually, finally worked with the forest as such. I let the forest become a metaphor of all of this. It's in the later poems at any rate. In *The Holy Forest* it's beginning to show that you're wandering through trees even as far back as Pleistocene where one is moving from where the change is . . .

NICHOLS: Proto-Indo-European —

BLASER: And that's headed for the apple. And the apple is not going to be the thing that caused all this trouble for all these years. That is a mere symbol.

NICHOLS: There is a weaving together then, of those things — the lyric, the seriality, and the investigation into violence?

BLASER: Yes.

NICHOLS: How to be in the twentieth-century.

BLASER: How to be in the twentieth-century.

NICHOLS: Or the twenty-first-century.

BLASER: We're headed for the twenty-first, aren't we? The serial poem is an interesting one because it can be used, and is used broadly by many, many people. You find it everywhere. And it works, I think, for that curiosity of the singular that has to hold on to the experience. The experience never is explanatory. It doesn't explain. It's exactly an event of what it is to move through a day, an hour, a year, a friendship, a lover, a whatever — moving with all of these things, and it's lovely if somehow or another a house turns up en route. It is actually a materiality, not a metaphysics, not something transparent . . . the words themselves as being your life and your work — to learn even to use the words — and as a consequence as soon as you come to realize that they are not constantly transparent to something, generally speaking thought to be out there, or in another, political range, that it's in the future and you get every fucking fortune teller in there pulling out the cards — they don't even know how to read cards — and then as for crystal balls, I mean skrying is a wonderful thing to do but you've got to watch it because —

NICHOLS: What was that word?

BLASER: Skrying. The word for reading crystal balls. Yes, to skry — S-K-R-Y-I-N-G — I think it is. We'll look it up to make sure. Anyway, so materiality of language. It is an experience to know that — to suddenly realize that the matter of the language and this is through all of them [the poets]. Really one of the finest and most delicious experiences of it is in translating, because it is there that you know immediately that the materiality of the language has changed in some form, and yet there is a materiality over there facing you and you work on that, and may play with it. You can do translation in that range, or you can do it in another range where it is assumed—Benjamin discusses that so well—that there is a language behind all of our languages. This is the secret of the Bible of course, that there's a language, God's language, behind everything. You get everybody busy preempting God's word.

NICHOLS: Would that be God and Capital?

BLASER: Well, capital is preempting as fast as it can and then turning it into a virtuality, which of course is another very, very chancy business of whether or not it's really a metaphysics of reality. . . .

NICHOLS: I'm thinking about perfect exchangeability, as being a kind of aim [of capital].

BLASER: Yeah, and it doesn't work that way. Language doesn't work that way. But that materiality of language is an extraordinary experience because then you begin to be much more respectful of it, caring of it, and even loving it. I mean, I think a poet always has this experience in some sense. I think of those who've worked with such grand . . . ability, say Byron and Shelley, for example—that if you go in there you want especially in that *Triumph of Life* of Shelley's—you want the way in which the materiality of what it is he's saying as he goes through the business of Rousseau and then finding that he looks like a—you know—a lump down here—he looks like a root or something. And what is driving the carriage that's going across and running over life and so on. Well, the poem's not finished, but you can see it. The first forty lines of *The Triumph of Life*, the stunning lyric, the beauty of them. And yet every movement . . . has an actual materiality and give[s the] experience of the materiality if you were able to write those in *terza rima*. Think of the experience of *terza rima*, what an extraordinary event that is. But the desire for matter. The example that I used in an abstract I was trying to give to some questions that were put to me and I never finished them because the questions were so difficult that it went on forever and every answer was an essay. And maybe that's just me, but I thought the questions deserved considerable answering and so never got finished with it. I ended up quoting *The Temptation of St. Anthony*, by Flaubert, which I think was just an astonishing book in the first place, and in the Penguin edition it has an astonishing introduction by this terrific woman who is able to go at this. It is Kitty Mrosovsky, and her introduction is worth attention. What she starts out by is the notion of Flaubert's ideas—I'm quoting her— of art as a type of martyrdom. Very interesting, because right there is a materiality. But then that's put alongside Baudelaire's idea of art as a type of prostitution, which I think is just absolutely delicious. Flaubert, she says, does not belong with the realists or art for art's sake, etc. When you come to the very end of it [*The Temptation of St. Anthony*] you have this incredible conversation between the sphinx and the chimera. Well, of course this would draw my attention. Death also has a few things to say, and so on and so forth. But the Sphinx and the Chimera are absolutely unforgettable, and I'm going to write my own conversation between the Sphinx and the Chimera. But when we get to [it] there's a griffin and oh my goodness—Anthony is of course a sinner—the temptations of St. Anthony. When he gets to the very end it's just—

> Oh happiness! happiness! I have seen the birth of life, I have seen the beginning of movement. The blood in my veins is beating so hard that it will burst them. I feel like flying, swimming, yelping, bellowing, howling. I'd like to have wings, a carapace, a rind, to breathe out smoke, wave my trunk, twist my body, divide myself up, to be inside everything, to drift away with odours, develop as plants do, flow like water, vibrate like sound, gleam like light, to curl myself up into every shape, to penetrate each atom, to get down to the depths of matter—to be matter! (232)

That is a passage that should go on poetic walls. This is a lovely edition, and she is not to be forgotten for the extraordinary, the beautiful way in which she [Mrosovsky] opens the gate and brings him there. This [edition] might still be available.

NICHOLS: So then seriality opens the lyric up—

BLASER: Opens, opens—

NICHOLS: —to that definition of matter.

BLASER: Yeah. And to the constant interweaving of what?—relations—it's such an abstract term, but interweaving of experiences, that nobody can preempt. And the voice of poetry consistently moves that place of the singularity within the world and its politics and its social forms and its exclusions and inclusions and its punishments. I mean you know death sentences these days are falling like dirty snowflakes, if you've ever seen a dirty snowflake. You just have to go to places like Boston, to see dirty snowflakes.

NICHOLS: Or Texas.

BLASER: [*laughs*] Well, in Texas, we might have to talk about dirty downpours—flash floods or something. Yes, yes, yes that was called . . .

NICHOLS: I was thinking of the death sentences.

BLASER: Yes, they called for the death sentence for homosexuals in Texas. I don't think that the one possible future President of the United States said anything about that.

[Tape change]

NICHOLS: I was trying to remember before a comment by Merleau-Ponty in *The Primacy of Perception*—that the perceived happening cannot be reabsorbed into the complex of relations. In other words, there is no abstraction that will hold an event, and I was putting that forward as a possible way of saying in a kind of abstract manner what would be going on in the writing of singularity in a poem.

BLASER: Oh, but that's very good. It's also very Whiteheadean, finally. It's so interesting that Whitehead is really quite similar to the postmodern thinkers, where he had no place in the modernist thinkers, though he was a modernist himself, and no place in philosophy, except for a group of—they're religionists that work with him—very well, they're scholarly and so on . . .

NICHOLS: Process theology.

BLASER: [The] process theology people are very tied to him and that went on, well, from—I think from the beginning of his career.

NICHOLS: I suppose it would be a complex occasion, is that the Whiteheadean term?[12]

BLASER: Yeah, it's a complex occasion. Whitehead is so very good on event, too. And what happens when there's an event, and really there's a—well, it's in Merleau-Ponty—that business of using the chiasm that he teaches us—and I think serial poems are particularly capable of chiasmatic experience.

NICHOLS: Robin, what was the relationship between the figure of the chiasm and the fold. The chiasm is still dipolar in its language, right?

BLASER: Yeah, which is one severe experience of singularity. But in the fold is that other possibility in which one then folds in—and I've begun working that very, very consciously in the latter poems with the use of people like [Henri] Michaux and . . .

NICHOLS: Deleuze?

BLASER: Deleuze, very particularly Deleuze, that beautiful book that he wrote—

NICHOLS: *The Fold?*

BLASER: It's called *The Fold*, yeah.

NICHOLS: —and the baroque?

BLASER: When I picked up the baroque it was because I thought of the baroque as being a major attention to something having happened to the great Christian tradition, and as a consequence you can even find the change in the line of painting, in the way in which sculpture folded itself together and of course also once it entered into poetry, it began to affect the imagery. It even affects syntax in somebody like Crashaw, whom I use. I use Traherne, because I take a whole passage praising the body, and Christ sings that, praising the body in my libretto. Very wonderful passage. These are Christian writers, English Christian writers out of the baroque period, but they're saying things they wouldn't have said before. It turns out that they kind of fold. The anti-perspectival aspect of Michelangelo moves over and doesn't become, I think, really conscious at all until Blake decides that he will move in. He never saw the original, he's got it all from an engraving. He decides to go also for that, that is, the perspectival begins to be one point, you know. And that of course is not really a singularity, because singularity doesn't identify itself by its having a single point in the world. In fact it has many points, and gets pointed at by many points, and poked at by many points, etc. etc.

NICHOLS: Well the way I understand Deleuze's discussion of it, it's a constant infolding of—

BLASER: Infolding, yeah. He uses the term rhizome, which is too complicated to get into, but it's very interesting stuff, and it's . . . been influential in music in particular, the Deleuzean. If we're going to make accusations, we could make accusations at a lot of contemporary music. In fact a lot doesn't have political—well, you see, I mean there's something very peculiar here. You've lost the singularity in the name of something else that very much needs working on: social justice.

⁜   ⁜   ⁜

NOTES

1. Robert Duncan was born in 1919; Blaser and Spicer in 1925. That would make Duncan six, not seven years older.

2. Peter Quartermain has supplied the following information in a telephone conversation, 24 August 1999.

Basil Bunting taught for a semester at the University of British Columbia, from September to December of 1970. On 29 November 1970, he read *Briggflatts* to an overflow audience. Peter Quartermain (Department of English) obtained Koerner Foundation funding to bring Robert Creeley, Allen Ginsberg, and Robert Duncan in for the *Briggflatts* reading. Bunting also taught at the University of Victoria on Vancouver Island for the 1971-72 academic year.

Robert Creeley taught at UBC as a sessional lecturer from 1962-63 (two sections of English 100, as Quartermain recalls). Creeley, of course, attended the Festival of Contemporary Arts (1962), and the Vancouver Poetry Conference (1963). In "Wonder Merchants," Warren Tallman places Creeley at the "Festival of Contemporary Arts" in February 1962 (175). Quartermain has explained to me that UBC held a festival of the arts every year from 1961 to 1965.

3. Robert Oppenheimer taught at the University of California, Berkeley and the California Institute of Technology before moving to Princeton in 1947. He worked on the Manhattan project (the harnessing of nuclear energy for military purposes) from 1942 to 1945, a project that culminated in the first nuclear explosion on 16 July 1945, Alamagordo, New Mexico. Oppenheimer's discussions with military security agents in 1942 led to the dismissal of a friend on the faculty at the University of California. In 1954, he called his discussions with the military a "tissue of lies." (URL: www.seorf.edu)

4. Henry Wallace was a socialist candidate in the 1948 presidential election.

5. Blaser, Robin. "out of the velvet—the denim—the straw of my mind," 99

Poets/1999: An International Poetics Symposium. Ed. Charles Bernstein. *Boundary 2,* 26:1 (Spring 1999): 52-53.
6. *Great Companion: Dante Alighiere.* The poem appears in this collection.
7. Blaser here refers to the Museo Guggenheim Bilbao, a museum of modern art in Bilbao, Spain, designed by architect Frank Gehry. The museum opened in 1997.
8. Fredric Jameson, *The Political Unconscious* (Ithaca, New York: Cornell UP, 1981); and *The Cultural Turn: Selected Writings on the Postmodern, 1983-1998* (London: Verso, 1998).
9. Badly put! I did not mean that public deliberation might take place at some future date in a better society, but that taking the future as underdetermined is a necessary precondition of opening a space for debate.
10. Žižek argues that the social, like the specular consciousness, has a heterogeneous "other" that is constitutive:

> . . . every ideological Universal—for example, freedom, equali-
> ty—is 'false' in so far as it necessarily includes a specific case
> which breaks its unity, lays open its falsity. Freedom, for exam-
> ple: a universal notion comprising a number of species (freedom
> of speech and press, freedom of consciousness, freedom of com-
> merce, political freedom, and so on) but also, by means of a
> structural necessity, a specific freedom (that of the worker to sell
> freely his own labour on the market) which subverts this univer-
> sal notion. That is to say, this freedom is the very opposite of
> effective freedom: by selling his labour 'freely', the worker *loses*
> his freedom—the real content of this free act of sale is the work-
> er's enslavement to capital. The crucial point is, of course, that it
> is precisely this paradoxical freedom, the form of its opposite,
> which closes the circle of 'bourgeois freedoms'. (22)

11. Blaser held a position in the Widener Library at Harvard from 1956 to 1958. The "awful job" consisted of assembling a display of historical materials on the Jewish holocaust of World War II.
12. I am wrong about the terminology. The term is "actual occasion," not "complex occasion." Donald Sherburne, in his *Key to Whitehead's Process and Reality*, explains:

> Whitehead's insight is to see that if one is to take the doctrine of
> evolution seriously and hold that sentient, purposive creatures
> gradually emerged out of the primordial ooze, then that ooze
> must be understood in such a way that the emergence from it of
> animals and human beings is intelligible. Hence he advocates a
> neutral monism in which actual entities are neither bits of mate-
> rial stuff nor Leibnizian souls, but, rather, units of process that
> may be linked to other actual entities to form temporal strands of
> matter, or perhaps linked with other sophisticated actual entities,

all of which are intricately involved with a complex society like the brain, to form a route of inheritance that we identify as the conscious soul of an enduring person. (205-06)

An event, in Whitehead's terminology, differs from an actual occasion because it may be temporally extended. It is:

> . . . a nexus of actual occasions interrelated in some determinate fashion in some extensive quantum: it is either a nexus in its formal completeness, or it is an objectified nexus. . . . An actual occasion is the limited type of an event with only one member. . . . For example, a molecule is a historic route of actual occasions; and such a route is an 'event.' (qtd. in Sherburne, 222-23)

What I had in mind was an event. Blaser comes up with the term in the next line.

WORKS CITED

de Vries, Hent. *Philosophy and the Turn to Religion.* Baltimore: Johns Hopkins UP, 1999.

Caddel, Richard and Peter Quartermain. *Other: British and Irish Poetry Since 1970.* Hanover and London: Wesleyan UP and the University Press of New England, 1999.

Flaubert, Gustave. *The Temptation of St. Anthony.* Trans. Kitty Mrosovsky. New York, Harmondsworth: Penguin Classics, 1980.

Lacan, Jacques. *Speech and Language in Psychoanalysis.* Trans. Anthony Wilden. Baltimore and London: Johns Hopkins UP, 1968.

Sherburne, Donald. *A Key to Whitehead's Process and Reality.* Chicago and London: U of Chicago P, 1966.

Tallman, Warren. "Wonder Merchants." *Open Letter* 3:6 (1976-1977): 175-207.

Žižek, Slavoj. *The Sublime Object of Ideology.* London, New York: Verso, 1989.

Robin Blaser in Florence, 1997

NOTES ON CONTRIBUTORS

GEORGE BOWERING is a poet, fiction writer, essayist and professor of contemporary literature at Simon Fraser University. He is the author of more than fifty books of poetry and prose. His most recent publications are *Egotists and Autocrats*, a history of Canadian Prime Ministers, forthcoming from Viking/Penguin and *His Life, A Poem* (ECW Press, 2000).

NORMA COLE's most recent works are *Desire & Its Double* (Instress 1998), *Spinoza in her Youth* (Abacus, February 1999), and *Scout*, a slide-text presentation. Her current translation work includes a selection of French writing and poetics called *Crosscut Universe* (Burning Deck, 2000). Cole has been the recipient of Gertrude Stein Awards as well as awards from The Fund for Poetry. She lives in San Francisco.

PAUL KELLEY teaches in Communications at Loyalist College in Kingston, Ontario. He is currently completing a study of Walter Benjamin. Some of his essays on philosophy, aesthetics, education, and culture have appeared in Canadian and U.S. journals. His poetry, too, has apppeared in Canadian and U.S. journals and anthologies, most recently in *Quarry* and *Public*.

KEVIN KILLIAN is a poet, novelist, critic and playwright. His books include *Bedrooms Have Windows, Shy, Little Men, Arctic Summer* and *Argento Series*. With Lewis Ellingham he has written *Poet Be Like God: Jack Spicer and the San Francisco Renaissance* (Wesleyan, 1998), the first biography of the important U.S. poet. With Peter Gizzi he is preparing an edition of Jack Spicer's correspondence. He lives in San Francisco.

PETER MIDDLETON teaches English at the University of Southampton. He is author of *The Inward Gaze: Masculinity and Subjectivity in Modern Culture*, and a forthcoming book from Manchester University Press (with Tim Woods) called *Textual Memory: History, Time and Space in Postwar British and American Literature*. He has written many articles on contemporary poetry and publishes poetry in little magazines both in the U.K. and North America.

ANDREW MOSSIN has published essays on contemporary poetry and poetics, including the work of Robert Duncan, Charles Olson, Robert Creeley, and

Nathaniel Mackey. His own poetry has appeared in *Talisman, River City, Lyric&*, and other publications. A chapbook, *The Epochal Body*, was recently published by Potes and Poets Press.

MIRIAM NICHOLS teaches contemporary literature and theory at the University College of the Fraser Valley. She has published on Robin Blaser in *Line, Sagetreib, Sulfur, Public, The Dictionary of Literary Biography, The Recovery of the Public World* (Talonbooks), and *The Reader's Encyclopedia* (forthcoming from the University of Toronto Press). Her most recent essays include studies of the Kootenay School, Steve McCaffery, bpNichol, Daphne Marlatt, Karen Mac Cormack, and Susan Howe, forthcoming from *Assembling Alternatives* (Wesleyan UP) and the Women and Texts conference series. Her next project is a biography of Robin Blaser. She lives in Vancouver.

SCOTT POUND is a PhD candidate in Poetics and Comparative Literature at the State University of New York at Buffalo. He recently co-edited (with Peter Jaeger) a special issue of the journal *Open Letter*. His poems have appeared in *Essex, Rampike, Torque* (Toronto) and *The Queen Street Quarterly*. He lives in Toronto.

DAVID SULLIVAN teaches film and literature at Cabrillo College in Aptos, California. He has published articles on Emily Dickinson, James Joyce, Kilarney Clary, and Robin Blaser, as well as interviews with Frank Bidart, C. K. Williams, and Reginald Gibbons. His poems have appeared in the *Grey City Journal, The Chicago Review, The Porter Gulch Review, The Beloit Poetry Journal*, and *Quarry West*. His manuscript of prose poems, "Half Life," is searching for a publisher. He lives near the ocean with his dog Alexy and cat Tralala.

FRED WAH has published poetry, prose-poems, biofiction, criticism and teaches creative writing and poetics at the University of Calgary. His book of prose-poems, *Waiting For Saskatchewan*, received the Governor-General's Award in 1986 and *So Far* was awarded the Stephanson Award for Poetry in 1992. *Diamond Grill*, a biofiction about hybridity and growing up in a small-town Chinese-Canadian cafe was published in 1996 and won the Howard O'Hagan Award for Short Fiction. His most recent book, *Faking It: Poetics and Hybridity*, was awarded the Gabrielle Roy Prize for Writing on Canadian literature.